SOCIOLOGY FOR A NEW CENTURY

# DEVELOPMENT AND SOCIAL CHANGE

## A GLOBAL PERSPECTIVE

### THIRD EDITION

◆

## PHILIP McMICHAEL

PINE FORGE PRESS
An Imprint of Sage Publications, Inc.
Thousand Oaks • London • New Delhi

*For information:*

 Pine Forge Press
An Imprint of Sage Publications, Inc.
2455 Teller Road
Thousand Oaks, California 91320
E-mail: order@sagepub.com

Sage Publications Ltd.
6 Bonhill Street
London EC2A 4PU
United Kingdom

Sage Publications India Pvt. Ltd.
B-42, Panchsheel Enclave
Post Box 4109
New Delhi 110 017  India

Printed in the United States of America

**Library of Congress Cataloging-in-Publication Data**

McMichael, Philip.

Development and social change : a global perspective / by Philip McMichael.—3rd ed.
      p. cm. — (Sociology for a new century)
Includes bibliographical references and index.
ISBN 0-7619-8810-6 (Paper)
    1. Economic development projects—History. 2. Economic development—History. 3. Competition, International—History. I. Title. II. Series.
HC79.E44 M25 2004
306.3'09—dc22                                    2003018184

This book is printed on acid-free paper.

03   04   05   06   07   10   9   8   7   6   5   4   3   2   1

| | |
|---|---|
| *Acquisitions Editor:* | Jerry Westby |
| *Editorial Assistant:* | Vonessa Vondera |
| *Production Editor:* | Kristen Gibson |
| *Copy Editor:* | Gillian Dickens |
| *Typesetter:* | C&M Digitals (P) Ltd. |
| *Cover Designer:* | Janet Foulger |

*For Karen,*
*with love and gratitude*

# Contents

# About the Author

**Philip McMichael** grew up in Adelaide, South Australia, and he completed his undergraduate studies at the University of Adelaide. After traveling in India, Pakistan, and Afghanistan and working in a community in Papua New Guinea, he pursued his doctorate in sociology at the State University of New York at Binghamton. He has taught at the University of New England (New South Wales), Swarthmore College, and the University of Georgia and is presently Professor and Chair of Development Sociology at Cornell University. His book, *Settlers and the Agrarian Question: Foundations of Capitalism in Colonial Australia* (1984), won the Social Science History Association's Allan Sharlin Memorial Award (1985). He is the editor of *The Global Restructuring of Agro-Food Systems* (1994) and *Food and Agrarian Orders in the World Economy* (1995). He has served as director of Cornell University's International Political Economy Program, as chair of the American Sociological Association's Political Economy of the World-System Section, and as President of the Research Committee on Agriculture and Food for the International Sociological Association. He currently serves on the Executive Board of the Global Studies Association and on a Scientific Advisory Committee in the Food and Nutrition Division of the United Nation's Food and Agricultural Organization (FAO). He and his wife, Karen Schachere, have two children, Rachel and Jonathan.

# Foreword

S ociology for a New Century offers the best of current sociological thinking to today's students. The goal of the series is to prepare students and—in the long run—the informed public for a world that has changed dramatically in the past three decades and one that continues to astonish.

This goal reflects important changes that have taken place in sociology. The discipline has become broader in orientation, with an ever growing interest in research that is comparative, historical, or transnational in orientation. Sociologists are less focused on "American" society as the pinnacle of human achievement and more sensitive to global processes and trends. They also have become less insulated from surrounding social forces. In the 1970s and 1980s, sociologists were so obsessed with constructing a science of society that they saw impenetrability as a sign of success. Today, there is a greater effort to connect sociology to the ongoing concerns and experiences of the informed public.

Each book in this series offers in some way a comparative, historical, transnational, or global perspective to help broaden students' vision. Students need to comprehend the diversity in today's world and to understand the sources of diversity. This knowledge can challenge the limitations of conventional ways of thinking about social life. At the same time, students need to understand that issues that may seem specifically "American" (e.g., the women's movement, an aging population bringing a strained Social Security and health care system, racial conflict, national chauvinism, etc.) are shared by many other countries. Awareness of commonalities undercuts the tendency to view social issues and questions in narrowly American terms and encourages students to seek out the experiences of others for the lessons they offer. Finally, students need to grasp phenomena that transcend national boundaries—trends and processes that are supranational (e.g., environmental degradation). Recognition of global processes stimulates student awareness of causal forces that transcend national boundaries, economies, and politics.

Reflecting the dramatic acceleration of the global economy, *Development and Social Change: A Global Perspective* explores the complex interplay between rich and poor countries over the post–World War II era. Its starting point is the view of international inequality predominant in the 1950s and 1960s. This thinking joined international organizations and Third World governments in a common ideology of state-managed economic and social change and championed the idea that, with a little help from rich countries and international organizations, poor countries could become developed countries, pulling themselves up by their own bootstraps. Reality, of course, fell far short of the vision that inspired development thinking, and this view, which McMichael calls the *development project*, gave way to *globalism*. Goals of integration with the world economy and openness to its forces supplanted goals of national development and "catching up with the West." McMichael's portrait of global interconnections spotlights the long reach of international markets and commodity chains and the many, often invisible, connections between producers and consumers worldwide.

# Preface to Third Edition

The third edition of this text updates the material in a world of fast-breaking news on the international front. The original perspective of the text remains since it appears that the argument of the previous editions has been essentially confirmed, namely, that the attempt to organize development as a global enterprise is fraught with instability and conflict. The world in the twenty-first century is an alarming one, given the rising use of terror (both stateless and state based) as a tactic of intimidation of populations and given the evident compromise and/or breakdown in multilateral negotiations among states. The World Trade Organization (WTO) Ministerial in Cancun, September 2003, marked the consolidation of a political bloc in the global South, the Group of 21, energized by a well-organized nongovernmental organization (NGO) movement, to render multilateral negotiations more democratic and more realistic and just in an increasingly unequal global economy.

This organizational current began during the 1990s, emerged at the WTO Ministerial in Seattle in 1999, and has gained coherence ever since. This is in part because of the intransigence of the global North on its agricultural protection and on WTO procedures, as well as its attempt to institutionalize a regime sanctioning foreign investment and privatized services in a *trade* organization. The promise of the so-called "Development Round," arising from the WTO Ministerial in Doha (2001), remained unfulfilled and perhaps served to focus attention on the need to change the balance of forces in the WTO to move the global development agenda forward. It remains to be seen how international relations in the development field will unfold since one consequence of the failed Cancun Ministerial is likely to be consolidation of bilateral and regional economic agreements based in more direct geopolitical relationships.

Bilateralism is also a product of the unipolarity of the twenty-first century, in which the world's remaining superpower state, the United States, moves to secure its power in the world, including its ability to finance its growing deficits. Rising terror attacks, compounded with the occupation of Iraq in 2003, elevate military expenditures and other costs of empire. This third edition addresses aspects of this new world disorder through discussions of the relationship between fundamentalism and modernity, as well as fundamentalism and terrorism. It also advances a provisional sketch of the emergence of a new, imperial project, alongside of the globalization project. Whether and to what extent such an imperial project will displace and/or subsume the globalization project remains to be seen. But there is no doubt that cross-cutting tensions between multilateralism and bilateralism, between Europe and the United States, and between the global North and the global South will shape the first decade of the twenty-first century.

The third edition, then, attempts to identify the discord in the project of global development to better understand the limits and possibilities of development. Part of this discussion includes a recognition of the growing presence and discursive power of the global justice movements (sometimes referred to as the "anti-globalization" movement). This text chooses to characterize these movements as "global countermovements," in the sense that they represent a cosmopolitan alternative to the singular view of corporate globalization—as expressed in the annual juxtaposition of the World Social Forum and the World Economic Forum, respectively. The interaction between these two forces reveals a struggle to (re)define development in a world defined by two powerful dynamics: integration/disintegration and inclusion/exclusion.

Other modifications to this third edition include a more conscious charting of the changing fortunes of the Third World as a political bloc; greater attention to political tensions within Third World states; inclusion of new developments in global labor migration and the role of remittance income; focus on the gendering of the global labor force; more coherent treatment of the protocols of the WTO, including privatization of services and knowledge; profile of the global AIDS crisis; and chronicling of the rise of a food sovereignty countermovement to the global food security regime centered on the dumping of agricultural surpluses and attempts to introduce transgenic foods through aid programs. Finally, in addition to the inclusion of new case studies, all case studies end with a question, often posed as a paradox, to introduce students to the question of whether and to what extent development is a process often realized through the intensification of inequalities, despite its stated intentions.

The subject of development is difficult to teach. Living in relatively affluent surroundings, students understandably situate their society on the "high end" of a development continuum—at the pinnacle of human economic and technological achievement. And they often perceive both the development continuum and their favorable position on it as "natural"—a well-deserved reward for embracing the values of modernity. (This is likely to be the case also for students from the so-called Third World, although their experiences will be different.) It is difficult to put one's world in historical perspective from this vantage point. It is harder still to help students grasp a world perspective that goes beyond framing their history as a simple series of developmental or evolutionary stages— the inevitable march of progress.

In my experience, until students go beyond simple evolutionary views, they have difficulty valuing other cultures that do not potentially mirror their own. When they do go beyond the evolutionary perspective, they are better able to evaluate their own culture sociologically and to think reflexively about social change, development, and international inequality. This is the challenge.

The narrative that follows presents an overview of social change and development as the twenty-first century takes hold. It is not organized around competing theories of social change and development, nor does it adhere to a single, all-encompassing perspective. Rather, my narrative retraces the story of development as an increasingly global enterprise.

This book introduces students to the global roots and dimensions of recent social changes and to the special role filled by the **development project.** It encourages them to think about development as a transnational project designed to integrate the world, and it helps them to see how this project is currrently undergoing dramatic revision via political and economic globalization, as well as by some powerful countermovements within this process. With these understandings in place, they will be better prepared for the many challenges that lie ahead.

Many of the available texts approach development through the lens of theory. Texts are usually organized around competing theories or perspectives (e.g., modernization vs. dependency vs. world systems theory, liberal perspectives vs. marxist perspectives, structuralism vs. neoliberalism, etc.). Students find themselves thrown into the task of evaluating abstract perspectives without proper grounding in knowledge of the post–World War II developmentalist era. While presenting competing theoretical perspectives is a fundamental part of teaching social change and development, students need a basic understanding of the context within which these competing theories arose and then collided.

The post–cold war world that students live in today is very different from the world that gave rise to development theories. The rapid pace of social change makes the task of understanding this world akin to shooting at a moving target. The established units of sociological analysis (e.g., national societies and citizens, individual rational actors, etc.) are now surrounded by competing organizing principles—subnational communities and supranational regions, transnational webs of exchange and transnational communities, ethnic and cultural entities, expressive politics, stateless refugees and terrorists, and so on. It is even questionable whether development theory, as it is now known and debated, will survive the dramatic social changes of the post–cold war world, as the ground is shifting—even degrading—under the globalization, and possibly an imperial, project.

This book has been designed with these new challenges in mind. My aim is to situate current changes historically, first presenting an overview of the development era (including its theoretical discourses) and then addressing its declining salience as a new global era emerges. Students who are already familiar with such social movements as consumerism, feminism, grassroots activism, and rain forest protection will find these issues here in the context of the shifting debates and challenges to the development project.

The text traces the steps in the gradual evolution of the development enterprise into an emerging **globalization project,** outlining the conditions under which the post–World War II managers of states and multilateral agencies institionalized development as a key organizing principle in the cold war era. A series of case studies concentrates on the Third World countries' experience of the development project, individualizing this experience and showing how it differed across Third World countries and regions while situating those individual experiences in a common process.

The common process of development itself has changed substantially. From the early 1970s, when new global trends began to override the 1940s Bretton Woods development institutions, a new project of globalization began, gradually supplanting the development project, dramatized by the debt crisis of the 1980s. The text lays out the main features of this trend, including some of the major countermobilizations, such as the feminist and the environmental movements. New questions arise in a world that is simultaneously integrating and disintegrating and grappling with environmental problems on a global scale. The scale and style of politics are changing, and new issues of human rights have emerged in a world that is experiencing an increasingly rapid circulation of money, people, goods, electronic impulses, and ideas. All of these issues complicate our once tidy view of development and the problem of international inequality. The goal of this presentation is to offer students an integrated perspective on the forces that have changed how "development" is understood at the turn of the twenty-first century.

By understanding the construction of the development era, students have a basis from which to begin to make sense of current trends of restructuring. These trends involve new discourses and new institutional developments, with a deep-rooted contention over the shape of the emerging world order.

## Organization and Language

In examining the experiences of the development project, I have interwoven global and national issues, which helps to both situate current limits to nationally managed development and show how even national development strategies had intrinsic global dimensions. I attempt to demonstrate that nation-states belong to and shape a transnational order, which in turn conditions their domestic experiences and possibilities. This includes charting the relative consequences of a bipolar, tripolar (three worlds), and now unipolar world and how the changing balance of geopolitical forces informs our understanding of "development."

Finally, a word about language. It has become commonplace to note that the Third World and the Second World have ended as coherent entities, and I have tried to record this change during the narrative by adding the epithet "the former" to each of these terms. Although they certainly violate a heterogeneous reality as omnibus terms, they are useful as shorthand and certainly recognizable to most people. I stick with *First World* for no other reason than convenience. Similarly, in some instances, I have used the terms *North* and *South* where these categories have a certain currency as political subdivisions of the contemporary world.

# A Timeline of Developmentalism and Globalism

| WORLD FRAMEWORK | Developmentalism (1940s-1970s) |
|---|---|
| POLITICAL ECONOMY | State-Regulated Markets<br>Keynesian Public Spending |
| SOCIAL GOALS | Social Entitlement and Welfare<br>Uniform Citizenship |
| DEVELOPMENT<br><br>[Model] | Industrial Replication<br>National Economic Sector Complementarity<br>[Brazil, Mexico, India] |
| MOBILIZING TOOL | Nationalism (Post-Colonialism) |
| MECHANISMS | Import-Substitution Industrialization (ISI)<br>Public Investment (Infrastructure, Energy)<br>Education<br>Land Reform |
| VARIANTS | First World (Freedom of Enterprise)<br>Second World (Central Planning)<br>Third World (Modernization via<br>    Development Alliance) |

| MARKERS | | | | |
|---|---|---|---|---|
| | Cold War Begins<br>(1946) | | Korean War<br>(1950-53) | Vietnam War<br>(1964-75) |
| | Bretton Woods<br>(1944) | Marshall Plan<br>(1946) | Alliance for<br>Progress<br>(1961) | |
| | United Nations<br>(1943) | Non-Aligned<br>Movement<br>(1955) | UNCTAD<br>(1964) | World Economic<br>Forum (1970) |
| | | FIRST<br>DEVELOPMENT<br>DECADE | SECOND<br>DEVELOPMENT<br>DECADE | |

```
- - - - - - - - - - •  •          •          •          •          •
     1940              1950        1960                   1970
```

| INSTITUTIONAL<br>DEVELOPMENTS | World Bank, IMF/GATT<br>(1944) (1964) | | | Group of 77<br>(G-77) |
|---|---|---|---|---|
| | US $ as<br>Reserve<br>Currency | PL-480<br>(1954) | Eurodollar/<br>Offshore<br>$ Market | |
| | COMECON (1947) | | | |

**Globalism (1980s-)**

Self-Regulating Markets (Monetarism)
Public Downsizing

Private Initiative and Global Consumerism
Identity Politics and Multilayered Citizenship

Participation in the World Market
Comparative Advantage
[Chile, South Korea; NAFTA]

Market Forces
Debt and Credit-Worthiness

Export-Orientation
Privatization
Entrepreneurialism
Public and Majority-Class Austerity

National Structural Adjustment (Opening Economies)
Regional Free Trade Agreements
Global Economic Management (Good Governance)

| Oil Crises (1973, 1979) | Cold War Ends (1989) | "New World Order" Begins | Imperial Wars (2001-) |
|---|---|---|---|
| | Debt Regime | WTO Regime | |
| New International Economic Order Initiative (1974) | Earth Summit (1992) | | WTO Ministerials Seattle (1999) Cancun (2003) |
| Chiapas Revolt (1994) | | World Social Forum (2001) | |

|  | DEBT CRISIS/ "LOST DECADE" | "GLOBALIZATION" DECADE |  |
|---|---|---|---|
| 1970 | 1980 | 1990 | 2000 |
| Group of 7 (G-7) (1975) | GATT Uruguay Round (1986) | NAFTA (1994) WTO (1995) | Group of 20 (G-20) (2003) |
| | Offshore Banking Structural Adjustment Loans | IMF/World Bank "Governance" Loans | |
| | | Glasnost/Perestroika | |

# Acknowledgments

I wish to express my thanks to the people who have helped me along the way, beginning with my graduate school mentor, Terence Hopkins. For the first two editions, which include acknowledgment of the various people who were so helpful, special mention still goes to original editor-in-chief, Steve Rutter, for his remarkable vision and his enthusiasm and faith in this project, as well as friends who contributed various insights—Fred Buttel, Harriet Friedmann, Richard Williams, Michell Adato, Dale Tomich, and Raj Patel—and my undergraduate and graduate students (particularly my teaching assistants) at Cornell.

For this third edition, I have received continual encouragment and valuable suggestions concerning presentation of the text from editor-in-chief, Jerry Westby. I extend my sincere thanks to him and to the production crew: my fastidious copyeditor, Gillian Dickens; graphics specialist, Vonessa Vondera; and my professional production editor, Kristen Gibson, who made the reproduction of the revised text possible. Cornell Presidential Scholar Sara Lee, assisted with background research, and Dana Perls was invaluable in producing a creative and diverse set of graphics to enhance this edition. I received thoughtful and provocative suggestions to improve this text from Doug Constance, Ann Baker Cottrell, Ed Crenshaw, Ben Crow, Ione Y. DeOllos, Jack Goldstone, and Robert Mazur—their collective good advice has certainly aided the revision, even if not always followed completely. I can only do so much.

Finally, very special thanks are due to two very special people: Dia Mohan—a colleague and former graduate student who has worked with me, and the text, over the past two editions and whose extraordinary intellectual insights have helped me develop a more nuanced understanding and presentation of the subject—and my daughter Rachel, whose thoughtful classroom challenge during the military occupation of Iraq encouraged me to include the emergence of the "imperial project" as a complicating factor in the project of globalization.

# Introduction: Development and Globalization

## What Is the World Coming To?

These days, the term *globalization* is on practically everyone's lips. Or so it would seem. One of the distinguishing features of this new century is the powerful apparatus of communication that presents an image of a world unified by global technologies and products and their universal appeal. It is almost as if there is no alternative to this image of globalization. And yet we know that while 75 percent of the world's population has access to daily television reception, only 20 percent of the world's population has access to consumer cash or credit.

We may see television commercials depicting the world's peoples consuming global commodities, but it is not as if everyone actually shares either this reality or this image. We know that the 20 percent of the world's people who do have consumer cash or credit consume 86 percent of all goods and services, while the poorest 20 percent consume just 1.3 percent.[1] The distribution of the world's material wealth is extraordinarily uneven. We also know that while we may be accustomed to a commercial culture, other cultures (e.g., Amish, Islamic, peasant, forest dweller) are either not commercial or not comfortable with commercial definition. Cultural meaning is not universally defined through the market, and so *globalization,* as it is currently understood, is not necessarily a universal aspiration.

Why, then, is there so much talk of "globalization"? There is no simple answer, but some of the explanations would be the following:

- While the world's peoples and continents have always been connected through exchanges of goods, literature, ideas, and fantasy, the recent communications revolution makes it possible to connect the world more intensively than ever before.

- Through the communications revolution, we gain access to and share knowledge of other cultures, and we evaluate different political cultures and their treatment of subgroups, such as children, women, subsistence dwellers, prisoners, homosexuals, indigenous people, and so forth.
- In the late twentieth century, *globalization* replaced *development* as a serious discourse and project of political and business elites.
- The increasingly finite world has become the object of powerful countries and corporations concerned with improving their competitive advantage by "capturing" world resources.
- The increasingly finite world has made itself known to us through the rising degradation of the environment.
- Tourism is currently the world's largest industry, especially cultural tourism, in which "otherness" is packaged as a cultural export to earn foreign currency.
- As the world and its natural and cultural resources are subjected to commercial speculation, media images prompt us to imagine its diversity as a source of wealth, simultaneously reducing it to a single, global entity.

Now, as hard as it might be, it is worth trying to imagine what globalization might mean to people who do not consume the material benefits or the images of globalization. There are some who aspire to consume, some who view "globalization" as privileging existing consumers, some who find meaning in their own culture but nevertheless feel somehow diminished by the comparison, and some who simply reject consumerism and affirm their culture. Let me illustrate these types, respectively:

- Some years ago, I attended a village meeting, in New Guinea, at which a well-known "cargo cult" member was instructing his fellow villagers to prepare for a shipment of goods from "the outside." Cargo cults construct millennial fantasies about seen or unseen foreign goods or gifts being bestowed on non-Western peoples, in the absence of being able to conceive of reorganizing their own culture to actually produce such items. This kind of perception is evident in the New Guinean Pidgin-English term for *helicopter—mixmaster belongim Jesus*—which suggests that divine providence is somehow connected to the artifacts of industrial civilization.
- In Judith Hellman's book, *Mexican Lives,* a street vendor named Rosario anticipates the impact of globalization (via the North American Free Trade Agreement [NAFTA]) on those Mexicans who survive by smuggling goods across the Texan border to sell in Mexico City: "You have to understand, thousands of people at the border live from collecting bribes. . . . If free trade comes, they'll find another way to shake us down, or maybe they won't let us cross at all. The NAFTA treaty isn't meant to rescue people like us, it's meant for the rich."[2]

- Helena Norberg-Hodge's book, *Ancient Futures,* describes how Ladakhi people, whose economy is not governed by money, perceive Western culture through contact with tourists, armed with cameras and seemingly infinite amounts of money, for which they evidently do not have to work: "In one day a tourist would spend the same amount that a Ladakhi family might in a year. Ladakhis did not realize that money played a completely different role for the foreigners; that back home they needed it to survive; that food, clothing, and shelter all cost money—a lot of money. Compared to these strangers they suddenly felt poor." Here, an invidious comparison with Western culture occurs through quite artificial contact. The author remarks that Ladakhis "cannot so readily see the social or psychological dimensions—the stress, the loneliness, the fear of growing old. Nor can they see environmental decay, inflation, or unemployment. On the other hand, they know their own culture inside out, including all its limitations and imperfections."[3]
- José Maria Arguedas, a South American Andean poet, writes, in "A Call to Certain Academics," the following:[4]

> They say that we do not know anything
> That we are backwardness
> That our head needs changing for a better one
> They say that some learned men are saying this about us
> These academics who reproduce themselves
> In our lives
> What is there on the banks of these rivers, Doctor?
> Take out your binoculars
> And your spectacles
> Look if you can.
> Five hundred flowers
> From five hundred different types of potato
> Grow on the terraces
> Above abysses
> That your eyes don't reach
> These five hundred flowers
> Are my brain
> My flesh

In juxtaposing these images, it is obvious that despite powerful images of a world converging on a common consumer culture, there are alternative currents of meaning and social organization. How the differences will be resolved is, of course, one of the key issues that frames the twenty-first century. There are many perspectives and voices expressing these tensions. Here I offer two such perspectives:

- Renato Ruggiero, the former director-general of the World Trade Organization (WTO), expressed the view of the proponents of economic globalization when he remarked in the late 1990s,

More than ever before, the world's prosperity . . . rests on maintaining an open international economy based on commonly agreed rules . . . by opening their economies . . . countries accelerate their development. . . . What is at stake as we contemplate the future of the multilateral system is much more than trade and economics. It involves questions of political and economic security. It is about how relations among countries and peoples are to be structured. It determines whether we foster international solidarity or descend into a spiral of global friction and conflict.[5]

- Richard Neville, a consultant to business on alternative futures, remarks in an article titled "The Business of Being Human,"

The point of business is to provide profit. The point of culture is to provide meaning. Can the two be reconciled? Not entirely; and we are doing our best to overlook the fact. This denial fuels our thirst for distraction, glorifies the ugly and endangers the ecosystem. On the other hand, it's kind of fun. Look at the queues outside Planet Hollywood. . . . Each year, the total corporate expenditure on advertising and marketing is more than $US620 billion, making it the boldest psychological project ever undertaken by the human race. It works out to more than $100 for every person on the planet, most of whom will never have the means to acquire the BMWs, the microwaves, the designer labels.[6]

Taking our cue from these statements, the twenty-first century appears to be shaping up as an elemental conflict between profits and meaning. While this scenario may be too simplified, it does seem to capture one of the key sources of tension attached to "globalization." In particular, it signals the conflict between the market culture that would unify the world and the popular cultures that differentiate the world as a mosaic of localized lifestyles. Of course, these two cultural types intermingle, but their horizons are "global" and "local," respectively, and the survival of each increasingly depends on limiting the autonomy (or power) of the other. An example of this tension is the controversy regularly generated by animated Disney films that attempt to appeal to consumers' multicultural impulses but via Westernized cultural images. Critics charge that the characters—whether Aladdin, Pocahontas or Mulan—reproduce ethnic stereotypes that privilege the commercial success of the global Disney corporation and diminish the dignity and complexity of the historical cultures depicted.

Another related tension concerns the social and environmental impact of the global market culture. In an article addressed to North American coffee drinkers, dated January 5, 1999, *The Washington Post* headlined "Where were your beans grown?" and bylined the observation that coffee farming in Central America is reducing the songbird population. Russell Greenberg, a scientist from the Smithsonian Institute, has documented that the decline of bird life in Central America is related partly to the boom in coffee drinking. As rain forests have disappeared, 150 species of migratory songbirds have relocated to the traditional shade trees that protect young coffee plants on the plantations. As coffee drinking intensifies, farmers remove the shade trees and substitute sunlight and chemicals to accelerate bean growth, thereby reducing bird habitats.[7]

This kind of environmental impact is widespread and indicates the conflict between rising market demand for globally produced goods and the sustainability of ecological and social systems at the points of production. The world was shocked when, in 1998, tropical hurricanes wrought widespread disaster in Central America as mudslides destroyed thousands of low-income dwellings and the lives of many of their inhabitants. Vulnerability to mudslides was a consequence of overlogging of the rain forests for timber, commercial cropland, and pastures to sustain lucrative exports to the world market. Central America was losing about 180 acres of trees an hour. And global warming was blamed for the torrential rains that fell that year in Central America as well as in China and Bangladesh.[8]

When people read about these disasters and their link to the market culture, inevitably they feel a sense of powerlessness in the face of such huge, transnational dilemmas. However, as awareness of the connections grows, people find ways and means to respond. For example, Russell Greenberg involved himself in the Smithsonian-sanctioned promotion of "shade-grown coffee" beans under a "Café Audubon" brand. He was emulating other consumer-led movements, such as the dolphin-safe tuna campaign and consumer boycotts of soccer balls stitched by children in Pakistan, to use consumer power to arrest social and ecological harm arising from unregulated market practices. In these ways, the tension between profits and meaning finds expression.

## The Global Marketplace

Much of what we wear, use, and consume today has global origins. Even when a product has a domestic "Made In . . ." label, its journey to market probably combines components and labor from production and assembly sites around the world. Sneakers, or parts thereof, might be produced in China or Indonesia, blue jeans assembled in the Philippines, a transistor radio or compact disk player put together in Singapore, and a watch made in Hong Kong. The fast food eaten by North Americans may include chicken diced in Mexico or hamburger beef from cattle raised in Costa Rica. And, depending on taste, our coffee is from Southeast Asia, the Americas, or Africa. We may not be global citizens, yet, but we are global consumers.

The global marketplace binds us all. The Japanese eat poultry fattened in Thailand with American corn, using chopsticks made with wood from Indonesian or Chilean forests. Canadians eat strawberries grown in Mexico with fertilizer from the United States. Consumers on both sides of the Atlantic wear clothes assembled in Saipan with Chinese labor, drink orange juice from concentrate made with Brazilian oranges, and decorate their homes with flowers from Colombia. The British and French eat green beans from Kenya, and cocoa from Ghana finds its way into Swiss chocolate. Consumers everywhere are surrounded and often identified by world products.

## Commodity Chains and Development

The global marketplace is a tapestry of networks of commodity exchanges that bind producers and consumers across the world. In any one network, there is a sequence of production stages, located in a number of countries at sites that provide inputs of labor and materials contributing to the fabrication of a final product. Sociologists call the networks **commodity chains.** Chains link each input stage, as a local combination of commodities, and together these phases form a finished good sold in the global marketplace. The chain metaphor illuminates the interconnections among producing communities dispersed across the world. And it allows us understand that when we consume a final product in a commodity chain, we participate in a global process that links us to a variety of places, people, and resources. While we may experience consumption individually, it is a fundamentally social (and environmental) act.

Not everything we consume has such global origins, but the trend toward these worldwide supply networks is powerful. It is transforming the scale of economic development, reaching beyond regional and national boundaries. Some researchers, for example, have noted that the ingredients of a container of yogurt—from the strawberries and milk to the cardboard and ink for the carton—travel more than 6,000 miles to the market in Germany, and yet all could be produced within a 50-mile radius.[9] As more and more goods and services are produced on this transnational scale, development assumes a different meaning. In the past, we understood development to be a process of economic growth organized nationally, but today, global economic integration is transforming development into a process of *globally organized economic growth.*

As the former WTO director, Renato Ruggiero, was quoted above as saying, globalization is now perceived as indispensable to development. This is a powerful idea that informs development policies made by national governments and international development agencies, such as the World Bank. Most governments across the world are participating in an opening of their economies to global competition or, in the case of the European Union, synchronizing their macroeconomic policies by adopting a common currency, the euro, to streamline the European economy and give it a global competitive edge. This initiative gathered steam when the United States, Canada, and Mexico signed NAFTA in 1994, providing the United States with a huge open market as a home base. The point is that *development* and *globalization* have become synonymous for business and political elites across the world.

However, as Rosario the street vendor observed, the marriage of development and globalization is spawning quite uneven offspring, as some regions and populations survive and prosper and others decline. On the margins, there are new currents of grassroots activity seeking to formulate and implement alternative, sustainable forms of development. In many cases, these forms of development have different goals: (1) They focus on basic needs rather than the rising material expectations that we associate with the consumer culture, and (2) they view participation, and therefore cultural meaning, as an indispensable part of the development process.

These are the two major currents of "development" today, and it is important to understand that they are very much related to one another. For one thing, the global marketplace is quite uneven in its consequences:

- With the collapse of Soviet communism in 1989, Russia joined the global capitalist club only to experience a dramatic compression of living standards for most Russians, as their gross domestic product declined 52 percent in the 1990s.[10]
- The 1998 United Nations (UN) *Human Development Report* noted, for example, that of the 4.4 billion people in developing countries, about 60 percent

lack access to safe sewers, 67 percent have no access to clean water, 25 percent have inadequate housing, and 20 percent have no access to modern health services of any kind.
- The average African household today consumes 20 percent less than it did a quarter of a century ago.
- The $17 billion spent annually in the United States and Europe on pet food exceeds by $4 billion the estimated annual additional cost of providing basic health and nutrition for everyone in the world![11]

In the context of globalization and rising global inequalities, many marginalized communities are responding by developing their own survival strategies, both material and cultural. Development agencies such as the World Bank are noticing this and channeling funds to nongovernmental organizations (NGOs) that are involved in these grass-roots endeavors, such as micro-credit distribution. Some say that the World Bank is merely trying to stabilize communities that have experienced marginalization from the global marketplace; nevertheless, the initiative of marginalized peoples is forcing the development establishment to alter the way it does business. In this sense, development expresses relations of power.

## Global Networks

In today's world, the interdependencies among people, communities, and nations are ever present. When we consume, we consume an image (of aesthetic or athletic dimensions, say) as well as materials and labor from many places in the global marketplace. Just as all humans eventually breathe the same air and drink the same water, consumers enjoy the fruits of others' labor.

The *global labor force* is dispersed among the production links of these commodity chains (see Figure 1). In the U.S.-based athletic shoe industry, the initial labor is related to the symbolic side of the shoe design—and marketing. This step remains primarily in the United States. Then there is the labor of producing the synthetic materials; of dyeing, cutting, and stitching; and of assembling, packing, and transporting. These forms of labor are all relatively unskilled and often performed by women, especially South Koreans, Taiwanese, Chinese, Indonesians, and Filipinos. Companies such as Nike *subcontract* with such labor forces through local firms in the regional production sites. South Korea and Taiwan are among the more reliable sites, generally having greater capacity and greater

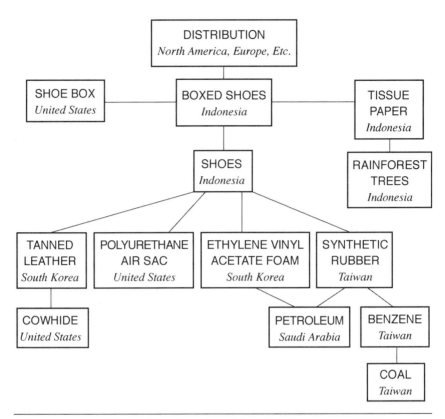

**Figure 1**    A Commodity Chain for Athletic Shoes

Source: Bill Ryan and Alan During, "The Story of a Shoe," *World Watch*, March/April 1998.

quality control than some other countries. But a shoe that costs Nike $20 on export from South Korea may cost only $15 if made in Indonesia or China. In fact, in the 1990s, Nike's expensive trainers, worth $150 dollars in the United States and Europe, were assembled by some 120,000 Indonesian contract workers earning less than $3 a day, which, although a starvation wage, met the legal minimum that applies to more than half of Indonesia's 80-million labor force. Depending on political and/or economic conditions, a company such as Nike will shift a substantial part of its production to these lower-wage sites.[12]

Relocating production is a routine part of any competitive firm's operations today. As fashion and design change, and with them labor costs and management patterns, so may the location of production. Firms reroute the production chains to stay competitive. Any shopper at The Gap, for example, knows that this clothing retailer competes by changing its styles on a six-week cycle. The key to this kind of flexible organization is to use far-flung subcontractors who can be brought on line or let go as the market changes. The people who work for these subcontractors often have little security, being one of the small links in this global commodity chain. Job security varies by commodity, firm, and industry, but rising employment insecurity across the world reflects the uncertainties of an increasingly competitive global market.

We hear a lot of discussion about whether the relocation of jobs from the United States, Europe, and Japan to the "developing countries" is a short-term or a long-term trend. The topic raises questions.

- First, are "mature" economies shedding their manufacturing jobs and becoming global centers of service industries (e.g., education, retailing, finance, insurance, marketing)?
- Second, do those jobs that shift "south" descend a wage ladder toward the cheapest labor, for example, in China?
- Third, are these only temporary competitive strategies by firms to reduce costs, or is the world being restratified into low- and high-wage regions, among and within nations (even the affluent ones)?

We examine such questions in the following chapters because the redistribution of jobs on a global scale is an indicator of a profound transformation under way in the world, a transformation that is redefining the parameters and meaning of development.

Another example from the global marketplace concerns conditions of work, illustrated in the global food industry. More and more fruits and vegetables are being grown under corporate contract by peasants and agricultural laborers around the world. Chile exports grapes, apples, pears, apricots, cherries, peaches, and avocados to the United States during the winter months. Caribbean nations produce bananas, citrus fruits, and frozen vegetables, and Mexico supplies American supermarkets with tomatoes, broccoli, bell peppers, cucumbers, and cantaloupes. Thailand grows pineapples and asparagus for the Japanese market, and Kenya exports strawberries, mangoes, and chilies to Europe. In short, the global fruit and salad bowl is bottomless. In an era when much of this production is organized by huge food companies that subcontract with growers and sell in consumer markets across the world, these growers face new conditions of work.

As discussed in Chapter 1, non-Europeans have been producing specialized agricultural products for export for some time, but the scale and profitability of export food production have expanded greatly in recent decades as the number and concentration of world consumers have grown. Firms must remain flexible to compete in the global marketplace. Not only does this need for flexibility bring growers across the world into competition with one another as firms seek to keep costs down, but it also means that the produce itself must meet high standards of quality and consistency. Growers find that their work is defined by the needs of the firm to maintain its market image and a predictable supply of products desirable to consumers across the world. So not only is the job insecure, but its very performance is also shaped by global market requirements.

Again, most contract growing of fruits and vegetables is done by women. Women are considered more reliable as workers than men; they can be trained to monitor plant health and growth and to handle fruit and work efficiently. Employers presume that women are more suited to the seasonal and intermittent employment practices (e.g., harvesting, processing, and packing) necessary to mount a flexible operation.[13] Increasingly, the needs of the global market shape the conditions of work and livelihoods in communities across the world.

## The Social Web of the Global Market

Globalization is ultimately experienced locally. It is difficult to imagine the changing web of social networks across the world that produce our market culture. We do not think about the global dimensions of the product we purchase at a supermarket or store. And we do not think about the power of transnational firms that shape the global market and its rules. The market, as well as its far-reaching effects on our lives, seems almost natural. But we disregard these connections at our peril for several reasons:

- We can no longer understand the changes in our society without situating them globally.
- We are likely to misinterpret social upheavals (including stateless or state-based terrorism) across the world if we ignore the contributions of global processes to political and economic instability.
- We cannot understand the consequences of disturbances in our complex biosphere without taking account of world-scale social transformations and stress on natural resources.

Along many of the commodity chains that sustain our lifestyle are people who experience globalization in quite different ways. Many are not consumers of commodities: Four-fifths of the roughly 6 billion people in the world do not have access to consumer cash or credit.[14] Even so, they are often the producers of what we consume, and their societies are shaped as profoundly by the global marketplace as ours, if not more so. We seldom remember this.

Rain forest destruction, for example, is linked to the expanding global market, although the connections are not always direct. Since the 1970s, Brazilian peasants have been displaced as their land has been taken for high-tech production of soybeans for export to feed Japanese livestock. These people have migrated en masse from the Brazilian southeast to the Amazon region to settle on rain forest land. Their dramatic encroachment on the forest captured the world's attention in the 1980s, lending impetus to the 1992 Earth Summit. It forced the industrialized world to see a link between poverty and environmental destruction.

Less obvious, however, is the precipitating connection between rising demand for animal protein in the Northern Hemisphere and rain forest destruction. And this connection is obscured by our customary view of development as a national process, making it even more difficult for us to view this episode as a global dynamic with particular local effects. The case study of the "hamburger connection" opposite outlines one such instance of world-scale social transformation with distinct local effects.

A brief examination of footwear and hamburgers demonstrates how products that may be everyday items of consumption, particularly in the wealthier segments of the global market, may have considerable effects on producers and producing regions where they are made. Figure 2 suggests that, even *within* the unequal relations between "developed" and "developing" societies, there are costs on both sides—in this case, to human physiological health as a consequence of two forms of malnutrition: (1) processed food and sedentary lifestyle malnutrition and (2) malnutrition from lack of adequate, nutritious food supplies. Not only are producers and consumers linked across space by commodity chains, but these links also have profound social implications.

As we begin to examine the social links, we see that they are often tenuous and unsustainable. The more links that are made, the more interdependent become the fortunes of laborers, producers, and consumers across the world. A change in fashion can throw a whole producing community out of work. A footloose firm seeking lower wages can do the same thing. A new food preference in one part of the world will intensify export agriculture somewhere else. Affluent consumer

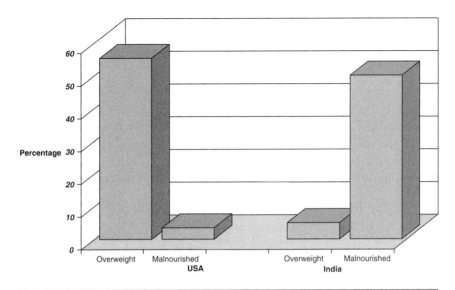

**Figure 2**    Percentage of Population Malnourished and Overweight

Source: *New Internationalist, 353* (2003): 20.

access to global food supplies reduces the supply of fresh, local, and healthy food choices everywhere (whether in supermarket cultures or in agrarian cultures converted to agri-exporting). Intensification may offer the security of a contract to a grower community for a time, but it may also increase that community's vulnerability to a more competitive producer elsewhere, given the variability of land fertility and wages and the mobility of firms. The intensification of beef exporting may displace not only a peasant community, but a local culture of mixed economy, interwoven with food crops and livestock, also may give way to specialized pasturing of steers. It also may affect the economic priorities of a nation as well as that nation's (and the world's) resource base.

## CASE STUDY
### The Hamburger Connection

Between 1960 and 1990, forests disappeared at alarming rates in Central America. During this time, more than 25 percent of the Central American forest was converted to pasture for cattle that were, in turn, converted into hamburgers. Deforestation was linked, by way of the global marketplace, to an expanding fast-food industry in the United States. About one-tenth of American burgers use imported beef, much of it produced under contract for transnational food companies by Central American meat-packing plants. The Central American beef industry has had powerful institutional support through government loans assisted by the World Bank, the Agency for International Development (AID), and the Inter-American Development Bank (IADB). The plan was to tie the development of Central American societies to this valuable export earner.

Few people realized that consuming a hamburger might also involve consuming forest resources or that Central America's new beef industry would have vast environmental and social consequences. These consequences include the displacement of peasants from their land and forest dwellers from their habitat because more than half of Central American land was committed to grazing cattle. As less land was available for farming, the production of peasant staple foods declined. The Costa Rican government had to use beef export earnings to purchase basic grains on the world market to compensate for the declining local food supply and to feed the country's people.

What, then, is the cost of a hamburger?

---

*Sources: Myers (1981:7); Place (1985:290-95); Rifkin (1992:192-93).*

## Dimensions of Social Change in the Global Marketplace

The changing composition and rhythms of the global marketplace connect people and development conditions across the world. Such interconnections have three dimensions:

- First, there is the integration of producers and consumers across space as commodities crisscross political boundaries.
- Second, this spatial integration introduces new dimensions of time as world market rhythms enter into and connect physically separate communities.

For instance, a firm that establishes an export site in a community brings new work disciplines in the production of goods for the global market.

- Third, once communities are integrated in the new time and space of the global market, they are increasingly subject to decisions made by powerful market agencies such as governments, firms, and currency or commodity speculators. If oil prices spike, for example, the effect is felt by a variety of groups in the global economy, from farmers to petrochemical firms to travelers. If there is a run on national currencies, as in the 1997 Asian financial crisis, whole populations can suffer as they have in Indonesia, Thailand, and South Korea.

The global market's continual reorganization dramatically affects the livelihoods of people and their life trajectories. Today, the athletic shoe industry, turning footwear into fashion, generates new and evolving employment opportunities in the United States (specialty shoe stores, product design, and marketing) and in East and Southeast Asia (production and assembly). Capturing market shares by designing fashion and finding cheap labor sites is the name of the game. But this game continually reshuffles the employment deck and people's futures. And although money makes this world go around, its accelerated circulation compresses people's lives into a unified social space (the global marketplace) and time (the rhythms and cycles of the global economy). As financial markets are deregulated, whole countries (e.g., Argentina in 2001) can plummet into material, psychological, and political crisis overnight.

Consider again the dynamics of the beef chain. Not only does rising hamburger consumption incorporate new grazing regions into the global marketplace, but this new space itself also has its own time. In the United States, beef consumption developed and grew throughout the century-long process of settling the American (rural and urban) frontier. The current fast-food demand, however, compresses the modernization process for forest dwellers and Indian peasants, forcing them to adapt in a single generation, converting their habitats to pasture, and displacing many of them to urban fringes. On the broader scale, the burning of forests and grazing of livestock intensify the threat to future generations of global warming. We are seeing the actions of humankind endangering the habitability of the planet. Here the long run, or rather our sense of it, is compromised by the finiteness of biospheric resources: perhaps the most dramatic effect of the compression of space and time.

# Development, Globalization, and Imperial Projects

This introduction illustrates, through examples of commodity chains and their social and environmental impacts, the global nature of economic activity. Development may still be pursued by individual nation-states, but less and less does it resemble the conventional definition of development as *nationally organized economic growth*. In this book, we examine the ways the world has moved from nationally organized growth toward *globally organized economic growth*.

Development and economic growth are active goals, rather than natural processes. We know this from observing still-existing communities of forest dwellers, who fashion their lives according to natural cycles. With the rise of modern European capitalism, state bureaucrats pursued economic growth to finance their military and administrative needs. But "development" as such was not yet a universal strategy. It became so only in the mid-twentieth century, as newly independent states joined the world community and the rush toward development, with quite varying success.

The 1991 UN *Human Development Report* states,

> The basic objective of human development is to enlarge the range of people's choices to make development more democratic and participatory. These choices should include access to income and employment opportunities, education and health, and a clean and safe physical environment. Each individual should also have the opportunity to participate fully in community decisions and to enjoy human, economic and political freedoms.[15]

We are now in an era of rethinking development, given the evident failure of many countries to fulfill this promise of development and the world's growing awareness of environmental limits. In this context, *sustainability* has become a popular issue, forcing a reevaluation of the development enterprise. This book traces the changing fortunes of development efforts, the shortcomings of which have produced two responses. One is to advocate a thoroughly global market to expand trade, under the aegis of powerful corporations, and spread the wealth. The other is to reevaluate the economic emphasis and growing global inequalities and to recover democratic and sustainable communities, at whatever scale necessary to sustain social life.

The development debate is re-forming around a conflict between privileging the global market and privileging human communities: Do we continue expanding industry and wealth indefinitely, or do we find a way that human communities (however defined) can recover social intimacy, spiritual coherence, healthy environments, and sustainable material practices? Both visions are confronting a changing world—possibly a declining world—of which each is increasingly well aware.

These visions echo the elemental conflict between profits and meaning stemming from the rise of Western rationalism, based in technology and market behavior. The globalization of this model, therefore, is likely to generate cultural tensions, especially where non-Western cultures are affected. The dilemma resides, partly, in the unequal power between Western states and firms and non-Western states, firms, and communities. This inequality is often expressed in the tension between the "haves" and the "have-nots," or between the North (Western Europe, Japan, and North America) and the South (Africa, Latin America, and Asia). But, interestingly, inequality and tension are growing within both North and South as globalization intensifies. The major thrust of this book is to make these tensions intelligible by situating them within a world-historical framework.

The world-historical framework is important because it allows us to link the changing trajectories of development across the world and those within particular countries. To that end, this account is organized by two major concepts: the *development project* and the *globalization project*. Each concept is an organizing concept, allowing two overlapping eras, and political-economic and discursive ways of ordering the world, to be juxtaposed with one another to evaluate their different goals, practices, and mechanisms. The globalization project succeeds the development project, partly because the latter failed and partly because the former became a new exercise of (market) power across the world (as transnational firms and banks grew and as neoliberal ideology took hold, restructuring states and societies everywhere). This is the legacy of the late twentieth century. As the twenty-first century takes hold, the world is confronted with a new formulation: an *imperial project*, arising out of a radical shift in the foreign policy of the United States, as the sole military superpower. We examine this briefly in Chapter 8.

# PART I

## The Development Project (Late 1940s to Early 1970s)

# 1

# Instituting the
# Development Project

Development emerged during the colonial era. While it may have been experienced by nineteenth-century Europeans as something specifically European, over time it came to be viewed as a universal necessity. But what *is* development?

In the nineteenth century, *development* was understood, *philosophically*, as the improvement of humankind. *Practically*, development was understood by political elites as social engineering of emerging national societies. It meant formulating government policy to manage the social transformations wrought by the rise of capitalism and industrial technologies. So development was identified with both industrial and market expansion and regulating its disruptive social effects. These effects began with the displacement of rural populations by land enclosures for cash cropping, creating undesirables such as menacing paupers, restless proletarians, and unpleasant factory towns.[1] Development meant balancing the apparent inevitability of technological change with social intervention—understood idealistically as assisting human society in its development and perhaps realistically as managing citizen-subjects experiencing wrenching social transformations.

Unsurprisingly, this social engineering impulse framed European colonization of the non-European world. Not only did colonial plunder underwrite European industrialization, but also colonial administrators assumed the task of developing, or controlling, their subject populations.

Here, development served a legitimating function, where, compared to Europeans, native peoples appeared backward. The proverbial "white man's burden" was an interpretation of this apparently natural relation of superiority and an invitation to intervene, in the name of development.

Development became, then, an extension of modern social engineering to the colonies as they were incorporated into the European orbit. Subject populations were exposed to a variety of new disciplines, including forced labor schemes, schooling, and segregation in native quarters. Forms of colonial subordination differed across time and space, but the overriding object was either to adapt or marginalize colonial subjects to the European presence. Punctuality, task specialization, and regularity were the hallmarks of the new discipline of adaptation, breaking down social customs and producing individual subjects who confronted a new, rational order, which they reproduced and/or resisted.

This draws attention to the relations of power in development. For example, in 1843, the Egyptian state (under suzerainty of the declining Ottoman, and rising British, empire) introduced the English "Lancaster school" factory model to the city of Cairo to consolidate the authority of its emerging civil service. Egyptian students learned the new disciplines required of a developing society that was busy displacing peasant culture with plantations of cotton for export to English textile mills and managing an army of migrant labor building an infrastructure of roads, canals, railways, telegraphs, and ports.[2] Across the colonial divide, industrialism was transforming English and Egyptian society alike, producing new forms of social discipline among laboring populations and middle-class citizen-subjects. As we shall see, while industrialism produced new class inequalities within each society, colonial development produced a racialized form of international inequality.

Non-European cultures were irrevocably changed through colonialism, and the postcolonial context was founded on inequality—embedded in modern ideals of sovereign nation-states, some of which were more equal than others, and in the domestic social inequalities introduced by colonialism. When newly independent states emerged, political leaders had to operate in an international framework that was not of their making but through which they acquired political legitimacy. How that framework emerged is the subject of this chapter. But first we must address the historical context of colonialism.

# Colonialism

Our appeal to history begins with a powerful simplification. It concerns the social psychology of European colonialism, built largely around stereotypes that have shaped perceptions and conflict for five centuries. (*Colonialism* is defined and explained in the following insert, and the European colonial empires are depicted in Figure 1.1.) One such perception was the idea among Europeans that non-European native people or colonial subjects were "backward," trapped in their tradition. The experience of colonial rule encouraged this image, as European and non-European cultures compared one another within a relationship in which Europe had a powerful social-psychological advantage rooted in its missionary and military-industrial apparatus. This comparison was interpreted, or misinterpreted, as European cultural superiority. It was easy to take the next step and view the difference as "progress," something the colonizers could impart to their subjects.

---

### What Is Colonialism?

*Colonialism is the subjugation by physical and psychological force of one culture by another—a colonizing power—through military conquest of territory and caricaturing the relation between the two cultures. It predates the era of European expansion (fifteenth to twentieth centuries) and extends to Japanese colonialism in the twentieth century and, most recently, Chinese colonization of Tibet. Colonialism has two forms: colonies of settlement, which often eliminate indigenous people (such as the Spanish destruction of the Aztec and Inca civilizations in the Americas), and colonies of rule, where colonial administrators reorganize existing cultures by imposing new inequalities to facilitate their exploitation. Examples of this are the British use of local landlords, zamindars, to rule parts of India; the confiscation of personal and common land for cash cropping; depriving women of their customary resources; and the elevation of ethnoracial differences (such as privileging certain castes or tribes in the exercise of colonial rule). The outcomes are, first, the cultural genocide or marginalization of indigenous people; second, the introduction of new tensions around class, gender,*

*(Continued)*

> (Continued)
>
> *race, and caste that continue to disrupt postcolonial societies; third, the extraction of labor, cultural treasures, and resources to enrich the colonial power, its private interests, and public museums; fourth, the elaboration of ideologies justifying colonial rule, including notions of racism, as well as backwardness versus modernity; and fifth, various responses by colonial subjects, ranging from death to submission and internalization of inferiority to a variety of resistances: from everyday forms to sporadic uprisings to mass political mobilization.*

Such a powerful misinterpretation—and devaluing—of other cultures appears frequently in historical accounts. It is reflected in assumptions made by settlers in the Americas and Australasia about the indigenous people they encountered. In each case, the Europeans perceived the Indians and aborigines as people who did not "work" the land they inhabited. In other words, they had no right of "property"—a European concept in which property is private and alienable. Their removal from their ancestral lands is a bloody reminder of the combined military power and moral fervor with which European colonization was pursued.

In precolonial Africa, as communities achieved stability within their environment, they developed methods for survival, relying on kinship patterns and supernatural belief systems. These methods were at once conservative and adaptive because, over time, African communities changed their composition, their scale, and their location in a long process of settlement and migration through the lands south of the equator. European colonists in Africa, however, saw these superstitious cultures as static and only occupying, rather than improving, the land. This perception ignored the complex social systems adapted first to African ecology and then to European occupation of that ecology.[3] Under these circumstances, the idea of the "white man's burden" emerged, a concept in which Europe viewed itself as the bearer of civilization to the darker races. French colonial historian Albert Sarraut claimed in 1923,

> It should not be forgotten that we are centuries ahead of them, long centuries during which—slowly and painfully, through a lengthy effort of research, invention, meditation and intellectual progress aided by the very influence of our temperate climate—a magnificent heritage of science, experience and moral superiority has taken shape, which makes us eminently entitled to protect and lead the races lagging behind us.[4]

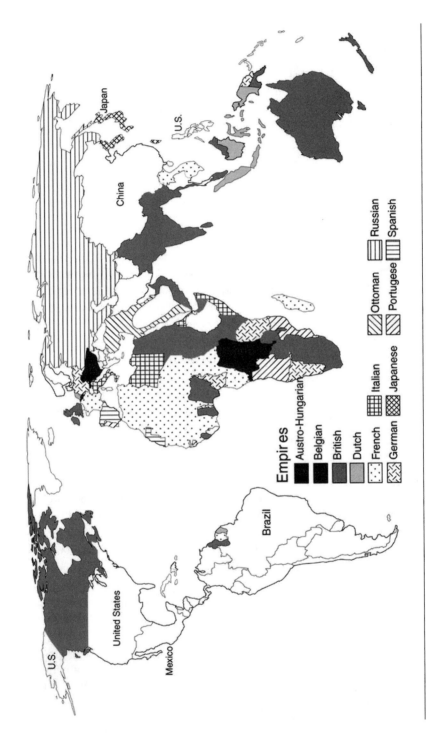

**Figure 1.1**    European Colonial Empires at the Turn of the Twentieth Century

The ensuing colonial exchange, however, was captured in the postcolonial African saying, "When the white man came he had the Bible and we had the land. When the white man left we had the Bible and he had the land." Under colonialism, when non-Europeans lost control of their land, their spiritual life was compromised insofar as it was connected to their landscapes. It was difficult to sustain material and cultural integrity under these degrading extractive processes and conditions.

---

### What Are Some Characteristics of Precolonial Cultures?

*All precolonial cultures had their own ways of satisfying their material and spiritual needs. Cultures varied by the differentiation among their members or households according to their particular ecological endowments and social contact with other cultures. The variety ranged from small communities of subsistence producers (living off the land or the forest) to extensive kingdoms or states. Subsistence producers, organized by kin relations, usually subdivided social tasks between men, who hunted and cleared land for cultivation, and women, who cultivated and processed crops, harvested wild fruits and nuts, and performed household tasks. These cultures were highly skilled in resource management and production to satisfy their material needs. They generally did not produce a surplus beyond what was required for their immediate needs, and they organized cooperatively—a practice that often made them vulnerable to intruders because they were not prepared for self-defense. Unlike North American Indians, whose social organization provided leadership for resistance, some aboriginal cultures, such as those of Australia and the Amazon, lacked leadership hierarchies and were more easily wiped out by settlers. By contrast, the Mogul empire in seventeenth-century India had a complex hierarchical organization based on local chiefdoms in which the chief presided over the village community and ensured that surpluses (monetary taxes and produce) were delivered to a prosperous central court and "high culture." Village and urban artisans produced a range of metal goods, pottery, and crafts, including sophisticated muslins and silks. Caste distinctions, linked to previous invasions, corresponded to divisions of*

*(Continued)*

(Continued)

*labor, such as trading, weaving, cultivating, ruling, and performing unskilled labor. Colonizers typically adapted such social and political hierarchies to their own ends—alienating indigenous political systems from their customary social functions and incubating tensions inherited by postcolonial states.*

Sources: Rowley (1974); Bujra (1992).

The non-European world appeared ancestral to the colonizers, who assumed that non-Europeans would and should emulate European social organization. Development came to be identified as the destiny of humankind. The systematic handicapping of non-Europeans in this apparently natural and fulfilling endeavor remained largely unacknowledged, just as non-European scientific and moral achievements and legacies in European culture were generally ignored. Being left holding the Bible was an apt metaphor for the condition of non-Europeans who were encouraged to pursue the European way, often without the resources to accomplish this.

Western secular and religious crusades in the forms of administration, education, and missionary efforts accompanied colonial rule to stimulate progress along the European path. The problem was that the ruling Europeans either misunderstood or denied the integrity of non-European cultures. And then there was the paradox of bringing progress to colonized peoples denied their sovereignty—a paradox experienced daily by the non-Europeans. This paradox fuelled the anticolonial movements seeking independence from Western occupation. Colonial subjects powerfully appropriated European discourse of the "rights of man," raising it as a mirror to their colonial masters and adopting it as a mobilizing tool for their independence struggle.

## The Colonial Division of Labor

From the sixteenth century, European colonists and traders traveled along African coasts to the New World and across the Indian Ocean and the China seas seeking fur, precious metals, slave labor, spices, tobacco, cacao, potatoes, sugar, and cotton. The European colonial powers—Spain, Portugal, Holland, France, and Britain—and their merchant companies

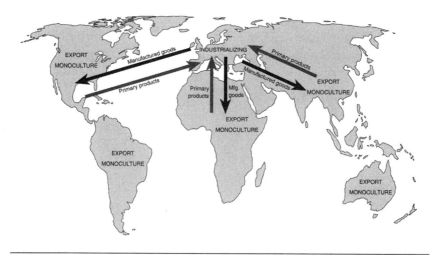

**Figure 1.2**    The "Colonial Division of Labor" between European States and Their Colonial Empires

exchanged manufactured goods such as cloth, guns, and implements for these products and for Africans taken into slavery and transported to the Americas. In the process, they reorganized the world.

The basic pattern was to establish in the colonies specialized extraction and production of raw materials and primary products that were unavailable in Europe. In turn, these products fueled European manufacturing as industrial inputs and foodstuffs for its industrial labor force. On a world scale, this specialization between European economies and their colonies came to be termed the **colonial division of labor,** illustrated in Figure 1.2.

While the colonial division of labor stimulated European industrialization, it forced non-Europeans into primary commodity production. Specialization disorganized non-European cultures, typically undermining local crafts and mixed-farming systems and alienating their lands and forests for commercial exploitation.

Not only did non-European cultures surrender their own handicraft industries in this exchange, but also their agriculture was often reduced to a specialized **export monoculture,** where local farmers produced a single crop, such as peanuts or cotton, for export.

Handicraft destruction was often deliberate and widespread. Perhaps the best-known destruction of native crafts occurred through Britain's conquest of India. Until the nineteenth century, Indian muslins and calicos were luxury imports into Europe (as were Chinese silks and satins). By that time, however, the East India Company (which ruled India for the British crown until 1858) undermined this Indian craft and, in its own words, "succeeded in converting India from a manufacturing country into a country exporting raw produce."[5] The company had convinced the British government to use tariffs of 70 to 80 percent against Indian finished goods and to permit virtually free entry of raw cotton into England. In turn, British traders flooded India with cheap cloth manufactured in Manchester. Industrial technology (textile machinery and steam engine) combined with political power to impose the colonial division of labor, as British-built railway systems moved Indian raw cotton to coastal ports for shipment to Liverpool and returned to the Indian countryside with machine-made products that undermined a time-honored craft.

### Social Reorganization under Colonialism

The colonial division of labor devastated producing communities and their craft- and agriculture-based systems. When the British first came to India, in the mid-eighteenth century, Robert Clive described the textile city of Dacca as "extensive, populous, and rich as the city of London." By 1840, Sir Charles Trevelyan testified before a British parliamentary committee that the population of Dacca "has fallen from 150,000 to 30,000, and the jungle and malaria are fast encroaching upon the town. . . . Dacca, the Manchester of India, has fallen off from a very flourishing town to a very poor and small town."[6]

While native industries declined under colonial systems, local farming cultures lost their best lands to commercial agriculture supplying European consumers and industries. Plantations and other kinds of cash-cropping arrangements sprang up across the colonial world, producing specialized tropical exports ranging from bananas to peanuts, depending on local agri-ecologies (see Table 1.1). In India, production of commercial crops such as cotton, jute, tea, peanuts, and sugar cane grew by 85 percent between the 1890s and the 1940s. In contrast, in that same period, local food crop production declined by 7 percent while the population grew by 40 percent, a shift that spread hunger and social unrest.[7] Using revenue and irrigation policies to force farmers into export agriculture, Britain came to depend on India for almost 20 percent of its wheat consumption by 1900. Worse than the fact that "Londoners were in fact eating India's bread" was the destruction of Indian food security by modern technologies. With the telegraph coordinating speculative price hikes, grain

**Table 1.1**    Selected Colonial Export Crops

| Colony | Colonial Power | Export Crop |
|--------|----------------|-------------|
| Australia | Britain | Wool, wheat |
| Brazil | Portugal | Sugar, coffee |
| Congo | Belgium | Rubber, ivory |
| Egypt | Britain | Cotton |
| Ghana | Britain | Cocoa |
| Haiti | France | Sugar |
| India | Britain | Cotton, opium, tea |
| Indochina | France | Rice, rubber |
| Indonesia | Holland | Rubber, tobacco |
| Ivory Coast | France | Cocoa |
| Kenya | Britain | Wool |
| Malaya | Britain | Rubber, palm oil |
| Senegal | France | Peanuts |
| South Africa | Britain | Gold, diamonds |

movements along a network of railways responded to London prices rather than local need. Thus, the technologies of the global market undermined the customary system of grain reserves organized at the village level as protection against drought and famine.[8]

The colonial division of labor developed European capitalist civilization (with food and raw materials) at the same time that it disrupted non-European cultures. As European industrial society matured, the exploding urban populations demanded ever-increasing imports of sugar, coffee, tea, cocoa, tobacco, and vegetable oils from the colonies, and the expanding factory system demanded ever-increasing inputs of raw materials such as cotton, timber, rubber, and jute. The colonists forced more and more subjects to work in cash cropping, employing a variety of methods such as enslavement, taxation, land grabbing, and recruitment for indentured labor contracts.

As the African slave trade subsided, the Europeans created new schemes of forced, or indentured, labor. Indian and Chinese peasants and handicraftsmen, impoverished by colonial intervention or market competition from cheap textiles, scattered to sugar plantations in the Caribbean, Fiji, Mauritius, and Natal; to rubber plantations in Malaya and Sumatra; and to British East Africa to build the railways that intensified the two-way extraction of African resources and the introduction of cheap manufactured goods. In the third quarter of the nineteenth century alone, more than one million indentured Indians went overseas. Today, Indians still outnumber native Fijians; they make up 50 percent of the Guyanese population and 40 percent of the residents of Trinidad. In the same period, 90,000 Chinese indentured laborers went to work in the Peruvian guano fields, and 200,000 went to California to work in the fruit industry, in the gold fields, and on the railways.[9]

---

### Colonialism Unlocks a Development Puzzle

*Colonialism was far-reaching and multidimensional in its effects. We focus here on the colonial division of labor because it isolates a key issue in the development puzzle. Unless we see the interdependence created through this division of world labor, it is easy to take our unequal world at face value and view it as a natural continuum, with an advanced European region showing the way for a backward, non-European region. But by viewing world inequality as relational (interdependent) rather than as sequential (catch-up), then the conventional, modern understanding of "development" comes into question. The conventional understanding is that individual societies experience or pursue development, in linear fashion, one after the other. If, however, industrial growth in Europe depended on agricultural monoculture in the non-European world, then development was more than a national process. This means that development is an international and unequal relationship (founded on some form of colonization). Whichever way we look at it, it is questionable to think of development as an isolated national activity. This, however, was the dominant conception in the mid-twentieth century, and our task is to consider why this was so then—and why now, in a rapidly integrating world, development is increasingly linked to globalization—in addition to examining the unequal foundations of each.*

---

Before moving to that task, it is important to summarize the unequal social structures of colonialism related to the colonial division of labor:

*Development and Underdevelopment.* Non-European societies were fundamentally transformed through the loss of resources and craft traditions as colonial subjects were forced to labor in mines, fields, and plantations to produce exports sustaining distant European factories. This was a *global* process, connecting slaves, peasantries, and laborers in the colonies with European proletarians—provisioned with cheap colonial products such as sugar, tea, and tropical oils and cotton clothing. Globally, development was realized through a racialized process of colonial "underdevelopment."

*Colonial Rule (New Systems of Inequality).* Colonial systems of rule secured supplies of colonial labor. For example, a landed oligarchy (the *hacendados*) ruled South America before the nineteenth century in the name of the Spanish and Portuguese monarchies, using an institution called *encomienda* to create a form of native serfdom. Settler colonialism also spread to North America, Australasia, and southern Africa, where settlers used military, legal, and economic force to wrest land from the natives for commercial purposes and to access slave, convict, and indentured labor. As the industrial era emerged, colonial rule (in Asia and Africa) grew more bureaucratic. By the end of the nineteenth century, colonial administrations were self-financing, depending on military force and the loyalty of local princes and chiefs, tribes, and castes (especially important, where, for instance, the British presence never exceeded 0.5 percent of the Indian population).[10] Native rulers were bribed with titles, land, or tax-farming privileges to recruit male peasants to the military and to force them into cash cropping to pay the taxes supporting the colonial state.

Male entry into cash cropping disrupted patriarchal gender divisions, creating new gender inequalities. Women's customary land-user rights were often displaced by new systems of private property, circumscribing food production, traditionally women's responsibility. Thus, British colonialism in Kenya fragmented the Kikuyu culture as peasant land was confiscated and men migrated to work on European farms, reducing women's control over resources and lowering their status, wealth, and authority.[11]

Elements of the modern state were deployed in the colonies, using industrial and/or military techniques to organize schooling, labor forces, and urban surveillance; to attach rural villages to commercial estates; to supervise public health; to regulate sexual relations; and so forth.[12] While the Europeans constructed a caricatured knowledge of their subjects ("Orientalism"), institutionalized in administration, universities, museums, and contemporary fiction, their exercise of power in the colonies refined methods of rule at home and abroad. In other words, colonial rule revealed the hard edge of power in the modern state.[13]

And just as the concentration of industrial labor in European factory towns produced labor organization, so these methods of rule produced resistances among subject populations, whether laborers, peasants, soldiers, or civil servants. These tensions fed the politics of decolonization, dedicated to molding inchoate resistance to colonial abuses into coherent, nationalist movements striving for independence.

*Diasporas.* The displacement of colonial subjects from their societies and their dispersion to resolve labor shortages elsewhere in the colonial world has had a lasting global effect—most notably in the African, Indian, and Chinese diasporas. This cultural mosaic has reconstituted the relations and meaning of race, ethnicity, and nationality—generating ethnopolitical tensions that shape national politics across the world today—and questioned the modernist ideal of the secular state.

## Decolonization

As Europeans were attempting to "civilize" their colonies, colonial subjects across the Americas, Asia, and Africa explored the paradox of European colonialism—the juxtaposition of the European discourse of rights and sovereignty against their own subjugation. In the French sugar colony of Haiti, the late eighteenth-century "Black Jacobin" revolt powerfully exposed the double standard of European civilization. Turning the rhetoric of the French Revolution successfully against French colonialism, the rebellious slaves of the Haitian sugar plantations became the first to gain their independence, sending tremors throughout the slaveholding lands of the New World.[14]

Resistance to colonialism evolved across the next two centuries, from the early nineteenth-century independence of the Latin American republics (from Spain and Portugal) to the dismantling of South African apartheid in the early 1990s. Although decolonization has continued into the present day (with the independence of East Timor in 2002 and the Palestinians still struggling for a homeland), the worldwide decolonization movement peaked as European colonialism collapsed in the mid-twentieth century, when World War II sapped the power of the French, Dutch, British, and Belgian states to withstand anticolonial struggles.

After millions of colonial subjects were deployed in the Allied war effort for self-determination against fascist expansionism from Europe to Southeast Asia, the returning colonial soldiers turned this ideal on their colonial masters in their final bid for independence. Veteran Nigerian anticolonialist and later president Nnamdi Azikiwe characterized African independence struggles by quoting Eleanor Roosevelt: "We are fighting a war today so that individuals all over the world may have freedom. This means an equal chance for every man to have food and shelter and a minimum of such things as spell happiness. Otherwise we fight for nothing of real value."[15] Freedom was linked to overcoming the deprivations of colonialism. And it took the form of the *nation*-state, understood as a product of struggle within these world-historical relations and, therefore, whose sovereign capacity to deliver development was shaped precisely by those relations (e.g., colonial division of labor, rules of the postwar international order)—as this chapter suggests.

## Colonial Liberation

Freedom also involved overcoming the social-psychological scars of colonialism. The racist legacy of colonialism deeply penetrated the psyche of colonist and colonized and remains with us today. In 1957, at the height of African independence struggles, Tunisian philosopher Albert Memmi wrote *The Colonizer and the Colonized,* dedicating the American edition to the (colonized) American Negro. In this work (published in 1967), he claimed,

> Racism . . . is the highest expression of the colonial system and one of the most significant features of the colonialist. Not only does it establish a fundamental discrimination between colonizer and colonized, a *sine qua non* of colonial life, but it also lays the foundation for the immutability of this life.[16]

To overcome this apparent immutability, West Indian psychiatrist Frantz Fanon, writing from Algeria, responded with *The Wretched of the Earth* (published 1967), a manifesto of liberation. It was a searing indictment of European colonialism and a call to people of the former colonies (the Third World) to transcend the mentality of enslavement and forge a new path for humanity. He wrote,

> It is a question of the Third World starting a new history of Man, a history which will have regard to the sometimes prodigious theses which Europe has put forward, but which will also not forget Europe's crimes, of which the most horrible was committed in the heart of man, and consisted of the pathological tearing apart of his functions and the crumbling away of his unity. . . . On the immense scale of humanity, there were racial hatreds, slavery, exploitation and above all the bloodless genocide which consisted in the setting aside of fifteen thousand millions of men. . . . Humanity is waiting

for something other from us than such an imitation, which would be almost an obscene caricature.[17]

Decolonization was rooted in a liberatory upsurge, expressed in mass political movements of resistance—some dedicated to driving out the colonists and others to forming an alternative colonial government to assume power as decolonization occurred. In Algeria (much as in Palestine today), the independence movement incubated within and struck at the French occupation from the native quarter. The use of terror against civilian populations symbolized the bitter divide between colonizer and colonized (portrayed in Pontecorvo's classic film, *Battle of Algiers*) and resonates today in al Qaeda terrorism against symbols of corporate and state military power and Western affluence.

## CASE STUDY

## The Tensions and Lessons of the Indian Nationalist Revolt

Perhaps responding to Fanon's plea for a new departure, Mahatma Gandhi's model of nonviolent resistance to British colonialism affirmed the simplicity and virtue in the ideal-typical premodern solidarities of Indian village life. Rather than embrace the emerging world of nation-states, Gandhi argued, didactically, that Indians became a subject population not because of colonial force but through the seduction of modernity. Gandhi's approach flowed from his philosophy of transcendental (as opposed to scientific or historical) truth, guided by a social morality deriving from human experience. Gandhi disdained the violent methods of the modern state and the institutional rationality of the industrial age. He regarded machinery as the source of India's impoverishment, not only in destroying handicrafts but in compromising humanity:

> We notice that the mind is a restless bird; the more it gets the more it wants, and still remains unsatisfied. . . . Our ancestors, therefore, set a limit to our indulgences. They saw that happiness is largely a mental condition. . . . We have managed with the same kind of plough as existed thousands of years ago. We have retained the same kind of cottages that we had in former times and our indigenous education remains the same as before. We have had no system of life-corroding competition. . . . It was not that we did not know how to invent machinery, but our forefathers knew that if we set our hearts after such things, we would become slaves and lose our moral fibres. They, therefore, after due deliberation decided that we should only do what we could with our hands and feet.

Gandhi's method of resistance included wearing homespun cloth instead of machine-made goods, foreswearing use of the English language, and mistrusting the European philosophy of self-interest. Gandhi viewed self-interest as undermining community-based ethics in the service of a modern state dominated by powerful economic and political interests. He advocated the decentralization of social power, appealing to grassroots notions of self-reliance, proclaiming,

> Independence must begin at the bottom. Thus, every village will be a republic or *panchayat* having full powers. It follows, therefore, that every village has to be self-sustained and capable of managing its affairs even to the extent of defending itself against the whole world.

While Gandhi's politics, anchored in a potentially reactionary Hindu religious imagery, galvanized rural India, Indian nationalism actually rode to power via the longstanding Indian National Congress and one of its progressive leaders, Jawaharlal Nehru. Nehru represented the formative national state, viewing Gandhian philosophy as inappropriate to the modern world but recognizing its importance in mobilizing the independence struggle. Infusing the national movement with calls for land reform and agrarian modernization to complement industrial development, Nehru declared,

> It can hardly be challenged that, in the context of the modern world, no country can be politically and economically independent, even within the framework of international interdependence, unless it is highly industrialized and has developed its power resources to the utmost.

Together, Gandhi and Nehru are revered as fathers of independence and the Indian national state, respectively. What is interesting for us is that the struggle against empire was woven out of two strands: an *idealist* strand looking back and looking forward to a transcendental Hinduism anchored in village-level self-reliance, as well as a *realist* strand looking sideways and asserting that Indian civilization could be rescued, contained, and celebrated in the form of a modern state. An unexpected third strand appeared at the moment of decolonization as Mohammed Ali Jinnah (switching allegiance from the Congress to the Muslim League in the 1930s) led a middle-class movement to secure a new fragment state, Pakistan, in return for his support of the British war effort. The bloody partition of India in 1947 is another story that continues to reverberate today in periodic violence between Hindus and Muslims, nuclear tensions between the two states, and rising Islamic fundamentalism in the militarized state of Pakistan.

Even though the world is different now than it was in the time of Indian independence, is it possible to see that a similar choice faces the world's peoples: between a path of centralized power, monoculture, and property rights versus a path of multilayered powers, diversity, and citizen rights?

*Sources: Chatterjee (2001:86, 87, 91, 97, 144, 151); Ali (2002:169–70).*

Other forms of resistance included militarized national liberation struggles (e.g., Portuguese African colonies, French Indo-China) and widespread colonial labor unrest. British colonialism faced widespread labor strikes in its West Indian and African colonies in the 1930s, and this pattern continued over the next two decades in Africa as British and French colonial subjects protested conditions in cities, ports, mines, and the railways. In this context, development was understood as a pragmatic effort to improve material conditions in the colonies to preserve the colonies—and there was no doubt that colonial subjects understood this and turned the promise of development back on the colonizers, viewing development as an entitlement. As British Colonial Secretary Malcolm MacDonald observed in 1940, "If we are not now going to do something fairly good for the Colonial Empire, and something which helps them to get proper social services, we shall deserve to lose the colonies and it will only be a matter of time before we get what we deserve."[18] In these terms, eloquent appeals to justice in the language of rights and freedom in international fora by the representatives of colonized peoples held a mirror up to the colonial powers, demanding freedom.

A new world order was in the making. From 1945 to 1981, 105 new states joined the United Nations (UN) as the colonial empires crumbled, swelling UN ranks from 51 to 156. The extension of political sovereignty to millions of non-Europeans (more than half of humanity) ushered in the era of development.[19] This era was marked by a sense of almost boundless idealism, as governments and people from the First and the Third Worlds joined together in a coordinated effort to stimulate economic growth; bring social improvements through education, public health, family planning, and transport and communication systems to urban and rural populations; and promote political citizenship in the new nations. Just as colonized subjects appropriated the democratic discourse of the colonizers in fueling their independence movements, so leaders of the new nation-states appropriated the idealism of the development era and proclaimed equality as a domestic and international goal, informed by the UN Universal Declaration of Human Rights (1948).

The UN declaration represented a new world paradigm of fundamental human rights of freedom, equality, life, liberty, and security to all, without distinction by race, color, sex, language, religion, political opinion, national or social origin, property, birth, or other status. The declaration also included citizenship rights, that is, citizens' rights to the **social contract:** Everyone "is entitled to realization, through national effort, and international co-operation and in accordance with the organization and resources of each State, of the economic, social and cultural rights indispensable for his dignity and the free development of his personality."[20]

## Decolonization and Development

Decolonization gave development new meaning, linking it to the ideal of sovereignty, the possibility of converting subjects into citizens, and the pursuit of economic development for social justice. Already independent Latin American states adopted similar goals and, in fact, offered a new model for national industrial development.

Latin American political independence occurred in the 1820s as the older Spanish and Portuguese empires declined. During the nineteenth century, Latin American commercial development centered on the prosperity gained through agricultural and raw material exports to Europe. Because of the profitability of export agriculture, Latin American political systems came to be dominated by powerful coalitions of landowners and urban merchants. The Latin American republics clothed their oligarchic regimes with the French and U.S. revolutionary ideologies of **liberal-nationalism,** which informed nineteenth-century European nation building via national education systems, national languages and currencies, and modern armies and voting citizens. These ideologies also informed the twentieth-century movements in Asia and Africa for decolonization, which occurred as the United States reached the height of its global power and prosperity. Eager to reconstruct the post–World War II world to expand markets and the flow of raw materials, the United States led an international project, inspired by a vision of development as a national enterprise to be repeated across a world of sovereign states.

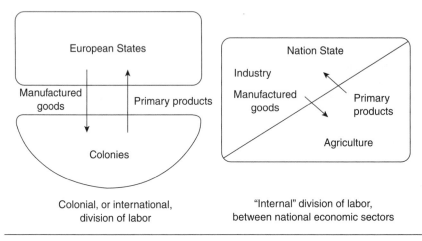

**Figure 1.3**    Distinguishing between an International and a National Division of Labor

U.S. development modeled this vision, being "inner directed" as opposed to the "outer-directed" British imperial model (based on its role as "workshop of the world"). The U.S. anticolonial lineage was compelling: the revolt of the North American colonies against British colonialism in the late eighteenth century, followed by a "civil war" against the last vestige of colonialism in the slave plantation system of the Old South. The New South was incorporated into a new national model of economic development, built on the interdependence of agricultural and industrial sectors. The division of labor between industry and agriculture, which had defined the global exchange between colonial powers and their colonies, was now internalized within the United States. Chicago traders, for instance, purchased midwestern farm products for processing, in turn selling machinery and goods to those farmers. City (industry) and countryside (agriculture) prospered together. The difference between the colonial and the national division between industry and agriculture is illustrated in Figure 1.3.

## Postwar Decolonization and the Rise of the Third World

In the era of decolonization, the world subdivided into three geopolitical segments. These subdivisions emerged after World War II (1939–1944) during the cold war, dividing the capitalist Western (**First World**) from the communist Soviet **(Second World)** blocs. The **Third World** included the postcolonial bloc of nations. Of course, there was considerable inequality across and within these subdivisions, as well as within their national units. The subdivision of the world is further explained in the following insert.

In this era, the United States was the most powerful state economically, militarily, and ideologically. Its superior standard of living (with a per capita income three times the average for Western Europe), its anticolonial heritage, and its commitment to liberal domestic and international relations lent it the legitimacy of a world leader, and it was the model of a developed society.

---

### How We Divide Up the World's Nations

*Division of the nations of the world is quite complex and extensive, and it depends on the purpose of the dividing. The basic division made in the early postwar era was into Three Worlds: The First was essentially the capitalist world (the West plus Japan), the Second was basically the socialist world (the Soviet bloc), and the Third was the rest—mostly former European colonies. The core of the Third World was the group of nonaligned countries steering an independent path between the First and Second Worlds, especially China, Egypt, Ghana, India, Indonesia, Vietnam, and Yugoslavia. In the 1980s, a Fourth World was named to describe marginalized regions. The United Nations and the development establishment use a different nomenclature: developed countries, developing countries, and least developed countries. A relational interpretation sees a division between the developed and the underdeveloped worlds. The* **Organization for Economic Cooperation and Development (OECD)** *represents the industrial states. In the 1970s, the oil-producing countries formed a producer cartel, becoming the* **Organization of Petroleum Exporting Countries (OPEC).** *At the same time, a group of rapidly industrializing Third World countries became known officially as* **newly industrializing countries (NICs).** *Alongside this group and overlapping it are the* **new agricultural countries (NACs),** *specializing in agro-industrial exports. Other groupings include the* **Group of 7 (G-7, or G-8)** *states (the core nations of the First World) and the* **Group of 77 (G-77)** *states (the collective membership of the Third World that formed in the mid-1960s).*

Ranged against the United States were the Soviet Union and an assortment of other communist states in Eastern Europe. The Second World was considered the alternative to First World capitalism.

The Third World, the remaining half of humanity and most of whom were still food-growing rural dwellers, was regarded as impoverished in standard comparative economic terms.

Frantz Fanon added political and cultural dimensions to the notion of impoverishment when he termed these people the "wretched of the earth." Whereas the First World had 65 percent of world income with only 20 percent of the world's population, the Third World accounted for 67 percent of world population but only 18 percent of its income. Many observers believe that much of the gap in living standards between the First and Third Worlds was a result of colonialism.[21]

This economic disparity between the First and Third Worlds generated the vision of development that would energize political and business elites in each world. Seizing the moment as leader of the First World, President Harry S. Truman included in a key speech on January 20, 1949, the following proclamation:

> We must embark on a bold new program for making the benefits of our scientific advances and industrial progress available for the improvement and growth of underdeveloped areas. The old imperialism—exploitation for foreign profit—has no place in our plans. What we envisage is a program of development based on the concepts of democratic fair dealing.[22]

The following year, a Nigerian nationalist echoed these sentiments:

> Self-government will not necessarily lead to a paradise overnight. . . . But it will have ended the rule of one race over another, with all the humiliation and exploitation which that implies. It can also pave the way for the internal social revolution that is required within each country.[23]

Despite the power differential between the United States and the African countries, the shared sentiments affirmed the connection between decolonization and development, where sovereign states could pursue national economic growth with First World assistance. The program of development pursued by new nations, dependence in independence, marked the postcolonial experience.

President Truman's proclamation confirmed this understanding in suggesting a new paradigm for the postwar era: the division of humanity between developed and undeveloped regions. This division of the world projected a singular destiny for all nations. Mexican intellectual Gustavo Esteva commented,

> Underdevelopment began, then, on January 20, 1949. On that day, two billion people became underdeveloped. In a real sense, from that time on, they ceased being what they were, in all their diversity, and were transmogrified into an inverted mirror of others' reality: a mirror that defines their identity . . . simply in the terms of a homogenizing and narrow minority.[24]

In other words, the proclamation by President Truman divided the world between those who were modern and those who were not. *Development/modernity* became the standard by which other societies were judged. It was a new and specific ideal of order (e.g., the bureaucratic state, industrial production, rational law, specialization, professionalism, technical innovation, price-based value) that, given the concentration of wealth and power in the First World, came to seem like order itself, assuming the status of a master concept. This was a way of looking at the world, a new paradigm. It assumed that with the end of the division of the world between the colonizers and the colonized, modernity was there for the taking by the underdeveloped world.

This new paradigm offered a strategy for improving the material condition of the Third World. It was also a strategy for reimposing order in the world, inscribing First World power and privilege in the new institutional structure of the postwar international economy. Development was simultaneously the restoration of a capitalist world market to sustain First World wealth, through access to strategic natural resources in the ex-colonial world, and the opportunity for Third World countries to emulate First World civilization and living standards. Because development was both blueprint for the world of nation-states and a strategy for world order, we shall call this enterprise the **development project.** The epithet *project* emphasizes that development is something pursued and incomplete, rather than an evolutionary outcome.

The power of the new development paradigm arose in part from its ability to present itself as universal, autonomous, and therefore uncontentious. The naturalization of development ignores the role of colonialism. In a postcolonial era, Third World states could not repeat the European experience of developing by exploiting the resources and labor of other societies. Development was modeled as a national process, initiated in European states. Its aura of inevitability devalued non-European cultures and discounted what the West learned from the non-European world. Gilbert Rist observed of postcolonial states, "Their right to self-determination had been acquired in exchange for the right to self-definition," [25] suggesting that they chose the fork in the road that proceeded toward a common (but Western-centered) future for the world and further legitimized (or naturalized) it. Of course, each state imparted its own particular style to this common agenda, such as African socialism, Latin American bureaucratic authoritarianism, or Confucianism in East Asia.

## Ingredients of the Development Project

The development project was a political and intellectual response to the condition of the world at the historic moment of decolonization. Under these conditions, development assumed a specific meaning. It imposed an essentially economic understanding of social change. In this way, development could be universalized as a market culture common to all. Its two universal ingredients were the nation-state and economic growth.

### The Nation-State

The **nation-state** was to be the framework of the development project. Nation-states were territorially defined political systems based on the government-citizen relationship that emerged in nineteenth-century Europe. Colonialism exported this model of political power (with its military shell), framing the politics of the decolonization movement, even where national boundaries made little sense. For example, the UN Economic Commission for Africa argued in 1989 that African underdevelopment derived from its arbitrary postcolonial geography, including 14 landlocked states, 23 states with a population below 5 million, and 13 states with a landmass of fewer than 50,000 hectares each.[26] The following insert illustrates the effects of these arbitrarily drawn boundaries, which continue to reverberate in world affairs of the present.

---

### How Was Africa Divided under Colonialism?

*The colonial powers inflicted profound damage on that continent, driving frontiers straight through the ancestral territories of nations. For example, we drew a line through Somalia, separating off part of the Somali people and placing them within Kenya. We did the same by*

*(Continued)*

(Continued)

*splitting the great Masai nation between Kenya and Tanzania. Elsewhere, of course, we created the usual artificial states. Nigeria consists of four principal nations: the Hausa, Igbo, Yoruba, and Fulani peoples. It has already suffered a terrible war which killed hundreds of thousands of people and which settled nothing. Sudan, Chad, Djibouti, the Senegal, Mali, Burundi and, of course, Rwanda are among the many other states that are riven by conflict.*

Source: Quoted from Goldsmith (1994:57).

During the 1950s, certain leading African anticolonialists doubted the appropriateness of the nation-state form to postcolonial Africa. They knew that sophisticated systems of rule had evolved in Africa before colonialism. They preferred an interterritorial, pan-African federalism that would transcend the arbitrary borders drawn across Africa by colonialism. But the pan-African movement did not carry the day. Geopolitical decisions about postcolonial political arrangements were made in London and Paris where colonial powers, looking to sustain spheres of influence, insisted on the nation-state as the only appropriate political outcome of decolonization. Indeed, a British Committee on Colonial Policy advised the prime minister in 1957, "During the period when we can still exercise control in any territory, it is most important to take every step open to us to ensure, as far as we can, that British standards and methods of business and administration permeate the whole life of the territory."[27] Some Africans who stood to gain from decolonization formed an indigenous elite ready to collaborate and assume power in the newly independent states.

### CASE STUDY

### Blaming the Victim? Colonial Legacies and State Deformation in Africa

Debates rage over Africa's global marginalization. Is the colonial legacy, or the instability of African states and societies, to blame? Is Africa's impoverishment a consequence of the political framework bequeathed by colonialism or the inability of Africans to embrace development? Was the nation-state an inappropriate political unit for Africa? Questions, posed in history, do not have simple answers. What we can do is consider how colonial rule may have shaped the ways in which postcolonial states emerged, limiting possibilities.

Collaboration with colonial rule by indigenous elites was inevitable following the colonists' practice of cultivating local elites as go-betweens to facilitate rule over subject populations. If such direct rule failed, indirect rule was used, based on the fracturing of "native" into several ethnicized minority identities called "tribes." The consequences were often debilitating—nurturing despotism and/or ethnic conflict. Fanon represents the African economic elites as a caricature of their Western counterparts, given their secondary role in servicing colonial exploitation of African resources. The colonial state in Africa was an alien, centralized apparatus of power. It managed land distribution, labor supply, taxation relationships, and the exporting of commodities, often organizing political authority along tribal identity lines. This coercive and fractious context shaped forms of postcolonial rule, where African elites reproduced arbitrary forms of authority, relying on their position in the state to accumulate wealth (not unique to Africa but pronounced) and sometimes cultivating ethnically driven conflict.

If modern Africa is characterized by fractious civil societies, where constructive recycling of social wealth is hampered by colonial legacies, can we say that African societies are simply at an earlier stage of *sequential* development, or is this more of a *relational* question that addresses Africa's world-historical positioning?

---

*Sources: Ake (1996:2–7); Fanon (1967); Mamdani (2003).*

Pan-Africanism was unsuccessful; nevertheless, it did bear witness to an alternative political and territorial logic. As historian Jean Suret-Canale wrote in 1970,

> Like most frontiers in Africa today, those inherited by Guinea from the colonial partition are completely arbitrary. They do not reflect the limits of natural regions, nor the limits of separate ethnic groups. They were shaped in their detail by the chances of conquest or of compromise between colonial powers.[28]

In addition, some of Guinea's rural areas were in fact attached as hinterlands to urban centers in other states, such as Dakar in Senegal and

Abidjan in the Ivory Coast. Considerable cross-border smuggling today is continuing testimony to these relationships. The pan-Africanists proposed regional political systems in which colonial states would be subsumed within larger territorial groupings—such as an East African federation of Uganda, Kenya, and Tanganyika (Tanzania).[29]

Fierce civil wars broke out in Nigeria in the 1960s and in Ethiopia in the 1970s, states such as Somalia and Rwanda collapsed in the early 1990s, and at the birth of the twenty-first century, conflict in the Congo among armies of six different nations threatened a more general repartition of Africa. These eruptions all included ethnic dimensions, rooted in social disparities and cross-border realities. In retrospect, they suggest that the pan-African movement had considerable foresight. Furthermore, ideas about the limits to the nation-state organization resonate today in the growing macro-regional groupings around the world.

## Economic Growth

The second ingredient of the development project was economic growth. Planning for development focused on economic transformation. The emphasis on economic growth allowed the application of a *universal quantifiable* standard to national development. The UN Charter of 1945 proclaimed "a rising standard of living" as the global objective. In national accounting terms, this "material well-being" indicator is measured in the commercial output of goods and services within a country: capita gross national product (GNP), or the national average of per capita income. While per capita income was not deemed the sole measure of rising living standards (health, literacy, etc.), the key criterion was measurable progress toward the goal of the "good society," popularized by economist and U.S. presidential adviser Walt Rostow's idea of the advanced stage of "high mass consumption."[30]

In the minds of Western economists, development required a kind of jump-start in the Third World. Cultural practices of wealth sharing within communities—which dissipated individual wealth—were perceived as a *traditional* obstacle to making the transition. The solution was to introduce a market system based on private property and wealth accumulation. A range of modern practices and institutions designed to sustain economic growth, such as banking and accounting systems, education, stock markets and legal systems, and public infrastructure (transport, power sources), was required. Rostow coined the term **take-off** for this transition.

**CASE STUDY**

**Development as Internal Colonialism, in Ladakh**

*Ancient Futures: Learning from Ladakh,* by Helena Norberg-Hodge, is a romanticized but telling description of how a traditional society (Buddhist in this representation) is transformed by the introduction of money. This was a society in which human relations were ordered by the rhythms of nature, high on the unforgiving steppes of the Himalayas. Work was performed collectively as Ladakhis built their annual and daily cultural rituals around the harvest cycle and viewed personal fulfillment as possible only through community life and reverence for the natural universe. Learning, or what we call education, was integral to cultural rituals and the work of manipulating a harsh environment. Extended kin relations and social cooperation ordered the lives of individuals and, according to Norberg-Hodge, produced a sense of joy in the satisfaction of essential needs through the community.

The nature of human relations changed dramatically when the Indian state built a road into this remote territory in the 1980s. Initially for military purposes, the new infrastructure introduced the market culture. Ladakhis now experienced transformations through formal education and commercial pressures associating money with fulfillment. Tourists appeared to have endless amounts of money without having to work for it. This they spent on cultural artifacts, which once defined Ladakhi social life. Young people drifted off the farms into Leh, the capital city, where they embraced the culture of consumerism with its media images of machismo for men and submission for women. The new education system schooled Ladakhi children in Western rationality, implicitly denigrating local culture and teaching them skills inappropriate for returning to that culture and often unrealizable in the emerging but unstable urban job market. Material items that were once simply exchanged for each other via community patterns of reciprocity now commanded a price in the new marketplace. Food prices, for example, were now governed by invisible market forces. The accumulation of money by individuals became the new rationality, discounting the custom of barter and sharing of skills and wealth. New and unequal social divisions emerged: urban/rural, Buddhist/Muslim, men/women, young/old, worker/professional, and so forth.

Modernity fundamentally altered the rationality of Ladakhi behavior: from collectivist to individualist, creating sharp divisions among people.

Invidious distinctions emerged, starting with Ladahki self-denigration when exposed to Western paraphernalia and the embrace of the market at the expense of customary practices. This parable returns us to the question in the Introduction about business versus culture: Must modernity involve the subordination of meaning to profit?

---

*Source: Norberg-Hodge (1992).*

As we learn from the case of Ladakh, the use of the *economic* yardstick of development, however, is fraught with problems. Average indices such as per capita income obscure inequalities among social groups and classes. Aggregate indices such as rising consumption levels, in and of themselves, are not accurate records of improvement in quality of life. Running air conditioners measures as increased consumption, but it also releases harmful hydrocarbons into the warming atmosphere. Hamburger consumption may improve national growth measures, but public health may suffer, and intensive resource consumption—of water, grain, and forestland—may compromise the quality of life elsewhere or in the future. Economic criteria for development have normative assumptions that often marginalize other criteria for evaluating living standards relating to the quality of human interactions, physical and spiritual health, and so forth. The emphasis on converting human interactions into measurable (and taxable) cash relations discounts the social wealth of nonmonetary activities (natural processes, people growing their own food, performing unpaid household labor and community service).

The principal shortcoming of the economism of development theory is its inability to acknowledge that states are first and foremost instruments of rule: Whether they can successfully "develop" their societies depends on their social structures and on historical circumstances, rather than the predictions of development theory and/or natural processes of development. Rule is accomplished in a variety of ways—via direct political domination (from state violence to education monologues to development discourses that impose definition and direction on cultural activity), via economic force (land expropriation, market competition, currency and price manipulation), via gender and ethnic relations that assign hierarchical identities and unequal opportunities to subject-citizens, via institutional rationality that devalues customary knowledges and practices, and so forth.

Under these circumstances, development is realized through inequality, and one universal form of inequality is the patriarchal state. Bina Agarwal describes the Malaysian state in these terms, where

Islamisation is backed by an autocratic "modern" State and . . . is observed to be used increasingly "as a source of moral education." Here Islamic movements are led exclusively by male religious specialists, and there "is a drive to emphasize the roles of women as wives and mothers, encourage them to forgo employment (where traditional culture emphasized work ethics for both sexes), tailor their reproductive choices to State directives, and curb their sexual independence (which has grown with their increasing absorption in urban industry since the early 1970s)."[31]

This "national mother" syndrome is deeply embedded in modern, patriarchal states.

# The Development Project Framed

Perhaps the most compelling aspect of the development project was a powerful perception by planners, governmental elites, and citizens alike that development was destiny. Both cold war blocs understood development in these terms, even if their respective paths of development were different. Each bloc took its cue from key nineteenth-century thinkers. The Western variant identified free enterprise capitalism as the high point of individual and societal development and was based in Jeremy Bentham's utilitarian philosophy of common good arising out of the pursuit of individual self-interest. The Communist variant, on the other hand, identified the abolition of private property and central planning as the goal of social development. The source for this was Karl Marx's collectivist dictum: "from each according to their ability, and to each according to their needs."

It is noteworthy that although the two political blocs subscribed to opposing representations of human destiny, they shared the same modernist paradigm. *National industrialization* would be the vehicle of development in each.

## National Industrialization: Ideal and Reality

"National industrialization" had two key assumptions. First, it assumed that development involved the displacement of agrarian civilization by an urban-industrial society. For national development policy, this meant a deliberate shrinking of the size and share of the agricultural sector as the manufacturing and service sectors grew. It also meant the *transfer of resources* such as food, raw materials, and redundant labor from the agrarian sector as agricultural productivity grew. Industrial growth would ideally feed back and technify agriculture. These two national economic sectors would therefore condition each other's development, as in the U.S. case discussed earlier in this chapter and illustrated in Figure 1.3.

Second, the idea of national industrialization assumed a *linear direction* for development. The goal of backward societies, therefore, was to play catch-up with the West. The Soviet Union's premier, Joseph Stalin, articulated this doctrine in the 1930s, proclaiming, "We are fifty or a hundred years behind the advanced countries. We must make good this distance in ten years. Either we do it or they crush us."[32] Stalin's resolve came from the pressures of military (and therefore economic) survival in a hostile world. The Soviet Union industrialized in one generation, "squeezing" the peasantry to finance urban-industrial development with cheap food.

The industrial priority dominated the development vision. Across the cold war divide, industrialization was the symbol of success in each social system, and beyond the ideological rivalry, each bloc shared the goals of the development project. Indeed, leaders in each bloc pursued industrial development to legitimize their power; the reasoning was that as living standards grew and people consumed more goods and services, they would subscribe to the prevailing philosophy delivering the goods and support their governments. Development is not just a goal; it is a method of rule.

### CASE STUDY

### National Development and the Building Blocs of the Global Economy

The cold war compelled leaders of each bloc to accelerate economic growth to secure their rule. Each system promoted its preferred industrial model, supported by economic aid and access to markets or resources, in the United States and the Soviet Union, respectively. These competing spheres of influence were, in effect, political and economic empires, dividing the world.

In the Second World, the Soviet system of self-reliant industrialization and collectivized agriculture was extended to East Central Europe. The goal was to reduce Eastern Europe's traditional agricultural exports to Western Europe and to encourage industrial self-reliance. In 1947, the

**Council for Mutual Economic Assistance (COMECON)** was established. It coordinated trade among the members of the East European bloc, exchanging primary goods for manufactured goods, and it also planned infrastructural energy projects for the bloc at large.

In the First World, much of the postwar economic boom depended on integration among market economies. Documents from the U.S. State Department and the Council for Foreign Relations reveal World War II plans for organizing the world according to Grand Area Planning, involving an investment sphere "strategically necessary for world control," including the entire Western Hemisphere, the former British empire, and the Far East. The United States opened these areas via export credits (reconstruction loans tied to imports of U.S. technology) and by encouraging foreign investment as (multinational) firms outgrew national borders.

In this way, economic integration "internationalized" domestic economies, either through patterns of foreign ownership or through the interdependence of commodity chains. The question that lies just below the surface in both the development and the globalization eras is the following: How can the empire of a superpower be reconciled with the ideals of a system of sovereign nation-states? Is it because of inequality among states, where some are more equal than others, or because an imperial power gets to define the rules of an unequal international order, or both?

*Sources: Chomsky (1981); Kaldor (1990:62, 67).*

The competitive—and legitimizing—dynamic of industrialization framed the development project across the cold war divide and propelled member states in the same general direction. Third World states climbed on the bandwagon. The ultimate goal was to achieve Western levels of affluence. If some states chose to mix and match elements from either side of the cold war divide, well and good. The game was still the same—catch-up. Ghanaian President Kwame Nkrumah claimed, "We in Ghana will do in ten years what it took others one hundred years to do."[33]

## Economic Nationalism

Decolonization involved a universal nationalist upsurge across the Third World. Such nationalism assumed different forms in different countries, depending on the configuration of social forces in each national political system. Nevertheless, the power of development was universal. Third World governments strove to build national development states—whether centralized like South Korea, corporatist like Brazil, or decentralized and populist like Tanzania. The **development state** organizes economic growth by mobilizing money and people. On the money end, it uses individual and corporate taxes, along with other government revenues such as export taxes and sales taxes, to finance public building of transport systems and to finance state enterprises such as steel works and energy exploration. On the people end, it forms coalitions to support its policies. Sometimes, state elites have used their power and the development ideal to accumulate wealth and influence in the state—whether through selling rights to public resources to cronies or capturing foreign aid distribution channels. In his study of the postcolonial Indian state, Sugata Bose remarked, "Instead of the state being used as an instrument of development, development became an instrument of the state's legitimacy."[34]

Just as *political* nationalism sought to regain sovereignty for Third World populations, so *economic* nationalism sought to *reverse the effects of the colonial division of labor*. Third World governments were interested in correcting what they perceived as underdevelopment in their economic systems, encouraging and protecting local efforts to industrialize with tariffs and public subsidies and reducing dependence on primary exports (increasingly viewed as "resource bondage").

## Import-Substitution Industrialization

Economic nationalism was associated with Raul Prebisch, an adviser in the 1930s to the Argentine military government and then founding director of the Argentine Central Bank. During the world depression of the 1930s, trade links weakened around the world. In Latin America, landed interests lost political power as shrinking primary export markets depleted their revenues, leading Prebisch to implement a policy of industrial protection. Import controls reduced expensive imports of manufactured goods from the West and shifted resources into domestic manufacturing.[35] In 1951, Prebisch was elected executive secretary of the UN **Economic Commission for Latin America (ECLA).** ECLA was central to the early formulation of a Third World posture on reform of the post–World War II global economy.

**Import-substitution industrialization (ISI)** largely framed initial economic development strategies in the Third World. Governments pursued ISI policies of discouraging imports through exchange rate manipulation and tariffs and by subsidizing "infant industries." The idea was to establish a cumulative process of domestic industrialization. For example, a domestic auto industry would generate parts manufacturing, road building, service stations, and so on, in addition to industries such as steel, rubber, aluminum, cement, and paint. In this way, a local industrial base would emerge.

ISI became the new economic orthodoxy in the postwar era.[36] While promoting economic nationalism in form, in substance it eventually encouraged direct investment by foreign firms.

---

### Foreign Investment and the Paradox of Protectionism

*When states erected tariffs in the mid-twentieth century, multinational corporations hopped over and invested in local, as well as natural resource, industries. For Brazil, in 1956, foreign (chiefly U.S.) capital controlled 50 percent of the iron and rolled-metal industry, 50 percent of the meat industry, 56 percent of the textile industry, 72 percent of electric power production, 80 percent of cigarette manufacturing, 80 percent of pharmaceutical production, 98 percent of the automobile industry, and 100 percent of oil and gasoline distribution. In Peru, a subsidiary of Standard Oil of New Jersey owned the oil that represented 80 percent of national production, and Bell Telephone controlled telephone services. In Venezuela, Standard Oil produced 50 percent of the oil, Shell another 25 percent, and Gulf one-seventh. In what Peter Evans has called the "triple alliance," states such as Brazil actively brokered relationships between foreign and local firms in an attempt to spur industrial development. In contrast, several decades later, in a different world, Evans's model of development became that of South Korea, where the state used its financial controls and business ties to nurture strategic domestic investments.*

---

Sources: de Castro (1969:241–42); Evans (1979, 1995).

## Development Alliance

To secure an expanding industrial base, Third World governments constructed political coalitions among different social groups to support rapid industrialization. In Latin America, for example, this coalition building formed a **development alliance**.[37] Its social constituency included commercial farmers, public employees, urban industrialists, merchants, and workers dependent on industrialization. Manufacturers' associations, labor unions, and neighborhood organizations signed on. Policymakers used price subsidies and public services such as health and education programs, cheap transport, and food subsidies to complement the earnings of urban dwellers and attract them to the cause of national industrialization.

The development alliance was a centralized and urban political initiative because governments could more easily organize social benefits for urban than for rural dwellers. Providing these social services was a way of keeping the social peace through ensuring affordable food and legitimizing the plan. The development alliance was also a vehicle of *political patronage,* whereby governments could manipulate electoral support. Mexico's Institutional Revolutionary Party (PRI), which controlled the state for much of the twentieth century, created corporatist institutions such as the Confederation of Popular Organizations, the Confederation of Mexican Workers, and the National Confederation of Peasants to channel patronage "downward" to massage loyalty "upward."

Employing these kinds of political patronage networks, development states aimed at shifting Third World economic resources away from specialization in primary product exports.

They redistributed private investment from export sectors to domestic production, and some states used mechanisms such as a development alliance to redistribute wealth at the same time. Brazil is often cited as a model of the former strategy, where the state fostered private investment without much redistribution of wealth. Brazil established a development bank to make loans to investors and state corporations in such central industries as petroleum and electric power generation.

Brazilian import substitution catered largely to the demand of relatively affluent urban consumers as well as the growing but less affluent industrial workforce. As local manufacturing of consumer products grew, Brazil had to import manufacturing technologies. When the domestic market was sufficiently large, multinational corporations invested directly in the Brazilian economy—as they did elsewhere in Latin America during this period. Latin America characteristically had relatively urbanized populations with expanding consumer markets.[38]

By contrast, the South Korean state centralized control of national development and the distribution of industrial finance. South Korea relied less on foreign investment than Brazil and more on export markets for the country's growing range of manufactured goods. Comprehensive land reforms equalized wealth among the rural population, and South Korean development depended on strategic investment decisions by the state that produced a development pattern in which wealth was more evenly distributed among urban classes and between urban and rural constituencies.

Whatever the form, the power of "development" was universal. Political elites embraced the development project, mobilizing their national populations around an expectation of rising living standards. In turn, political elites expected economic growth to legitimize them in the eyes of their emerging citizenry.

In accounting for and evaluating the development project, this book gives greatest attention to the Western bloc. There are several reasons for this focus:

- Western affluence was the universal standard.
- Western history proposed and realized the concept of "modernity" and theories of development.
- Much of the Third World was fully exposed to the Western development project, and today this extends to the countries of the now-defunct Second World.
- Western development is viewed in the post–cold war era as the only game in town that is eligible for multilateral financial assistance.

## Summary

The development project arose in a specific historical context in which the West represented itself as a model for the future of economic growth. The idea of development emerged during the colonial era, even though it contradicted the practice of colonialism. Our brief examination showed that colonialism had a profoundly disorganizing impact on non-European societies through the reorganization of their labor systems around specialized export production. It also had a disorganizing social-psychological effect on colonial subjects. But part of this impact included exposure of non-European intellectuals, workers, and soldiers to the European liberal discourse on rights, fueling anticolonial movements for political independence.

The political independence of the colonial world gave birth to the development project. Colonialism was increasingly condemned as individual countries sought their own place in the sun. Finding that place meant (1) accepting the terms of the development project and (2) finding ways to realize those terms in specific national contexts. Those terms included acceptance of the discursive and institutional relationships that reproduced international inequalities. Third World states may have become individually independent, but they also were defined collectively as "underdeveloped," within an imperial world.

Newly independent nations responded by playing the catch-up game—on an individual basis but, as the next chapter shows, within an international framework. The pursuit of rising living standards inevitably promoted Westernization in political, economic, and cultural terms as the non-European world emulated the European enterprise. The influential terms of the development project undercut Frantz Fanon's call for a non-European way, qualifying the sovereignty and diversity that often animated the movements for decolonization. It also rejected the pan-African insight into alternative political organization. Both of these ideas have reemerged recently, and they have a growing audience.

Third World elites, once in power, had little choice but to industrialize. This was the measure of independence from the colonial division of labor. It was also the measure of their success as political elites. The mirrored image of the West was materializing, both in the direction of Third World development and in an international development community emerging through aid and trade ties between First and Third World peoples.

The development project came under increasing scrutiny during the 1990s, losing considerable credibility among members of Third World (now southern) states. It has had quite mixed success, and there is a growing reaction to its homogenizing thrust. Ethnic or cultural identity movements have begun to reassert their political claims in some parts of the world. There is also a growing movement to develop alternative livelihood strategies beyond formal economic relations—to explore new ways of community living or simply to recover older ways of life that preceded the specializing thrust of modern commercial systems. These movements express a loss of faith in the ideals of the development project.

The remainder of this book explores how these ideals have worked out in practice, how they have been reformulated, and how a new project has emerged out of these changes. The next chapter examines the development project in action.

# 2

# The Development Project: International Dimensions

The development project was introduced as a postcolonial initiative, framed in national terms. We now focus on its international dimensions. The development project spanned roughly a quarter of a century, during which time the world economy experienced a steady upswing. The project sought to universalize the Euro-American understanding of modernity, characterized as an industrial civilization. However, since the model was an idealized version of development, it was unlikely to succeed. Third World resource needs were met, not through colonization (like the West) but through dependence on First World finance and technology. Whether this dependence was a new form of colonialism is a question raised in Third World circles, and it draws attention to the international relationships embedded in the development project.

When countries became independent nation-states, they joined the international relations of the development project. How could a national strategy be simultaneously international?

- First, the colonial division of labor left a legacy of "resource bondage" embedded in Third World social structures. There, trading classes of landowners and merchants, enriched by primary goods exports, favored this historic relationship. And of course, the First World still needed to import raw materials and agricultural goods and to market their industrial products.

- Second, as newly independent states sought to industrialize, they purchased First World technology, for which they paid with loans or foreign exchange earned from primary exports.
- Third, nation-states formed within an international framework, including the normative, legal, and financial relationships of the United Nations (UN) and the Bretton Woods institutions, which integrated states into universal political-economic practices.

National economic growth depended, then, on the stimulus of these new international economic arrangements. The UN declared the 1960s and 1970s "Development Decades," to mobilize international cooperation in various development initiatives designed to strengthen development at the national level and to mitigate the effects of the colonial division of labor. In this chapter, we examine the construction of the Bretton Woods system and how its multilateral arrangements shaped national development strategies. We then look closely at the ways the development project affected and reshaped the international division of labor.

## The International Framework

The pursuit of national economic growth by all countries required international supports, both material and political-legal. Material supports included foreign aid, technology transfer, stable currency exchange, and international trade. Aid and trade relationships often followed well-worn paths between ex-colonial states and their postcolonial regions. Superimposed on these historic relationships were the new relations embodied in the **Bretton Woods** institutions and the political, military, and economic relationships of the new capitalist superpower, the United States, as it sought to contain the rival Soviet empire.

In the context of reviving and stabilizing the world economy after a severe 1930s depression and a devastating second world war (1939–1945), the United States spearheaded two initiatives to reconstruct the world economy: the bilateral **Marshall Plan** and the multilateral Bretton Woods program. The development project emerged within the bilateral Marshall Plan and became formalized under the multilateral Bretton Woods program. It did not become a full-fledged operation until the 1950s, the peak decade of Third World political independence. To understand the international origins of the development project, we shall briefly examine the Marshall Plan.

## U.S. Bilateralism: The Marshall Plan

In the post–World War II years, the United States focused on European reconstruction as the key to stabilizing the Western world and rendering it "safe for capitalism." European grain harvests in 1946 were expected to reach only 60 percent of prewar levels. Scarcity of labor skills and certain goods depleted transport and communication networks, and countless refugees posed enormous problems. There was also a growing popular desire for social reform.[1] Indeed, on returning from Europe in 1947, U.S. Assistant Secretary of State for Economic Affairs Will Clayton stated in a memorandum,

> Communist movements are threatening established governments in every part of the globe. These movements, directed by Moscow, feed on economic and political weakness. . . . The United States is faced with a world-wide challenge to human freedom. The only way to meet this challenge is by a vast new programme of assistance given directly by the United States itself.[2]

In these political circumstances, the United States hoped to use financial aid to stabilize discontented populations and rekindle economic growth in strategic parts of the world. The other side of this strategy was to contain communism—primarily in Europe, where the Soviet Union had laid claim to territories east of Berlin, but also in the Far East, where communism had gained ground first in China and then in North Korea. The United States sought to gain nations' allegiance to the Western free enterprise system by promoting their economic growth through financial assistance. In 1950, Secretary of State Dean Acheson stressed the urgency of concentrating such assistance in Western Europe, to counter the consolidation of Eastern Europe under Soviet rule: "We cannot scatter our shots equally all over the world. We just haven't got enough shots to do that. . . . If anything happens in Western Europe the whole business goes to pieces."[3]

Meanwhile, the United Nations had organized a multilateral program of international relief. U.S. bilateral initiatives—increasingly important in the cold war—complemented and sometimes conflicted with these multilateral initiatives. U.S. bilateral policy overrode the proposals of two UN agencies established in 1943: the **Food and Agricultural Organization (FAO)** and the United Nations Relief and Rehabilitation Administration (UNRRA). When these agencies proposed a World Food Board in 1946 to organize reserves and regulate international trade in food, President

Truman's administration declined support. It chose instead to pursue bilateral aid programs where the United States was in control. In the Far East, U.S. food aid replaced UNRRA aid in an effort to bolster Chiang Kai-shek's anticommunist forces in China. And in Europe, the Marshall Plan replaced UNRRA aid.[4]

The Marshall Plan was a vast, bilateral transfer of billions of dollars to European states and Japan, serving U.S. geopolitical goals in the cold war. The plan restored trade, price stability, and expanded production. It aimed at securing private enterprise in these regions to undercut socialist movements and labor militancy. Dollar credits, allowing recipients to purchase American goods, closely integrated these countries' economies with that of the United States, solidifying their political loyalty to the "free world"—the Western bloc of the cold war world.

U.S. bilateral strategy aimed to consolidate this Western bloc under American leadership. The U.S. State Department considered the economic integration gained through dollar credits a way to stem the Western European trend toward economic self-reliance. The Europeans desired social peace and full employment, to be achieved through closely regulated national economies, but the U.S. government wanted an open world economy. The Marshall Plan solved this dilemma, using bilateral aid to facilitate international trade and encourage U.S. direct investment in European national economies.

Since Europe ran a serious trade deficit with the United States (which imported little from Europe), an ingenious triangular trade was established to enable Europe to finance imported American technology and consumer goods. This arrangement also provided the United States access to raw materials from European colonial territories, paying in dollars deposited in European accounts in London banks. From these accounts, European states could finance imports from the United States. In turn, U.S. investments in colonial and postcolonial territories stimulated demand for European manufactured goods. The triangle was complete.[5]

By 1953, the Marshall Plan had transferred $41.3 billion to the First World economies and had sent $3 billion in bilateral aid to the Third World. Post–World War II global economic reconstruction meant containment of communism first, spearheaded by the United States. Military and economic aid complemented each other and, in fact, were typically recorded together. During the two decades following World War II, the United States regarded the following countries as key to its containment policy, some of which contributed land for military bases: Greece, Iran, Turkey, Vietnam, Formosa (Taiwan), Korea, Philippines, Thailand, Spain,

Portugal, and Laos.[6] With containment in place, further reconstruction would be accomplished by a complex multilateral arrangement whereby infusions of American dollars stimulated the world economy.

## Multilateralism: The Bretton Woods System

The idea for an international bank was part of the plan to reconstruct the world economy in the 1940s. Trade was to be restored by disbursing credit to revitalize regions devastated by war or colonialism. Through a global banking operation, funds would be redistributed to these regions to stimulate new production. The famous July 1944 conference of 44 financial ministers at Bretton Woods, New Hampshire, provided the opportunity to create such an international banking system. Here, the U.S. Treasury steered the conference toward chartering the foundation of the "twin sisters": the **World Bank** and the **International Monetary Fund (IMF).**

Each institution was based on member subscriptions. The World Bank would match these subscriptions by borrowing money in international capital markets to raise money for development. The IMF was to disburse credit where needed to stabilize national currency exchanges. Once the ministers approved formation of these Bretton Woods institutions, the conference president, Henry Morgenthau, foresaw the

> creation of a dynamic world economy in which the peoples of every nation will be able to realize their potentialities in peace . . . and enjoy, increasingly, the fruits of material progress on an earth infinitely blessed with natural riches. This is the indispensable cornerstone of freedom and security. All else must be built upon this. For freedom of opportunity is the foundation for all other freedoms.[7]

These were the key sentiments of the development project: multinational universalism, viewing natural bounty as unlimited, and a liberal belief in freedom of opportunity as the basis of political development. Human satisfaction was linked to rising living standards.

The functions of the Bretton Woods agencies were as follows:

- to stabilize national finances and revitalize international trade (IMF),
- to underwrite national economic growth by funding Third World imports of First World infrastructural technologies,
- to expand Third World primary exports to earn foreign currency for purchasing First World exports (industrial technology and consumer goods).

In effect, then, the Bretton Woods system managed an international exchange between the First and Third Worlds that resembled the colonial division of labor, in a more intensive way. This was not surprising, as this international division of labor was already structured into the very social and economic organization of states across this divide and shaped how they participated in international trade.

The World Bank's mandate was to make large-scale loans to states for national infrastructural projects such as dams, highways, and power plants. These projects undergirded national economic integration and growth, complementing smaller scale private and public investments. In its first 20 years, two-thirds of the Bank's loans purchased inputs to build transportation and electric power systems. Indeed, the World Bank's *Eleventh Annual Report* stated, "Most of the Bank's loans are for basic utilities . . . which are an essential condition for the growth of private enterprise." At the same time, the Bank invested in large-scale cash crop agriculture, such as cacao, rubber, and livestock, deepening the international division of labor.[8]

The Bretton Woods institutions lubricated the world economy by moving funds to regions that needed purchasing power. Expanded trade stimulated economic growth across the First World/Third World divide. At the same time, these agencies disseminated the technologies of the development project, tempting Third World states to adopt the capital-intensive methods of the West. Whereas Europe had taken several centuries to industrialize, Third World governments expected to industrialize rapidly with multilateral loans and so reduce their specialization in primary goods exporting. Industrialization often substituted capital-intensive for labor-intensive production technologies (the difference is explained in the following insert).

---

### Capital-Intensive versus Labor-Intensive Production

*The difference between capital- and labor-intensive activities has to do with the ratio of labor to capital, or tools. The latter lighten labor's load. Ancient pyramid building was a labor-intensive activity, as the proportion of slaves to tools was high. Modern dam building tends to be capital intensive because it uses explosives and earth-moving machinery rather than armies of diggers, although large amounts of labor may be used for certain parts of the project—such as erecting scaffolding. In general, as production processes are mechanized, they become capital intensive; that is, they substitute capital for labor.*

The Bretton Woods system was unveiled as a universal and multilateral attempt to promote rising living standards on a global scale. Of the 44 nations in attendance at Bretton Woods, 27 were from the Third World. Nevertheless, the system had a predictable First World bias. First, control of the World Bank was dominated by the five biggest (First World) shareholders—beginning with the United States, whose representatives appointed their own executive directors to the board. The remaining seven directors represented the 37 other member states. This asymmetry, including overwhelming male representation, still exists; in the 1990s, the 10 richest industrial states controlled 52 percent of the votes, and 45 African countries controlled just 4 percent of the votes. Second, the president of the World Bank is customarily an American, just as the managing director of the IMF is customarily a European. Third, the Bank finances only foreign exchange costs of approved projects, encouraging import dependence (in capital-intensive technologies) in development priorities. Finally, the IMF adopted a "conditionality" requirement, requiring applicants to have economic policies that met certain criteria for them to obtain loans. International banks and other lenders inevitably adopted IMF conditionality as their own criterion for loans to Third World countries. In this way, Third World development priorities were tailored toward outside (i.e., First World) evaluation.[9] Thus, national strategies had international dimensions.

World Bank lending, however effective in its own terms, reflected First World priorities. The Bank emphasized what were considered to be productive investments, such as energy and export agriculture, rather than social investments, such as education, health services, water and sanitation facilities, and housing. In addition, as a global agency, the Bank found it more convenient to invest in large-scale, capital-intensive projects that might, for example, have common technological inputs and similar appraisal mechanisms.[10] In this way, early Bank lending priorities established large-scale technologies as the basis for borrower country participation in the development project. Not only has the Bank sponsored Western **technological transfer,** but it has also established an *institutional presence* in Third World countries.[11] When the Bank finances infrastructural projects, these are often administered through agencies with semi-autonomous financial and political power within host countries, as the case study shows.

**CASE STUDY**
**Banking on the Development Project**

The World Bank has always been the premier development institution. In providing loans and expertise, it has exerted considerable influence over domestic development policy. For example, in the late 1950s, as a condition for further power loans, the Bank insisted that the Thai government establish the Electrical Generating Authority of Thailand (EGAT). EGAT then supervised a series of loans for large-scale dams, from 1964 (the Bhumibol hydroelectricity project) through the 1970s and 1980s. Thousands of Thai peasants were displaced and resettled under the terms of the dam project, often on poorer lands and at considerable cost to their livelihood. Given EGAT's semi-autonomous status, however, the agency was immune to demands by these displaced peasants for compensation. Such semi-autonomous agencies (*parastatals*) often override domestic political process in the name of technical efficiency.

In Malaysia, a similar parastatal agency, called the Federal Land Development Authority (FELDA), was created by the Bank to administer three loans between 1968 and 1973. The purpose of the loans was to finance the clearing of sections of tropical rain forest and the resettling of 9,600 families who would grow oil palms and rubber trees. By 1982, by the Bank's own account, FELDA had developed 1.3 million acres (6.5 percent of Malaysian forest cover in the 1970s) and resettled 72,600 families. And in Colombia, between 1949 and 1972, more than 70 percent of Bank loans supported such autonomous development agencies. Despite the likelihood that World Bank projects would short-circuit the political process, Third World elites embraced them in the interest of development. India's first prime minister, Jawarharlal Nehru, referred to the Rihand dam project as one of "the temples of modern India," especially in generating power for the Singrauli region, India's "Switzerland." The Bank was a leading donor in this project, funding the National Thermal Power Corporation (NTPC) as an alternative to India's infamously inefficient public bureaucracy.

The question is whether the embrace of Western-style large-scale infrastructural projects was development, an instrument of legitimacy for ruling elites, or a trojan horse for foreign interests.

*Source: Rich (1994:75).*

In examining how the development project issued from the Bretton Woods institutions, we have focused on the World Bank as the key multilateral agency responsible for underwriting Third World development. In addition to its influence through the parastatals, the Bank framed development priorities through its on-site project agencies and its encouragement of large-scale power generation and transport projects. Such projects stimulated industrialization on a Western scale, often financed by private investments, increasingly made by foreign corporations and complemented by Bank funds. The Bank also channeled loans into intensive agriculture, requiring fossil fuel, energy-dependent technical inputs such as fertilizers, pesticides, and hybrid seeds. In addition, the Bank catalyzed the central ideas of the development project. For example, it created the Economic Development Institute in 1956, which trained Third World officials (soon to be prime ministers or ministers of planning or finance in their own countries) in the theory and practice of development as understood in the First World.[12] Finally, Bank lending became a model for other multilateral banks and aid agencies, as they determined priorities for assistance.

In short, multilateralism, Bank style, characterized the Bretton Woods system—Bank policy set the parameters of development. Third World elites by and large embraced these parameters since they were not in a position to present an alternative. When individual governments did try socialist alternatives, loan funds rapidly dried up. Multilateral funding was committed to extending the realm of free enterprise.

## Politics of the Postwar World Order

As the realm of free enterprise expanded, the political dynamics of the cold war deepened. These dynamics had two aspects: (1) the competition between the U.S.-led (First World) bloc and the Soviet (Second World) bloc for spheres of influence and (2) Third World attempts to avoid becoming pawns in this geopolitical game. While the United States and the Soviet Union were busy dividing the world, the countries of the Third World came together to assert their own presence in the international system. We explore the interplay of all these forces in the following sections.

*Foreign Aid.* An examination of the patterns of Western foreign aid in the postwar era shows that patterns of development assistance contradicted the universalism of the development project. All states could not be equal, as some were more significant players than others in the maintenance of order in the world market system. Western aid concentrated on undercutting competition from states or political movements that espoused rival (i.e., socialist) ideologies of development. Its priority was to use economic and military aid and trade to stabilize geopolitical regions through regionally powerful states such as South Korea, Israel, Turkey, and Iran. These states functioned as military outposts in securing the perimeters of the so-called free world and in preventing a "domino effect" of defections to the Soviet bloc.

Cold war rivalry governed much of the political geography of the development project. In the 1950s, the Soviet Union appeared to be challenging the United States in military and space technology. When the Soviet satellite *Sputnik* was first to fly into outer space in 1957, followed by manned Soviet space flights, Second World industrial rivalry gained credibility in both the First and Third Worlds. The Soviet Union was expanding economic and political relations with Third World states, especially newly independent states in Asia and Africa. Political rivalry intensified in 1956, when the Soviet Union financed and built the Aswan Dam in Egypt. This Soviet initiative followed U.S. pressure on the World Bank not to fund the project, in opposition to the "Arab socialism" of Egypt's new leader, Gamal Abdel Nasser. By 1964, the Soviet Union had extended export credits to about 30 states, even though 8 received most aid. Under the Soviet aid system, loans could be repaid in local currencies or in the form of traditional exports, a program that benefited states short of foreign currency. Not only was the Soviet Union offering highly visible aid projects to key states such as Indonesia and India, but aid policies also clearly favored states pursuing policies of central planning and public ownership in their development strategies.[13]

For the United States and its First World allies, then, the development project was more than a transmission belt for Western technology and economic institutions to the Third World. So long as the Third World, a vital source of strategic raw materials and minerals, was under threat from an alternative political-economic vision such as socialism, First World survival was at stake. In 1956, this view was articulated clearly by Walt Rostow, an influential development economist:

> The location, natural resources, and populations of the underdeveloped areas are such that, should they become effectively attached to the Communist bloc, the United States would become the second power in the world. . . . Indirectly, the evolution of the underdeveloped areas is likely to determine the fate of Western Europe and Japan, and therefore, the effectiveness of those industrialized regions in the free world alliance we are committed to lead. . . . In short, our military security and our way of life as well as the fate of Western Europe and Japan are at stake in the evolution of the underdeveloped areas.[14]

The United States' foreign aid patterns between 1945 and 1967 confirm this view of the world. Yugoslavia, for instance, received considerable aid as the regional counterweight to the Soviet Union on the western perimeter of Eastern Europe. Elsewhere, aid to geopolitically strategic states (including Iran, Turkey, Israel, India, Pakistan, South Vietnam, Taiwan, South Korea, the Philippines, Thailand, and Laos) matched the total aid disbursement to all other Third World countries.[15]

*The Non-Aligned Movement.* Parallel with this cold war world order was an emerging Third World perspective that advocated a more independent vision. As decolonization proceeded, the composition of the United Nations shifted toward a majority of non-European member states. In 1955, the growing weight of the Third World in international politics produced the first conference of "nonaligned" Asian and African states at Bandung, Indonesia, forming the **Non-Aligned Movement (NAM).** Key players were the leaders of Indonesia (Sukarno), India (Nehru), Ghana (Nkrumah), Vietnam (Ho Chi Minh), Egypt (Nasser), and China (Zhou Enlai). The NAM used its collective voice in international fora to forge a philosophy of noninterference in international relations. At a subsequent meeting of NAM, President Nyerere of Tanzania articulated this position in terms of economic self-reliance:

> By non-alignment we are saying to the Big Powers that we also belong to this planet. We are asserting the right of small, or militarily weaker, nations to determine their own policies in their own interests, and to have an influence on world affairs. . . . At every point . . . we find our real freedom to make economic, social and political choices is being jeopardised by our need for economic development.[16]

The subtext of this statement, and indeed of the final Bandung communiqué, was a questioning of the legitimacy of the economic model of development embedded in the multilateral institutional order. The first bone of contention was the paucity of multilateral loans. By 1959, the World Bank had lent more to the First World ($1.6 billion) than to the Third World ($1.3 billion). Also, loan terms were tough. Third World members of the UN pressed for expanded loans, with concessions built in, proposing that a UN facility perform these multilateral development functions. Third World members expected to exert some control over a Special United Nations Fund for Economic Development (SUNFED). The First World's response was to channel this demand away from the United

Nations and toward the World Bank. Here a new subsidiary, the International Development Association (IDA), was established to make loans at highly discounted rates (called "soft loans") to low-income countries. Between 1961 and 1971, the IDA lent $3.4 billion, representing about one-quarter of total Bank lending. In addition, several regional banks modeled on the World Bank were established—including the Inter-American Development Bank (IDB) in 1959, the African Development Bank (AfDB) in 1964, and the Asian Development Bank (ADB) in 1966.[17]

*The Group of 77.* The next contentious issue was the organization of international trade. The **General Agreement on Tariffs and Trade (GATT),** founded in 1947, enabled states to negotiate reciprocal trade concessions. Because the GATT assumed a level playing field, rather than one marked by histories of inequality and colonialism, speakers for the Third World regarded it as discriminatory, as many Third World states were unable to make such reciprocal concessions.[18] In fact, during the 1950s, the Third World's share of world trade fell from one-third to almost one-fifth, with declining rates of export growth associated with declining terms of trade.[19] Third World pressure, led by Latin America, founded the **United Nations Conference on Trade and Development (UNCTAD)** in 1964.

UNCTAD was the first international forum at which Third World countries, formed into a caucus group called the **Group of 77 (G-77),** collectively demanded economic reform in the world economy. They declared that reform should include stabilizing and improving primary commodity prices, opening First World markets for Third World manufactures, and expanding financial flows from First World to Third World. Once UNCTAD was institutionalized, it served as a vehicle for Third World demands.

While UNCTAD had a limited effect on world economic relations, its membership of scholars and planners from the Third World infused international agencies with a Third World perspective. Perhaps its most concrete influence was on the World Bank under its president, Robert McNamara (1968–1981), who linked economic growth to the redistribution of wealth. "Growth with equity" was the new catch-cry, and for a while, planners embraced the idea of investing in "basic needs." Infrastructural lending continued, but new Bank funds were directed into poverty alleviation projects, with rural development and agricultural expenditure rising from 18.5 percent of Bank lending in 1968 to 33.1 percent in 1981.[20]

As we shall see in Chapter 4, the solidarity of the G-77 lasted until the mid-1970s. At this point, the organization of the world economy changed drastically, unraveling the tidy subdivision of the international system into its Three Worlds. This was the beginning of the end of the Third World as a credible term for a region of the world sharing common historical conditions. It was also a time when the isolation between First World and Second Worlds began breaking down. But until then, the development project framed national economic growth in the Third World in a close relationship between international institutions and national policies.

We now take leave of the institutional side of the development project and examine its impact on the international division of labor.

## Remaking the International Division of Labor

If the development project was an initiative to promote Third World industrialization, then it certainly had some success. The result, however, was uneven, and in some respects, industrialization was quite incomplete. Nevertheless, by 1980, the international division of labor had been remade, if not reversed. The Third World's exports included more manufactured goods than raw materials, and the First World was exporting 36 percent more primary commodities than the Third World.[21] In the remainder of this chapter, we examine the shift in the international division of labor, as well as its impact on the *world food system*.

In world manufacturing, the European First World lost its core position in this period. Japan and a middle-income group of Third World states improved their share of world manufacturing, from 19 to 37 percent.[22] In the next chapter, we examine the implications of this rising group of middle-income Third World states. Here we focus on the redivision of the world's labor.

In agriculture, the Third World's share of world agricultural exports fell from 53 to 31 percent between 1950 and 1980, while the American "breadbasket" consolidated its role as the pivot of world agricultural trade.[23] By the 1980s, the United States produced 17 percent of the world's wheat, 63 percent of its corn, and 63 percent of its soybeans; the U.S. share of world exports was 36 percent in wheat, 70 percent in corn, and 59 percent in soybeans.[24] On the other side of the globe, between 1961 and 1975, Third World agricultural self-sufficiency declined everywhere except in centrally planned Asian countries (China, North Korea, and Vietnam). In all regions except Latin America, self-sufficiency dropped below 100 percent. Africa's self-sufficiency, for instance, declined from 98 percent in 1961 to 79 percent in 1978.[25]

Two questions arise:

- Why did commercial agriculture concentrate in the First World, while manufacturing dispersed to the Third World?
- Is there a relation between these trends?

The answer lies in the political structures of the development project. For one thing, Third World import-substitution industrialization (ISI) protected "infant" industries. In addition, First World agriculture was protected by farm subsidies, sanctioned by the GATT. These policies complemented one another, substantially reshaping the international division of labor. In considering the impact of these intersecting policies on the remaking of the international division of labor, we focus on the shaping of the world food order. Our focus on the food order offers one view of the global conditions promoting industrialization and agro-industrialization, making food a central part of understanding the ordering of the world by the development project. Food also provides a unique lens as it is such an important vehicle for the transformation of social systems, diets and health, and power relations internal to nations and internationally.

### CASE STUDY

### South Korea in the Changing International Division of Labor

South Korea is arguably the most successful of the middle-income newly industrializing countries (NICs), transforming its economy and society in the space of one generation. In 1953, agriculture accounted for 47 percent of its gross national product (GNP), whereas manufacturing accounted for less than 9 percent. By 1981, these proportions had switched to 16 percent and 30 percent, respectively. At the same time, the contribution of heavy and chemical industries to total industrial output matured from 23 percent in 1953–1955 to 42 percent in 1974–1976. How did this happen?

South Korea was heavily dependent on injections of American dollars following the Korean War in the early 1950s, during which it pursued the ISI strategy. By 1973, the Korean government's Heavy Industry and Chemicals Plan encouraged industrial maturity in shipbuilding, steel, machinery, and petrochemicals. The government complemented ISI with export-oriented industrialization, beginning with labor-intensive consumer goods such as textiles and garments. In the early 1960s, manufactured goods accounted for 17 percent of exports. This figure rose to 91 percent by the early 1980s as increasingly sophisticated electronics goods were added to the basket of exports and as Korean manufacturers gained access to foreign markets (especially the massive U.S. market) for their products.

South Korea exemplifies a development state whose industrial success depended on a rare flexibility in policy combined with the unusually repressive political system of military ruler Park Chung Hee (1961–1979). Koreans worked extremely long hours only to find their savings taxed away to support government investment policies. Industrial labor had no rights. Confucianism was a social cement. As an ethic promoting consensus and the authority of education and the bureaucratic elite, it provided a powerful mobilizing cultural myth. Being situated on the front line of the cold war helped, as the United States opened its markets for Korean exports.

Meanwhile, cheap food imports from the United States played a key role. Before 1960, virtually no Western-style bread was consumed in Korea—rice is cherished, and at that time, the country was self-sufficient in food. By 1975, however, South Korea was only 60 percent food self-sufficient, and by 1978, it belonged to what the U.S. Department of Agriculture calls "the billion dollar club." That is, South Korea was purchasing $2.5 billions worth of farm commodities from the United States, much of which was wheat. In addition, the government was providing free lunch bread to schoolchildren, and thousands of Korean housewives were attending sandwich-making classes, financed by U.S. aid counterpart funds.

Considering South Korea's history, this was indeed a dramatic transformation, not only in the country's diet and economic organization but also in its international relations, as South Korea began to import food and export manufactured goods. Under Japanese occupation, Korea had been turned into an industrial colony—and rice bowl—for the Japanese empire (1910–1945). The South Korean farming population diminished by 50 percent as industrial expansion attracted rural migrants to the cities. This shift, however, was not because rice farming modernized—it remained extremely small scale, retaining an average farm size of 1 hectare (2.471 acres) during this time, because the government closely husbanded a small-scale farming system with farm credit and price supports.

Since the South Korean "miracle" depended significantly on the subsidy to its industrialization strategy provided by cheap American food, as well as on access to U.S. markets for its manufactured exports, was its development ultimately a domestic or an international process?

---

*Sources: Harris (1987:31–36); Wessel (1983:172–73); Evans (1995).*

# The Postwar Food Order

In the post–World War II era, the United States set up a *food aid program* that channeled food surpluses to Third World countries. Surpluses arose out of the farm model pursued in the United States, heavily protected by tariffs and subsidies (institutionalized in the GATT). In this model, farmers specialized in one or two commodities (such as corn, rice, sugar, and dairy products), and, with technological support from the public purse, American farming entered an era of overproduction. Farm subsidies encouraged this by setting prices for farm goods above their price on the world market. The resulting surpluses subsidized Third World industrial labor forces with cheap food. It was a massive transfer of agricultural resources to the Third World urban-industrial sectors. This postwar food order[26] set in motion the rural-urban prescriptions of development economists, but with a difference: It operated on a global, rather than a national, scale.

## The Public Law 480 Program

To dispose of farm surpluses, the U.S. government instituted the **Public Law 480 Program (PL-480)** in 1954. It had three components: commercial sales on concessionary terms, such as discounted prices in local currency (Title I); famine relief (Title II); and food bartered for strategic raw materials (Title III). The stated goal of PL-480 was "to increase the consumption of U.S. agricultural commodities in foreign countries, to improve the foreign relations of the U.S. and for other purposes." By 1956, almost half of U.S. economic aid was in the form of food aid. In 1967, the U.S. Department of Agriculture reported, "One of the major objectives and an important measure of the success of foreign policy goals is the transition of countries from food aid to commercial trade."[27]

Title I sales under the U.S. PL-480 program anchored the food regime, accounting for 70 percent of world food aid (mostly wheat) between 1954 and 1977. By the mid-1960s, this food aid accounted for one-quarter of world wheat exports, a quantity sufficient to stabilize the prices of traded food goods. The management of these food surpluses stabilized food prices, and this, in turn, stabilized two key parts of the development project: (1) the American economy and its breadbasket and (2) Third World government industrial plans. Through market expansion, each came to depend on the other. The 1966 annual report on PL-480 to the U.S. Congress noted its positive impact on the U.S. balance of payments: "This increase in commercial sales is attributable in significant part to increased familiarity with our products through the concessional sales and donations programs. . . . [T]he economic development built into food aid programs measurably improves U.S. export sales opportunities."[28]

At this point, 80 percent of U.S. wheat exports were in the form of food aid. During the 1960s, the U.S. share of world food aid was more than 90 percent, although this fell to 59 percent by 1973.[29] By then, aid had become increasingly *multilateral*, building on a supplementary system of food aid to needy countries that was established in the 1960s at the initiative of the United States. It was funded with financial pledges from the **Organization for Economic Cooperation and Development (OECD)** and administered by the United Nation's Food and Agricultural Organization (FAO).[30]

## Food Importing

Under the aid program, wheat imports supplied burgeoning Third World urban populations. At the same time, Third World governments intervened in the pricing and marketing of food, establishing distribution programs to pass on the international subsidies to urban consumers (recall the discussion in Chapter 1 of the "development alliance," composed of manufacturers, labor unions, urban professionals, and middle classes). Cheap food thus supported consumer purchasing power and subsidized the cost of labor, stabilizing urban politics and improving the Third World environment for industrial investments.

Returning to the South Korean case, wheat imports in that country quadrupled between 1966 and 1977,[31] while rice consumption began a gradual but steady decline. Cheap imported food allowed the government to maintain low grain prices to hold down industrial wages. Low wages subsidized the industrial export strategy, beginning with labor-intensive manufactures of clothing items. Meanwhile, from 1957 to 1982, more than 12 million people migrated from the rural sector to work in industrial cities such as Seoul and Pusan.[32] Thus, rapid industrialization in South Korea, fueled by labor transfers from the countryside, depended on a cheap food policy underwritten by food aid.[33] In this way, the postwar food order sponsored economic development in one of the "showcase" countries of the cold war.

The impact of food aid varied elsewhere in the world, depending on the resources of particular countries and their development policies. South Korea was a success story largely because the government centralized management of its rice culture, its industrial development (balancing establishment of an industrial base with export manufacturing), and the supply of labor to the industrial centers. By contrast, urbanization in Colombia followed the collapse of significant parts of its agriculture under the impact of food aid and commercial imports of wheat. The Colombian government did not protect its farmers. Stimulated by the food aid program, imports of wheat grew tenfold between the early 1950s and 1971. Cheap food imports cut by half the prices obtained by Colombian farmers. They reduced their wheat production by about two-thirds, and other food crops, such as potatoes and barley, virtually disappeared. Displaced peasants entered the casual labor force, contributing to the characteristic urban underemployment and low-wage economy of Third World countries.[34]

Between 1954 and 1974, major recipients of U.S. food aid were India, South Korea, Brazil, Morocco, Yugoslavia, South Vietnam, Egypt, Tunisia, Israel, Pakistan, Indonesia, Taiwan, and the Philippines (see Figure 2.1). Usually, it was cheaper and easier for governments to import wheat to feed their growing urban populations than to bankroll long-term improvements in the production, transportation, and distribution of local foods.[35] Food aid allowed governments to purchase food without depleting their scarce foreign currency.

Shipments of food were paid for in counterpart funds, that is, local currency placed in U.S. accounts in local banks by the recipient government. These funds could be spent only by U.S. agencies within the recipient country. They financed a range of development activities, such as infrastructural projects, supplies for military bases, loans to U.S. companies (especially local agribusiness operations), locally produced goods and services, and trade fairs. Counterpart funds were also used to promote *new diets* among Third World consumers in the form of school lunch programs and the promotion of bread substitutes. As U.S. Senator George McGovern predicted in 1964,

> The great food markets of the future are the very areas where vast numbers of people are learning through Food for Peace to eat American produce. The people we assist today will become our customers tomorrow.... An enormous market for American produce of all kinds will come into being if India can achieve even half the productivity of Canada.[36]

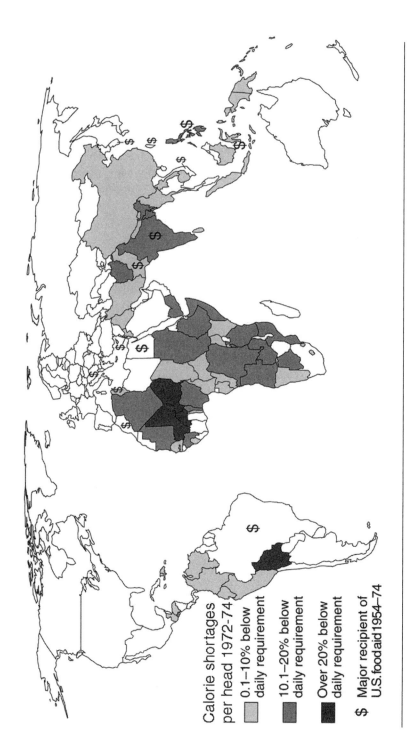

**Figure 2.1**    Food Shortage Regions and Food Aid Recipients

Source: Michael Kidron and Ronald Segal, *The State of the World Atlas*. London: Pan, 1981.

Thus, as the food aid program wound down in the early 1970s, commercial sales of American farm commodities continued, not only because Third World consumers had become dependent on such foods but also because they were mostly newly urbanized consumers. In the case of South Korea, rice consumption per capita continues its annual decline as Koreans continue to shift to flour-based products and animal protein. In Colombia, where commercial sales were prominent earlier and production of local staples collapsed, imported wheat became the substitute staple food. As we shall see below, when governments can no longer afford such food dependency and food supplies dwindle, their urban populations may riot.

## Food Dependency

Across the Third World in general (with the exception of Argentina), wheat importing rose from a base of practically zero in the mid-1950s to almost half of world food imports in 1971. By 1978, the Third World was receiving more than three-quarters of American wheat exports.[37] At the same time, Third World per capita consumption of wheat rose by almost two-thirds, with no change in First World wheat consumption patterns. And Third World per capita consumption of all cereals except wheat increased 20 percent while per capita consumption of traditional root crops declined by more than 20 percent.[38] In Asian and Latin American urban diets, wheat progressively replaced rice and corn. Wheat (and rice) imports displaced maize in Central America and parts of the Middle East and millet and sorghum in West Africa. Subsidized grain imports also undercut the prices of traditional starches (potatoes, cassava, yams, and taro). Thus, traditional "peasant foods" were replaced by the new "wage foods" of grains and processed foods consumed by urban workers.[39]

The rising consumption of imported wheat in Third World countries was linked to two far-reaching changes in this period:

- the increasingly tenuous condition of peasant agriculture, as government-organized urban food markets enabled subsidized wage foods to outcompete peasant foods;
- the expansion of an industrial labor force, as small producers (outside the agro-export sector) left the land and sought low-wage jobs in the rapidly growing cities.

In the conventional economic development model, these social trends occur within a national framework. In reality, via the development project, they assumed international dimensions as First World farmers supplied Third World industrial labor (remaking the international division of labor).

## Green Power

By the 1970s, Third World reliance on imports for modernized diets was considerable. PL-480 contracts offered incentives to governments receiving food aid to eventually expand their commercial imports of food. The food aid program subsided in the early 1970s in part because Third World commercial imports were swelling. In fact, Third World cereal imports more than tripled during the 1970s. By 1980, the structure of the grain trade had significantly altered, with the Soviet bloc joining the Third World (including China) as the major importing regions and the European Community becoming a major grain exporter, rivaling the American breadbasket.[40] This phase in the international food order (1973 to the present) has involved cutthroat competition for Third World markets among the grain-exporting countries. Here, commercial exports of food replace concessional exports of food aid, giving rise to a *global food regime* based in trade rules that privilege corporate power in the organization of the world food economy.[41]

The centerpiece of this new commercial phase was the U.S. government strategy of green power, a strategy of aggressive agro-exporting to consolidate America's role as "breadbasket of the world."[42] The strategy was recommended to President Nixon in 1971 for resolving America's growing balance of payments difficulties—as the United States began losing its industrial edge in world markets. The Williams Commission recommended that the United States should specialize in high-technology manufactured goods (machinery, computers, armaments) and agriculture. And so the government removed constraints on the use of American farmland and encouraged export agriculture under the slogan of planting "hedgerow to hedgerow." The green power strategy envisioned a reorganized world agriculture, based in a simple global division of agricultural labor: The United States would expand sales of cheap grain to the Third World, which would pay with exports of labor-intensive crops such as fruit, vegetables, and sugar.[43]

The green power strategy doubled the U.S. share of world trade in grains (peaking at 60 percent) through the 1970s. Between 1975 and 1989, the United States and the European Community used ever-increasing export subsidies to try to corner world grain markets, reducing world agricultural prices by 39 percent.[44] Such food dumping intensified Third World food dependency and destabilized international trade. It is not surprising that the GATT Uruguay Round, which began in 1986, focused on establishing new rules for agricultural trade (see Chapter 5). To put this in perspective, we need first to examine how green power affected farming in the Third World.

## Remaking Third World Agricultures

Given the development project's emphasis on industrialization, food aid turned out to be quite fortuitous; by keeping food prices low, it subsidized Third World industrial strategies. Cheap food fed urban populations, leaving urban consumers more income to spend on products of the new industries springing up behind state protection. The intent of the U.S. PL-480 program was also to create future markets for commercial sales of U.S. grains as Third World consumers shifted to wheat-based diets.

Consumption of final products, however, was only part of the strategy. The other thrust of the food aid program was to expand consumption of other agricultural goods, such as feed grains and agricultural technology. Export of these products followed a logic similar to that of the food aid program: finding outlets for surplus products. Behind this stood the massive state-sponsored expansion in American agricultural productivity, which more than doubled that of manufacturing during the period of the postwar food regime (1950s–1970s). The management of agricultural overproduction made disposal of surpluses a matter of government policy.

### The Global Livestock Complex

Surplus grain was sufficiently cheap and plentiful to feed livestock rather than people. In this section, we consider how expanding supplies of feed grains stimulated the growth of commodity chains linking specialized feed producers with specialized livestock producers across the world. After shifting to a wheat-based diet, more affluent Third World consumers shifted up the food chain, from grain to fresh vegetables to animal protein (beef, poultry, and pork). But what historical forces have brought this about? An examination of the dynamics of the food regime suggests that "dietary modernization" is as much the result of policy as it is the consequence of rising incomes.

U.S. grain-processing industries followed the movement of cattle from open-range feeding to grain feeding (75 percent by the early 1970s). The grain companies that had formerly sold and processed wheat diversified into the mass production of processed feeds (corn, barley, soybeans, alfalfa, oats, and sorghum) for cattle and hog feedlots as well as poultry motels. Consumption of animal protein became identified with "the American way of life," as meat came to account for one-quarter of the American food bill by 1965.[45]

Poultry consumption more than tripled between the 1930s and 1970, and beef consumption roughly doubled between the turn of the century and 1976.[46] Under the auspices of Marshall Plan export credits for U.S. agribusiness products, this agri-food model spread to Europe and Japan. The European *Common Agricultural Policy* (*CAP*) allowed free entry to feedstuff imports (cereal substitutes), and the Japanese livestock industry became almost completely dependent on feed grain imports.

Under the food aid program, exports of feed grains also flourished as animal protein consumption took hold among urban middle classes in the Third World. The U.S. Feed Grains Council routinely channeled counterpart funds into the development of local livestock and poultry industries. Loans were made to more than 400 agribusiness firms to establish subsidiary operations in 31 countries as well as to finance trade fairs and educational programs introducing livestock feeds and feeding techniques. By 1966, feed grains were the biggest single earner of export dollars for food companies.[47] In 1969, for example, four South Korean firms entered joint ventures with U.S. agribusiness companies (including Ralston-Purina and Cargill) to acquire technical and marketing expertise. According to the PL-480 annual report of 1970, these enterprises would use counterpart funds "to finance construction and operation of modern livestock feed mixing and livestock and poultry production and processing facilities. As these facilities become fully operational, they will substantially expand the market for feedgrain and other feed ingredients."[48]

## CASE STUDY
### Food and Class Relations

The growing feed grains trade traces changing social diets and, therefore, the transformation of social structures. Animal protein consumption reflects rising affluence in the Third World as the people of these countries embraced First World diets beyond those staple (grain, primarily wheat) diets promoted directly through food aid. The German statistician Ernst Engel formulated a law correlating the dietary move from starch to grain to animal protein and fresh vegetables with rising incomes. But instead of just reflecting individual choice and mobility, the difference in diets reflects who holds the power to produce certain foods and how patterns of consumption are distributed among social classes.

An example of such intervention in shaping the food chain comes from Costa Rica, a Central American state with a history of government and multilateral support of beef production. Between 1963 and 1973, in Guanacaste province, cattle herds increased by 65 percent while peasant bean production fell 41 percent. Declining food security for the poorer segments of Costa Rica forced its government to use foreign exchange earnings from exported beef to purchase basic grains on the world market to feed its citizens. On the global level, Engel's law may be in effect, as different classes of people dine on different parts of the food chain, but it is a *managed* effect. As wealthy (often foreign) consumers dine "up" on animal protein, local peasants, displaced by cattle pastures, face an increasingly tenuous low end of the food chain, typically depending on low-protein starchy diets.

On the occasion of the World Bank's $93.5 million loan to China for 130 feedlots and five processing centers for its nascent beef industry, in 1999, Neal Barnard, president of the Physician's Committee for Responsible Medicine, observed, "While smart Americans recognize the need to 'Easternize' their own diets with rice, soy products and more vegetarian options, World Bank bureaucrats decided to promote a Westernization of China's diet."

In an age when the "global epidemic of malnutrition" refers to the matching of the 1.2 billion underfed by the 1.2 billion overfed, we might wonder why, or how, development has come to be identified with affluent diets centered on animal protein.

*Sources: Place (1985:293–95); Gardner and Halweil (2000); McMichael (2001).*

With livestock production expanding throughout the Third World, specialized feed grain supply zones (primarily of maize and soybeans) concentrated in the First World and in "middle-income" countries such as Brazil and Argentina. Between the late 1940s and 1988, world production of soybeans increased sixfold. At the same time, maize production was revolutionized as a specialized, capital-intensive agro-industry. In the late 1980s, the value of the maize trade was six times that of the world wheat trade.[49] In other words, livestocking came to be linked, through the grain companies, with crop farming elsewhere in the world. Thus, specialized agricultures were linked by chains of commodities organized in global complexes—a pattern common to both agriculture and manufacturing. Indeed, the livestock complex was as central to postwar development and consumption patterns as the automobile complex.

## The Green Revolution

The other major contribution to the remaking of Third World agriculture was the **green revolution.** This was a "package" of plant-breeding agricultural technologies originally developed under the auspices of the Rockefeller Foundation (in Mexico in the 1940s) and then in a combined venture with the Ford Foundation (in the Philippines in the 1960s). Scientists focused on producing high-yielding varieties (HYVs) of seeds that allowed intensified cropping patterns. The new hybrid seeds were heavily dependent on disease- and pest-resisting chemical protections in the form of fungicides and pesticides. Intensive irrigation and fertilization were required to optimize yields, a practice that promoted weeds, which then had to be killed with herbicides. In other words, the HYVs came with a considerable package of chemical and infrastructural inputs, encouraging a modern, specialized form of commercial farming. The differences between traditional and modern farming are explained in the following insert.

---

### What "Traditional" and "Modern" Farming Look Like

*The major difference between customary and modern agriculture is specialization. Customary farming is mixed farming that complements crops with livestock that is used as a source of animal power, dung fuel, postharvest stubble grazing, and various items of subsistence, such as milk, hides, and tallow. Family or village labor is usually the norm. In*

*(Continued)*

(Continued)

*contrast, modern farms specialize in one or two particular crops or livestock activities. This practice was very pronounced in colonies, where sugar plantations or coffee farms would replace traditional agriculture. With specialization and increasing scale comes capital intensity, as producers add mechanical, biotechnical, and chemical inputs. Agriculture becomes industrialized and may depend on hired labor to complement farm machinery.*

*In an important trend, a growing number of farmers around the world are redefining modern agriculture along organic and diverse lines (still using some modern technology) because it is a more sustainable form of farming and can produce much more (variety of) food per unit of land than industrial agriculture. A resurgence of customary agricultural practices, such as crop rotation and South American raised-bed agriculture, has also enhanced sustainability.*

The expansion of green revolution agriculture in the Third World embodied the two sides of the development project: the national and the international. From a *national* perspective, governments sought to improve agricultural productivity and the delivery of maize, wheat, and rice to urban centers. In the context of the international food regime, this was an *import-substitution* strategy. The green revolution produced dramatic yields, but they have been highly concentrated in a few ecologically advantaged regions of the Third World. Asia and, to a much lesser degree, Latin America have captured the benefits from the new grain varieties, while Africa has charted few gains. Maize, emphasized early, was not a very successful green revolution crop. The major wheat-producing countries in the Third World—India, Argentina, Pakistan, Turkey, Mexico, and Brazil—planted the bulk of their wheat acreage in the new hybrid varieties, accounting for 86 percent of the total green revolution wheat area by the 1980s. Meanwhile, six Asian countries—India, Indonesia, the Philippines, Bangladesh, Burma, and Vietnam—were cultivating more than 87 percent of the rice acreage attributed to the green revolution by the 1980s. Because little commercial wheat or rice is grown in much of Africa, the green revolution largely bypassed that continent. Stagnant food production in Africa stimulated soaring imports of wheat destined largely for the growing urban classes.[50]

From an *international* perspective, the food aid program helped to spread green revolution technology. A reformulation of PL-480, in 1966, included provisions for "self-help" measures in the contract for food aid. Although varying by recipient, these provisions always included "creating a favorable environment for private enterprise and investment, . . . development of the agricultural chemical, farm machinery and equipment, transportation and other necessary industries, . . . [and use of] available technical know-how." Counterpart funds routinely promoted agribusiness and green revolution technologies, complemented with loans from institutions such as the United States Agency for International Development (USAID) and the World Bank.[51] These agencies aimed to weave First World agricultural technologies into Third World commercial farming.

As it increased crop yields, the green revolution was realized through the increase of rural income inequalities. In parts of Latin America, such as Mexico, Argentina, Brazil, and Venezuela, as well as in irrigated regions of India, this high-input agriculture nurtured a process of economic differentiation among, and often within, farming households. Within households, women typically have less commercial opportunity. The green revolution package of hybrid seeds and supporting inputs had to be purchased; to buy them, participants needed a regular supply of money or credit. Women, particularly poor women, usually found themselves "out of the loop"—not only because of the difficulty of obtaining financing but also because of institutional barriers in agricultural extension traditions of transferring technology to male heads of households. In Muslim cultures where the tradition of *purdah* keeps women confined, "male agents do not have easy access to the women farmers, and female agents are . . . difficult to recruit."[52]

Among farming households, the wealthier ones were more able to afford the package—and the risk—of introducing the new seed varieties. They also prospered from higher grain yields, often with easier access to government services than their poorer neighbors who lacked the political and economic resources to take full advantage of these technologies. The rising incomes and higher yields of the wealthier households gave them a competitive advantage over their poorer neighbors. Rising land values often hurt tenant farmers by inflating their rent payments. Some poor households were forced to rent their land to their richer neighbors or lost it through foreclosure to creditors. Finally, the mechanical and chemical technologies associated with the green revolution either reduced farmhand employment opportunities for poor or landless peasants (where jobs were mechanized) or degraded working conditions where farmhands were exposed to toxic chemicals, such as herbicides.[53]

Generalizing, *the spread of agribusiness typically exacerbates social inequalities* in Third World countries. These inequalities take a number of forms. At the village level, gender and household differentiation have occurred, deepening inequities that began with the privatization of formerly communal lands under colonialism. Private property distribution often favors males at the expense of women, whereas commercial agriculture exposes peasants to competitive and unpredictable market forces, often to the disadvantage of poorer and therefore more vulnerable households. At the regional level, yield disparities increase between irrigated and nonirrigated districts. Such disparities and the emphasis on marketing wage foods for urban consumers discriminate against the production of rainfed grains, beans, and root crops that provide all-important staple peasant foods.[54] Perhaps most significantly, agribusiness' exacerbation of inequalities is qualitative because the social protections within precapitalist inequalities are systematically eroded with the promotion of the agribusiness market culture and the exporting of food.

## Antirural Biases of the Development Project

Within the framework of the development project, Third World governments wanted to feed growing urban populations cheaply, both to maintain their political support and to keep wages down. Indeed, the term **urban bias** has been coined to refer to the systematic privileging of urban interests, from health and education services through employment schemes to the delivery of food aid.[55] This bias was central to the construction of development political coalitions in the postwar era. Such coalitions were firmly based in the cities of the Third World.

Attention to the urban areas, however, did not go unnoticed in the countryside, which was neither silent nor passive. Growing rural poverty, rural dissatisfaction with urban bias, and persistent peasant activism over the question of land distribution put **land reform** on the political agenda in Asia and Latin America. When the Cuban Revolution redistributed land to poor and landless peasants in 1959, land reforms swept Latin America. Between 1960 and 1964, Brazil, Chile, Costa Rica, the Dominican Republic, Ecuador, Guatemala, Nicaragua, Panama, Peru, and Venezuela all enacted land reforms. The **Alliance for Progress** (1961)—a program of nationally planned agrarian reform coordinated across Latin America— provided an opportunity for the United States to support land reforms as part of a strategy to undercut radical insurgents and stabilize rural populations. Land reforms attempted to reproduce the American family farm model, first introduced in the late 1940s in East Asia, which was at that time under occupation by U.S. military forces. These land reforms were a model in two senses: first, as interventions to quell peasant militancy and, second, as a method of reducing tenancy and promoting owner occupancy on a smallholding basis.[56]

### CASE STUDY
### What Produces a Development Mentality?

One of the underexplored dimensions of development is the way people think and act in or on the world. Most studies, including this one, foreground the social-structural changes, leaving changes in systems of thought and identity in the background. This is perhaps because of the ingrained rationalism of the categories through which we conceptualize the world, categories such as "market," "class," "peasant," and "urban" that sociologize individuals and their relationships. As Dia Mohan shows in a perceptively provocative study of West Bengali cultural politics, individual negotiation of dominant systems of meaning and representation is fundamental to how the experience of power contributes to the perpetuation and/or transformation of power relations.

In examining the adoption of green revolution technology in the Colombian coffee industry, Christopher London shows how coffee growers rethink their identity in the process of technification of coffee production. London's archetype grower, Santiago Mejía, reproduces in his production practices and in his self-understanding the essential ingredients of the conception of development advocated by the National Federation of Coffee Growers of Colombia (FEDECAFE). In an interview, Mejía expresses the shift in his beliefs, devaluing farming with the traditional coffee variety, *pajarito,* now that he has adopted the scientific practices of FEDECAFE-style technification:

> Before . . . [we planted] *pajarito* because there wasn't any other more productive variety, so indisputably it had to be the one we used. What else could a coffee grower sow? . . . One cultivated *pajarito* in a rustic manner, rudimentary, with whatever resources one happened to have because he didn't have anyone who could say "we have a much better system," or that "it's already been tested and proved" like the extension agents do. . . . So,

for that reason we and our grandfathers had to do it that way because it was the first thing that appeared. But as all things evolve so one has to be in agreement with development.

London observes that, in embracing the new agricultural technology, the grower is also embracing, to a greater or lesser extent, the modern mentality, where "his own past . . . is seen as being primitive and better for having been left behind. One has to be in agreement with development."

While there are powerful institutions such as the state, development agencies, the market, and private property that shape the possibilities and understandings of development, under what conditions do people either accept official versions of development or reject them as forms of rule and proceed to explore alternative practices of development?

---

*Sources: London (1997); Mohan (2003).*

---

The land reform movement, however, focused on redistributing only the land that had not already been absorbed into the agribusiness complex. In effect, the reforms exempted farmland undergoing modernization and dealt with what was left, including frontier lands. Indeed, alongside the strengthening of the agribusiness sector, considerable "re-peasantization" occurred during this period. In Latin America, two-thirds of the additional food production between 1950 and 1980 came from frontier colonization, and the number of small farmers with an average of two hectares of land grew by 92 percent. Arable land overall increased by as much as 109 percent in Latin America and 30 percent in Asia but possibly declined in Africa.[57] Resettlement schemes on frontiers, including forests, were typically financed by the World Bank, especially in Indonesia, Brazil, Malaysia, and India. These strategies sometimes simply relocated rural poverty and resembled "a war against the earth's rapidly dwindling tropical forests." In Brazil, for example, between 1960 and 1980, roughly 28 million small farmers were displaced from the land by the government's sponsorship of agro-industrialization to enhance foreign exchange earnings from agricultural exports, notably soy products. The displaced farmers spilled into the Amazon region, burning the forest to clear new and often infertile land.[58]

Persistent rural poverty through the 1960s highlighted the urban bias of the development project. At this point, the World Bank, under President McNamara, devised a new poverty alleviation program. It was a multilateral scheme to channel credit to smallholding peasants and purportedly to stabilize rural populations where previous agrarian reforms had failed or been insufficient. The Bank itself acknowledged that almost half of its 82 agricultural projects between 1975 and 1982 were unsuccessful in alleviating poverty. Instead, the outcomes included displacement of hundreds of millions of peasants throughout the Third World, leakage of credit funds to more powerful rural operators, and the incorporation of surviving peasant smallholders, via credit, into commercial cropping at the expense of basic food farming.[59]

The lesson we may draw from this episode of reform is that neither the resettlement of peasants nor their integration into monetary relations is always a sustainable substitute for leaving peasant cultures to adapt to their surrounding environment themselves. The assumptions of the development project heavily discriminated against the survival of peasant culture, as materially impoverished as it may have seemed.

Through a combination of state neglect and competition in national and world markets, the long-term decline of Third World peasant agriculture, begun in the colonial era, has accelerated. Land reforms and land resettlement programs (mainly in Latin America and Asia) notwithstanding, these interventions typically have done little to halt the deterioration of the peasant economy.[60] The commercialization of agriculture undermines the viability of household food production as a livelihood strategy for peasant populations and a subsistence base for the rural poor. The environmental stress associated with population growth and land concentration steadily downgrades survival possibilities for the rural poor as common lands and forest timbers for fuel disappear. The result is a growing stream of peasants migrating to overcrowded metropolitan centers of Latin America, Asia, and Africa.

## Summary

The development project was a multilayered enterprise; its components are delineated in the following insert. National strategies of economic growth, extending all the way down to farming technology, dovetailed with international assistance. The Bretton Woods institutions complemented bilateral aid programs in providing the conditions for Third World countries to pursue a universal goal of "catch-up." Third World governments embraced national industrial growth as the key to raising living standards. Third Worldism came to mean correcting the distortions, or imbalances, of the colonial division of labor. The key was industrialization.

In this way, the Third World as a whole was incorporated into a singular project, despite national and regional variations in available resources, starting point, and ideological orientation.

Aid programs bound Third World development to the overall enterprise of global reconstruction. Military and economic aid programs shaped the geopolitical contours of the "free world" by integrating countries into the Western orbit. They also shaped patterns of development through technological transfer and subsidies to industrialization programs. We have reviewed here the significance of food aid in securing geopolitical alliances as well as in reshaping the international division of labor. As development economists had predicted, Third World industrialization depended on the transfer of rural resources. But this transfer was not confined to national arenas. Indeed, exports of First World food and agricultural technology revealed a *global* rural-urban exchange.

---

### What Are the Ingredients of the Development Project?

*The development project was an organized strategy for pursuing nationally managed economic growth. As colonialism collapsed, political elites of newly independent states embraced development as an enterprise for growth, legitimacy, and revenue generation. The Western experience provided the model, and an international institutional complex provided financial and technical assistance for national development across the world, protected by cold war military relations. Some ingredients were the following:*

- *an organizing concept with universal claims (e.g., development as rising living standards, rationality and scientific progress);*
- *a national framework for economic growth;*
- *an international framework of aid (military and economic) binding the developing world to the developed world;*
- *a growth strategy favoring industrialization;*
- *an agrarian reform strategy encouraging agro-industrialization;*
- *development-state initiatives to stimulate and manage investment and mobilize multiclass political coalitions into a development alliance supporting industrial growth;*
- *realization of development through gender, race, and ethnic inequalities, embedded in states and spread through markets.*

The international dimension is as critical to our understanding of the development processes during the postwar era as is the variety of national forms. We cannot detail such variety here, and that is not the point of this story. Rather, we are interested in understanding how the development project set in motion a global dynamic that embedded national policies within an international institutional and ideological framework. This framework was theoretically in the service of national economic growth policies. But on closer examination, the reverse was also true. Social changes within Third World countries had their own local face; nevertheless, much of the stimulus derived from a common global process, which linked changes in the First World to changes in the Third World. One could say that all change under these circumstances was conditioned by international relationships, especially transfers of economic resources and ideologies.

In this chapter, we have examined one such example of these transfers, and we have seen how they condition the rise of new social structures. Transfers included basic grains directly supplying working-class consumers and feed grains indirectly supplying more affluent consumers through the livestock complex. In this way, First World agricultural expansion was linked with the rise of new social classes in the Third World. At the same time, the export of green revolution technology to Third World regions stimulated social differentiation among men and women and among rural producers, laborers, and capitalist farmers. Those peasants who were unable to survive the combined competition of cheap foods (priced to subsidize urban consumers) and high-tech farming in the countryside commonly migrated to the cities, further depressing wages. Not surprisingly, this scenario stimulated a massive relocation of industrial tasks to the Third World, reshaping the international division of labor. This is the subject of Chapter 3.

# PART II

## From National Development to Globalization

# 3

# The Global Economy Reborn

The development project held out the promise of parallel national programs of industrial development. Rising standards of living would depend on producing "national products" in an economy in which industrialization linked national manufacturing and agricultural sectors. The development state would partner private enterprise, assisted by programs of multilateral and bilateral aid.

The development project also involved reconstructing the world economy. U.S. President Franklin D. Roosevelt invoked an image of "one worldism," where international unity would be expressed politically in the United Nations and organized economically through the Bretton Woods institutions. However, as the cold war intensified in the late 1940s, Roosevelt's "one worldism" yielded to President Truman's "free worldism." This marked the rise of a U.S.-centered world economy in which American governments deployed military and economic largesse to secure and expand an informal empire as colonialism receded. With the West's focus now on *containing* Soviet and Chinese power, the development project settled on the twin foundations of *freedom of enterprise* and the U.S. *dollar as the international currency.* In this arrangement, bilateral disbursements of dollars wove together the principal national economies of the West and Japan. As the source of these dollars, the U.S. Federal Reserve System led those countries' central banks in regulating an international monetary system.[1]

Under cold war conditions, Third World political elites participated in a development project shaped by geopolitical security concerns, expressed in substantial military and financial aid packages. Countries differed in their resource endowments and in the character of their political regimes—ranging from military dictatorship to one-party states to parliamentary rule. Nonetheless, the expressed goal was of a *convergent* world of independent states at different points along a single path of development. However, divergent forces soon appeared. These included a growing, rather than diminishing, *gap between First and Third World living standards* and a substantial *differentiation among states within the Third World* as the newly industrializing countries shot ahead. In this chapter, we consider how these divergent forces came about—suggesting that they signaled a dramatic reorganization of the world as an emerging global production system spun a giant web across nation-states.

## Divergent Developments

Between 1950 and 1980, the rate of Third World economic growth exceeded that of the First World. It also exceeded the rate of growth of European countries during their early, comparable phases of development. However, when we take into account population growth rates and per capita income, the motive to "catch up" appears to have been somewhat illusory.

In the postwar era, the per capita income of the Third World, as a proportion of that of the First World, remained steady—about 7 percent to 8 percent—but the difference in gross national product (GNP) per capita between First and Third Worlds widened from $2,191 in 1950 to $4,839 in 1975 (in constant 1974 dollars).[2] In the mid-1970s, the official multilateral definition of the absolute poverty line was an annual income of $50. At the time, about 650 million people were estimated to be living in absolute poverty around the world, with another 300 million living in relative poverty—with annual incomes between $50 and $75. By 1980, the numbers of the world's absolute poor had increased to 1 billion, according to calculations from the 1983 Brandt Commission's report, *Common Crisis: North, South & Cooperation for World Recovery*.

These estimates may overstate poverty because per capita income calculations cannot account for cultural practices that generate alternative livelihood possibilities. Nevertheless, they do express the unequal global distribution of income as purchasing power, and, because purchasing power commands resources, such international inequality is cumulative.[3] Thus, the evidence in the late 1960s to early 1970s suggested that most Third World countries were running to stay increasingly behind. *The wealth gap between First and Third Worlds was evidently enlarging, despite the promise of the development project.* Moreover, the figures cited earlier do not reveal the growing inequalities of income and access to resources *within* these countries.

Industrial growth fueled by international assistance often relied on imported capital-intensive techniques and neglect of food production. The typical social consequence of these patterns was that growing numbers of rural and urban poor were deprived of the benefits of economic growth. The severity of this pattern often depended on the character of the particular country's political regime. The so-called Brazilian economic miracle followed the pattern described above, with the economy expanding at an annual rate of around 10 percent during the decade of military rule after 1964.[4] But there was also a *net loss* of industrial jobs, a rising share of the total income gained by the top 10 percent of the population, and a growing number of people living at or below the poverty line, variously estimated at 50 percent to 80 percent of the population.[5] Despite, or perhaps because of, Brazil's well-known extremes of wealth and poverty, its "miracle" growth depended also on vast resource endowments.

By contrast, South Korea, with a much smaller population (it had two-thirds fewer people than Brazil), followed a different course. The South Korean regime enlarged consumer purchasing power by controlling the differentiation of income between rich and poor, which was roughly one-quarter of the distributional spread of income in Brazil.[6] As authoritarian as the South Korean state was, its pattern of industrialization depended on a comprehensive land reform program, stabilizing rural incomes, and preferential access to the U.S. market for manufactured exports. In other words, while development itself is realized through inequalities, their extent and significance depend on government economic and social policy.

## The Newly Industrializing Countries (NICs)

Differentiation among Third World countries increased, too, as a select few played the catch-up game more successfully than others and sprinted ahead. The average growth rate for the Third World in the 1960s was 4.6 percent, with per capita growth rates of 1 percent or less; six Third

World newly industrializing countries (NICs),[7] however, grew at rates of 7 to 10 percent, with per capita growth rates of 3 to 7.5 percent.[8] These six countries were Hong Kong, Singapore, Taiwan, South Korea, Brazil, and Mexico.

The rise of the NICs revealed two sides of the development project. On one hand, NICs fulfilled the expectation of rising living standards and upward mobility in the international system, legitimizing the development project. They belonged to the group of middle-income Third World countries whose annual manufacturing growth rates (7.6 percent in the 1960s and 6.8 percent in the 1970s) exceeded those of their low-income Third World associates (6.6 percent and 4.2 percent, respectively), as well as those of the First World (6.2 percent and 3.3 percent, respectively).[9] The other middle-income countries—especially Malaysia, Thailand, Indonesia, Argentina, and Chile—expected to follow the same path.

On the other hand, the NICs also demonstrated the *selectivity* of the forces released by the development project. They cornered the bulk of private foreign investment.[10] Much of this was concentrated in developing export production facilities in textiles and electronics in South Korea, Taiwan, Mexico, and Brazil. In 1969, for instance, most of the foreign investment in electronic assembly centered on the Asian NICs—Hong Kong, South Korea, Taiwan, and Singapore.[11] Between 1967 and 1978, the share of manufactured exports from the NICs controlled by transnational corporations (TNCs) was 20 percent in Taiwan, 43 percent in Brazil, and 90 percent in Singapore.[12] The distribution of industrial growth in the Third World was also highly concentrated. Between 1966 and 1975, more than 50 percent of the increase in value of Third World manufacturing occurred in only four countries, while about two-thirds of the increase was accounted for by only eight countries: Brazil, Mexico, Argentina, South Korea, India, Turkey, Iran, and Indonesia.[13]

Across the Third World, countries and regions differed in levels of industrialization (the measure of development): The manufacturing portion of the gross domestic product (GDP) in 1975 was 5 percent in Africa, 16 percent in Asia, and 25 percent in Latin America and the Caribbean.[14] By 1972, the Organization for Economic Cooperation and Development (OECD) reported, "It has become more and more clear that measures designed to help developing countries as a group have not been effective for [the] least-developed countries. They face difficulties of a special kind and intensity; they need help specifically designed to deal with their problems."[15] The notion of a universal blueprint was clearly fading.

### CASE STUDY
### The NICs: An Exception that Disproved the Rules?

The NICs demonstrated success at the same time as they demonstrated departures from the model of national development. Economic growth was supposed to stimulate democracy, but the NICs appeared to compromise this expectation. Neither were they an arbitrary grouping of middle-income states; *strong geopolitical forces contributed to their industrial success.* In the Bretton Woods system, all states may have been equal, but some states were more equal than others in their global position.

Hong Kong and Singapore have functioned historically as entrepôts (port cities) in South China and the Malaccan Straits, respectively. In the East Asian expansion of the last quarter of the twentieth century, they served as vital centers of marketing, financial, and producer services. In addition, they coordinate the regional entrepreneurial networks of the Chinese diaspora.

Within the context of the cold war, the other four states—Taiwan, South Korea, Mexico, and Brazil—held strategic regional geopolitical positions. Their higher rates of economic growth were fueled by enormous transfers of economic assistance from the Western powers. Military aid and preferential access to the U.S. market helped sustain authoritarian regimes that stabilized economic growth conditions through such measures as investment coordination and the political control of labor, whether through repressive forms in East Asia or corporatist forms in Latin America. During the period of maximum growth, South Korea and Taiwan garrisoned U.S. troops, given their proximity to North Korea and China, respectively, and Taiwan, South Korea, Mexico, Singapore, and Brazil were distinguished by one-party or military rule. The term **bureaucratic-authoritarian industrializing regimes (BAIRs)** was coined to describe this type of government. The former prime minister of Singapore, Lee Kuan Yew, justified the BAIR regime in his paternalist way: "I do not believe that democracy necessarily leads to development. I believe that what a country needs to develop is discipline more than democracy. The exuberance of democracy leads to indiscipline and disorderly conduct which are inimical to development." He may have meant that when different classes put conflicting demands on the state—industrialists seeking propitious business conditions, workers demanding higher wages, farmers requesting subsidies—ruling elites have less flexibility.

What does it mean to consider the NICs as showcases of development when their industrial success and leadership depended on conditions not predicted in the development model?

---

*Sources: Cumings (1987); The Economist (August 27, 1995:15).*

## Third World Industrialization in Context

The rise of the NICs appeared to confirm that the colonial legacy was in retreat and that industrialization would inevitably spread from the First and Second Worlds into the Third World. Each of the NICs, with some variation, moved through the low-value industries (processed foods, clothing, toys) to higher-value industries (steel, autos, petrochemicals, machinery). Whereas the Latin American NICs (Mexico and Brazil) began the early phase in the 1930s and graduated to the more mature phase in the 1950s, the Asian NICs (Taiwan and South Korea) began manufacturing basic goods in the 1950s and did not move to higher value manufacturing until the 1970s. The other regional variation was that the Asian NICs financed their import-substitution industrialization (ISI) via the export of labor-intensive products because they lacked the resource base and domestic markets of the Latin NICs.[16]

With the exception of Hong Kong, most of the NICs had strong development states that guided public investment into infrastructure development and industrial ventures with private enterprise. The South Korean state virtually dictated national investment patterns.[17] Industrialization depended on the size of a country's domestic market as well as access to foreign exchange for purchasing First World capital equipment technologies. As their technological rents rose, Latin NICs adopted the **export-oriented industrialization (EOI)** model of the Asian NICs to earn foreign exchange.

Widespread EOI signaled a significant change in strategies of industrialization, organized increasingly by TNC investment and marketing networks. For First World firms, EOI became the means of relocating the manufacturing of consumer goods, and then machinery and computers, to the Third World. Third World states welcomed the new investment with corporate concessions and a ready supply of cheap, disorganized labor. At the same time, First World consumption patterns were intensified with easy credit and a mushrooming of shopping malls and fast food in the 1970s. *The global consumer and the global labor force reproduced each other.*[18]

Third World manufacturing exports outpaced the growth in world manufacturing trade during this period, increasing their share of world trade from 6 to 10 percent between 1960 and 1979. The NICs accounted for the bulk of this export growth, and its composition broadened from textiles, toys, footwear, and clothing in the 1960s to more sophisticated exports of electronics and electrical goods (First World bound), as well as machinery and transport equipment (Third World bound), by the 1970s.[19] Asian NIC development was achieved by rooting their industrial base in the world economy. Thus,

> Mexico, Brazil, Argentina, and India . . . accounted for over 55% of all Third World industrial production but only about 25% of all Third World manufactured exports (narrowly defined). Hong Kong, Malaysia, Singapore and South Korea . . . were responsible for less than 10% of Third World production but 35% of all Third World manufactured exports (narrowly defined).[20]

The Asian NICs were exceptional in their export orientation for geopolitical reasons. First, the East Asian perimeter of the Pacific Ocean was a strategic zone in the U.S. cold war security system. As noted in the previous case study, military alliances opened U.S. markets to exports, often of goods assembled for U.S. corporations. Second, Japan's historic trade and investment links with this region have deepened as Japanese firms have invested in low-wage assembly production offshore. In each case, the Asian NICs have reaped the benefits of access to the near-insatiable markets of the United States and Japan. Global and regional context has been as influential in their growth as domestic policy measures and economic cultures.

## The World Factory

The expanding belt of export industries in the Third World, led by the NICs, provides a clue to a broader transformation occurring within the world at large. There was a new "fast track" in manufacturing exports, which was superseding the traditional track of exporting processed resources. This heralds the rise of the *world factory:* involving the proliferation of export platforms producing *world*, rather than national, products. Often, the production steps are separated and distributed among geographically dispersed sites in assembly-line fashion, producing and assembling a completed product, as depicted in the athletic shoe commodity chain diagram in the Introduction. World products (an automobile, a cell phone, a miniature computer, a pair of jeans, or an electronic toy) emerge from a single site or a global assembly line of multiple sites organizing disparate labor forces of varying skill, cost, and function.[21]

The phenomenal growth of export manufacturing using labor-intensive methods in the East Asian region, as well as regions such as Mexico's border-industrial zone, signaled the rise of *a global production system and a world labor force*. In Asia, the stimulus came from the relocation of the Japanese industrial model of hierarchical subcontracting arrangements to sites across the region. The Mexican Border Industrialization Program (BIP) paralleled this "decentralization" of industrial production, whereby unfinished components would come to this new industrial enclave for assembly to be sold on the world market as a world product. In 1965, the Mexican government implemented the BIP to allow entirely foreign-owned corporations to establish labor-intensive assembly plants (known as **maquiladoras**) within a 12-mile strip south of the border. Concessions to firms, employing Mexican labor at a fraction of the U.S. wage and paying minimal taxes and import duties to the Mexican government, were part of a competitive world factory strategy. In the *Wall Street Journal* of May 25, 1967, the Mexican minister of commerce stated, "Our idea is to offer an alternative to Hong Kong, Japan and Puerto Rico for free enterprise."[22] The *maquiladoras* earn about one-third of Mexico's scarce foreign currency income.

U.S. firms establishing assembly plants in the BIP concentrated on garments, electronics, and toys. By the early 1970s, 70 percent of the operations were in electronics, following a global trend of U.S. firms relocating electronic assembly operations to southern Europe, South Korea, Taiwan, and Mexico, seeking low-cost labor in response to Japanese penetration of the transistor radio and television market. The 168 electronics plants established by 1973 on the Mexican border belonged to firms such as General Electric, Fairchild, Litton Industries, Texas Instruments, Zenith, RCA, Motorola, Bendix, and National Semiconductor. There were also 108 garment shops, sewing swimsuits, shirts, golf bags, and undergarments; some subsidiaries of large companies such as Levi Strauss; and other small sweatshops (unregulated workplaces) subcontracted by the large retailers.[23]

### CASE STUDY
### The World Factory in China

China has become perhaps the prime location for low-wage production in the global economy. The government anticipated this development by establishing "special economic zones" in coastal regions in the 1980s to attract foreign investment. By the mid-1990s, when the East Asian NICs had emerged as "middle-income countries" with relatively high-skilled labor forces, China became the preferred site for foreign investors—especially Korean and Taiwanese investors, who were experiencing rising labor costs at home. In 1995, the ratio of factory wages in China to South Korea/Taiwan to Japan was approximately 1:30:80.

In her investigations of shoe factories (producing Reebok and Nike products, among others) in Dongguan City, sociologist Anita Chan observes that vast concrete industrial estates have mushroomed on former rice paddies. Local farmers now live off the rents from the factories, while tens of thousands of migrants from China's poorer hinterland swell the low-wage workforce. Twelve-hour shifts (with enforced overtime) and seven-day workweeks are common, with Korean or Taiwanese managers using militaristic methods to break in and control the migrant labor force (in addition to requiring a deposit of two to four weeks' wages and confiscation of migrant ID cards). As the cash economy has expanded in China, a huge migrant labor force has gravitated toward coastal industrial regions, attracting foreign investment. Between 1985 and 1996, the portion of Chinese exports from foreign-owned plants grew from 1 to 40 percent. And during the 1990s, China took 45 percent of direct foreign investment in Asia.

China now produces about half of the world's shoes and a proliferating array of electronic items, toys, and garments for the global economy. While this may appear to be an impressive "industrial revolution" in China, in fact it is of absolute global significance. As China attracts global assembly-line jobs away from other countries (Mexican jobs, now overpriced at $1.50 an hour, are relocating to the 25 cents an hour jobs in China), it is steadily dismantling the belief and expectation that all nations develop through stages: from labor-intensive industries, such as clothing and toys, to capital-intensive industries, such as steel, autos, and semiconductors. If both stages of production are fragmented into low-skill tasks and shifted offshore to export-processing zones, they are already reconstituted as world factory jobs.

As world factory jobs, is it possible that China's 1.2 billion educated but impressively cheap and well-regimented labor force threatens to puncture national development illusions—especially those of prominent economists, who consider today's sweatshops as just the first steps for developing countries?

---

*Sources: Chan (1996:20); Faison (1997:D4); Greider (2001); Myerson (1997).*

The global proliferation of low-wage assembly marked the strategic use of export platforms chiefly in the Third World by competing TNCs from the United States, Europe, and Japan and, later, from some Third World countries. As these companies seek to reduce their production costs to enhance their global competitiveness, so export platforms have spread. Thus, the NICs' strategy of export-oriented industrialization sparked the world factory phenomenon: from sweatshops in Los Angeles to subcontractors in Bangladesh, Ireland, Morocco, and the Caribbean.

## The Strategic Role of Information Technologies

The world factory system is nourished by the technologies of the "information age." Especially important in the latest of these revolutions is the semiconductor industry. Semiconductors—notably the integrated computer chip—are the key to the new information technologies that undergird the accelerating globalization of economic relations. Advances in telecommunication technologies enable firms, headquartered in global cities such as New York, London, or Tokyo, to coordinate production tasks distributed across sites in several countries. Information technologies allow rapid circulation of production design blueprints among subsidiaries, instructing them in retooling their production to accommodate changing fashion or reorganize production methods in their offshore plants. Thus, we find global assembly lines stretching from California's Silicon Valley or Scotland's Silicon Glen to assembly sites in Taiwan, Singapore, Malaysia, or Sri Lanka.[24] What *appears* to be an expansion of industrial exporting, from a national (accounting) perspective, is increasingly a globally organized production system. As participants in global assembly lines, nations may specialize in producing just airplane wings, or automobile dashboards, or shoe soles, or buttonholes. And, to the extent that the export platforms are substitutable, nationally located production loses permanence.

How has this come about? Microelectronics. This was a leading industry in establishing the world factory, given the low skill in much electronic assembly and its dispersion to export platforms across the world. In turn, electronic *products* such as computers and digital telecommunications technology enable the global dispersion and coordination of production and circulation in other industries, from banking to textiles to automobiles. Thus, information technology globalizes the production of goods and services.

## The Global Production System

The consolidation of the world factory system has spun a giant web of exchanges across the world. But the web lacks the symmetry of the spider's creation. Economic globalization is neither uniform nor stable. Global production systems consist of multilayered divisions of labor among plants sited in global or regional networks. Relations across and among these plants are vertically and/or horizontally ordered, depending on the relative hierarchies of skill involved in producing the commodity.

The global network features in Robert Reich's portrayal of a U.S. corporation that coordinates multinational inputs in an integrated transnational assembly of a "world car." He views the corporation as "no longer even American. It is, increasingly, a façade, behind which teems an array of decentralized groups continuously subcontracting with similarly diffuse working groups all over the world." His example is the $10,000 Pontiac:

> Of which about $3000 goes to South Korea for routine labor and assembly operations, $1,750 to Japan for advanced components (engines, transaxles and electronics), $750 to West Germany for styling and design engineering, $400 to Taiwan, Singapore, and Japan for small components, $250 to Britain for advertising and marketing services, and about $50 to Ireland and Barbados for data processing. The rest, less than $4000 goes to strategists in Detroit, lawyers and bankers in New York, lobbyists in Washington, insurance and health care workers all over the country, and General Motors shareholders—most of whom live in the United States, but an increasing number of whom are foreign nationals.[25]

With the opportunity for global coordination (and mobility) embedded in informational technologies, TNCs subdivide production sequences according to technological or labor skill levels and shift labor-intensive activities to offshore export platforms or processing zones. Thus, General Motors drastically cut costs in 1999 by subcontracting with South Korean and Japanese tool makers. Parent firms tend to monopolize high technologies, with component processes (assembling, etching, and testing computer chips), component goods (pharmaceutical stock, engines, and auto parts), and consumer goods (cameras, electronic games, TVs, and video recorders) moved offshore for production in cheaper sites, export processing zones, or sweatshop districts. TNCs often organize production hierarchies and alliances based on joint ventures with firms in other

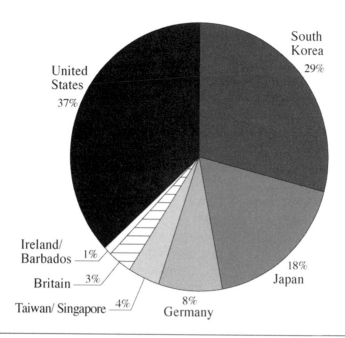

**Figure 3.1**     Global Sourcing: A $10,000 "American Pontiac"—Where the
Money Goes

Source: Robert Reich, *The Work of Nations: Preparing Ourselves for 21st Century Capitalism*
(Vintage Press, 1992), p. 11.

countries. These may be used to gain access to technology, markets, or
finance—for example, Hyundai improved its computer memory chip production capacity through a joint venture with Texas Instruments in the
1980s, and, in 1999, Renault exchanged its finance for Nissan technology
to form the world's fourth largest auto firm after General Motors, Ford,
and Toyota.[26]

   The global production system depends on a *technical division of labor*
among specialized processes located in different world sites. Here,
instead of *countries* specializing in an export industry (manufacturing or
agriculture), world production *sites* specialize as part of a chain linking
sites in several countries. From the end of the 1960s, there was a marked
relocation of *manufacturing* investment from the First World to the Third
World. Such "decentralization" of manufacturing was the combined
result of declining profitability on investments in the First World, as well
as Third World state entrepreneurship to attract foreign investment into
local industrialization programs, some of which involved sponsorship of

industrial (and agricultural) export zones. In the 1970s, 50 percent of all manufactured exports from U.S.-based TNCs were from Brazil, Mexico, Singapore, and Hong Kong.[27] And there was a shift from producing a national product to producing a world product, as illustrated in the case study of the world car.[28]

**CASE STUDY**

**The World Car: From Ford and Mitsubishi**

In the postwar era, the Ford Motor Company invested directly in a United Kingdom affiliate that produced the British Ford Cortina for local consumers; it had a British design and was assembled locally with British parts and components. At that time, no matter where the capital came from, supply linkages and marketing services were generated locally through import-substitution industrialization. Governments actually encouraged foreign investment in the domestic product.

However, this pattern has since changed. The Ford Cortina has now become the Ford Escort, the "world car" version of the original British "national car." Assembled in multiple national sites (including Britain), the Escort is geared to production for the world market. It uses parts and components from 14 other countries, including Germany, Switzerland, Spain, the United States, and Japan. Given the larger production run of a world car, Ford claimed a saving of 25 percent over the earlier method of building new cars separately for the North American and European markets.

Similarly, the Mitsubishi Motor Corporation, which is headquartered in Japan, has subsidiaries producing components in South Korea, Indonesia, Thailand, Malaysia, the Philippines, Australia, and even the United States (as joint ventures with the Chrysler Corporation and the Ford Motor Company). Mitsubishi cars, assembled in Thailand or Japan, are sold in the United States, Canada, the United Kingdom, New Zealand, and Papua New Guinea as Dodge or Plymouth Colts.

In the twenty-first century, world car factories are smaller and cleaner and involve networks of suppliers coordinated by car firms (retaining only core tasks of design, engineering, and marketing) that are becoming known as "vehicle brand owners." In context of the 25 to 30 percent overcapacity in the global auto industry, car firms are intensifying their outsourcing activities. Led by Honda, huge car plants are being dismantled and their operations further decentralized to handle variation in demand for high-volume vehicles and a growing requirement for low-cost, flexible manufacturing for low-volume production closer to their markets. Honda, having installed a single global manufacturing system, can now switch models overnight by changing software in its robots.

With the rise of global production systems that seem to "denationalize" development, how should we understand development: as a strategy of capturing value added by attracting higher skill nodes of a global commodity chain to a country or simply as a global corporate activity?

*Sources: Jenkins (1992:23–25); Stevenson (1993:D1); Borthwick (1992:511); Sivanandan (1989:2); The Economist (February 23, 2002:71-73).*

## The Export Processing Zone

**Export processing zones** (EPZs) (otherwise known as free trade zones [FTZs]) are specialized manufacturing export estates with minimal customs controls, and they are usually exempt from labor regulations and domestic taxes. EPZs serve firms seeking lower wages and Third World governments seeking capital investment and foreign currency to be earned from exports. The first EPZ appeared at Shannon, Ireland, in 1958; India established the first Third World EPZ in 1965, and as early as the mid-1980s, roughly 1.8 million workers were employed in a total of 173 EPZs around the world. By the century's end, more than 800 EPZs employed millions of workers.[29]

The dynamics of EPZs run counter to the development project since they favor export market considerations over the development of domestic markets (local production capacity and consumption). Export processing zones typically serve as enclaves—in social as well as economic terms. Often physically separate from the rest of the country, EPZs are built to receive imported raw materials or components and to export the output directly by sea or air. Workers are either bused in and out daily or inhabit the EPZ under a short-term labor contract. Inside the EPZ, whatever civil rights and working conditions that hold in the society at large are usually denied the workforce. It is a workforce assembled under conditions analogous to those of early European industrial history to enhance the profitability of modern, global corporations.

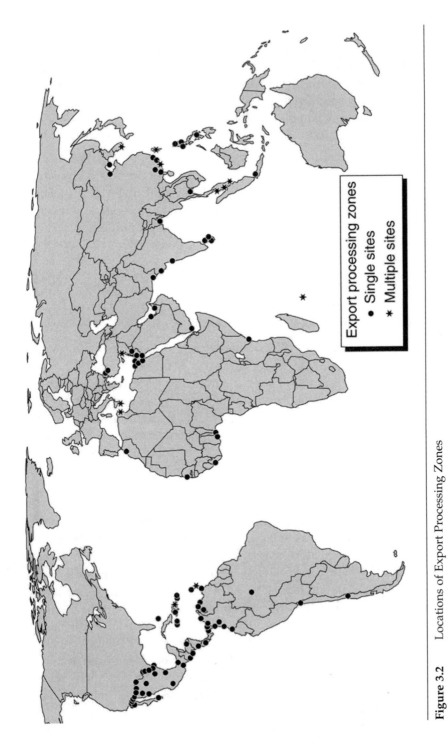

**Figure 3.2** Locations of Export Processing Zones

Source: Adapted from Peter Dicken, *Global Shift: Transforming the World Economy* (Guilford Press, 1998), p. 131.

Much of the world's 27 million strong EPZ labor force is composed of women.[30] Between 1975 and 1995, garment production spawned 1,200,000 jobs in Bangladesh, with women taking 80 percent (with considerable impact on Islamic culture). In Mexico, young women account for roughly 85 percent of the workforce of the *maquiladoras*, supposedly more docile, agile, and reliable than men in routine assembly work—and certainly cheaper. When Motorola shifted its electronics plant 200 miles south from Phoenix to Nogales, its annual wage for assembly work fell from $5,350 to $1,060. The following description of a worker at an electronics *maquiladora* near Tijuana captures the conditions of this kind of labor:

> Her job was to wind copper wire onto a spindle by hand. It was very small and there couldn't be any overlap, so she would get these terrible headaches. After a year some of the companies gave a bonus, but most of the girls didn't last that long, and those that did had to get glasses to help their failing eyes. It's so bad that there is constant turnover.[31]

The transnational corporations that employ workers in export processing zones obtain other concessions, such as free trade for imports and exports, infrastructural support, tax exemption, and locational convenience for reexport. For example, for *maquila* investment in Sonora, one of the poorest border states, the Mexican government's most favorable offer was 100 percent tax exemption for the first 10 years and 50 percent for the next 10.[32] In short, the EPZ is an island in the country within which it is located, separated from domestic laws and contributing little to the host economy, other than foreign currency earned via export taxes levied by host states. It belongs instead to an archipelago of production sites across the world (concentrating in Latin America, the Caribbean, and Asia), serving world markets.

## The Rise of the New International Division of Labor (NIDL)

The formation of a global labor force began during the development project. The effects of urban bias, agrarian class polarization accelerated by the green revolution, and cheap food imports combined to expel peasants from the land. From 1950 to 1997, the world's rural population decreased by some 25 percent, and roughly half of the world's population dwells in and on the margins of sprawling cities.[33] European depeasantization was spread over several centuries. Even then, the

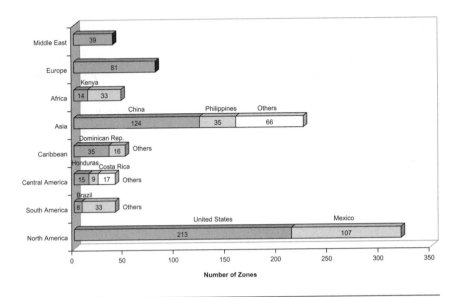

**Figure 3.3**    Number of Free Trade Zones across the World

Source: World Economic Processing Zones Association (www.wepza.org) and the International Labor Organization (1997, www.ilo.org).

pressure on the cities was relieved as people immigrated to settler colonies in North America and Australasia. But for Third World societies, this process has been compressed into a few generations, a little longer for Latin America. Rural migrants in many places overwhelm the cities.

Depeasantization does not by itself create a global labor force; it simply swells the ranks of displaced people lacking means of subsistence and needing wage work. Wage work for a global labor force stems from the *simplification* of First World manufacturing work and *relocation* of these routine tasks as low-cost jobs to form a global assembly line linking sites across the world.

Initially, First World mass production developed around large production runs using assembly lines of work subdivided into specialized tasks. Each worker on the line performed a routine task contributing to a final product. Such simplification deskills work on the assembly line. Today, such tasks as cutting, sewing, and stitching in the garment or footwear industry or assembly, machine tending, or etching in the electrical, automobile, or computer chip industry are typically located in cheap labor regions. At the same time, the technologies to coordinate those tasks generate needs for new skilled labor, such as managerial, engineering, or design labor, often retained in the First World. That is, the *global labor force is actually bifurcated,* where skilled labor tends to concentrate in the First World, and unskilled labor concentrates in the Third World. TNCs started coordinating this bifurcation via their "internal" labor hierarchies as early as the 1970s, as detailed in the following description:

> Intel Corporation is located in the heart of California's "Silicon Valley." . . . When Intel's engineers develop a design for a new electronic circuit or process, technicians in the Santa Clara Valley, California, plant will build, test, and redesign the product. When all is ready for production of the new item, however, it doesn't go to a California factory. Instead, it is air freighted to Intel's plant in Penang, Malaysia. There, Intel's Malaysian workers, almost all young women, assemble the components in a tedious process involving hand soldering of fiber-thin wire leads. Once assembled, the components are flown back to California, this time for final testing and/or integration into a larger end product. And, finally, they're off to market, either in the United States, Europe, or back across the Pacific to Japan.[34]

In the 1970s, the relocation of deskilled tasks to lower-wage regions of the world was so prevalent that the concept of a **new international division of labor (NIDL)** was coined to describe this development. NIDL referred to an apparent decentralization of industrial production from the First to the Third World. The conditions for this movement were defined as endless supplies of cheap Third World labor, the new technical possibility of separating and relocating deskilled manufacturing tasks offshore, and the rise of transport and informational technologies to allow coordination of global production systems.[35]

**CASE STUDY**
**Gendering the Global Labor Force**

"Endless supplies of cheap Third World labor" needs definition. In fact, the labor is often gendered, and the endless supply depends on complex patriarchal and subcontracting hierarchies. Labor-intensive export platform industries prefer young, unmarried, and relatively educated women. Women comprise more than 80% of the EPZ labor forces in Taiwan, the Philippines, Sri Lanka, Mexico, and Malaysia. While employers argue that women are suited to the jobs because of their dexterity and patience, the qualities assumed of female employees are required as much by the construction of the jobs as by patriarchal and repressive cultural practices reproduced within the factories, sweatshops, and homework units. Job construction also depends on changing conditions; as Laura Raynolds has shown in research on Dominican Republic plantations, in times of economic downturn, displaced men may in turn displace women via the use of local patronage networks, with work being regendered to reward masculine competition.

Women are typically subjected to long work days and lower wages compared to men. High turnover, lack of union rights, sexual harassment, and poor health characterize the female workforce that has mushroomed across the Asian, Central American, and Middle Eastern regions. Under these conditions, patriarchal states, competing for foreign investment, encourage women to enter the workforce at the same time as the new female workforce may be under official (especially Islamic) scrutiny for loose morals, and governments withhold maternity benefits, child care, and education opportunities on the grounds that they are "secondary workers" in a male-dominated labor market. Rural families propel, sometimes sell, their teenage girls into labor contracts, viewing their employment as a daughterly duty or a much-needed source of income.

Where young women and children work in family production units (proliferating in China today), subcontractors rely on patriarchal pressures to discipline the workers. In the workplace, teenage girls are often forced to take birth control pills to eliminate maternity leave and payments or are forced to have abortions if they get pregnant. Labor contractors and managers routinely demand sexual favors from young women for awarding jobs, giving rise to a "factory harem mentality." The endless nature of the supply of female labor comes from their short working life in many of these jobs—because of the eye-hand coordination of girls that peaks at age 16; the physical deterioration from low wages, poor health, and nutrition; the high turnover due to harassment; the steady experience of having the life sucked out of them by long working hours and no advancement in skills; and the steady stream of new cohorts of younger women to follow, whether from the countryside, the children of the working poor, or international traffickers in labor. These are some of the compelling conditions that enable a particular kind and scale of casual labor to form around the world to supply the brand owners the brands to sell to the global consumer.

What kind of development is realized through the manipulations of (international and national) gender inequalities?

---

*Sources: Agarwal (1988); Fernandez-Kelly (1983:129); Kernaghan (1995); Ong (1997); Raynolds (2001); Pyle (2001).*

Skilled labor concentrates in the north and also where enterprising states such as the NICs of East Asia (South Korea, Taiwan, Singapore, and Hong Kong) have used public investment to upgrade workforce skills. The upgrading was necessary as their wage levels were rising in relation to other countries that were embracing export production, such as Malaysia, Indonesia, and the Philippines. In 1975, if the hourly wage for electronics work in the United States was measured at 100, the relative value for equivalent work was 12 in Hong Kong and Singapore, 9 in Malaysia, 7 in Taiwan and South Korea, 6 in the Philippines, and 5 in Indonesia and Thailand.[36] This wage differentiation made the East Asian NICs' labor-intensive production less competitive, forcing them to upgrade their segment of the global labor force.

These Asian countries improved their competitiveness by specializing in more sophisticated export manufacturing for First World markets, using skilled labor rather than semiskilled and unskilled labor. After upgrading their labor force, the NICs attracted skilled labor inputs as a regional growth strategy. As the skilled work came, these states became headquarters, or cores, of new regional divisions of labor patterned on the production hierarchy between Japan and its East and Southeast Asian neighbors.

An East Asian division of labor in the semiconductor industry for U.S. firms formed by 1985 through the upgrading of the production hierarchy. Final testing of semiconductors (capital-intensive labor involving computers with lasers) and circuit design centers were located in Hong Kong, Singapore, and Taiwan; wafer fabrication in Malaysia; and assembly in Malaysia, Thailand, the Philippines, and Indonesia. In the 1970s, semiconductors were assembled in Southeast Asia and then flown back to the United States for testing and distribution, but by the 1980s, Hong Kong imported semiconductors from South Korea and Malaysia to test them for reexport to the First World and for input in Hong Kong's fabled watch assembly industry.[37]

Patterns of global and regional sourcing have mushroomed across the world, particularly under the stimulus of informatics. Firms establish subsidiaries offshore or extensive subcontracting arrangements—in

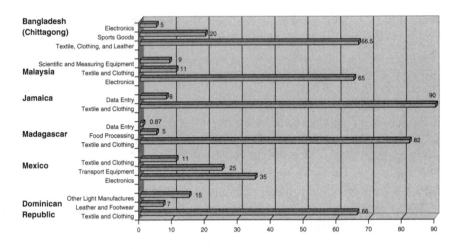

**Figure 3.4**    Percentage of Workforce Involved in Making Products, Provisions, and Services Exported from Selected EPZ Host Countries, 1994

Source: International Labor Organization (1995, www.ilo.org) and the International Confederation of Free Trade Unions (1995, www.cftu.org).

labor-intensive consumer goods industries such as garments, footwear, toys, household goods, and consumer electronics. The Nike Corporation produces most of its athletic shoes through subcontracting arrangements in South Korea, China, Indonesia, and Thailand; product design and sales promotion are reserved for its U.S. headquarters, where the firm "promotes the symbolic nature of the shoe and appropriates the greater share of the value resulting from its sales."[38] U.S. retailers of every size also routinely use global subcontracting arrangements in the Asia-Pacific and the Caribbean regions to organize their supplies and reduce their costs, as illustrated in the case study on Saipan.

### CASE STUDY
### Global Subcontracting in Saipan

One of the production sites used over the past two decades as a supplier in global subcontracting is the tiny island of Saipan, in the western Pacific.

Saipan has been a U.S. territory since 1945, and the islanders are American citizens. In the early 1980s, new federal rules for the garment industry allowed duty-free (and virtually quota-free) imports from Saipan into the United States as well as liberal foreign investment conditions. Companies involved in garment production on Saipan include The Gap, Geoffrey Beene, Liz Claiborne, Eddie Bauer, and Levi Strauss. For some, Saipan has strategic importance. While its exports make up only about 1 percent of all clothing imports into the United States, they account for roughly 20 percent of sales for some large American companies.

Saipan (like American Samoa) has a "comparative advantage": Although the "Made in USA" label can legitimately be used here, the island was exempted from the federal minimum wage in 1976. The commonwealth government has maintained a minimum wage of $2.15 an hour since 1984 (compared with the federal minimum of $4.25 on Guam, 120 miles to the south).

Despite the label, more than half the labor force contributing to these exports is foreign—predominantly Chinese recruits, who expect to work in the United States but find themselves in Saipan barracks surrounded by barbed wire and patrolled by uniformed guards. The clothing factories resemble sweatshops, and they have recently attracted the attention of American labor unions and investigators from the U.S. Department of Labor and the Occupational Safety and Health Administration. Inspectors found Chinese workers whose passports had been confiscated and who were working 84-hour weeks at subminimum wages. Workers, with legal assistance, filed a class-action suit against their employers (including firms from the region) in 1999. Four U.S. retailers (Nordstrom, Gymboree, Cutter and Buck, and J. Crew) settled with 50,000 current and former workers, committing to monitor improvements in wages and working conditions. Other lawsuits followed, with one of the companies, Levi Strauss, agreeing to new codes requiring improved conditions, to be implemented also in other sites in Myanmar and China.

How can codes of corporate conduct be enforced in sweatshops when host governments are complicit, employers are often subcontractors, union organization is often disallowed, and firms can move on to the next cheap labor site, at the drop of a hat?

---

*Sources: Shenon (1993:10); Udesky (1994); The Economist (June 3, 1995:58); Dickinson and Schaeffer (2001:212); Fickling (2003).*

The Saipan case study illustrates the dark side of subcontracting—a pattern of abuse commonly experienced by unprotected labor throughout the world. In 1999, the United Nations estimated about 20 million bonded laborers worldwide, with half that number in India. Similarly, the International Labor Organization estimates about 80 million children younger than age 14 working across the world in conditions hazardous to their health—in farming, domestic labor, drug trafficking, fireworks, manufacturing, fishing, brick making, carpet weaving, sex work, stone quarrying, and as soldiers. Many of these children work 14-hour days in crowded and unsafe workplaces.[39] Regardless of whether transnational corporations offer better conditions than local firms, the rise of global subcontracting eliminates and/or undermines regulation of employment conditions.

## From the NIDL to a Truly Global Labor Force

The rise of global subcontracting transformed the tidy bifurcation of labor between the First World (skilled) and the Third World (unskilled labor), captured in the NIDL concept, into a bifurcation of labor everywhere. That is, the division is no longer simply a geographical division (north-south), mainly because of the recursive effect of global subcontracting bringing pressure to bear on organized workforces in the First World. Bifurcation is the separation of a core of relatively stable, well-paid work from a periphery of casual, low-cost labor, wherever. We see it occurring in tertiary education, across and within institutions, where teaching is divided between tenured professors and part-time lecturers. This relationship has no particular geography, although its most dramatic division remains a north-south one.

As firms restructure and embrace **lean production** (see insert), they may trim less skilled jobs and fulfill them through subcontracting arrangements that rely on casual labor, often overseas. The U.S. automobile sector outsourced so much of its components production from the late 1970s that the percentage of its workforce belonging to unions fell from two-thirds to one-quarter by the mid-1990s. Not only did outsourcing bifurcate auto industry labor, but the expansion of this nonunion workforce also eroded wages, such that between 1975 and 1990, the low-wage workforce grew by 142 percent, from 17 to 40 percent of the automobile workforce. And for the U.S. workforce as a whole, industrial restructuring reduced real average weekly earnings by 18 percent from the mid-1970s to the mid-1990s. Meanwhile, union density fell from 25 to 14.5 percent across 1980 to 1995 (and, in the private sector, to 10.2 percent by 1996).[40]

---

### What Is Lean Production?

---

*Lean production is a mixed bag of information technologies, craft work, and archaic or repressive forms of work organization, including self-employment, subcontracting, and piece-rate work. Responding to "just-in-time" supply patterns, it bifurcates labor forces between stable cores of full-time employment and unstable peripheries of "flexible," part-time, or temporary workers. It derives from the Toyota model of a subcontracting pyramid, where a base of insecure, low-paid, and labor-intensive jobs supports a stable core of employees. The hierarchy offers production flexibility and the possibility of disciplining core workers with the threat of outsourcing.*

*At the turn of the twenty-first century, the U.S. economic boom was expressed in expanding high-end managerial and computer systems jobs. But temporary and part-time labor is a defining feature of the twenty-first-century labor market. By 1995, the largest employer in the United States was no longer General Motors but Manpower, Inc., a firm coordinating "temps." Thirty percent of the temporary workforce was located in manufacturing, construction, transportation, and utilities. The U.S. labor market represents a model of lean production, where companies can hire part-time employees without traditional full benefits, creating millions of second-class jobs (most workers prefer full-time work). Women comprise 70 to 90 percent of the temps in the First World. The proportion of part-time workers in the workforce grew between 1979 and 1995 from 16.4 to 24.1 percent in the United Kingdom, from 8.1 to 15.6 percent in France, from 11.4 to 16.3 percent in Germany, and from 13.8 to 18.6 percent in Canada. By a European Union requirement, European governments are relaxing labor laws and generating new part-time jobs, at the rate of 10 percent a year, to improve the flexibility of European firms competing in the world market.*

---

Sources: Cooper and Kuhn (1998:A1); Moody (1999:97–99).

---

From 1970 to 1994, manufacturing employment fell 50 percent in Britain, 8 percent in the United States, 18 percent in France, and 17 percent in Germany, with many of these jobs being "low-tech," such as footwear, textiles, and metals. In 1995 alone, the U.S. apparel industry lost 10 percent of its jobs and, with jobs lost in the fabrics industry, accounted for 40 percent of manufacturing jobs lost that year. More than 50 percent of the U.S. clothing market is accounted for by cheap imports from Asia and Latin America. Around 65,300 U.S. footwear jobs disappeared in the 1980s—associated with, for example, Nike's decision to stop making athletic shoes in the United States and relocating most of its production to South Korea and Indonesia. In the early 1990s, a worker, usually female, in the footwear industry in Indonesia earned $1.03 per day compared to an average wage in the U.S. footwear industry of $6.94 per *hour*.[41]

Even as postindustrial work (retailing, health care, security, finance, restaurants) has filled the gap left by industrial manufacturing across the First World, employment in the proliferating service sector is not immune to relocation. Many new jobs in the Caribbean, for example, are data-processing jobs that large U.S. insurance, health industry, magazine subscription renewal, consumer credit, and retailing firms have shifted offshore at a lower cost. Swissair, British Airways, and Lufthansa relocated much of their reservations to Indian subcontractors in Bangalore, where "the staff are well educated at English-speaking universities yet cost only a fraction of what their counterparts are paid in the North." According to a spokesperson for Swissair, "We can hire three Indians for the price of one Swiss." The relocation of revenue accounts preparation saved 8 million francs and 120 jobs in Zurich. And since 1990, Eastern Europe has become an increasingly competitive site (with India) for labor-intensive computer programming.[42]

 **CASE STUDY**

**High Heels and High Tech in Global Barbados**

In an innovative study of "pink-collar" work and identities in the Caribbean, Carla Freeman decenters modernity by exploring how an Afro-Caribbean workforce has embraced the international division of labor in the informatics industry. Disadvantaged by Mexico's stranglehold on trade preferences with North America, the export-oriented countries of Barbados, Jamaica, and Trinidad offer a "comparative advantage" in the service industry, given their English-speaking tradition and tourist orientation.

Barbados, with a literacy rate of 98 percent and a reputation for order and polite service, turned itself into a haven for offshore information-based data-processing work, globally sourced by Multitext and Data Air (subsidiaries of British and U.S. telecommunication corporations, respectively):

> On a typical shift . . . between about fifty and one hundred Barbadian women sit in partitioned computer cubicles of a given production floor from 7:30 in the morning until 3:30 in the afternoon, taking a half-hour break for lunch and sometimes a fifteen-minute stretch in between. Their key-strokes per hour are monitored electronically as they enter data from airline ticket stubs, consumer warranty cards, or the text of a potboiler novel for top U.S. airlines, appliance houses and publishers. In each case, the surveillance of the computer, the watchful eye of supervisors, and the implementation of double-keying techniques are all aspects of the production process integral to the companies' guarantee of 99 percent accuracy rates.

While such work is deskilled, demoted, and gendered, globally, Freeman finds that even though they could earn more in the canefields, the women themselves are attracted to these pink-collar jobs because, through them, they identify with office work and informatics technology (and with the firms' imported female Indian computer engineers) and because the Barbados Development Plan (1988–1993) and its vision of development via information-based exports guarantees basic employment benefits, such as maternity and sick leave and three weeks of paid vacation.

Here we glimpse a portion of the feminized global labor force identifying, professionally, with work that is devalued and tightly disciplined—is this about informatics being an exception to the rule or whether these are the conditions in a tourist haven, or does it tell us that we cannot expect to find homogeneous conditions in the global economy, especially when local participants project their own meaning onto what they do?

---

*Source: Freeman (2000:23–48).*

Manufacturing labor has lost considerable organizational as well as numerical power to corporate strategies of restructuring, leading to the qualitative restructuring of work discussed in the insert on lean production. After a decade of conservative government restructuring of the British labor force (weakening union rights, eliminating minimum wages, reducing jobless benefits), Britain in the 1990s became a new site for offshore investment from Europe—mostly in part-time jobs (electronic assembly, apparel, clerical tasks) undertaken by women at considerably lower wages than would be paid in Europe.[43] Typically, "Third World" working conditions are just as likely to appear in the global centers via the practice of lean production. Garment sweatshops are a recurring phenomenon, for example, in New York City, and a range of "Third World" jobs has spread in First World cities over the past two decades. In other words, the *global labor force* is well entrenched across the world.

Global integration habitually marginalizes people and their communities, as jobs are automated, shed, or relocated by corporations under global competitive pressures. Competition compels firms not only to go global but also to keep their sourcing flexible and, therefore, their suppliers—and their workers—guessing. The women's wear retailer Liz Claiborne, which divides its sources mainly among the United States, Hong Kong, South Korea, Taiwan, the Philippines, China, and Brazil, claims, "The Company does not own any manufacturing facilities: all of its products are manufactured through arrangements with independent suppliers. . . . The Company does not have any long-term, formal arrangements with any of the suppliers which manufacture its products."[44] As the world market has been corporatized, firms that once organized "company towns," with considerable paternalism toward their workers, have shed that responsibility as they have reached out to the more abstract (flexible and expendable) global labor force.

 **CASE STUDY**
**The Corporatization of World Markets**

Export markets concentrate in the First World, where markets are a great deal denser than Third World markets and consumer culture is well entrenched. Export, or world, markets are typically organized by TNCs. UN data reveal that transnational corporations account for two-thirds of world trade. Fifty of the largest 100 economies are run by TNCs, not countries: For instance, General Motors is larger than Thailand, Norway, or Saudi Arabia, and Mitsubishi is larger than Poland, South Africa, or Greece. TNCs control most of the world's financial transactions, (bio) technologies, and industrial capacity—including oil and its refining, coal, gas, hydroelectric and nuclear power plants, mineral extraction and processing, home electronics, chemicals, medicines, wood harvesting and processing, and more.

The top 5 TNCs in each major market (such as jet aircraft, automobiles, microprocessors, and grains) typically account for between 40 and 70 percent of all world sales, with the 10 largest corporations in their field controlling 86 percent of telecommunications and 70 percent of the computer industry. Furthermore, about 50 percent of world trade takes place inside the TNCs, as components move within corporate networks, including subsidiaries of allied firms and parent corporations in the construction of a final product. By 1991, according to estimates from the United Nations Conference on Trade and Development (UNCTAD), sales internal to transnationals exceeded their overall trade in final products, including services. At century's end, the combined annual revenues of the 200 largest corporations exceeded those of the 182 states with 80 percent of the world's population. At the same time, corporate tax rates have declined significantly in most First World states (a decline from 30 to 7 percent of government funds in the United States since the early 1950s), forcing governments to shift tax burdens to personal income and sales.

From 1970 to 1995, the number of TNCs rose from 7,000 to 40,000. The combined sales of the largest 350 TNCs in the world total almost one-third of the combined GNPs of all industrialized countries and exceed the individual GNPs of *all* Third World countries. The majority of these firms are headquartered in France, Germany, Japan, the United Kingdom, and the United States, accounting for 70 percent of all transnational investment and about 50 percent of all the companies themselves. Wal-Mart is now the largest corporation in the world and the largest importer of Chinese-made products, with an annual revenue of $220 billion, $7 billion in profits. Of the 10 richest people in the world, 5 are Waltons from the Wal-Mart empire, with S. Robson Walton now topping Bill Gates as No. 1. Wal-Mart has more than 1 million un-unionized employees (three times that of General Motors), a large proportion of whom are employed part-time (with minimal benefits).

Under these circumstances of globalization, the framework and content of development appears to have been redefined: not in terms of governments pursuing social equity in the national citizen-state but in terms of the corporate pursuit of efficiency and choice for the global consumer-citizen.

If the consumer-citizen represents only one-fifth of the world's population, what kind of development (and globalization) do we have?

---

*Sources: Baird and McCaughan (1979:135-36); M. Brown (1993:47); Ellwood (1993:5, 2001:55-63); Korten (1996:323); Karliner (1997:5); Daly and Logan (1989:67); Martin and Schumann (1997:12); The Economist (July 16, 1994); Beams (1999); Hightower (2002); Alperovitz (2003:15).*

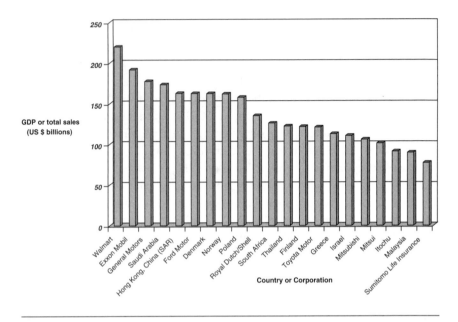

**Figure 3.5**    Corporate versus Country Economic Graph

Sources: Sales: *Fortune* (July 22, 2002). Gross domestic product: *Human Development Report* (United Nations, 2002).

As corporations shuffle the global employment deck, the United States has experienced further declines in real wages (a trend since 1972), rising poverty rates, increased family stress and social disorder, rising public health costs, and so on. A 1995 study, titled *Families in Focus,* found that family decay is worldwide—attributed largely to the trend of women assuming a greater role as income earners. These jobs are usually inferior, requiring longer hours of work than men's work and leading to new stresses in households.[45] Proposed retraining schemes to help workers adjust to a shifting employment scene are often ineffectual, as most replacement jobs are low paid and low- or no-benefit service work.[46]

Retraining is likely to be ineffectual when governments surrender the prerogative to regulate investment and labor markets to global market forces. In the global marketplace, product cycles are unstable, as consumer fashions and sourcing sites change relentlessly. The loss of jobs is not simply an economic transfer from one nation to another; more fundamentally, it represents the "hollowing out" of a nation's economic base and the erosion of social institutions that stabilize the conditions of employment and habitat associated with those jobs. A century of institution building in labor markets, in corporate/union relations, and in communities can disappear overnight when the winds of the market are allowed to blow across uneven national boundaries. Those who have work find they are often working longer hours to make ends meet, despite remarkable technological advances.

## Global Agribusiness

Just as the manufacturing transnational corporations use global sourcing strategies, so do agribusiness firms. The food trade is one of the fastest growing industries in the world today, especially in processed foods such as meat and flour products and in fresh and processed fruits and vegetables. Food companies stretch across the world, organizing producers on plantations and farms to deliver products for sale in the higher value markets. As we have seen, the livestock complex was one of the first segments of the food industry to internationalize, producing what has been called the "world steer."

### CASE STUDY
### Agribusiness Brings You the World Steer

The "world steer" resembles the "world car." It is produced in a variety of locations with global inputs (standardized genetic lines and growth patterns) for global sale (standardized packaging). Like the world car, the world steer is the logical extension of the mass production system. The beef industry is subdivided into two branches: intensive lot feeding for high-value specialty cuts and extensive cattle grazing for low-value lean meat, supplying an exploding fast-food industry.

In Central America, Brahman bulls (or their semen) imported from Florida and Texas, crossed with native criollo and fed on imported African and South American pasture, produce a more pest-resistant, more heat-resistant, and beefier breed of steer. From conception to slaughter, the production of the steer is geared entirely to the demands of a global market. Animal health and the fattening process depend on medicines, antibiotics, chemical fertilizers, and herbicides supplied from around the world by transnational firms. Foreign investors in this industry include TNCs such as International Foods, United Brands, Agrodiná mica Holding Company, and R. J. Reynolds.

Development strategies favored agro-exporting for foreign exchange to purchase industrial technologies. Central American states complemented their traditional exports (coffee and bananas) with beef, obtaining loans from the World Bank, the Agency for International Development (AID), and the Inter-American Development Bank (IADB) to fund the expansion of pasture and transport facilities. World steer production has redistributed cattle holdings and open-range woodland from peasants to the ranchers supplying the export packers. More than half the rural population of Central America (35 million) has been unable to survive as a peasantry.

World steer production not only reinforces inequality in the producing regions but also threatens craftwork and food security. Domesticated animals traditionally have provided food, fuel, fertilizer, transport, and clothing, in addition to grazing on and consuming crop stubble. In many ways, livestock have been the centerpiece of rural community survival over the centuries. Peasants have always used mixed farming as a sustainable form of social economy, hunting on common lands to supplement their local diets with additional protein. Elimination of woodlands reduces hunting possibilities, shrinks wood supplies for fuel, and destroys watershed ecologies. Also, development policies favoring other cattle breeds over the traditional criollo undermine traditional cattle raising and hence peasant self-provisioning. Peasants forfeit their original meat and milk supplies and lose access to side products such as tallow for cooking oil and leather for clothing and footwear.

The promise of globalization is a cornucopia of commodities, including beef. But this promise works for some, not those whose disappearing cultures and agro-ecologies subsidize affluent food production. What kind of development rewards such specialization at the expense of sustainable peasant cultures, generating, rather than eliminating, deprivation?

Sources: Sanderson (1986b); Williams (1986:93–95); Rifkin (1992:192–93).

Global sourcing also sustains the intensive form of livestock raising that requires feedlots. Three agribusiness firms headquartered in the United States operate meat-packing operations across the world, raising cattle, pigs, and poultry on feedstuffs supplied by their own grain marketing subsidiaries elsewhere in the world. Cargill, headquartered in Minnesota, is the largest grain trader in the world, operating in 70 countries with more than 800 offices or plants and more than 70,000 employees. It has established a joint venture with Nippon Meat Packers of Japan, called Sun Valley Thailand, from which it exports U.S. corn-fed poultry products to the Japanese market. ConAgra, headquartered in Nebraska, owns 56 companies and operates in 26 countries with 58,000 employees. It processes feed and animal protein products in the United States, Canada, Australia, Europe, the Far East, and Latin America. Tyson Foods, headquartered in Arkansas, runs a joint venture with the Japanese agribusiness firm C. Itoh, which produces poultry in Mexico for both local consumption and export to Japan. Tyson also cuts up chickens in the United States, using the breast meat for the fast-food industry and shipping leg quarters to Mexico for further processing (at one-tenth the cost of preparing them in this country) for the Japanese market.[47]

## The New Agricultural Countries (NACs)

Despite the far-flung activities of these food companies, agribusiness investments have generally concentrated in select Third World countries (e.g., Brazil, Mexico, Argentina, Chile, Hungary, and Thailand), known as the **new agricultural countries** (NACs).[48] They are analogous to the NICs insofar as their governments promote agro-industrialization for urban and export markets. These agro-exports have been called *nontraditional exports* because they either replace or supplement the traditional tropical exports of the colonial era. Nontraditional exports tend to be high-value foods such as animal protein products and fruits and vegetables. And, to carry the analogy further, the term *new international division of labor* has been extended to these agro-exports because they supersede the exports associated with the colonial division of labor.

Thailand's traditional role in the international division of labor as an exporter of rice, sugar, pineapples, and rubber is now complemented with an expanding array of nontraditional primary exports: cassava (feed grain), canned tuna, shrimp, poultry, processed meats, and fresh and processed fruits and vegetables. Former exports, corn and sorghum, are now mostly consumed domestically in the intensive livestock sector. Raw agricultural exports, which accounted for 80 percent of Thailand's exports in 1980, now represent 30 percent; processed food makes up 30 percent of manufactured exports. In other words, Thailand has become an NAC.[49]

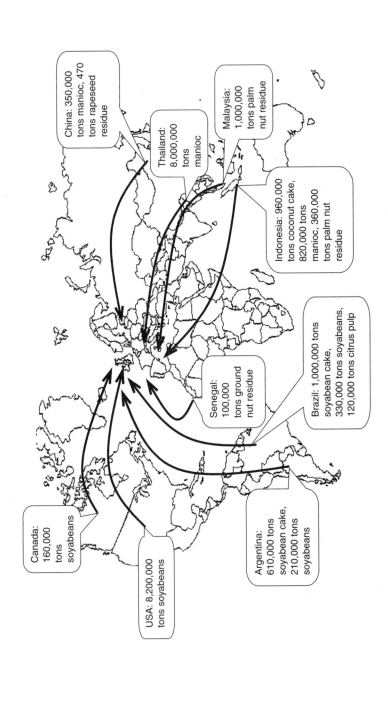

**Figure 3.6** Europe's Global Sourcing of Animal Feed Ingredients

Source: Tim Lang, "Dietary Impact of the Globalization of Food Trade." *International Forum on Globalization News*, 3(1998): 10–12.

Viewed as Asia's supermarket, Thailand expanded its food processing industry on a foundation of rural smallholders under contract to food processing firms. Food companies from Japan, Taiwan, the United States, and Europe use Thailand as a base for regional and global export-oriented production. For example, Japanese firms form joint ventures with Thai agribusinesses to expand feed (soybeans and corn) and aquaculture supply zones for Japanese markets. Thailand's agro-exports are linked to the affluent markets in the Pacific Rim (especially those of Japan, South Korea, and Taiwan), and these markets accounted for more than 60 percent of Thailand's foreign exchange in the 1990s. Thai poultry production is organized around small growers who contract with large, vertically integrated firms. To facilitate this, the Thai government organized a complex of agribusinesses, farmers, and financial institutions with state ministries to promote export contracts, distributing land to landless farmers for contract growing and livestock farming.[50] Thailand's mature feed industry, coupled with low-cost labor, helped Thai poultry producers compete with their U.S. counterparts in the Japanese market, the latest competitor being China. Thailand is the world's largest producer of farmed shrimp[51]— symbolizing the symbiosis whereby consumer affluence and the NAC phenomenon reproduce one another in what has been called the second green revolution.

## The Second Green Revolution

As we saw in Chapter 2, the green revolution encouraged agribusiness in the production of wage foods for urban consumers in the Third World. Since then, agribusiness has spread from basic grains to other grains, such as feedstuffs, to horticultural crops, such as fresh fruits and vegetables. More recently, agribusiness has created feed-grain substitutes such as cassava, corn gluten feed, and citrus pellets, and biotechnology is creating plant-derived "feedstocks" for the chemical industry. This kind of agriculture depends on hybrid seeds, chemical fertilizers, pesticides, animal antibiotics and growth-inducing chemicals, specialty feeds, genetically modified plants, and so forth. It is a specialized, high-input agriculture servicing high-value markets, in addition to food processors and agrochemical firms. It extends green revolution technology from basic to luxury foods and agro-industrial inputs and has been termed the *second green revolution*.[52]

The second green revolution is a reliable indicator of high-income consumers adopting affluent First World diets, wherever they are located.

It involves, most notably, substituting feed crops for food crops and the exacerbation of social inequalities (in access to land and basic foods). In Mexico, for example, U.S. agribusiness firms promoted the use of hybrid sorghum seeds among Mexican farmers in the late 1950s. Then, in 1965, the Mexican government established a support price favoring sorghum over wheat and maize (products of the green revolution). As sorghum production doubled (supplying 74 percent of Mexican feedstuffs), wheat, maize, and even bean production began a long decline. In the 1970s, meat consumption rose among wealthier Mexicans, with increases of 65 percent in pork, 35 percent in poultry, and 32 percent in beef. At the same time, no kind of meat was available for about one-third of the population.[53] In other words, *development is realized through inequality.*

The second green revolution contributes to the globalization of markets for high-value foods such as off-season fresh fruits and vegetables. This market is one of the most profitable for agribusinesses. As global markets have deepened and transport technologies have matured, "cool chains" maintain chilled temperatures for transporting fresh fruit and vegetables grown by Third World farmers to supermarket outlets across the world. U.S. firms such as Dole, Chiquita, and Del Monte have moved beyond their traditional commodities such as bananas and pineapples into other fresh fruits and vegetables, joined by British firms Albert Fisher and Polly Peck. By coordinating producers scattered across different climatic zones, these firms are able to reduce the seasonality of fresh fruits and vegetables and thus create a *global supermarket.* Year-round produce availability is complemented with exotic fruits such as breadfruit, cherimoya (custard apple), carambola (star fruit), feijoa (pineapple guava), lychee, kiwi, and passionfruit; vegetables such as bok choy, cassava, fava beans, and plantain; and salad greens such as arugula, chicory, and baby vegetables.[54]

In this new division of world agricultural labor, transnational corporations typically subcontract with or hire peasants to produce specialty horticultural crops and off-season fruits and vegetables for export processing (canning, freezing, gassing, boxing, juicing, and dicing) to supply expanding consumer markets located primarily in Europe, North America, and Pacific-Asia. However, as the commodification of agriculture for global markets proceeds, it impinges on women's livelihoods, their food security, and that of their families. Most food consumed across the world is produced by women: accounting for 45 percent in Latin America, 65 percent in Asia, and 75 percent in Sub-Saharan Africa. Women's lack of security and rights in land means that commercialization easily erodes women's role in and control of food production.

### CASE STUDY

 The Global Labor Force and the Link
between Food Security and Food Insecurity

The global fruit and vegetable industry depends on flexible contract labor arrangements. Coordination of multiple production sites, for a year-round supply of fresh produce, is achieved through information technologies. These global commodity chains disconnect producers and consumers with interesting consequences: consumer ignorance of conditions under which their goods are produced, as well as producer experience of growing food for (firms for) distant consumers rather than for their own communities.

Deborah Barndt's research retraces the journey of the tomato from Mexico to the ubiquitous fast-food and retailing outlets of North America. Naming it "Tomasita," to foreground its labor origins in ethnic and gendered terms, she describes the Sayula plant of one of Mexico's largest agro-exporters, Santa Anita Packers, where, in the peak season, Sayula employs more than 2,000 pickers and 700 packers. The improved seed varieties originate in Mexico but are developed and patented in Israel or the United States. Such seeds need heavy doses of pesticides,

> but the company did not provide any health and safety education or the protective gear. Perhaps a more visually striking indicator of monocultural production was the packing plant, employing hundreds of young women whom the company moved by season from one site to another as a kind of "mobile maquiladora." . . . the only Mexican inputs are the land, the sun, and the workers. . . . The South has been the source of the seeds, while the North has the biotechnology to alter them . . . the workers who produce the tomatoes do not benefit. Their role in agro-export production also denies them participation in subsistence agriculture, especially since the peso crisis in 1995, which has forced migrant workers to move to even more scattered work sites. They now travel most of the year—with little time to grow food on their own plots in their home communities . . . with this loss of control comes a spiritual loss, and a loss of a knowledge of seeds, of organic fertilizers and pesticides, of sustainable practices such as crop rotation or leaving the land fallow for a year—practices that had maintained the land for millennia.

What is instructive about this agribusiness strategy is that the food security of northern consumers (via the global supermarket) is obtained through the food *in*security of Mexico—converted from a food self-sufficient nation (relinquished in 1982 with the dismantling of the national food system) to one that imports one-third of its food needs (staple grains). Displaced maize farmers (especially indigenous women) move to the new *agro-maquilas* or to North American orchards or plantations, where what they earn in a week in Mexico is what they earn in a day in the United States.

What are the long-term consequence of a global food system that destabilizes peasant communities and exacerbates southern food dependency, for no good reason other than profit and a year-round supply of tasteless tomatoes?

*Source: Barndt (1997:59-62).*

## Global Sourcing and Regionalism

Global sourcing is a strategy used by transnational corporations and host governments alike to improve their world market position and secure predictable supplies of inputs. Because of the formation of an infinitely available global labor force, firms have been able to reorganize marketing strategies to allow them to segment consumer markets. This means substituting flexible for standardized mass production, using smaller and less specialized (multitasking) labor forces. Whether **flexible production** is actually replacing mass production is not entirely clear. In fact, flexible, or lean, production is reorganizing mass production to allow the segmentation or differentiation of consumer markets. Marketing now drives production, and a system of "mass customization" has developed to allow firms to mass produce essentially similar products with multiple variations to suit individual needs—the sneaker industry, with its endless variations in style, is a clear case in point.

The size of market segments depends on social class incomes. Recently, we have seen a considerable stratification of consumption—in the broad quality range of cars and clothing items, as well as in the segmentation of the beef market into high-value beefsteak and low-value hamburger. With a global market, firms are increasingly under pressure to respond to changing consumer preferences as the life span of commodities declines (with rapidly changing fashion and/or technologies). Shifting consumer tastes require greater flexibility in firms' production runs, use of inputs, use of inventory, and in selling strategies.

In the 1980s, the Toyota Company introduced the just-in-time (JIT) system of "destandardized or flexible mass production."[55] With JIT (premised on informatics), simultaneous engineering replaces the sequencing of mass production—the "just-in-case" system in which materials are produced on inflexible assembly lines to supply standardized consumer markets. By contrast, simultaneous engineering allows quicker changes in design and production, so firms can respond to volatile consumer markets. The Gap, for example, changes its inventory and "look" every six weeks. As the company's Far East vice president for offshore sourcing remarked, "The best retailers will be the ones who respond the quickest, the best . . . where the time between cash register and factory shipment is shorter."[56]

The JIT system promotes both global *and* regional corporate strategies. In the clothing industry, shoes and garments commodity chains can be dispersed globally and centrally coordinated by the parent firm. In the garments trade, a global fashion designer typically purchases a Paris-designed shirt for U.S.$3 to $4 in Bangladesh, Vietnam, or Thailand and sells the shirt in the European market at 5 to 10 times its price. In the shoe trade, Vietnamese workers make about U.S.$400 a year stitching sneakers, while corporate celebrities are paid U.S.$10 to $20 million a year to "sell" these products. Changing fashions favors flexible subcontracting arrangements in the "field," where flexible labor costs are so cheap. In more capital-intensive sectors, where automated technologies are less transferable, firms tend to invest in regional sites so they can respond quickly to local/regional market signals as fashions change.[57]

Recent concentration of investment flows in the denser First World regions of the world market reflects this corporate strategy. These are the regions with the largest markets, where an integrated production complex based on the JIT principle has the greatest chance to succeed. Even if the commodity life cycle has quickened, demanding greater production flexibility, mass consumption of such commodities still occurs. So firms locate near the big markets, where strategic countries act as nodes for trade and investment circuits. Thus, countries such as Mexico and Malaysia become important investment sites precisely because of the new regional complexes of the North American Free Trade Agreement (NAFTA) and the Asia-Pacific Economic Conference (APEC).

The new industrial corridor in Mexico (from Mexico City north to Monterey) demonstrates this effect. U.S. and Japanese auto companies are currently expanding their operations there, with the North American market in mind. Car and light truck production in Mexico was projected to triple between 1989 and 2000. The city of Saltillo, which used to manufacture appliances and sinks, built one of North America's larger auto-making complexes, including two General Motors plants, a new Chrysler assembly plant, a Chrysler engine plant, and several parts facilities. One consequence of this process is a stratification of Mexican industrial workers, as wages for some auto work on the border drift up with rising skill levels—on the order of a 40 percent increase in the first half of the 1990s, even though the pay differential across the border is still more than 6 to 1.[58] While some *maquila* jobs have already moved to China (an entry-level factory worker in Tijuana earns $1.50 to $2 an hour vs. 25 cents an hour in parts of China), Mexico retains the advantage in automobile production since cars are costly to transport. As Tijuana's mayor, Jose de Jesus Gonzales Reyes, declared, "This is our new strategy, selling the Tijuana–San Diego region."[59] Meanwhile, in Southeast Asia, General Motors opened 23 factories in the Southeast Asian region in the mid-1990s—15 in China, 4 in South Korea, 3 in Malaysia, and 1 in Indonesia; Ford expects to match this by capturing 10 percent of the Asian market by the end of the first decade of the twenty-first century, and Toyota and Honda continue their interest in this regional market.[60]

In the context of NAFTA, U.S., Japanese, and European firms rush to invest in food-processing operations in Mexico, consolidating its status as an NAC supplying the North American market—similar to Thailand's new regional supermarket role. Firms such as Coca-Cola, Pepsico, General Foods, Kraft, Kellogg's, Campbell's, Bird's Eye, Green Giant, Tyson Foods, C. Itoh, Nestlé, and Unilever are investing in fruits and vegetables, meat, dairy products, and wheat milling to supply regional markets.[61]

### CASE STUDY

### Regional Strategy of a
### Southern Transnational Corporation

We tend to think of TNCs as northern in origin. The Charoen Pokphand (CP) Group was formed in Bangkok in 1921 by two Chinese brothers to trade in farm inputs, including seeds. In the 1960s, CP expanded into animal feed production, from which it began to vertically integrate poultry production, providing inputs (chicks, feed, medicines, credit, extension services) to farmers and, in turn, processing and marketing poultry domestically and then regionally in East Asia. In the 1980s, CP entered retailing, acquiring a Kentucky Fried Chicken (KFC) franchise for Thailand, and now CP controls about one-quarter of the Thai fast-food market as an outlet for its poultry, including 715 Seven-Eleven convenience stores. By the mid-1990s, CP was Thailand's largest TNC and Asia's largest agri-industrial conglomerate, with 100,000 employees in 20 countries. It was an early investor in China, establishing a feed mill in Shenzhen in 1979, in a joint venture with Continental Grain. In 1995, CP was operating 75 feedmills in 26 of China's 30 provinces; controlled the KFC franchise rights for China, operating in 13 cities; and its poultry operations accounted for 10 percent of China's broilers, producing 235 million day-old chicks per annum.

By now, CP has investments in fertilizers, pesticides and agro-chemicals, vehicles, tractors, supermarkets, baby foods, livestock operations in poultry and swine, milk processing, crop farming and processing, seed production, aquaculture, and jute-backed carpets, as well as in telecommunications, real estate, retailing, cement, and petrochemicals. CP produces poultry in Turkey, Vietnam, Cambodia, Malaysia, Indonesia, and the United States, as well as animal feed in Indonesia, India, and Vietnam; through a public joint venture, CP is involved in China's fourth and sixth largest motorcycle manufacturing operations and in the development of an industrial park and satellite town in Shanghai. CP's current initiative is in shrimp farming, where it controls 65 percent of the Thai market and is the world's largest producer of farmed shrimp. CP has used joint ventures to expand shrimp farming to Indonesia, Vietnam, China, and India, which are likely to replace Thailand as the regional source of shrimp since they are cheaper sites for an industry that is beset by ecological stress.

When we see the extent of a TNC's concentration of power over regional or global economic activity, where is this kind of development going, and whose future does it serve?

---

*Source: Goss, Burch, and Rickson (2000).*

New strategies of regional investment partly explain the repatterning of investment flows in the 1990s. As that decade began, foreign direct investment (FDI) in the Third World increased as global FDI declined.[62] Just as in the 1970s, when the NICs were the locus of world economic expansion, the majority of foreign investment concentrated in regionally significant states such as China, Mexico, Indonesia, and South Korea. These states are significant because they have large and growing domestic markets and/or they are located near other large, affluent markets in East Asia and North America. Meanwhile, there is a new vision of economic regionalism under way in the *Plan Puebla de Panama* complex: an industrial corridor linking the south of Mexico to Panama to mobilize the pool of displaced, cheap indigenous labor.[63]

Different firms have different production strategies, whether regional or global, depending on the need for proximity (e.g., automated technologies or fresh vegetables) or on sourcing from cheap labor zones (e.g., low-skill labor processing). In the service industry, regional strategies may be necessary to accommodate cultural preferences. McDonald's, for instance, may sell Big Macs and Happy Meals in Vienna, Indonesia, and South Korea, but in Vienna, it caters to local tastes in blended coffee by selling "McCafes"; in Jakarta, rice supplements French fries on the menu; and in Seoul, McDonald's sells roast pork with soy sauce on a bun. However, the low- to mid-value retailer Wal-Mart has broad, standardized consumer segments in mind, with one spokesperson remarking, "With trade barriers coming down, the world is going to be one great big marketplace, and he who gets there first does the best."[64] Thus, McDonald's, the firm with the global brand, deploys flexible menus to retain local market share, while Wal-Mart sees the consumer world as its oyster.

World capitalism has tendencies toward both global and regional integration. Regional integration may anticipate global integration since it promotes trade and investment flows among neighboring countries. But it also may reflect a defensive strategy by firms and states that distrust the intentions of other firm/state clusters. At present, the global economy is subdivided into three macroregions, centered on the United States, Japan, and Germany/Western Europe—each with hinterlands in Central and Latin America, Southeast Asia, and Eastern Europe/North Africa, respectively. But within those macroregions, there are smaller free trade agreements in operation, often based on greater economic affinity among the members in terms of their GNPs and wage levels. How the future will unfold—with global or regional integration as the dominant tendency—is not yet clear.

## Summary

This chapter has examined the rise of the NICs critical to the emergence of a global production system. The rise of the NICs did not simply represent a possibility of upward mobility for individual states in the world economic hierarchy. It also altered the conditions for "development." Until the 1970s, *development* was understood as primarily a national process of economic and social transformation. But by then, two trends were becoming clear: (1) The First World was not waiting for the Third World to catch up—indeed, the gap between these two world regions was expanding—and (2) one strategy emerging among some Third World states was to attempt to reduce that gap by aggressive exporting of manufactured goods.

By 1980, the World Bank redefined *development* as "successful participation in the world market." The prescription for Third World countries was to adopt the NICs' strategy of export-oriented industrialization. Specialization in the world economy, rather than replication of economic activities within a national framework, emerged as the criterion of "development."

Export expansion in the Third World can now be understood from two angles. On one hand, it was part of a governmental strategy of export growth in both manufacturing and agricultural products. Successful governments have converted liberalized policies regarding foreign investment into a recipe for what some term *upward mobility*. Indeed, the real exponents of this strategy, the Southeast Asian NICs (South Korea, Taiwan, Singapore, and possibly Malaysia), have displayed an unusual capacity for a flexible form of state capitalism, accompanied by considerable political authoritarianism, including labor repression. They attracted foreign capital with promises of stable political conditions and anticipated world-economic technological upgrading, developing workforce skills, improving their export composition, and securing the benefits of riding the world economic curve. The result was a growing differentiation among Third World countries, in conventional development terms.

On the other hand, export expansion was part of a global strategy used by transnational corporations to "source" their far-flung activities. Some middle-income Third World states such as Brazil and South Korea converted domestic production into export production on their own as domestic markets matured. Meanwhile, the transnational corporations were building global production systems—in manufacturing, agriculture, and services. Global sourcing merged with the export-oriented strategy, especially as a result of the debt regime (see Chapter 4). In effect, a new global economy was emerging, beyond trade among national economies. The global economy was embedded in those parts of national societies producing or consuming world commodities. It is organized chiefly by transnational corporate webs of economic activity, linking sites of labor differentiated along skill and gender/ethnic lines. For any one state, the corporate-based global economic system is unstable and beyond its ability to control or regulate.

As states absorb global economic activity into their social fabric, they subordinate their political and social futures to the global economy. Development has begun to shed its national identity and to change into a global enterprise in which individual states must participate—but quite tenuously as we shall see.

# 4

# Demise of the Third World

The consolidation of a global economy undid the Third World as a political entity, as a condition for the project of globalization. More than a matter of economic integration, the laying of the foundations of globalization was an exercise of First World power in shifting international development discourse from economic nationalism to world market participation. This involved more than two decades of military and financial disciplining of Third World initiatives that restricted foreign corporate access to Third World resources and markets and threatened default on First World loans. Beginning, perhaps, with the installation of General Suharto in Indonesia in 1965, U.S.-led Western intervention introduced a new model of development, premised on an open-door policy across the Third World, culminating in the debt regime in the 1980s. This regime imposed financial disciplines via structural adjustment that completed the rollback of economic nationalism and the political dismantling of the Third World.

Within the Third World, the separation of the newly industrializing countries (NICs) from their Third World peers led to a reevaluation of the economic nationalism of the development project, undermining Third World unity. Export-oriented industrialization fueled rapid economic growth and legitimized a new development model characterized as the "free market" model, and in the 1980s, this was represented as the solution to the debt crisis. *Development*, which had been defined as nationally managed economic growth, was redefined in the World Bank's *World Development Report 1980* as "participation in the world market."[1]

The redefinition prepared the way for superseding economic nationalism and embracing globalization. *The global economy was emerging as the unit of development.* This was made possible by the rise of a global banking system in the 1970s, spurred on by a process of financial liberalization that eased the cross-border movement of money. Money became increasingly stateless and easy to borrow. In the 1970s, Third World states borrowed from global banks as if there were no tomorrow. Banks lent money as if there were no risks in bankrolling Third World governments. In the 1980s, this mountain of debt crumbled as interest rates were hiked to relieve an oversubscribed dollar. The resulting debt crisis drastically reframed the development agenda: The World Bank and the International Monetary Fund (IMF) imposed new loan-rescheduling conditions on indebted states, compelling them to look outward, rather than inward, for their development stimulus.

This chapter surveys these various ways in which the debt crisis transformed the development project into a globalization project. It is essentially about the transition between projects and suggests that this transition had several related political and economic strands, including the following:

- elaboration through military and economic aid of a cold war empire of containment,
- defeat of a final effort at Third World unity (the New International Economic Order initiative),
- financial deregulation and the rise of a global money market,
- First World sponsorship of profligate borrowing by often corrupt Third World elites, and
- financial disciplining of indebted countries by the Bretton Woods institutions, bringing extensive austerity and Third World charges of a "lost decade."

## The Empire of Containment and the Political Decline of the Third World

Just as the Third World was born as a political entity, so it died as a political entity, symbolizing the rise and fall of the development project. But this passage traversed four decades, beginning in the 1950s, when, even in its formative years, the first symbolic blow to Third World economic nationalism came in the form of a CIA-led coup in 1953 against Iranian

Prime Minister Mossadegh after he nationalized British oil holdings. By the time of Indian Prime Minister Jawaharlal Nehru's death in 1964, the non-alignment strategy of Third Worldism was weakening. Many Third World regimes and nationalist movements were aligned with one or both of the superpowers. In addition, China, critical of the bureaucratic-industrial model of the Soviet Union, offered a different model, reversing urban bias and "modernizing" the peasantry via the Great Leap Forward in the 1950s. The United States, concerned that the Chinese experiment would overshadow the Indian model of state-guided (nevertheless capitalist) development, moved to strengthen its alliance with India to anchor the Western development project. Another key figure in the Non-Aligned Movement (NAM), Indonesian President Sukarno, nurtured a state- and military-sponsored form of development, supported by a complex coalition of nationalist, Muslim, and communist parties, forming what he called a "Guided Democracy."[2] Sukarno's regime had mobilized more than 15 million citizens to join parties and mass organizations that challenged Western influence in the region.[3]

In 1965, President Sukarno was overthrown in a bloody coup, including a pogrom claiming between 500,000 to a million lives—mostly members of Indonesia's huge and popular communist party (the PKI). The CIA reported, "In terms of the numbers killed, the massacres rank as one of the worst mass murders in the 20th century." General Suharto, leader of the coup, used the pretext of an internecine struggle between the Indonesian army and the PKI to unleash a violent "year of living dangerously."[4] Declassified documents reveal that a British Foreign Office file in 1964 called for the defense of Western interests in Southeast Asia because it is "a major producer of essential commodities. The region produces nearly 85 percent of the world's natural rubber, over 45 percent of the tin, 65 percent of the copra and 23 percent of the chromium ore." And two years earlier, a CIA memo recorded an agreement between the British Prime Minister Macmillan and U.S. President Kennedy to "liquidate president Sukarno, depending on the situation and available opportunities."[5]

Not unlike the U.S. government's awarding of private contracts to rebuild Iraq in 2003, following regime change, Time-Life, Inc. sponsored a 1967 meeting in Geneva between General Suharto, his economic advisers, and corporate leaders representing "the major oil companies and banks, General Motors, Imperial Chemical Industries, British Leyland, British-American Tobacco, American Express, Siemens, Goodyear, the International Paper Corporation, and US Steel." With Ford Foundation help, General Suharto reformulated a development partnership with foreign investment. Billed "To Aid in the Rebuilding of a Nation," the conference nevertheless invited the corporations to identify the terms of their involvement in the Indonesian economy. James Linen, president of Time-Life, Inc., expressed the *birth of this new global order* when he observed in his opening remarks, "We are here to create a new climate in which private enterprise and developing countries work together . . . for the greater profit of the free world. This world of international enterprise is more than governments. . . . It is the seamless web of enterprise, which has been shaping the global environment at revolutionary speed."[6]

These events marked a turning point in the trajectory of Third World nationalism, introducing new forms of state developmentalism and forging a new discourse of global development partnership. Such intervention was quite consistent with the containment policy articulated for that region by U.S. President Eisenhower in 1959:

> One of Japan's greatest opportunities for increased trade lies in a free and developing Southeast Asia. . . . The great need in one country is for raw materials, in the other country for manufactured goods. The two regions complement each other markedly. By strengthening of Vietnam and helping insure the safety of the South Pacific and Southeast Asia, we gradually develop the great trade potential between this region . . . and highly industrialized Japan to the benefit of both. In this way freedom in the Western Pacific will be greatly strengthened.[7]

The war waged in Vietnam by a U.S.-led coalition during the next two decades confirmed this policy, and it was followed up with strategic interventions in Chile, El Salvador, Nicaragua, Panama, Granada, and Iraq, as well as disbursements of military and economic aid to secure the perimeter of the "free world" and its resource empire. Military power was thus part of the mix, securing and prying open the Third World to an emerging project of global development orchestrated by the United States as the dominant power.

## The New International Economic Order

The Vietnam War (early 1960s to 1975) came to symbolize global inequality. The world was deeply divided over the war, as a confrontation between foreign high-tech and peasant armies, as well as between the ideologies of free enterprise and socialism, and as an issue of empire versus sovereignty. Just as terrorism of the twenty-first century is often identified as a product of poverty, so communism and/or national liberation struggles were linked to underdevelopment. This was the time of the "second-generation Bandung regimes," displaying a more radical, social-ist Third Worldism than the first-generation regimes that pioneered the NAM at Bandung in 1955 and informing a radical dependency theory that sought to explain the evident crisis of Third World development in terms of the continued exploitation by the informal relationships of First World empire.[8]

Between 1974 and 1980, national liberation forces came to power in 14 different Third World states, perhaps inspired by the Vietnamese resis-tance. The possibility of a united South presented itself in two forms in this decade: first, the formation of the **Organization of Petroleum Exporting Countries (OPEC)**, representing the possibility of Third World control over strategic commodities such as oil, and, second, the 1974 pro-posal to the United Nations (UN) General Assembly by the G-77 for a **New International Economic Order (NIEO)**.[9] This proposal demanded reform of the world economic system to improve the position of Third World states in international trade and their access to technological and financial resources.

The NIEO included the following program:

- opening northern markets to southern industrial exports,
- improving the terms of trade for tropical agricultural and mining products,
- providing better access to international financing, and
- facilitating more technology transfers.[10]

The NIEO initiative was consistent with the dependency perspective, namely, that First World structural power stunted Third World develop-ment. For example, the United Nations Conference on Trade and Development (UNCTAD) put pressure on the First World to reduce tariffs on Third World manufactured exports, which reduced protection only on goods originating in transnational corporation (TNC) production sites. Despite exceeding the growth target of 5 percent per annum set by the United Nations for the second development decade of the 1960s, eco-nomic and social indices showed that most Third World countries were not achieving the rising living standards promised by the development project. Refocusing on *basic needs* via the elevation of rural development funding for 700 million smallholders, in 1974, the World Bank reported,

It is now clear that more than a decade of rapid growth in underdeveloped countries has been of little or no benefit to perhaps a third of their population.

Paradoxically, while growth policies have succeeded beyond the expectations of the first development decade, the very idea of aggregate growth as a social objective has increasingly been called into question.[11]

The Third World representatives argued that focusing on inequalities within the Third World as the source of poverty neglected global inequalities. Of course, both sets of relationships were responsible and mutually conditioning, but the interpretive stakes were high. Algerian president Honari Boumedienne told the UN General Assembly in 1974,

> Inasmuch as [the old order] is maintained and consolidated and therefore thrives by virtue of a process which continually impoverishes the poor and enriches the rich, this economic order constitutes the major obstacle standing in the way of any hope of development and progress for all the countries of the Third World.[12]

The NIEO was a charter of economic rights and duties of states, designed to codify global reform along Keynesian lines (public initiatives). It demanded reform of international trade, the international monetary system (to liberalize development financing, debt relief, and increased financial aid), and technological assistance. In addition, it proclaimed the economic sovereignty of states and the right to collective self-reliance among Third World states.[13] Although the NIEO included the Second World, the Soviet Union declined involvement on the grounds that the colonial legacy was a Western issue.

The NIEO initiative was perceived as "the revolt of the Third World." It was indeed the culmination of collectivist politics growing out of the NAM. But it was arguably a movement for reform at best and, at worst, a confirmation of dependency insofar as the proposal depended on northern concessions that would, in turn, increase external revenues available to Third World elites. Interestingly enough, its prime movers were the presidents of Algeria, Iran, Mexico, and Venezuela—all oil-producing nations distinguished by their very recently acquired huge oil rents, as opposed to the impoverished "least developed countries" (LDCs) and the NICs.[14]

Coinciding with the G-77's proposal for global reform was a new development in the core of the First World. This was the formation of what would become the **Group of Seven (G-7)** states. The finance ministers of the original members—the United States, the United Kingdom, France, and West Germany—met in the White House Library in 1973. By 1975, Japan, Italy, and Canada were included in the G-7, which had annual secret meetings in which the first five finance ministers shaped economic policy for the seven states (which, in turn, set the northern agenda). Also, in 1974, central bankers of the G-10 (G-7 plus Sweden, the Netherlands, and Belgium) responded to a financial crisis, stemming from the deregulation of international finance, by agreeing to use the Bank for International Settlements (BIS) to organize a "lender of last resort" function in the event of future crises.[15]

While the G-7 only went public in 1986, it played a key role behind the scenes in *crisis management*. Its origins coincided with a profound shift in the organization of the world economy: the demise of the Bretton Woods regime, the excess liquidity during the mid-1970s when the First World stagnated and the world was awash in stateless money and petrodollars, and Third World unruliness. The G-7 provided First World backbone, ensuring that the NIEO and its symbolic politics would not amount to anything.

The First World's official response was to affirm cooperation and to assist the Third World cause—where it strengthened the world economic order, that is. There were several parts to this response, including the World Bank's basic needs strategy. This included stabilization of rural populations and extension of commercial cropping, stabilization of the conditions of private foreign investment by improved coordination of economic policy across the North-South divide, and a U.S. strategy of buying time by trying to institutionalize the dialogue within forums such as the French-initiated Conference on International Economic Cooperation (1975–1977), which met several times but reached no agreement.[16]

The First World response combined moral themes with governance. But the master theme was really time; as it passed, so did the energy of the NIEO initiative. In the short term, the unity of the Third World fragmented as the prospering OPEC states and the NICs assumed a greater interest in *upward mobility* in the international order. In the long term, the redistributive goals of the NIEO would be overridden by the new doctrine of **monetarism** that ushered in the 1980s debt crisis through drastic restrictions in credit and, therefore, social spending by governments. An official of the U.S. National Security Council articulated the expectation that the differentiation among Third World states would promote a form of *embourgeoisement* as prospering states sought to distance themselves from their poorer neighbors.[17]

The moral of this story is that Third World elites attempted to assert political unity in the world just as economic disunity grew with the divergence of middle-income and poorer states. *The ease of debt financing via the offshore capital markets was a key to promoting individual mobility and fracturing collective solutions among the Third World states.* The First World's representatives had an interest in fostering private solutions, as expansion of the global production system was necessary to First World economic health. The idea of encouraging a country's participation in the world market as the new development strategy was already strongly rooted. In short, the First World managed to sidetrack the Third World's collective political initiative and assert the market solution to development problems.

In the meantime, the goal of the NIEO in redistributing wealth from First to Third Worlds in some ways actually came to pass. Although much of the wealth was oil money, recycled through bank lending to the Third World, it nevertheless met the demands of Third World elites for development financing (in addition to financing rising costs of imported fuel as well as rising military expenditure, which accounted for one-fifth of Third World borrowing). Much of this money was concentrated in the middle-income states and considerably undercut Third World political unity. The marked differentiation in growth patterns of countries intensified in the ensuing debt crisis of the 1980s, which amplified global power relations.

## Financial Globalization

Transnational banks (TNBs) formed in the 1970s with the help of a burgeoning *offshore capital market* beyond the regulatory power of states. The TNBs were banks with deposits outside the jurisdiction or control of any government, usually in tax havens in places such as Switzerland, the Bahamas, or the Cayman Islands. TNBs used these deposits to make massive loans to Third World governments throughout the 1970s. International bank lending, at $2 billion in 1972, peaked in 1981 at $90 billion, then fell to $50 billion in 1985 as a debt crisis followed the orgy of overextended or undersecured loans.[18] To learn why this financial globalization occurred, we need to look at the duality of the Bretton Woods system, where national economic growth depended on the international circulation of American dollars.

The Bretton Woods arrangement maintained stable exchanges of currency between trading countries. To accomplish this stability, the American dollar served as the international reserve currency, with the multilateral financial institutions (the World Bank and the IMF) and the U.S. Federal Reserve Bank making disbursements in dollars. At the same time, fixed currency exchanges stabilized countries' domestic interest rates and, therefore, their economies. Governments could thus implement macroeconomic policy "without interference from the ebb and flow of international capital movements or flights of hot money," said J. M. Keynes, the architect of the postwar world economic order.[19] Within this stable monetary framework, Third World countries were able to pursue development programs with some predictability.

## The Offshore Money Market

Foreign aid and investment underwrote national economic growth during the 1950s and 1960s, breeding a growing offshore dollar market (accessed also by the Soviet Union). This was the so-called Eurocurrency market, initially centered in London's financial district. By depositing earnings in this foreign currency market, transnational corporations evaded Bretton Woods controls on the cross-border movement of capital (as a currency-stabilizing mechanism).

Eurodollar deposits ballooned with the expansion of U.S. military and economic spending abroad during the Vietnam War. Between 1960 and 1970, they grew from $3 billion to $75 billion, rising to more than $1 trillion by 1984. As overseas dollar holdings mushroomed, dwarfing U.S. gold reserves, they became a U.S. liability if cashed in for gold. With mounting pressure on the dollar, President Nixon burst the balloon by declaring the dollar nonconvertible in 1971. This was the end of the gold-dollar standard by which all currencies were *fixed* to a gold value through the U.S. dollar. From now on, currencies would *float* in relative value, with the dollar as the dominant (reserve) currency. The termination of the Bretton Woods system of fixed currency exchanges was the beginning of the end of the development project.

Just as the rise of the development project was politically managed, through the superiority of the United States and its development model, so the demise of the development project was politically managed. In the early 1970s, contrary to the wishes of Western Europe and Japan, the United States unilaterally liberalized international financial relations. Removal of exchange controls was designed to protect the autonomy of U.S. policy, allowing the United States to shift the adjustment burden associated with its large deficits onto other states and investors as they purchased U.S. assets and dollars needed for participation in global markets.

The deregulation of the international financial system signaled a change in the balance of forces internationally and domestically. *Internationally*, U.S. power was waning with the emergence of rival economies, the bloodletting of the Vietnam War, and mounting financial deficits associated with the war and multinational corporate investments. *Domestically,* conservative political forces, including an increasingly coherent neoliberal coalition, and multinational corporate interests favored financial liberalization—viewed as a mechanism to reassert U.S. power in the post–Bretton Woods era.[20]

Deregulation ushered in an era of uncontrolled—and heightened— capital mobility as currency speculators bought and sold national currencies. Financial markets, rather than trade, began to determine currency values, and speculation on floating currencies destabilized national finances. By the early 1990s, world financial markets traded roughly $1 trillion in various currencies daily, all beyond the control of national governments.[21] For example, the mid-1990s saw massive speculation in the Mexican *peso,* when investors expected the North American Free Trade Agreement (NAFTA) to strengthen the Mexican economy. When it did not, traders sold their *peso* holdings, a move that severely destabilized the Mexican economy and was so threatening to world financial markets that the United States stepped in to support the Mexican currency with billions of dollars of new loans. The bailout deal required Mexican oil revenues to be deposited in the U.S. Federal Reserve system, as a *quid pro quo* in the event Mexico defaulted on its repayments.

The loss of currency control by governments threatens nations' economic and political sovereignty. Speculation destabilizes currency values, compromising planning. In 1992, the former chairman of Citicorp described the currency traders, facing 200,000 trading room monitors across the world, as conducting "a kind of global plebiscite on the monetary and fiscal policies of the governments issuing currency." He found this system to be "far more draconian than any previous arrangement, such as the gold standard or the Bretton Woods system, because there is no way for a nation to opt out."[22]

## Banking on Development

Fueled by the dollars earned on the 1973 spike in oil prices engineered by OPEC, the offshore capital market grew from $315 billion in 1973 to $2,055 billion in 1982. The seven largest U.S. banks saw their overseas profits climb from 22 to 60 percent of their total profits in the same time period.[23] By the end of the 1970s, trade in foreign exchange was more than 11 times the value of world commodity trade. The instability of currencies, and therefore of profitability conditions, forced TNCs to diversify their global operations to reduce their risk.[24] In this way, the financial revolution, combined with a flood of petro-dollars, accelerated the formation of a global production system, redistributing economic growth to the Third World. With the First World in an oil price–induced recession, the global banks turned to Third World governments, eager to borrow and considered unlikely to default. By encouraging massive borrowing, the banks brokered the 1970s expansion in the middle-income Third World countries, which functioned now as the engine of growth of the world economy.

In the early 1970s, bank loans accounted for only 13 percent of Third World debt, while multilateral loans made up more than 33 percent and export credits accounted for 25 percent.[25] By the end of the decade, the composition of these figures had reversed, with banks holding about 60 percent of the debt. The departures from the original development model are summarized in the following insert.

---

### Departures from the Development Model in the 1970s

*The 1970s was a decade of transition, as the development project unwound. First, financial deregulation challenged national sovereignty by opening national markets to cross-border capital flows, which, along with currency speculation, destabilized macroeconomic planning. Second, unregulated private bank lending displaced official, multilateral lending to Third World states, but this kind of debt financing was unsound—too much money was lent on the assumption that countries could not go bankrupt. When the debt crisis hit, austerity measures undid many of the gains of the development project. Third, under TNC leadership, more and more manufactured goods and agricultural products were produced for world, rather than domestic, markets. Fourth, development discourse in the early 1970s targeted poverty alleviation, in recognition of the shortcomings of the two development eras, but by the 1980s, the discourse accepted the idea of world market participation as the key to development.*

---

The presence of willing private lenders was a golden opportunity for Third World states to exercise some autonomy from the official financial community. Until now, they had been beholden to powerful First World states for foreign aid and to multilateral agencies for funding of their development programs. Even though official lending continued to rise through the 1970s, from $8 billion to $45 billion,[26] money borrowed from the global banks came not only with no strings attached but also with easy repayment terms because there was so much money to lend. By 1984, all nine of the largest U.S. banks were lending more than 100 percent of their shareholders' equity in loans to Mexico, Brazil, Argentina, and Venezuela, while Lloyds of London lent a staggering 165 percent of its capital to these countries.[27]

Loans typically served several functions. Elites sought to legitimize rule with grand public development projects represented in nationalist terms, to strengthen their militaries, and to enrich their patronage networks with lucrative contracts resulting from loans. In Brazil, between 1964 and 1985, a string of military generals pursued the characteristic Latin American nationalist model, using loans to build the public sector in steel, energy, and raw material production. With debt financing, Brazil transformed itself from a country earning 70 percent of its export revenue from one commodity, coffee, into a major producer and exporter of a multiplicity of industrial goods—including steel, pulp, aluminum, petrochemicals, cement, glass, armaments, and aircraft—and processed foodstuffs such orange juice and soybean meal. Rio de Janeiro and São Paulo have new subway systems, railroads have been built to take ore from huge mines deep in the interior to new ports on the coast, and major cities are linked by a modern telecommunications network.[28]

Of the 21 Latin American nations, 18 were ruled by military regimes in the 1970s, committed to investing in huge infrastructural projects, particularly in the energy sector. At the same time, between 1976 and 1984, the rise in public foreign debt roughly matched a parallel outflow of private capital to banks in New York, the Cayman Islands, and other financial havens.[29] The composition of Latin American borrowing shifted dramatically between the 1960s and the late 1970s, as official loans fell from 40 to 12 percent, private foreign direct investment fell from 34 to 16 percent, and foreign bank and bond financing rose from 7 to 65 percent.[30] Much of this expansion was organized by public- or state-owned enterprises (like a national postal service), and much of it was designed to generate export earnings. Between 1970 and 1982, the average share of gross domestic investment in the public sector of 12 Latin American countries rose from 32 to 50 percent. State managers borrowed heavily to finance the expansion of public enterprise. Often, this was done to establish a counterweight to the foreign investor presence in these economies, which accounted for about 50 percent of the Brazilian and 28 percent of the Mexican manufacturing sectors in 1970.[31]

During the 1970s, public foreign debt grew twice as fast as private foreign debt in Latin America. In Mexico, state enterprises expanded between 1970 and 1982 from 39 to 677 under the rule of the Institutional Revolutionary Party (PRI). By 1978, foreign loans financed 43 percent of the Mexican government's budget deficit and 87 percent of state-owned companies. All across Latin America, public largesse supplemented and complemented foreign and local private investment and even subsidized basic goods and services for the largely urban poor. Regarding the Argentine military's holding company, Fabricaciones Militares, an Argentine banker claimed, "No one really knows what businesses they are in. Steel, chemicals, mining, munitions, even a whore house, everything."[32]

### CASE STUDY
### Containment and Corruption

Assigning blame for the debt crisis is complicated. Certainly, the old colonial tactic of surrogate rule died hard—for much of the development era, the military was the rule rather than the exception in the Third World, where dictators were bankrolled as client regimes of the West in the cold war context. Powerful military leaders, such as Ferdinand Marcos of the Philippines, Saddam Hussein of Iraq, and Chile's Augusto Pinochet, ruled through fear and squandered the national patrimony. It was estimated that 20 percent of loans by non-oil-exporting countries went to imports of military hardware.

In the Congo, the CIA helped bring President Mobutu to power in 1965 for a rapacious, 31-year rule. Mobutu renamed his country Zaire, authenticating his rule in the name of African nationalism, but he traded away Zaire's vast natural resources, including a quarter of the world's copper and half its cobalt, for bank loans totalling billions of dollars and half of U.S. aid to sub-Saharan African in the late 1970s. From the spoils, he stashed $4 billion by the mid-1980s, in addition to a dozen European estates to which he traveled on chartered Concorde flights. Under his rule, Zaire gained 500 British double-decker buses, the world's largest supermarket, and an unwanted steelworks. Deposed in 1996, Mobutu's family holds his fortune, and the country holds his $12 billion debt.

Two years later, when General Suharto was forced to resign, his severance pay was estimated at $15 billion, 13 percent of Indonesia's debt, owed mostly to the World Bank. During Suharto's dictatorship of 30 years, the World Bank loaned more than $30 billion, some of which went into constructive literacy programs, while more than $630 million underwrote the regime's infamous "transmigration" program to colonize the archipelago, including massacres in East Timor. In 1997, a secret World Bank memorandum from Jakarta disclosed a monumental development scandal: that "at least 20 to 30 percent" of the Bank's loans "are diverted through informal payments to GOI [Government of Indonesia] staff and politicians."

If containment encouraged military rule and corruption was rife, why should the burden of debt repayment be borne disproportionately by the citizen-subjects of Third World states?

---

*Sources: Pilger (2002:19-20); Roodman (2001:5-6, 27).*

As public foreign debt grew in the Third World, regimes reached beyond the terms of the development project, borrowing to enrich their patronage networks, strengthen their hold on power through militarization or grand projects, or simply make up lost ground. During the 1970s, state enterprises across the Third World enlarged their share of the gross domestic product (GDP) by almost 50 percent. Because it was so uncontrolled, *debt financing inflated the foundations of the development state.* Borrowing was an effective counterweight to corporate foreign investment, even when it enabled states to insist on joint ventures with the transnationals.[33] But it also deepened the vulnerability of the development state to the banks and the multilateral managers, who appeared on the scene in the 1980s.

## The Debt Regime

The 1980s debt crisis consolidated two distinct trends that had been emerging in the 1970s: (1) the undoing of the Third World as a collective entity, as economic growth rates diverged among states, and (2) *global governance,* in which individual national policies were subjected to coordinated, rule-based procedures that strengthened the grip of the global political economy. We shall call this latter process the **debt regime.** The breakup of the Third World enabled global elites in the Bretton Woods institutions and the First World to argue that the international economic order was not responsible for the crisis centered in Latin American and African states. They claimed that the experience of the Asian NICs was proof of this pudding. In other words, debt stress and economic deterioration in the poorer zones of the world, they said, stemmed from a failure to copy the NICs' strategy of export diversification in the world market. As we know, however, the NICs, although held up as examples of market virtue (to justify the emerging neoliberal project), were in fact state-managed economies. Furthermore, we now know that the debt crisis was visited upon East and Southeast Asia a decade later, in the 1997 regional financial collapse.

The export-led strategy informed the 1989 World Bank report *Sub-Saharan Africa: From Crisis to Sustainability*—regardless of whether the world market could absorb such a proliferation of exports:

> Declining export volumes, rather than declining export prices, account for Africa's poor export revenues. . . . If Africa's economies are to grow, they must earn foreign exchange to pay for essential imports. Thus it is vital that they increase their share of world markets. The prospects for most primary commodities are poor, so higher export earnings must come from increased output, diversification into new commodities and an aggressive export drive into the rapidly growing Asian markets.[34]

Debt was of course not new to these regions of the world. Between 1955 and 1970, several countries (including Argentina, Brazil, Chile, Ghana, Indonesia, Peru, and Turkey) had the terms of their debt rescheduled—sometimes several times—to ease the conditions of payment. And debt servicing (paying off the interest) was consuming more than two-thirds of new lending in Latin America and Africa by the mid-1960s. The difference now was the combination in the 1970s of inflated oil prices and unsecured lending by the banks, intensifying debt.[35]

The debt crisis began in 1980 when the U.S. Federal Reserve Board moved to stem the fall in the value of the dollar resulting from its over-circulation in the 1970s lending binge. The United States reduced the money supply with an aggressive monetarist policy. Credit contracted, raising interest rates as banks competed for dwindling funds. Lending to Third World countries slowed, and shorter terms were issued—hastening the day of reckoning on considerably higher cost loans. Some borrowing continued, nevertheless, partly because oil prices had risen sharply again in 1979. Higher oil prices actually accounted for more than 25 percent of the total debt of the Third World. Previous debt had to be paid off, too, especially the greater debt assumed by overconfident oil-producing states such as Nigeria, Venezuela, and Mexico.[36]

Third World debt totaled $1 trillion by 1986. Even though this amount was only half the U.S. national debt in that year, it was a significant problem because countries were devoting new loans entirely to servicing previous loans.[37] Unlike the United States, cushioned by the dollar standard (the de facto international reserve currency preferred by countries and traders), Third World countries were not in a position to continue this debt servicing—their dollar reserves lost value as real interest rates spiked, First World recession reduced consumption of Third World products, and Third World export revenues collapsed as primary export prices dived 17 percent relative to First World manufactured exports.[38]

The World Bank estimated the combined average annual negative effect of these "external" shocks in 1981–1982 to be 19.1 percent of GDP in Kenya, 14.3 percent in Tanzania, 18.9 percent in the Ivory Coast, 8.3 percent in Brazil, 29 percent in Jamaica, and more than 10 percent in the Philippines.[39] Third World countries were suddenly mired in a *debt trap:* Debt was choking their economies. To repay the interest (at least), they would have to drastically curtail imports and drastically raise exports. But reducing imports of technology jeopardized growth. Expanding exports was problematic, as commodity prices were at their lowest in 40 years and slid further with the glut of exports. Some commodities lost markets to First World substitutes. Since the mid-1970s sugar price boom, the soft drink industry had steadily replaced sugar with fructose corn syrup, a biotechnological substitute. Other substitutes included glass fiber for copper in the new fiber-optic telecommunications technology, soy oils for tropical oils, and synthetic alternatives to rubber, jute, cotton, timber, coffee, and cocoa.[40] The market could not solve these problems alone.

## Debt Management

The chosen course of action was debt management. The Bretton Woods institutions once again were in the driver's seat, even though around 60 percent of Third World debt was with private banks. The IMF took charge because its original task was to evaluate a country's financial condition for borrowing (even though this function broke down in the 1970s). The IMF now had a supervisory status that individual banks did not have in the financial system at large.

Debt management took several forms. Initial stabilization measures focused on financial management (lowering imports to reduce imbalance of payments). **Structural adjustment** measures followed: a comprehensive restructuring of production priorities and government programs in a debtor country—basically reorganizing the economy. Along with the World Bank and its structural adjustment loan (SAL), the IMF levied restructuring conditions on borrowers in return for loan rescheduling. By the mid-1980s, loan conditions demanded policy restructuring, whereby debtor states received prescriptions for political-economic reforms, including *austerity* measures, to stimulate economic growth and regular debt service. The debt managers drew on the Chilean model of the 1970s, where a military junta experimented with monetarist policies, slashing social expenditures to reduce debt. In 1989, the executive director of the United Nations Children's Fund (UNICEF), James P. Grant, observed,

> Today, the heaviest burden of a decade of frenzied borrowing is falling not on the military or on those with foreign bank accounts or on those who conceived the years of waste, but on the poor who are having to do without necessities, on the unemployed who are seeing the erosion of all that they have worked for, on the women who do not have enough food to maintain their health, on the infants whose minds and bodies are not growing properly because of untreated illnesses and malnutrition, and on the children who are being denied their only opportunity to go to school. . . . It is hardly too brutal an oversimplification to say that the rich got the loans and the poor got the debts.[41]

Under this regime, the responsibility for irredeemable debt fell on the borrowers, not the lenders—unlike U.S. bankruptcy law. Debt was defined as a liquidity problem (shortage of foreign currency) rather than a systemic problem.[42] That is, the debt managers placed the blame on the policies of the debtor countries rather than on the organization of the global financial system. Why? First, the IMF had the power to insist that debt rescheduling (including further official loans) was possible only if countries submitted to IMF evaluation and stabilization measures, including World Bank structural adjustment loans. Second, despite attempts at debt strikes (e.g., by Peru), collectively, debtors were in a weak bargaining position, given the differentiation among Third World states in growth and debt. Furthermore, an individual solution for debt rescheduling was often preferred by indebted governments to the uncertainty of a collective debtors' strike.

### CASE STUDY
### Debt Regime Politics: Debt Collection as Development?

Mexico was the first "ticking bomb" in the global financial structure, with an $80 billion debt in 1982. More than three-quarters of this amount was owed to private banks (U.S. bank loans were more than 50 percent exposed in Mexico). Mexican political forces were divided between a "bankers' alliance" and the "Cárdenas alliance"—representing a national-ist coalition rooted in the labor and peasant classes. The outgoing president, José López Portillo, allied with the latter group, linked the huge capital flight from his country ($30 billion between 1978 and 1982) to the international financial order, recommending controls on "a group of Mexicans . . . led and advised and supported by the private banks who have taken more money out of the country than the empires that exploited us since the beginning of time." Portillo opposed debt man-agement proposals by nationalizing the Mexican banking system and installing exchange controls against capital flight. He shocked the international financial community when he declared in his outgoing speech,

> The financing plague is wreaking greater and greater havoc throughout the world. As in Medieval times, it is scourging country after country. It is trans-mitted by rats and its consequences are unemployment and poverty, indus-trial bankruptcy and speculative enrichment. The remedy of the witch doctors is to deprive the patient of food and subject him to compulsory rest. Those who protest must be purged, and those who survive bear witness to their virtue before the doctors of obsolete and prepotent dogma and of blind hegemoniacal egoism.

Portillo's conservative successor, Miguel De La Madrid, campaigned on guaranteeing a reversal, forcing Portillo to back down and concede to an IMF accord, initiated by the U.S. government and the Bank of International Settlements. To effect the bailout, the IMF put up $1.3 bil-lion, foreign governments $2 billion, and the banks $5 billion in "invol-untary loans." A global condominium—including the banks, the multilateral financial community, and the First World governments—put together the bailout package.

In 1986, Mexico was rewarded for refusing to participate in a regional effort to form a debtors' club.

The Mexican bailout became a model for other bailout programs, primarily because the Mexican government effectively implemented the austere measures the IMF demanded in return for debt rescheduling. As in Mexico, in other middle-income nations (e.g., Brazil, Thailand, Turkey), it has been documented that development alliance constituencies, particularly ruling elites and middle classes who benefited from the original loans, used their political power to shift repayment costs onto the working poor via austerity cuts in social services. As World Bank chief economist, Stanley Fischer, noted in 1989, "Most of the burden has been borne by wage earners in the debtor countries."

But if the debt regime was a politicized method of debt collection, how is it that its prescriptions served as a new model of development under the emerging project of globalization?

*Sources: Helleiner (1996:177); George (1988:41, 49); Barkin (1990:104-5); Bienefeld (2000); Roodman (2001:34-35).*

## Reversing the Development Project

As countries adopted the debt regime rules and restructured their economies, they reversed the path of the development project. These rules had two key effects. First, they institutionalized the new definition of development as participation in the world market. In particular, the debt managers pushed for export intensification via "comparative advantage"—as we saw in the World Bank's 1989 report on sub-Saharan Africa above. Second, the rescheduling conditions brought dramatic adjustments in economic and social priorities within indebted countries. These adjustments overrode the original development goal of managed national economic growth. Rescheduling bought time for debt repayment, but it came at a heavy cost.

Adjustment measures included the following:

- drastic reduction of public spending (especially on social programs, including food subsidies),
- currency devaluation (to inflate prices of imports and reduce export prices, thereby improving the balance of trade in the indebted country's favor),
- privatization of state enterprises, and
- reduction of wages to attract foreign investors and reduce export prices.

Most of these measures fell hardest on the poorest and least powerful social classes—those dependent on wages and subsidies. While some businesses prospered, poverty rates climbed. Governments saw their broad development alliances crumble as they could no longer afford to subsidize urban constituencies.

In Mexico, as part of the IMF loan rescheduling conditions in 1986, food subsidies for basic foods such as tortillas, bread, beans, and rehydrated milk were eliminated. Malnourishment grew. Minimum wages fell 50 percent between 1983 and 1989, and purchasing power fell to two-thirds of the 1970 level. The number of Mexicans in poverty rose from 32.1 to 41.3 million, matching the absolute increase in population size during 1981–1987. By 1990, the basic needs of 41 million Mexicans were unsatisfied, and 17 million lived in extreme poverty.[43] Meanwhile, manufacturing growth rates plummeted, from 1.9 in 1980–1982 to 0.1 in 1985–1988, leading to a considerable decline in formal employment opportunities.[44] Coupled with drastic cuts in social services, the reduction in manufacturing led to further deterioration of living standards. By 1987, 10 million people could not gain access to the health system, a situation that contributed to the "epidemiological polarization" among social classes and regions—such as the difference between the infant mortality rates of northern and southern Mexico, as well as between those of rural and urban areas and lower and upper classes.[45] Mexico assumed the role of a new agricultural country (NAC), with extensive state-sponsored agro-industrialization. By 1986, Mexico was exporting to the United States more than $2 billion worth of fresh fruits, vegetables, and beef but also importing from that country $1.5 billion in farm products, largely basic grains and oil seeds. IMF strictures made dependency on staple foods more expensive and reduced the government's role in subsidizing food staples.[46]

In Africa, the severity of the debt burden meant that Tanzania, the Sudan, and Zambia were using more than 100 percent of their export earnings to service debt in 1983. In Zambia, the ratio of outstanding debt to gross national product (GNP) increased from 16 to 56 percent in 1985. African economies were particularly vulnerable to the fall in commodity prices during the 1980s: Copper accounted for 83 percent of Zambia's export earnings and 43 percent of Zaire's, coffee for 89 percent of Burundi's export earnings and 64 percent of Ethiopia's, cotton for 45 percent of Sudan's and 54 percent of Chad's export earnings, and cocoa for 63 percent of Ghana's total exports. With falling commodity prices, an African coffee exporter had to produce 30 percent more coffee to pay for

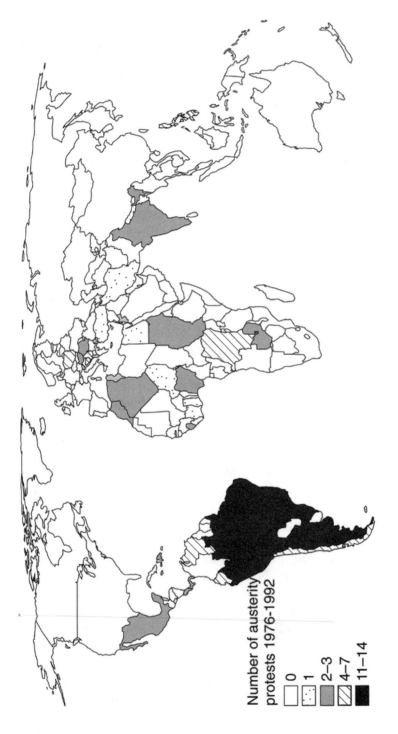

**Number of austerity
protests 1976-1992**

- 0
- 1
- 2–3
- 4–7
- 11–14

**Figure 4.1**    Locations of Riots against Austerity Programs

Source: John Walton and David Seddon, *Free Markets and Food Riots* (Blackwell, 1994).

one imported tractor and then produce more coffee to pay for the oil to run it.[47]

IMF/World Bank adjustment policies in Africa reduced food subsidies and public services, leading to urban demonstrations and riots in Tanzania, Ghana, Zambia, Morocco, Egypt, Tunisia, and Sudan. In Zambia, for example, the price of cornmeal—a staple—rose 120 percent in the mid-1980s following adjustment. And since corn is a crop controlled by men, they expanded cultivation of corn at the expense of peanuts, a cash crop grown by women. School enrollments declined, as skilled Africans migrated in droves. Between 1980 and 1986, average per capita income declined by 10 percent, and unemployment almost tripled.[48] In effect, all the "development" indicators, including infant mortality, took a downturn under the impact of adjustment policies. Oxfam reported in 1993 that World Bank adjustment programs in sub-Saharan Africa were largely responsible for reductions in public health spending and a 10 percent decline in primary school enrollment. In the late 1980s, UNICEF and the UN Commission for Africa reported that adjustment programs were largely the cause of reduced health, nutritional, and educational levels for tens of millions of children in Asia, Latin America, and Africa.[49]

 **CASE STUDY**

**The IMF Food Riots: Citizens versus Structural Adjustment**

The so-called "IMF riots" swept across the former Second and Third Worlds, expressing with them the demise of the development project. Between 1976 and 1992, some 146 riots occurred in 39 of the approximately 80 debtor countries, including Romania, Poland, Yugoslavia, and Hungary. These large-scale, often coordinated, urban uprisings protested the austerity measures of their governments, with the rioters often breaking into food banks to help themselves. Walton and Seddon define these austerity protests as "large-scale collective actions including political demonstrations, general strikes, and riots, which are animated by grievances over state policies of economic liberalization implemented in response to the debt crisis and market reforms urged by international agencies."

These riots contested the unequal distribution of the means of livelihood, targeting policies that eroded urban dwellers' social contract with the development state. Collapsing social entitlements included a range of subsidized services necessary to members of hyper-urbanized environments, including food, health care, education, transportation, housing, and others.

The *classical* food riot, which signaled the destabilization of traditional food markets during the transition from customary to market society, occurred during the era of European state building in the eighteenth and nineteenth centuries. By contrast, the *contemporary* food riot signals a new transition, occurring across a world experiencing the hollowing out of the national economic project. The welfarist conception of the public household arose in the First World as states replaced communities. This conception also shaped Second and Third World state policies of national economic development. Structural adjustment austerity reverses this policy. Austerity protests seek to restore lost social rights within the national project. At the same time, they bear witness to and, in some cases, identify the project of globalization as the driving force behind the shrinking of the public household.

The IMF riots symbolized the link made by protestors between IMF conditions and state shrinking. Björn Beckman observed that the logic of the structural adjustment program "is to further weaken the motivation of the state to respond to the popular demands that have been built into the process of postcolonial state formation."

When citizens organize such large-scale riots, should we understand them simply as material protests about the withdrawal of resources or also as cultural protests about "voice" in state-society relations?

*Sources: Walton and Seddon (1994); Kagarlitsky (1995:217); Beckman (1992:97).*

Much has been written about the "lost decade" of the 1980s for the poorer regions of the world economy, meaning that the debt crisis set them back considerably. If we combine per capita GDP figures with changes in terms of trade and debt rescheduling, average per capita income is estimated to have fallen 15 percent in Latin America and 30 percent in Africa during the 1980s. But in South and East Asian countries, by contrast, per capita income rose. These states were more in step with the global economy, benefiting from the oil boom in the Middle East, the most rapidly growing market, to which they exported labor, receiving lucrative remittances in turn. The Asian states were relatively immune to the "lost decade" because the ratio of their debt service to exports was half that of the Latin American countries during the 1970s.[50] Besides their geopolitical advantage, they were less vulnerable to credit contraction in the new monetarist world economic order.

The debt crisis exacerbated the demise of the Third World. It continued to lose collective political ground as debt management eroded national sovereignty, and it fractured into several zones, including what some refer to as the "Fourth World"—impoverished regions, especially countries in sub-Saharan Africa. At the same time, the debt crisis expanded the reach of global governance, to which we now turn.

## Global Governance

Global governance involves the adoption by nation-states of policies and rules that favor global circuits of money, capital, and goods. While adopted by countries (with variation), the policies and rules stem from the **global managers**—officials of the multilateral institutions (IMF, World Bank), G-7 political elites, executives of transnational corporations, and global bankers. The conditions laid down during the debt regime initiated this form of surrogate global government. Indebted states, for the most part, implemented certain policy changes and restructuring of economic priorities to reestablish creditworthiness in the eyes of the global financial community. For example, when a state gives priority to export production over production of domestic goods to repay debt, it appears to be putting its national financial house in order. This policy may affect the flow of money, but it also attaches that country's future to the global economy—for example, in allowing foreign investment to shift resources into export production. Global governance is not simply an external force; it shapes national strategies for repositioning producers in the global market.

Global governance embraces the whole world, not just the formerly colonial countries. Indeed, IMF debt-rescheduling measures were common in the First and Second Worlds, beginning with Britain in the 1970s. Poland's massive debt and subsequent austerity programs had much to do with destabilizing it and the perimeter of the Second World, leading to the collapse of the Soviet bloc in the late 1980s. From 1978 to 1992, more than 70 countries of the former Third World undertook 566 stabilization and structural adjustment programs imposed by the IMF and the World Bank to control their debt.[51] All this restructuring did not necessarily resolve the debt crisis. In fact, the debtor countries collectively entered the 1990s with 61 percent more debt than they had held in 1982.[52]

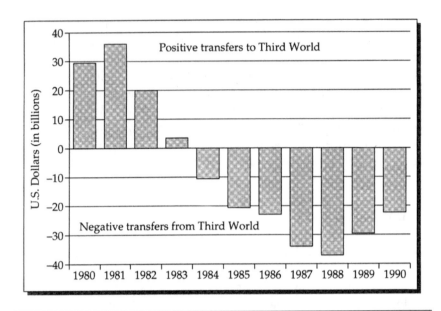

**Figure 4.2**    Net Transfers of Long-Term Loans to Third World States

Source: UN, *Human Development Report 1997*, p. 64.

As a consequence of growing debt, many countries found themselves under greater scrutiny by global managers, in addition to surrendering greater amounts of their wealth to global agencies. The turning point was 1984. In that year, the direction of capital flows reversed—that is, the inflow of loan and investment capital into the former Third World was replaced by an *outflow* in the form of debt repayment (see Figure 4.2). The (net) extraction of financial resources from the Third World during the 1980s exceeded $400 billion.[53] At the same time, massive bank debt had become public debt, the repayment of which now fell on the shoulders of the governments themselves, especially their more vulnerable citizens. The banks wrote off some debt, but they were protected from complete debt loss by the First World governments, whose central bankers had agreed in 1974 (with the Bank of International Settlements) to stand behind commercial bank loans, as lenders of last resort.[54]

## Challenging the Development State

The procedures of the debt regime eroded national economic management and, by extension, the social contract that development states had with their citizens. Keynesian (state interventionist) policies had steadily eroded through the 1970s in the First World as the ideology of economic liberalism spread its message of giving the market a free rein. Public expenditure fell; so did wage levels as organized labor lost ground when firms moved offshore and/or cheaper imports from the NICs flooded domestic markets.

Under the new monetarist doctrine in the 1980s, this trend was extended south. The debt regime directly challenged the development state. Debt managers demanded a *shrinking* of states of the former Third World, both through reduction in social spending and through the **privatization** of state enterprises. To reschedule their debt, governments sold off the public companies that had ballooned in the 1970s. As a result, the average number of privatizations in this region of the world expanded tenfold across the decade. From 1986 to 1992, the proportion of World Bank SALs demanding privatization rose from 13 to 59 percent, and by 1992, more than 80 countries had privatized almost 7,000 public enterprises—mostly public services such as water, electricity, or telephones.[55]

Although there is no doubt that development state elites had pursued excessive public financing, privatization accomplished two radical changes:

- it reduced public capacity in developmental planning and implementation, thereby privileging the corporate sector, and
- it extended the reach of foreign ownership of assets in the former Third World—precisely the condition that governments had tried to overcome in the 1970s.

Between 1980 and 1992, the stock of *international* bank lending rose from 4 to 44 percent of the GDP of the countries of the Organization for Economic Cooperation and Development.[56] Rather than losing the money they had loaned in such excessive amounts, banks earned vast profits on the order of 40 percent per annum on Third World investments alone.[57] Foreign investment in the Third World resumed between 1989 and 1992, increasing from $29 billion to $40 billion (especially in Mexico, China, Malaysia, Argentina, and Thailand).[58] The restructured global South was apparently now quite profitable for private investment: Wages were low, governments were not competing in the private capital markets, and an export boom in manufactured goods and processed foods was under way.

Through a case-by-case adjustment, the debt regime transformed the conditions of development. Austerity measures lowered wages to encourage foreign investment, privatization revived the principle of freedom of enterprise, and export expansion sustained the flow of products to the wealthier zones of the global economy. Martin Khor, director of the Third World Network, Malaysia, views structural adjustment as

> a mechanism to shift the burden of economic mismanagement and financial mismanagement from the North to the South, and from the Southern elites to the Southern communities and people. Structural adjustment is also a policy to continue colonial trade and economic patterns developed during the colonial period, but which the Northern powers want to continue in the post-colonial period.[59]

Each measure either undermined the coherence or commercialized the sovereignty of national economies. Lowered wages reduced local purchasing power. Wage earners had to tighten their belts; as a result, the market for local goods contracted. Privatization of public enterprises reduced state capacity. They were no longer in a position to enter into joint ventures with private firms and lay plans for production priorities; rather, private firms appropriated formerly public functions (those that were profitable). Finally, export expansion often displaced local production systems—as we saw, for example, in the case study about the "world steer" in Chapter 3. The case study of the Dominican Republic offers a parallel example of the challenge to state developmentalism under the conditions of the debt regime.

**CASE STUDY**

**Turning the Dominican Republic Inside Out?**

Ever since the Dominican Republic achieved independence from Spain in the nineteenth century, it has been a "sugar republic," with secondary exports of coffee, cocoa, and tobacco. In the 1980s, the contribution of these primary commodity exports to total export earnings fell from 58 to 33 percent. Under pressure from the IMF, the government responded with an *export-substitution strategy* to generate new export revenues to service its substantial foreign debt. This strategy fit with the 1980s U.S. Caribbean Basin Initiative (CBI) to promote foreign investment in agro-exports. Nontraditional exports included tropical root crops such as yams and taro; vegetables and horticultural crops such as peppers, tomatoes, green beans, and eggplants; and tropical fruits such as melons, pineapples, and avocados. Beef products were the most significant agro-industrial export.

The adoption of this broad agricultural restructuring involved policy reversals that removed government supports for basic food production, with the result that more than 50 percent of the Dominican household food basket was now imported. In addition, social programs that redistributed some wealth were undermined in the rush to subsidize firms in the nontraditional agricultural sector. As in most countries, domestic food production depended on state support, restriction of imports, subsidized credit and technical assistance for small producers, and stabilization of prices for the poorer classes. Credit for these social programs dried up following structural adjustment. Rice, heavily subsidized for low prices, was "liberalized" in 1988, undermining a national crop and creating greater reliance on rice imports.

Meanwhile, the government leased old sugar plantation lands to transnational corporations, such as Chiquita and Dole, for the production of pineapples. With plantations elsewhere—in Hawaii, Thailand, the Philippines, Guatemala, and Honduras—these transnationals are able to negotiate favorable conditions from host governments. Laura Raynolds observes that "most of the roughly 2,000 workers in the new pineapple plantations are casual day laborers who are unprotected by national labor legislation. These workers, many of whom are women, have no job security and are paid less than even the subminimum wage. Labor unions have either been crushed outright or co-opted by the combined forces of the state and the transnational corporations." Regarding government concessions to attract the TNCs, she adds that "these concessions increase the likelihood that production will relocate if the state does not maintain a satisfactory level of subsidization. . . . The Dominican state has forfeited direct control over critical national land resources and rural labor forces."

If governments expand agro-industrial production to improve their participation in the world market, can this new form of neoliberal development be equitable and sustainable?

---

*Sources: Raynolds (1994:218, 231–32); Raynolds et al. (1993:1111).*

As economic activity was embedded more deeply in global enterprise, the reach of the global forces strengthened at the expense of national economies. This outcome was not unique to the 1980s, but the mechanisms of the debt regime institutionalized the power and authority of global governance within nation-states' very organization and policy repertoire. *This was a turning point in the story of development.*

## Restructuring States and Societies

Internalizing global governance involves two significant (and related) changes in power relations:

- debt rescheduling conditions actively reorganize the structure and priorities of states and societies, and
- reorganization is unrepresentative, as global bureaucrats, responding to financial signals rather than citizen scrutiny, often decide how states should conduct their economic affairs.

Chapter 2 reported that the World Bank routinely establishes local agencies to administer its projects. During the debt regime, this practice blossomed under the pretext of shaking markets loose from government regulation. Giving the market free rein is arguably a euphemism for allowing global actors (bureaucrats, banks, firms) a stronger hand in determining what should be produced, where, and for whom.

Global governance is typically institutionalized through the administration of adjustment programs. Throughout the Bretton Woods era, the IMF shaped national fiscal management, applying conditions to the loans it made to adjust the short-term balance of payments.[60] But this influence involved merely financial stabilization measures. Structural adjustment loans, by contrast, restructure national economies and redistribute power within the state. The latter involves privileging the central bank and trade and finance ministries over program-oriented ministries (social services, agriculture, education).[61] This power shift removes resources from state agencies that support and regulate economic and social sectors affecting the majority of the citizenry, especially the poorer classes. These resources are shifted to the agencies more directly connected to global enterprise: Global economic criteria override national social criteria. Perhaps the most dramatic example of state restructuring in recent years is that of Mexico.

Between 1980 and 1991, Mexico negotiated 13 SALs with the World Bank and 6 agreements with the IMF. The Bank proposed an agricultural SAL in 1986 to assist in the elimination of tariffs on imported food, privatization of rural parastatal agencies, liberalization of trade and domestic food prices, "sound" public investment, and cutbacks in the agricultural

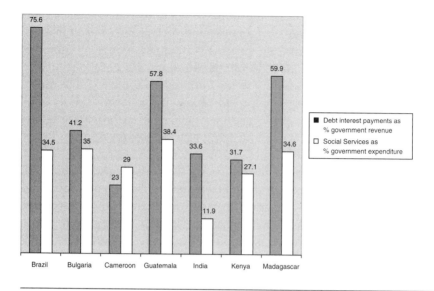

**Figure 4.3**     Government Spending on Foreign Debt and Social Services
(Selected Countries, 1995)

Source: World Bank, *World Development Report*, 1998–1999.

Note: Social Services includes health, education, social security, welfare, housing,
and community services.

ministry. These were the conditions of the loan. Rural social services were
subordinated to agro-industrial priorities. In 1991, a follow-up sectoral
adjustment loan further liberalized food importing, privatized state-
owned monopolies, and eliminated price guarantees on corn—a drastic
step. Deteriorating social conditions forced the Bank to subsidize national
Pronasol and Procampo programs, offering financial assistance to poor
rural producers. Mexico experienced a decade of liberal reforms, man-
dated by the global managers and pursued by the government to maintain its creditworthiness—a dress rehearsal for NAFTA. The state
abandoned its husbanding of the national agricultural sector, shifting
financial support from *campesinos* to agro-export production.[62]

In another part of the world, structural adjustment policies pursued by
the multilateral agencies in Africa reveal a telling rethinking of the state's
role in development. Initially, as presented in the World Bank's 1981
(Berg) report, the goal of "shrinking" the state was justified as a way to
improve efficiency and reduce urban bias.[63] Structural adjustment

programs directly challenged the political coalitions and goals of the national development state. At the same time, SAPs strengthened finance ministries in the policymaking process.[64] In other words, within the African countries, power moved from the development coalitions (urban planning, agriculture, education) to the financial group, which was most concerned with a country's ability to obtain international credit. The report revealed a shift in Bank lending practices from providing assistance for development concerns to tying aid to "comprehensive policy reform."[65]

The World Bank's premise for the policy shift was that development states were overbureaucratic and inefficient, on one hand, and unresponsive to their citizenry, on the other. In the World Bank's major report of 1989 on sub-Saharan Africa, it reinterpreted "shrinking" the state to mean a reorganization of state administration to encourage populist initiatives. Of course, some of these observations are credible; there are many examples of authoritarian government, corruption, and "hollow" development financing—such as Zaire President Mobutu's lavish global-set lifestyle and Ivory Coast President Félix Houphouët-Boigny's construction in his home village of a larger-than-the-original replica of St. Peter's basilica in the Vatican. Nevertheless, the solutions proposed and imposed by the Bank substitute growing external control of these countries in the name of financial orthodoxy.[66]

In its 1989 report titled *Sub-Saharan Africa from Crisis to Sustainable Growth: A Long Term Perspective Study,* the Bank advanced the idea of "political conditionality." It proposed "policy dialogue" with recipient states, leading to "consensus forming." This is a sophisticated way of constructing political coalitions within the recipient state that embrace economic reforms proposed by the multilateral agencies.[67] One observer noted, "It has become an explicit target of the institutions, and the World Bank in particular, to shift the balance of power within governments towards those who expect to gain from the policy reforms encouraged by the institutions and/or those who are in any case more sympathetic towards such changes."[68]

This strategy is actually a way of remaking states, through "institution building." It continues the practice discussed in Chapter 2, whereby the administration of Bank projects gives greatest weight to the input of technical experts in national planning. This new phase of Bank involvement deepens by organizing coalitions in the state that are committed to the redefinition of the government's economic priorities. The state sheds accountability to its citizens, who lose input into their own government.

One response is to withdraw into a "shadow" economy and society, as illustrated in the Tanzanian case study.

 **CASE STUDY**

**Tanzanian Civil Society Absorbs Structural Adjustment**

While structural adjustment involves standard prescriptions, its implementation varies from country to country, depending on government capacity and the level of social and political resistance from the citizenry. Resistance takes both formal and informal paths. Political democratization may be one outcome of urban grassroots resistance to their government's betrayal of the development alliance's social pact in implementing austerity measures. Another outcome may involve retreating to the "informal economy" as a survival strategy. This is the case in Tanzania, a country founded in President Nyerere's vision of a benevolent state anchored in rural villages practicing an African socialism of shared property, collective labor, and a social ethic derived from the traditional African family.

Aili Mari Tripp shows that Tanzania experienced deepening economic crisis at the turn of the 1980s, so that the state, with an already weakened capacity to extract resources, initiated a policy of economic liberalization prior to a 1986 agreement with the IMF, which deepened economic distress. While public-sector managers and the mass party organizations opposed structural adjustment, urban dwellers in general were surprisingly quiescent. Between 1974 and 1988, with real wages falling by 83 percent, Tanzanians intensified their income-generating activities "off the books"—involving crop sales on parallel markets in the agricultural sector; sideline incomes for wage workers such as baking, carpentry, or tailoring; schoolchildren absenteeism so that children could work for family income; supplementary tutorials by school teachers; moonlighting physicians; and so forth. As Tripp remarks, austerity "was somewhat softened by the fact that more than 90 percent of household income was coming from informal businesses, primarily operated by women, children and the elderly. By providing alternatives to the state's diminishing resource base, these strategies diverted demands that otherwise might have overwhelmed the state. . . . In the end, little was demanded of a state that had placed itself at the center of the nation's development agenda and had established itself as the guarantor of society's welfare."

Does this kind of self-organizing activity represent the realization of the original social contract in the development state and offer us a glimpse of an alternative, sustainable conception of development?

*Sources: Rist (1997:130-32); Tripp (1997:3-6, 13).*

One consequence of the debt regime has been an expanding "trustee-ship" role for the multilateral agencies. This procedure compromises national sovereignty and illustrates the reach of global regulatory mechanisms that may override national policymaking. Under these conditions, the World Bank, now the principal multilateral agency involved in global development financing, has played a definite governing role. It "dictate[s] legal and institutional change through its lending process," and, since its 1989 report, it now asserts that evaluating governance in debtor countries is within its jurisdiction.[69]

Despite the new emphasis on human rights and democratization as conditions for reform and financial assistance, the World Bank remains unaccountable to the citizenry in developing countries. And when the IMF and the Bank stabilize and make long-term loans to a debtor, they assume "a governance role that may best be likened to that of a trustee in bankruptcy," except that trustees are accountable to the bankruptcy court. The IMF and the Bank remain accountable to no one other than their powerful underwriters.[70] Furthermore, after a loan is approved, U.S. corporations and citizens are given access to economic—and political—intelligence reports prepared by the Bank. The political asymmetry is obvious, lending support to the idea that global rule without law is being institutionalized.[71]

In sum, the debt regime reformulated the terms of economic management, relocating power within states and from states in the former Third World to global agencies. World Bank and IMF programs of adjustment substituted for a true multilateral management of the debt crisis. These conditions imposed standard rather than locally tailored remedies on indebted states. Governments and business elites in the former Third World countries collaborated in this enterprise, often for the same reasons they had promoted development financing in previous decades: They are well placed to benefit from infusions of foreign capital, some of which is used for patronage. Meanwhile, the debt burden is borne disproportionately by the poor.

## Summary

The demise of the Third World as a political bloc had political and economic origins. Politically, its subordination came about through the politics of containment, whereby Western intervention and military alliances secured client regimes in strategic world regions. Democracy was less important than showcasing development favoring a free enterprise model and "economic openness." As the NAM lost influence, the Third World regrouped to pressure the First World to reform the architecture of the international economy. The defeat of this political initiative dovetailed with the economic differentiation among Third World countries. Divergence of growth patterns in the Third World intensified through the 1980s. According to the World Bank, the East Asian share of Third World real incomes rose from 22 to 33 percent while all other regions had lower shares, especially Latin America and sub-Saharan Africa, where income share fell by 6 and 5 percentage points, respectively.[72]

Two trends were emerging. One was the further polarization of wealth and growth rates within the Third World. The rising tide was lifting some regions and swamping others. The countries of the Third World, which had stood together as the Group of 77, were no longer able to identify and pursue common interests because some were experiencing a level of prosperity so much greater than that of others. The defeat of the New International Economic Order initiative was a turning point in Third World politics. The other trend was the consolidation of the organizational features of the global economy, with the lending institutions adopting a powerful trusteeship role in the debtor nations in the 1980s.

Global financial organization matched global production systems emerging via Third World export strategies. Offshore money markets redistributed private capital to governments as loans, and transnational corporations invested in export production. A frenzy of development projects ensued, as Third World states sought to equal the success of the NICs. Public investments complemented and underwrote private enterprise. When credit dried up in the 1980s, debt repayment schemes reversed both aid-for-development programs and investment by the transnationals. Debt rescheduling was conditioned on the privatization of state agencies and projects, as well as erosion of the social contract. And the rescheduling process concentrated financial power in the hands of the multilateral agencies.

Development states turned inside out. New institutional mechanisms of global governance emerged as the multilateral agencies initiated the restructuring of policy priorities and administrations in these states, and they gathered ideological force in the growing faith in the authority of the market. In short, the debt crisis was a rehearsal for the globalization project, which we discuss in Chapter 5.

# PART III

## The Globalization
## Project (1980s– )

# 5

# Implementing
# Globalization as a Project

The globalization project succeeded the development project—not because development is dead but because its coordinates changed. Development, once a public project, has been redefined as a private, global project. Why not just "globalization" (without the project)? Isn't globalization obvious and here to stay? It is tempting to think of globalization as inevitable, or as destiny, until we notice that it only includes one-fifth of the world's population as beneficiaries. To call it a project emphasizes its political dimensions. We hear a lot about the free market, but this is because "freeing" markets is a political act. Markets are no more natural than nations—they have to be constructed, accepted as real, and reproduced. Here globalization is considered as a political intervention, to overcome the limits of the development project.

As we saw in the previous chapter, economic nationalism came to be viewed as limiting development because it obstructed the transnational mobility of goods, money, and firms in the service of efficient allocation of global resources. And so, with national sovereignty in decline, the development mantle has been assumed by powerful corporate players in the world market. Alongside of them are the multilateral institutions, such as the World Trade Organization (WTO), that seek to govern this new global project. The founding director-general of the WTO, Renato Ruggiero, expressed this when he observed in 2000,

It is a new world. . . . The Cold War is over. Even more significant is the rise of the developing world as a major power in the international economy as a result of the shift to freer markets and open trade—an event that could rank with the industrial revolution in historical significance. All this is taking place against the backdrop of globalization—the linking together of countries at different levels of development by technology, information, and ideas, as well as by economics.

To be more explicit, the future of development lay with the world market, linked by the rules of neoclassical economic discourse. Ruggiero went on to say,

More than ever before, trade and the rules of the trading system intersect with a broad array of other policies and issues—from investment and competition policy to environmental, developmental, health, and labor standards. . . . If we want real coherence in global policymaking and a comprehensive international agenda, then coordination has to come from the top, and it must be driven by elected leaders . . . progress in resolving the challenge of the new century will hinge on our ability not just to build a coherent global architecture, but to build a political constituency for globalization. . . . Without the WTO, we will go back to a world of national barriers, protectionism, economic nationalism, and conflict.[1]

Thus, the director-general of the WTO articulated the vision of the globalization project: the implementation of the rule of the market via the restructuring of policies and standards across the nation-state system. Trade (two-thirds of which is controlled by transnational corporations [TNCs]) was to be privileged as the motor of development. The genuine ideals of internationalism stem from the view that trade brings peace. But does this axiom hold, and what kind of trade relationships do we mean? After two decades of trade liberalization, the world order is marked by war, terror, and various forms of fundamentalism (economic, religious, ethnic) responsible for an array of social exclusion and conflict. This section of the book seeks to understand these contradictory happenings.

The development project had offered a blueprint for all nations, linking foreign aid and technology transfer to state-managed industrialization programs. As we have seen, the blueprint had mixed success, being compromised by a combination of colonial legacies in dependence on cash cropping, corruption of the development state by military aid and despotic rule, unequal relationships in the international economy, and debt and structural adjustment that punctured the illusion of upward mobility for much of the Third World.

The debt regime imposed new disciplines on Third World states—disciplines representing a fundamental shift in the world order. National governments are less and less development managers; more and more, they manage their portion of the world market according to efficiency criteria. Modernity is less a national property expressed in citizenship and more a global property expressed in consumption. Freedom has come to be identified less with membership in the national polity and more with participation in the global marketplace. The shift was sufficiently profound to spawn a new discourse of "globalization" from the mid-1980s on.

The globalization project did not begin on any particular date, but it signifies a new way of thinking about development (represented in the timeline introducing this book). Global governance has its roots in the Bretton Woods and cold war institutions, which coordinated a framework for nationally managed programs of capitalist development. Global management of capitalism emerged privately in the 1970s (in the form of the G-7) and publicly in the 1980s when the Bretton Woods institutions made explicit claims about *managing a global economy.*

The global managers include the Bretton Woods institutions, governments restructured around the goals of debt rescheduling, and transnational corporate elites (arguably a global ruling class, whose interest in privileging corporate rights inform the restructuring of national institutions to facilitate market rule). Among these political and economic elites, a consensus emerged, redefining development in the new terms of the world market. It was backed with the financial coercion institutionalized during the management of the debt crisis by the International Monetary Fund (IMF) and the World Bank. Thus, the globalization project was born.

As we shall see, the globalization project rests on unstable foundations, expressed in a growing array of alternatives and articulated by mushrooming resistance movements and by disaffected members of the so-called Washington Consensus. Here we focus on the institutional dimensions and tensions of the globalization project to illustrate the new global politics of development.

# The Globalization Project

The development project dovetailed with nation building in the postcolonial world. It had a definite political arena: the national territory. This arena of development is now yielding to alternative arenas: communities, cities, bioregions, fair trade networks, global commodity chains, macroregions, and flexible international corporate coalitions. And the initiative is passing from national governments to nongovernmental organizations (NGOs) committed to special development concerns at community or international levels (e.g., Oxfam, Friends of the Earth, Public Citizen, Grameen Bank), to free trade agreements (e.g., European Union [EU], North American Free Trade Agreement [NAFTA], Free Trade Agreement for the Americas [FTAA]), and to institutions of global governance such as the WTO.

Officially, globalization is considered a global development strategy—in World Bank terms, this means *successful participation in the world economy*. The newly industrializing countries were held up as exemplars of the new strategy of export-led growth. During the 1980s, the definition of development was extended to include a policy of broad *liberalization*—in particular, privatization of public functions and the application of market principles to the administration of wages, prices, and trade. President Reagan reiterated this theme in his 1985 State of the Union address: "America's economic success . . . can be repeated a hundred times in a hundred nations. Many countries in East Asia and the Pacific have few resources other than the enterprise of their own people. But through free markets they've soared ahead of centralized economies."[2] While this was historically inaccurate (the newly industrialized countries [NICs] combined strong states with protectionism), nevertheless this ideal served to guide the structural adjustment measures imposed on debtor nations by the debt managers in the 1980s.

The export orientation of the East Asian NICs thus was idealized to legitimize market rule across the world. In fact, the Reagan administration turned the free market ideal *against* the economic nationalism of Japan and the Asian NICs to open their markets. Meanwhile, the United States led a parallel attempt to build a free market global consensus—focusing on breaking down the resistance of the Soviet empire (the Second World) to market capitalism. This was central to the emerging globalization project.

### CASE STUDY
### Incorporating the Second World into the Globalization Project

The restructuring of the Second World marked its demise, with the cold war ending in 1989. This set the stage for globalization, as it could only be realized in a unilateral, rather than a bipolar, world order.

In 1986, Hungary, Romania, the former Yugoslavia, and Poland were subject to IMF supervision of their economies. Many of these states had started borrowing from Western financial institutions during the 1970s, often to pay for basic consumer items demanded by their increasingly restive civilian populations. By 1986, Soviet President Mikhail Gorbachev was formulating plans for *perestroika* (restructuring) in exchange for membership in the Bretton Woods institutions.

Earlier, in 1982, the IMF had tendered an austerity plan in Hungary on the condition that centrally planned production be replaced by "market-responsive" and "financially disciplined" enterprises, along with reductions in subsidies of food, transportation, heating fuel, and housing. These subsidies were the foundation of the well-established basic *economic* rights of the socialist systems. During the 1980s, small-scale state enterprises were privatized, and workers were now earning piece rates determined not by the work performed (as with a normal union contract) but by the profit rate of the enterprise. Social equality was being redefined along Western lines as the equality of private opportunity. Former public officials in the Second World had the lock on opportunity, enriching themselves and their relatives as public property was privatized. Joyce Kolko remarked, "There was growing resentment in the general population at the rising prices, falling living standards, and the new rich."

Deregulation throughout these once centrally regulated social systems led to what is called "Third Worldization." By the early 1990s, Eastern European per capita income levels resembled those of the former Third World. The per capita incomes of Poland and Mexico were about the same, as were those of Hungary and Brazil. Because Eastern European populations have higher levels of education and stable population growth rates, they differ from former Third World societies. In far-eastern Russia, South Korean companies outsource garment production to beat quotas on apparel imports into the United States under the Multi-Fiber Agreement. Just 440 miles from Seoul, where average hourly apparel labor costs were $2.69 in 1998, Vladivostock labor cost only 56 cents an hour—and some of that labor is Chinese! Because Chinese workers are used to 12-hour days and 2 days off a month, Korean employers use Chinese labor to pressure desperate Russian seamstresses and cutters into accepting sweatshop working conditions.

The incorporation of Eastern Europe into the project of globalization reveals a deep compromise of citizens' basic needs in the name of the market. Does the precipitous decline in Russian living standards, with an explosion of organized crime and AIDS, portend development under globalization?

---

*Sources: Kolko (1988:278–96); Kagarlitsky (1995); Working (1999:D1, 23).*

With the advent of the globalization project, development has not disappeared; rather, its meaning has changed. No longer identified as a universally national project, twenty-first-century development is a much more contested notion. Global elites have reframed development as globally managed growth, centered on (world) market principles as the most efficient allocation of resources. National governments are necessarily caught between the pressures of globalization and protection. Governments are on the twin horns of a dilemma: balancing the needs of citizens affected differentially by exposure to world market competition and their own legitimacy needs—expressed in the national accounts for corporate investment and export markets (foreign exchange). Most countries are riven by protectionist coalitions opposing powerful forces favoring liberalization. The globalization project involves political choices to (re)define the bearings and future of states and their civic responsibilities. If competing in the world market requires policies reducing public expenditure that may lower national standards of employment, health care, and education, then globalization is a political, not a natural, phenomenon.

The choices implicit in the globalization project call forth different interpretations of the purpose of development—whether it is governed by economic efficiency or social justice, corporate or social welfare, resource exploitation or ecological sustainability, or centralized political-economic power or participatory economic democracy. We are witnessing a massive tug-of-war across the world between proponents of these various positions. The tug-of-war has simplified into two camps, symbolized by the annual meetings of the **World Economic Forum** (representing officialdom: state managers and the global corporate elite) and the **World Social Forum** (representing a host of alternative movements of resistance against the dominant corporate model). We return to this tug-of-war in Chapters 7 and 8.

These new frames of reference express the demise of the singular vision of the development project and provide the ingredients of an intensifying debate over the appropriate scale, goals, and social content of development. At this point, it is important to identify the organizing concept of the globalization project.

## Liberalization and the Dismantling of the Development Project

The globalization project arose via the dismantling of the development project. Its key strategy of liberalization was first applied to indebted states via the debt regime. Debtor governments that shrunk the state and implemented other austerity measures were rewarded by the debt managers with credit released in tranches (staggered portions) to ensure their continuing compliance with loan conditions. Liberalization, then, involved the *downgrading* of the social goals of national development, combined with the *upgrading* of participation in the world market (tariff reduction, export promotion, financial deregulation, relaxation of foreign investment rules). Together, these policies reformulated development as a global project—implemented through liberalized states incorporated into a world market constructed by transnational banks and firms, informatics, and multilateral institutions dedicated to a vision of corporate globalization. As suggested in the following case study of Chile, liberalization also involved new forms of social inequality, perhaps heralding the globalization project.

 **CASE STUDY**

**Chile—The Original Model of Economic Liberalization**

Chile is perhaps the model case of economic liberalization. A military coup in 1973 eliminated the democratically elected socialist president Salvador Allende, followed by detention, torture, and execution of thousands of Chileans as part of an eight-year period of debilitating authoritarian rule. General Augusto Pinochet pursued a radical free market reform, otherwise known as "shock treatment," masterminded by economists trained at the University of Chicago, a center of neoclassical economics. Over the next two decades, 600 of the country's state enterprises were sold; foreign investment expanded into strategic sectors such as steel, telecommunications, and airlines; trade protection dwindled; and the dependence of the Chilean gross domestic product

(GDP) on trade grew from 35 percent in 1970 to 57.4 percent in 1990. In other words, *Chile was structurally adjusted before structural adjustment became fashionable.* Sergio Bitar, Allende's minister of mining, remarked that privatization was "the greatest diversion of public funds that has occurred in our history, without the consultation of public opinion or accountability to a congress."

Chile was known as the most democratic of Latin American nations prior to the assault on its parliamentary and civil institutions by the Pinochet military junta and its economic reforms. Debt restructuring in the 1980s increased social polarization. The share of national income of the richest 10 percent of the people rose from about 35 percent to 46.8 percent, while that of the poorest half of the population declined from 20.4 percent to 16.8 percent. Social spending continued to fall, wages were frozen, and the peso was seriously devalued. Deindustrialization set in, unemployment levels rose to 20 to 30 percent, and real wages suffered a 20 percent reduction. Meanwhile, an export boom occurred, retiring some of the debt and earning the Chilean experiment a reputation as a miracle. U.S. President Bush declared in Chile in 1990, "You deserve your reputation as an economic model for other countries in the region and in the world. Your commitment to market-based solutions inspires the hemisphere."

By 1990, about 40 percent of the 13 million Chilean people were impoverished in a country once known for its substantial middle class. The pursuit of global efficiency had weakened the domestic fabric of social security and local production. In consequence, a sustained grassroots movement, centered in the *poblaciones* (slums) and active from the mid-1970s, succeeded—through painstaking organization and bloody uprisings in the 1980s—in regaining elections in 1988, when Pinochet was defeated. Since then, Chilean political parties have become centrist and disconnected from the grassroots movement. Cathy Schneider observed, "The transformation of the economic and political system has had a profound impact on the world view of the typical Chilean. . . . It has transformed Chile, both culturally and politically, from a country of active participatory grassroots communities, to a land of disconnected, apolitical individuals." In this context, Chile recently privatized its health and social security system—again modeling the new "market state," now informing U.S. domestic policy. With privatization, the working poor disproportionately subsidize the health needs of the 2 million poorest Chileans, and pensions have declined (sharpened by the informalization of the workforce).

Why is it that military rule, the rundown of public goods, disregard for human rights, and new forms of social polarization all conditioned the Chilean embrace of the project of globalization?

---

*Sources: Bello (1994:42, 44–45, 59); George (1988:131–32); Schneider, quoted in Chomsky (1994:184); Schneider (1995:3, 194, 201); Collins and Lear (1996:157, 162).*

Liberalization combines domestic restructuring with opening markets. Theoretical justification for the strategy of market opening derives from nineteenth-century English political economist David Ricardo's concept of **comparative advantage**—that prosperity derives from maximizing advantage in international trade through specialized production reflecting a nation's relative resource endowments. When countries exchange their most competitive products on the world market, national and international economic efficiency results.[3] This theorem obviously contradicts the development project's ideal of a series of integrated national economies, as the world market becomes the unit of development. And the theorem did not allow for capital mobility, which today, arguably, *constructs* comparative advantage for countries.

Until the 1970s, "comparative advantage" represented a minority strand of economic thought. This was mainly because it was out of step with social history since movements of organized labor and an engaged citizenry demanded social entitlements and protections from the free market, especially after the Great Depression of the 1930s. The globalization project has foregrounded liberalization's promise of greater economic efficiency, relegating Keynesian ideas of state economic intervention and public investment to the background. The evidence is all around us in various guises—in welfare reform/reversal, in wage erosion, and in privatization schemes. It is a universal process, most dramatically played out in the former Second World countries, where public resources have been sold at rock-bottom prices to well-placed new capitalists (usually former state officials) and markets have been released from government regulation. The globalization project came to maturity in the wake of the collapse of Soviet communism and the ending of the cold war in 1990. Symbolically, this represented the new global reach of neoliberal capitalism or corporate globalization.

## CASE STUDY

 **Mini-Dragon Singapore
Constructs Comparative Advantage**

Singapore is an exceptional city-state, highly dependent on foreign investment. Ruled by a paternalistic People's Action Party (PAP) since gaining independence in 1959 from Britain and its 1965 expulsion from the Malaysian federation, it is known as one of the Pacific Asian "minidragons." Its NIC status depended on centralized planning between state bureaucracies, public enterprise, and TNCs, as well as on a corporatist (developmentalist) political system that silenced political opposition, turned labor unions into agents of the state, and elaborated a social discipline based on Confucian ethics of loyalty.

In 1985, at the height of a local recession and the reorganizations under way in the global economy, a government economic committee recommended a new strategy to liberalize the economy. Beginning with Singapore Airlines, the government began a gradual process to privatize its substantial public sector and to foster local enterprise and high-tech foreign investment. The recent technological upgrading in financial services and manufacturing is part of a strategy to position Singapore as the source of specialized exports (including producer services such as computer technologies) to the fastest growing region of the world economy, the Pacific Asian region. Restructuring also involves relocating lower value and "dirty" pork production for the Singapore consumer to agroexport platforms in nearby Indonesia and Malaysia, as well as developing high-value and "clean" agro-technology parks within Singapore. Meanwhile, the PAP's strategy of using social investments—in nearly universal public housing, universal public health services and education, and vocational retraining—allows it to coordinate wage levels with economic strategies and, most important, to continue its tradition of low unemployment levels and social cohesion.

If "comparative advantage" is an attribute of a country's endowments, then Singapore's planning and skilled labor force must be counted, but how should foreign investment feature in the calculus?

*Sources: Deyo (1991); Ufkes (1995).*

Beyond liberalization's downward pressure on social rights, it intensifies exporting, consistent with the doctrine of comparative advantage. Commercial extraction of natural resources has intensified across the world under these conditions, threatening environments, habitats, and resource regeneration.

The close correlation between debt, export liberalization, and high rates of deforestation is well known.[4] In Canada, home to 10 percent of the world's forests, about 1 million hectares of woodland disappear annually to logging. In the province of British Columbia, the Mitsubishi Corporation has the largest chopstick factory in the world, converting aspen stands into chopsticks at the rate of 7 to 8 million pairs a day.[5] In Chile, timber exports doubled in the 1980s, reaching beyond industrial plantations to the logging of natural forests.[6] Chile's export boom overexploited the country's natural resources beyond their ability to regenerate.[7] In Ghana, the World Bank's African model of structural adjustment, exports of mining, fishing, and timber products were accelerated to close the widening gap between cocoa exports and severely declining world prices of cocoa. From 1983 to 1988, timber exports increased from $16 million to $99 million, reducing Ghana's tropical forest to 25 percent of its original size.[8] The NGO, Development GAP, reported that deforestation

> threatens household and national food security now and in the future. Seventy-five per cent of Ghanaians depend on wild game to supplement their diet. Stripping the forest has led to sharp increases in malnutrition and disease. For women, the food, fuel, and medicines that they harvest from the forest provide critical resources, especially in the face of decreased food production, lower wages, and other economic shocks that threaten food security.[9]

After 70 countries underwent structural adjustment, the resulting *glut* of exports produced the lowest commodity prices seen on the world market since the 1930s. For example, in West Africa, between 1986 and 1989, cocoa producers expanded their exports by 25 percent, only to suffer a 33 percent price fall on the world market. The NGO, Oxfam, named this syndrome the "export-led collapse."[10] Between 1990 and 2000, the world coffee industry doubled in value to $60 billion—but farmers received half as much as in 1990. Across the world, today, 20 million households produce coffee, but the overproduction has brought the price of beans to a 30-year low. For a $2.70 cup of coffee, farmers receive on average 2.3 cents, while the transnationals (such as Proctor & Gamble, Philip Morris, and Nestlé) receive $1.33 on average.[11]

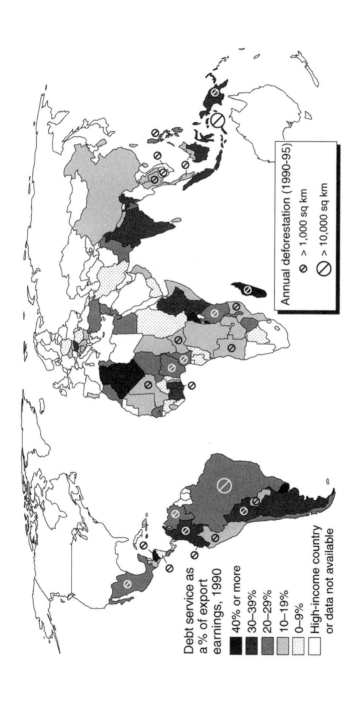

**Figure 5.1**    Debt and Deforestation

Sources: Alan Thomas et al., *Third World Atlas* (1994); World Bank, *World Development Report* (1998–99.)

Exporting to earn foreign exchange involves three dynamics: (1) selling domestic resources to firms supplying global markets and delivering the revenues to multilateral lenders as debt repayment, (2) re-creating "resource bondage," and (3) depleting and undermining the sustainability of natural resources that provide subsistence security to the poor ("the commons") and, in the case of forests, threaten the well-being of the planet. Depletion of the Brazilian Amazon forest has intensified, recently, under the *Avanca Brasil,* a $40 billion state-supported project to open the Amazon for its timber and farmland. Cargill, the global agribusiness, has the contract to build a new port terminal in the Amazon delta, to connect the huge Mato Grosso soy fields with the insatiable appetite of the ballooning middle class of China, which entered the twenty-first century as the world's largest importer of soy oil, meal, and beans. The Brazilian government has introduced a deforestation licensing system in the Mato Grosso state, but neighboring states of Para and Rondonia remain even more frontier-like in yielding the forest to loggers, sawmill operators, cattle ranchers, and speculators expecting to profit from the continuation of Brazil's export boom.[12]

As a development strategy, export reliance is problematic, especially where primary commodity prices remain low (especially compared to higher value manufactured goods and services)—and *The Economist* declared in 1999 that commodity prices were at an all-time low for the past century and a half. Export reliance is compounded by biotechnical substitution. For example, many prepared foods and drinks now substitute high-fructose corn syrup for sugar, resulting in a collapse of the world sugar market as sugar imports decline. As a result, producers in Brazil, India, the Philippines, Thailand, and several African and Caribbean countries lost markets just at the time when their debt servicing demanded increased exports.[13]

Contrary to neoclassical theory, export reliance often puts regions in the global South at a *comparative disadvantage.* Liberalization substitutes reliance on the world market for self-reliance as the organizing principle of development. The flow of credit to debt-stressed nations usually depends on renunciation of national development norms, including protection of local producers, labor forces, communities, environments, and social entitlements. All of these norms are viewed as impediments to the market, which is why the globalization project begins with market liberalization as the touchstone of efficiency. Scaling back public capacity transformed nation-states into market states concerned with improving globally driven economic activity. It is not surprising, therefore, that during the 1990s, private foreign investment became the main source of supply of capital to the global South, growing by more than five times.[14]

The globalization project includes an explicit vision of global order, quite distinct from that of the era of the development project:

- In the development project era, the slogan was "Learn from, and catch up with, the West." Now, under comparative advantage, the slogan is "Find your niche in the global marketplace."
- While the development project held out *replication* as the key to national development, the project of globalization presents *specialization* as the path to economic prosperity.

But specialization in monoculture, or the global assembly line, does not alter the reality that the mechanisms of specialization—wage cutting, foreign investment concessions, privatization, and reduction of social entitlements—are repeated everywhere, intensifying market competition. Short-term efficiencies are sought at the long-term expense of the social contract. In theory, this may produce greater productivity but at the cost of considerable and irreversible economic and social marginalization, impoverishment, environmental stress, and displacement.

## Global Governance

In the shifting tensions between development and globalization, states face a world order in which global institutions have assumed a more powerful governing role. This role is by no means absolute, and it requires compliance from the states themselves. The question of compliance is central, as there are two ways of guaranteeing compliance: consensus and coercion.

- Consensus is achieved to the extent that governments and citizens accept the legitimacy of neoclassical economic theory: that market rule is neutral and efficient.
- Coercion is necessary where liberalization is questioned or resisted.

Ultimately, the most effective way of guaranteeing compliance is to institutionalize market rule, where individual governmental functions are recomposed as global governance functions and enforced through the WTO. Indeed, at the first ministerial meeting of the WTO in December 1996, Director-General Renato Ruggiero remarked that preparing a global investment treaty was similar to "writing the constitution of a single global economy." Here we examine how global governance has evolved.

The governance mechanisms of today were anticipated in World Bank loan policy changes in the midst of the debt crisis. Traditionally, the Bank focused on *project* loans for public infrastructure in Third World states. Project loans continue into the present, but in the 1980s, the Bank shifted its emphasis from project to *policy* loans. It linked loans to policies that pursued market-oriented economic growth strategies, especially the structural adjustment loan (SAL). In 1983, World Bank President Clausen remarked, "The fundamental philosophy of our institution is to help countries diversify their exports . . . and to have an export orientation."[15] The priority had shifted to stabilizing global financial relations and opening up southern economies to accelerated resource extraction, rather than funding national projects.

By the 1990s, global debt management was firmly institutionalized in the World Bank and the IMF. As these institutions were ultimately beholden to the so-called Group of 7 (G-7) "northern" powers (the United States, Britain, France, Germany, Italy, Canada, and Japan), the newly formed South Commission (an organ of the global South) made a provocative declaration in 1990:

> What is abundantly clear is that the North has used the plight of developing countries to strengthen its dominance and its influence over the development paths of the South. . . . While adjustment is pressed on them, countries in the North with massive payments imbalances are immune from any pressure to adjust, and free to follow policies that deepen the South's difficulties. The most powerful countries in the North have become a *de facto* board of management for the world economy, protecting their interests and imposing their will on the South. The governments of the South are then left to face the wrath, even the violence, of their own people, whose standards of living are being depressed for the sake of preserving the present patterns of operation of the world economy.[16]

While identifying global governance, perhaps narrowly, with the North-South power relation, the South Commission's declaration draws attention to a new dimension in development discourse: the priority given to managing the world economy as a *singular entity*. In other words, the World Bank/IMF partnership in structurally adjusting particular states is a method of governing and an attempt to resolve the instability in a deregulated global money market. Ongoing management of global financial relations has become a practical necessity to stabilize economies and open or "denationalize" them in the process.

### CASE STUDY

### Mexican Sovereignty Exposed: From Above and Below

Mexico's admission into the Organization for Economic Cooperation and Development (OECD) via its participation in NAFTA precipitated the January 1, 1994, *Zapatista* uprising in Chiapas. In protest of President Salinas's decision, *Zapatista* spokesperson, Subcomandante Marcos, claimed it was a "death sentence for indigenous peoples." The *Zapatistas* declared, "When we rose up against a national government, we found that it did not exist. In reality we were up against great financial capital, against speculation and investment, which makes all decisions in Mexico, as well as in Europe, Asia, Africa, Oceania, the Americas—everywhere." Having exposed the question of Mexican sovereignty, the uprising unsettled regional financial markets. The *Zapatistas* suggested that NAFTA was a confidence trick of the globalization project:

> At the end of 1994 the economic farce with which Salinas had deceived the Nation and the international economy exploded. The nation of money called the grand gentlemen of power and arrogance to dinner, and they did not hesitate in betraying the soil and sky in which they prospered with Mexican blood. The economic crisis awoke Mexicans from the sweet and stupifying dream of entry into the first world.

The Mexican peso responded by losing 30 percent of its value in December 1994, generating a negative "tequila effect" throughout Latin American financial markets. International financiers hastily assembled a financial loan package of $18 billion to stabilize the peso. The United States committed $9 billion (and more), while the Bank for International Settlements in Switzerland, owned by the European Central Banks, provided $5 billion. Canada also contributed $1 billion, and a dozen global banks, including Citibank, added a $3 billion line of credit. Finally, the IMF was called in to lend both money *and* its stamp of approval to restore investor confidence in the Mexican economy. U.S. President Clinton remarked in 1995, "Mexico is sort of a bellwether for the rest of Latin America and developing countries throughout the world." Confidence in NAFTA was also at stake.

If the Mexican bailout was to stabilize the global economy and legitimize the globalization project, the question remains why Chiapas has been occupied by the Mexican federal army ever since? What is it about the globalization project that it values foreign investment over minority rights?

---

*Sources: Bradsher (1995:D6); Starr (2000).*

Global circuits (of debt, money, and pension funds) are so embedded in national economies (and vice versa) that stabilizing these destabilizing financial relations now dominates national policymaking. In this way, the new forms of global governance seek, at one and the same time, to ensure open economies and the institutional mechanisms to manage the volatile side effects—evidenced in domino-like financial crises.

## GATT: The Making of a Free Trade Regime

The debt regime elevated the Bretton Woods institutions to a governance role, targeting the Third World. During 1986 to 1994, the *whole world* became the target of the Uruguay Round of the General Agreement on Trade and Tariffs (GATT). The Uruguay Round was to establish a set of new and binding rules concerning free trade, freedom of investment, and protection of intellectual property rights. Once formulated, these rules formed the framework of the WTO. In this section, we focus on agriculture because it was central to the Uruguay Round's challenge to national developmentalism.

The United States engineered the creation of the GATT in 1948 as an alternative to the International Trade Organization (which included provisions from the United Nations [UN] Declaration of Human Rights concerning full employment, working conditions, and social security).[17] *Through GATT, trade expansion was delinked from the social contract.* From 1948 through 1980, GATT reduced tariff rates on trade in manufactured goods by more than 75 percent.[18] Agriculture had been excluded from the GATT on the insistence of the United States. In the 1980s, at a time of recession and declining industrial leadership, the United States initiated the Uruguay Round, with the aim of liberalizing agriculture and services (banking, insurance, telecommunications), in which the First World held a competitive advantage. Third World countries were skeptical, as their cheaper exports of steel products, footwear, electronic products, and agricultural products were limited by First World protections. India and Brazil led the resistance to broadening GATT, but First World pressure and the promise of open markets, including agricultural markets, won the day.[19]

The liberalization movement was supported by an activist lobby of "free trader" agro-exporting states, called the Cairns Group: Argentina, Australia, Brazil, Canada, Chile, Colombia, Fiji, Hungary, Indonesia, Malaysia, the Philippines, New Zealand, Thailand, and Uruguay. It was expected that free trade would enhance the farm commodity exports of the Cairns Group and of the United States. Not surprisingly, transnational corporations supported liberalization. In fact, 14,000 firms—including General Motors, IBM, and American Express—formed a multinational trade negotiations coalition to lobby GATT member nations.

Agribusinesses such as Cargill, Ralston-Purina, General Mills, Continental Grain, RJR Nabisco, and ConAgra supported GATT's challenge to trade barriers, domestic price supports for farm products, and supply-management policies that restrict the demand for farm inputs such as fertilizer and chemicals. Such regulations constrain the ability of transnationals to profit from expanded trade and access to low-cost producers through global sourcing and use of cheap products as a competitive market weapon against high-priced producers. Corporations produce and sell farm products across the world—they take advantage of seasonal variation and dietary variation and engage in redundant food swaps (see Figure 5.2). Alternatively, farmers are spatially fixed and depend on national farm policy—input and price subsidies, farm credit, risk insurance, and import controls—for their economic viability. Unless they are corporate farmers, they do not favor liberalization, which exposes them directly to volatile world prices.

Accordingly, a GATT ministerial meeting recognized an "urgent need to bring more discipline and predictability to world agricultural trade."[20] The *absence* of trade rules during the closing years of the development project showed in the widespread use of export subsidies. Farm subsidies quadrupled in the United States and doubled in the European Community in the early 1980s, generating ever larger surpluses to be dumped on the world market and depressing world agricultural prices, which declined 39 percent between 1975 and 1989.[21] Many Third World farm sectors were adversely affected by dumping, which devalued their agro-exports and deepened food import dependency, especially in sub-Saharan Africa. In Zimbabwe, for example, U.S. corn dumping forced that country's grain marketing board to cut domestic producer prices almost in half in 1986 and to reduce its purchase quota from these producers.[22]

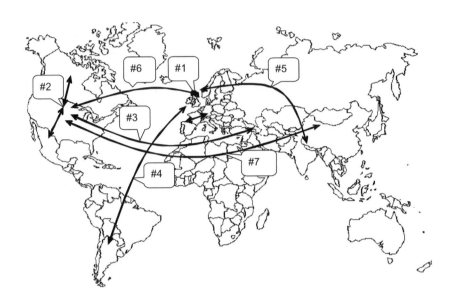

**Figure 5.2**    The Global Food Swap

Sources: U.S. International Trade Commission (2000, www.itc.org); Food and Agricultural Organization of the UN (2000, www.fao.org/trade/); Lucas (2001); U.S. Department of Agriculture, Foreign Agricultural Services (2000, www.usis.usemb.se/Agriculture/).

Note: #1: In 1998, Britain exported 33,100 tons of poultry meat to the Netherlands and imported 61,400 tons of poultry meat from the Netherlands. #2: In 2002, the United States exported 16,899,033 kg of fresh or chilled tomatoes to Mexico and imported 143,828,042 kg of fresh or chilled tomatoes from Mexico. The United States also exported 112,687,375 kg of these same tomatoes to Canada and imported 68,720,041 from Canada. #3: In 2002, the United States exported 31,541 kg of shelled walnuts to Turkey and imported 35,471 kg of shelled walnuts from Turkey. #4: In 1999, the European Union (EU) imported 44,000 tons of live bovine animals and meat from Argentina. That same year, the EU exported 874,211 tons of live bovine animals and meat to other countries across the world. #5: Between 2001 and 2002, India imported $56.60 million worth of coffee, tea, mate, and spices from the United Kingdom. In that same time period, India exported $51.08 million worth of those same products to the United Kingdom. #6: In 2001, Denmark exported 51,000 whole salmons to the United States and imported 70,000 whole salmons from the United States. #7: In 2002, the People's Republic of China imported 435,000 metric tons of broiler poultry to the United States and exported 438,000 metric tons of broiler poultry to the United States.

GATT-style liberalization of agricultural trade claims to stabilize commodity markets, but it does not guarantee survival of farmers in the global South.[23] Global firms control roughly three-quarters of all global trade in primary commodities,[24] enabling price manipulation to secure markets. Identifying the governance implications, leaders of the European Ecumenical Organization for Development claimed, "With four grain corporations controlling over 80% of world cereals trade . . . market liberalization would simply transfer authority from governments to corporate leaders whose activity is guided by the profit motive."[25]

Such transfer of authority was implicit in the redefinition of **food security**. The goal of food security is to provide populations with sufficient and predictable food supplies. Natural endowments and colonial history complicate how individual states pursue food security. At its inception, GATT's Article XI included food security provisions that permitted member nations to prohibit food exporting in the event of critical shortages of foodstuffs.[26] In the Uruguay Round, however, the United States challenged this provision on the grounds of the superior efficiency of free world markets in food:

> The U.S. has always maintained that self-sufficiency and food security are not one and the same. Food security—the ability to acquire the food you need when you need it—is best provided through a smooth-functioning world market. . . . In the food security context, we have also proposed that the permission to restrict or inhibit exports of agricultural food products to relieve critical food shortage be removed from Article XI.[27]

This *global conception of food security* stemmed from the institutionalized superiority of U.S. agro-exporting via the postwar international food regime, a 1970s green power strategy, and a 1985 Farm Bill that drastically cheapened U.S. agro-exports. In 1986, Agricultural Secretary John Block remarked,

> The push by some developing countries to become more self-sufficient in food may be reminiscent of a bygone era. These countries could save money by importing food from the United States. . . . The U.S. has used the World Bank to back up this policy, going so far as making the dismantling of farmer support programs a condition for loans, as is the case for Morocco's support for their domestic cereal producers.[28]

Globally managed food security, based on the idea of "comparative advantage," depends on three political conditions: (1) trade liberalization measures, (2) subsidized "breadbasket" regions, and (3) corporate-managed food circuits. From the global South, this is perceived as promoting "recolonization"[29]—despite the membership of some southern states such as Malaysia, the Philippines, and Thailand in the Cairns Group of agro-exporters, which favor free trade because of their palm oil, coconut oil, and rice exports, respectively. Even so, their domestic staple grain producers are threatened by liberalization.

In short, the making of a free trade regime reconstructed "food security" as a global market function, privileging corporate agriculture and placing noncorporate farmers at a comparative disadvantage. Food security would now be "governed" through the market by corporate, rather than social, criteria. In this way, unprotected southern farmers are subjected to the "disciplines" (e.g., efficiency) of an unequal global market anchored in northern agricultural protectionism and managed by transnational agribusiness corporations.

## The World Trade Organization

The singular achievement of the GATT Uruguay Round was the creation of the **World Trade Organization** (WTO) on January 1, 1995. The WTO, with 146 voting members (and 26 claimants), assumes unprecedented power to enforce GATT provisions. It is unprecedented because, as below, the WTO is arguably less about trade rule consistency than about weakening member state sovereignty via liberalization. *Free trade* is a misnomer for the reach of WTO rules. In combination, they represent a challenge to national democratic governance, removing decision making to nontransparent tribunals located in Geneva, Switzerland, using an abstract market logic to override individual government policy.

Unlike the GATT (a trade treaty only), the WTO has independent jurisdiction like the United Nations. That is, it has the power to enforce its rulings on member states, and these include rulings going beyond simply cross-border trade into the realm of "trade-related" issues. This means setting rules regarding the movement of goods, money, and productive facilities across borders—rules that restrict countries from enacting legislation or policies discriminating against such movement. The WTO is dedicated to privileging corporate rights to compete internationally. This means ensuring that TNCs receive treatment equal to that received by domestic firms and removing local restrictions (e.g., labor, health, environmental laws) on trade and investment that might interfere with corporate competitiveness in the global marketplace. As World Bank economist Herman Daly warned in 1994, establishing such rules to override national governments' capacity to regulate commerce "is to wound fatally the major unit of community capable of carrying out any policies for the common good."[30]

The WTO has an *integrated dispute settlement* mechanism. If a state is perceived to be distorting trade obligations in one area, such as curbing investments in timber cutting to protect a forest, it can be disciplined through the application of sanctions against another area of economic activity, like some of its manufactured exports. Member states can lodge complaints through the WTO, whose decision holds automatically unless every member of the WTO votes to reverse it. Should states refuse to comply, the WTO can authorize the plaintiff to take unilateral action. The ambit of the dispute settlement mechanism is wide: covering trade, investment, services, and intellectual property. That is, in seeking to "harmonize" trade relationships, the WTO sponsors the diluting of national sovereignty in economic and social policy. Martin Khor, director of the Third World Network, suggests, in claiming to reduce "trade-distorting" measures, that the WTO becomes "development-distorting."[31]

The WTO's first trade complaint, in 1996, involved a challenge to the U.S. Clean Air Act regulations by Venezuela and Brazil on behalf of their petroleum-refining corporations against domestic oil refiners. The Environmental Protection Agency had the choice of replacing the regulation with a WTO-consistent rule that weakened environmental protection or facing trade sanctions totaling $150 million a year. This case "inspired a run of successful challenges against hard-won environmental and public health laws."[32] The very *threat* of such challenges has had the effect also of diluting national laws protecting human and environmental health.

The WTO's dispute mechanism thus can require nations to alter such domestic laws to bring them in line with its provisions, overriding national regulatory powers. Furthermore, the WTO staff are unelected bureaucrats who answer to no constituency other than those corporate entities that benefit from "free trade." WTO proceedings are secret, denying citizen participation in making and evaluating policy. In its confidential bureaucratic guise, such global governance, framed by the discourse of economic theory, subordinates the sovereignty of the nation-state, the historic site of the social contract and democracy.

The WTO, in enforcing market freedoms, seeks to depoliticize economic activity. As the outgoing director general of GATT, Peter Sutherland, declared in 1994, "Governments should interfere in the conduct of trade as little as possible."[33] This implies a *general* challenge to national laws and regulations regarding the environment, health, preferential trade relations, social subsidies, labor legislation, and so on. While the challenge does not eliminate all laws, it seeks to *harmonize* regulation internationally, lowering the ceiling on democratic initiatives within the national polity, especially those involving subnational jurisdictions.[34] As we shall see, the goal of depoliticizing the economy can backfire, and this explains in large part the mushrooming global social justice movement.

In this sense, although implementation is uneven, the WTO expresses the essence of the globalization project. That is, global managers assume extraordinary powers to govern the web of global economic relations lying across nation-states, often at the expense of the national and/or democratic process. What is so remarkable is that the reach of economic globalization is so limited in terms of the populations it includes, and yet its impact is so extensive. The impact is extensive precisely because states collaborate, or have no choice but to collaborate, in the project. Just as nation-states were the ideal vehicle of the development project, so restructured states convey the globalization project to their populations.

We now turn to a summary examination of the four principal and mutually reinforcing protocols of the WTO: the Agreement on Agriculture (AoA), Trade-Related Investment Measures (TRIMs), Trade-Related Intellectual Property Rights (TRIPs), and the General Agreement on Trade in Services (GATS).

### 1. The Agreement on Agriculture (AoA)

The 1995 Agreement on Agriculture advocated universal reductions in trade protection, farm subsidies, and government intervention. Deregulation of farm price supports compromises the ability of many countries to meet their commitments to the AoA. Their farmers have been unable to recover the cost of their production in the face of collapsing prices since world prices for farm goods fell 30 percent or more in the first half decade since the AoA was instituted.[35] Hypocritically, countries with the capacity to pay (U.S. and European states) retained subsidies, to the despair of countries with significant farm populations, threatened daily with the dumping of cheap farm commodities.

Declining world prices for agricultural commodities is symptomatic of the growing power of agribusiness to enhance profitability through global sourcing. With liberalization, farmers everywhere are under pressure to compete by selling cheap. Corporate farmers survive by subsidized "scale economy." In the mid-1990s, 80 percent of farm subsidies in the OECD countries concentrated on the largest 20 percent of (corporate) farms, rendering small farmers increasingly vulnerable to a deregulated (and increasingly privately managed) global market for agricultural products. In 1994, 50 percent of U.S. farm products came from 2 percent of the farms, and only 9 percent came from 73 percent of the farms.[36] Between 1998 and 1999, U.K. farm income fell by about 75 percent, driving 20,000 farmers out of business, and U.S. farm income declined by almost 50 percent between 1996 and 1999. In the global South, conservative estimates are that between 20 and 30 million people have lost their land from the impact of AoA trade liberalization, including 1,750,000 rural Mexicans.[37]

### CASE STUDY
### Global Comparative Disadvantage: The End of Farming as We Know It?

A recent report from the Public Citizen's *Global Trade Watch* documents a common process of elimination of small farmers across the whole North American region as the legacy of NAFTA. While millions of Mexican *campesinos* have lost their maize farms to cheap and heavily subsidized corn exports from the North, U.S. farmers are also faced with an intensification of competitive imports from Mexico and Canada, replacing crops grown in the United States such as fruit, vegetables, and other labor-intensive foodstuffs. Since 1994, 33,000 U.S. farms with under $100,000 annual income have disappeared (six times the decline for 1988–1993). During the 1990s, a massive demographic shift occurred in Mexico—overall population growth was 20 percent, but urban population grew 44 percent and rural only 6 percent. Half of the rural population earns less than $1.40 a day (insufficient to feed themselves), and so about 500 people leave the countryside daily.

Policy changes such as these express and enhance agribusiness power. The ethos of liberalization is that exporting makes agricultural protections unnecessary because of expanding global food flows. As Public Citizen observes with respect to U.S. policy,

> Proponents of the legislation contended it would make farming more efficient and responsive to market forces; in reality it essentially handed the production of food to agribusiness.... Congress has had to appropriate

emergency farm supports—in massive farm bailout bills—every year since the legislation went into effect.

Fifty-six percent of U.S. emergency taxpayer assistance went to the largest 10 percent of the farms. Meanwhile, agribusiness restructured, with input industries and output industries consolidating alliances to "encircle farmers and consumers in a web . . . from selling seeds and bioengineering animal varieties to producing the pesticides, fertilizers, veterinary pharmaceuticals and feed to grow them to transporting, slaughtering, processing and packaging the final 'product.'" The Canadian National Farmers Union testified that "almost every link in the chain, nearly every sector, is dominated by between two and ten multi-billion-dollar multinational corporations." Once NAFTA opened Mexico's door to 100 percent foreign investor rights, Pillsbury's Green Giant subsidiary relocated its frozen food processing from California to Mexico to access cheap wages, minimal food safety standards, and zero tariffs on reexport to the United States. Cargill purchased a beef and chicken plant in Saltillo, and Cargill de Mexico invested nearly $200 million in vegetable oil refining and soybean processing in Tula. Anticipating continent-wide liberalization, Tyson Foods has operations in Mexico, Brazil, Argentina, and Venezuela; ConAgra processes oilseed in Argentina; Archer Daniels Midland crushes and refines oilseed, mills corn and flour, and bioengineers feeds in Mexico, Central America, and South America; and Wal-Mart is in Argentina and Brazil. Public Citizen remarks,

> Multinational agribusinesses were positioned uniquely to take advantage of trade rules that force countries to accept agricultural imports regardless of their domestic supplies. The companies utilized their foreign holdings as export platforms to sell imported agriculture goods in the U.S., and by thus increasing supply, put negative pressures on U.S. agriculture prices.

When liberal policy and northern government subsidies enable corporations to construct their own comparative advantages, by rendering family/peasant farming "inefficient" and redundant, how can "market-based resource allocation" retain credibility in the face of a social catastrophe involving destabilization of rural communities, large-scale displacement of people, and food insecurity?

*Sources: Public Citizen (2001:ii-iv, 10, 13, 16, 19-21); Jordan and Sullivan (2003:33).*

Liberalization is less about freeing trade than about facilitating agribusiness: consolidating corporate agriculture and cheapening farm products to enhance agro-exports. The AoA normalized export subsidies for 25 of 130-odd WTO members, including the United States and the European Union, which intensified export dumping such that "just 3 (members) are responsible for 93% of all subsidized wheat exports and just 2 of them are responsible for subsidizing 94% of butter and 80% of beef exports."[38]

Through the AoA, the WTO institutionalized the global meaning of *food security*. Under the AoA, states no longer have the right to full self-sufficiency as a national strategy. Rather, the minimum market access rule guarantees the "right to export" (therefore the requirement to import), even under conditions of subsidized exports. Southern states signed the AoA expecting to improve their foreign currency earnings from expanded agro-exports so that they could retire foreign debt. However, since northern commodities are cheapened by export subsidies and economies of mechanized scale, and since 70 percent of the global food trade is internal to TNC transactions, trade liberalization favors agro-exports from the global North.

*Food security*, then, is not food self-reliance but food import dependency for a large minority of southern states—those adversely affected by world market dumping of northern food surpluses. By the mid-1990s, half of the foreign exchange of the 88 low-income food deficit countries went to food imports.[39] Food-dependent states' food bills grew, on average, 20 percent between 1994 and 1999, despite record-low prices in the late 1990s. Meanwhile, northern states continue farm support. In the absence of public capacity in the South, unprotected farmers are at a comparative disadvantage. In 2000, Oxfam asked, "How can a farmer earning US$230 a year (average per capita income in LDCs [least developed countries]) compete with a farmer who enjoys a subsidy of US$20,000 a year (average subsidy in OECD countries)?"[40] In India, Devinder Sharma observes, "Whereas for small farmers the subsidies have been withdrawn, there is a lot of support now for agribusiness industry. . . . The result is that the good area under staple foods is now shifting to export crops, so we'll have to import staple food."[41] While 90 percent of agricultural research expenditures in Latin America went to food crop research in the 1980s, 80 percent focused on export crops during the 1990s.[42] In Kenya, 40 percent of the nation's children (6- to 16-year-olds) work on plantations, which export pineapple, coffee, tea, and sugar. While these foodstuffs supply European markets, 4 million Kenyans face starvation.[43]

The substitution of export crops for domestic crops is only an approximate measure of the dismantling of national farm sectors, or of the "commons": The foundation of rural life, it nevertheless symbolizes the conversion of agriculture to a market good and the privatization of a public good, food security. As local producers and markets are scuttled by the removal of public protections, marginalized by the privileging of export cropping, and swamped by artificially cheapened food imports, rural populations are displaced into casual labor, and rural cultures are dismantled in the name of free trade.

## 2. Trade-Related Investment Measures (TRIMs)

TRIMs arose within the context of the GATT Uruguay Round, in an attempt to reduce "performance requirements" imposed on foreign investment by host governments. Such requirements might include expecting a TNC to invest locally, hire locally, buy locally, and transfer technology as a quid pro quo for investment access.[44] The WTO uses TRIMs to manage the cross-border movement of goods and services production, especially, as the WTO Web site explains, since trade is closely linked with investment via "the fact that one-third of the $6.1 trillion total for world trade in goods and services in 1995 was trade within companies—for example between subsidiaries in different countries or between a subsidiary and its headquarters." The point of TRIMs is to secure investor rights at the expense of domestic development measures. As one proponent, Theodore H. Moran, argues, "The multinational corporate community would then be able to rationalize their regional and global sourcing strategies on the basis of productivity, quality, and cost considerations in place of the political dictates that now disrupt their operations."[45]

**CASE STUDY**
**Corporate Property Rights in India**

In June 2000, the United States (followed by the European Union) deployed the WTO disputes mechanism against India on the grounds that its auto industry violates the TRIMs protocol. India opened its auto sector in 1996 to joint ventures with investors such as Fiat, Daimler-Benz, General Motors, Ford, Toyota, Honda, and Hyundai. Complaints from these firms of local content restrictions and export requirements to generate foreign exchange precipitated the WTO challenge. The conflict is essentially between an Indian industrial policy using export requirements to stem a glutted car market, already 50 percent over capacity, and foreign auto firms eager to capture one of the world's largest potential markets. The TRIMs initiative illustrates the tension between the urgency of corporate property rights, as championed by the WTO, and the planning and/or transitional needs of individual countries. India's industry minister, Murasoli Maran, observed, "Third World countries are worried that what they keep out of the front door may find its way into the WTO through the back door." Meanwhile, wealthy Indians use the side door: Mercedes Benz launched its S320-L model in 2000 at $150,000, with 84 orders already in hand. In 2001, BMW, Jaguar, and Alfa Romeo followed.

The tensions in this case raise the following question: If a country has a policy to stabilize its domestic economy and its trade balance, why would the WTO threaten that policy and invite instability?

---

*Source: Devraj (2001:17).*

The argument in favor of TRIMs is that they reduce domestic content requirements that misallocate local resources, raise costs, penalize competitive investment, and burden consumers, in addition to slowing technological adoption, reducing quality, and retarding management practices.[46] In other words, the role of TRIMs is to enhance conditions for transnational investment by reducing the friction of local regulations. Greater freedom for investors under TRIMs is justified by evidence of "higher-than-average wages and benefits, advanced technology, and sophisticated managerial and marketing techniques," as well as a stronger "integration effect" with the local economy. It is exemplified in the Mexican auto industry, where parent firms invested in local supply firms for self-interest and not because of local content requirements, resulting in the creation of globally competitive Mexican auto part suppliers. Also, in the Malaysian semiconductor industry, an indigenous machine tool firm matured from supplying parts to foreign investors to supplying high-precision computer-numeric tools and factory automation equipment to international and domestic markets.[47] But the "integration effect" favors integration the other way: of local producers into the world market, rather than foreign investors integrating into a program of domestic industrialization.

The TRIMs protocol includes reducing the escalating cost and beggar-thy-neighbor practice of "locational incentive packages"—where countries compete for business through concessions. In a commissioned OECD study (1994), the "Irish model" emerged as a paradigmatic case—where Ireland used incentives (grants of 60 percent of fixed assets, 100 percent of training costs, free building sites and rent subsidies in industrial parks, and extremely low tax rates) to attract more than 1,000 TNCs, generating nearly 100,000 jobs: more than 50 percent of Irish industrial output and 75 percent of manufactured exports.[48] In the 1990s, Ireland emerged as a prosperous export platform for the European market (building on a period of labor disorganization via deindustrialization). This model was copied by Mexico and Brazil vis-à-vis the North American and global markets. Remember, Shannon, Ireland, was the site of the first export processing zone (EPZ) in 1958. While TRIMs may attempt to regulate export platform concessions to preserve the principle of comparative advantage, in challenging domestic requirements on foreign investment, TRIMs encourage EPZs, whose sole domestic link is labor, minus its civil rights. As we have seen, cheap, disorganized labor is the one "comparative advantage" many governments in the global South have to offer.

## 3. Trade-Related Intellectual Property Rights (TRIPs)

The WTO Web site defines **intellectual property rights** as "rights given to persons over the creations of their minds. They usually give the creator an exclusive right over the use of his/her creation for a certain period of time." The TRIPs protocol was defined by a coalition of 12 major U.S. corporations, a Japanese federation of business organizations, and the agency for European business and industry. Based on a synthesis of European and U.S. patent laws, intellectual property rights protection is to be administered by the WTO. Advocates claim that it simplifies the protection of property rights across national borders and protects and promotes innovation for everyone by guaranteeing profits from technological developments, such as computer software, biotechnological products and processes, and pharmaceuticals. But critics contest this corporate definition of intellectual rights, arguing that bio/diverse and generic knowledges should remain available to human kind as a global "commons."[49]

At the turn of the twenty-first century, when a scientist from Abbott Laboratories isolated a frog secretion to develop a painkiller, the Ecuadorian government demanded compensation on behalf of Ecuador and the Amazonian Indians, who use the chemical as poison on their hunting arrows. It did so under the terms of the 1992 Convention on Biological Diversity, which confirms national sovereignty over genetic resources, affirming the principle that nations are entitled to "fair and equitable sharing of the benefits." Many commercial drugs these days derive from chemicals found in tropical flora and fauna. Our lifestyle is directly connected to the extraction of these sorts of resources, such as drugs from the rosy periwinkle of Madagascar to fight childhood leukemia and testicular cancer, Brazzein, a powerful sweetener from a West African berry, biopesticides from the Indian neem tree, and human cell lines to identify genes causing illnesses such as Huntington's disease and cystic fibrosis.[50]

It seems rational that the world's biodiversity should service humankind, such as the frog secretion. This is why so much attention is being paid to preserving the tropical rain forests, for example, given their rich biological variety. But the greater the attention, the more controversy that erupts. At issue is the question of control of resources. And it often comes down to the relationship between the lifestyle of the global North and the rights of indigenous peoples in the developing nations, mostly in the global South.

The global South contains 90 percent of global biological wealth, and scientists and corporations of the North account for 97 percent of all patents. Patents on biological wealth give patent holders exclusive control over use of the genetic materials. In many cases, a corporation has patented genetic material obtained from a southern country without payment or obligation, turned it into a commodity such as a medicine, and then charged a fee for use of the genetic resource in local production or charged high prices for the commodity—even to the country where the material was originally in use, perhaps for centuries. Critics view this appropriation of genetic material by foreigners as **biopiracy.** A London-based organization, ActionAid, defines biopiracy as

> the granting of patents on plant varieties or individual genes, proteins and gene sequences from plants in the South by commercial and industrial interests. This privatisation of living organisms often involves companies taking indigenous plant varieties from developing countries and using these species for the extraction of genes, or genetically modifying . . . existing plants.[51]

In this sense, TRIPs are yet another weapon in the WTO corporate property rights ("comparative advantage") arsenal. Biopiracy need not be limited to plant varieties. Attempts have been made to acquire human and other animal genetic material, as well as nonplant microbiological material. The entire living world is very much up for grabs in this particular vision of commodifying natural endowments and resources.

TRIPs grew out of an attempt to stem intellectual property pirating of Western products (watches, CDs, etc.) in the global South but, ironically, now appears to sanction a reverse biological form of piracy on a disproportionate scale, threatening livelihood, rather than commodity, rights. About 1.4 billion people in the global South depend primarily on farm-saved seeds and on crop genetic diversity as the basis of cultural and ecological sustainability. Farmers express concern that if firms can patent traditional seed stock, planting of traditional crops may be liable for patent infringement.[52] This concern arises because firms such as I.C. Industries and Pioneer Hi-bred sought licensing rights to use a gene from an African cowpea. When inserted into crops such as corn and soybeans, the gene increases pest resistance. As the Rural Advancement Foundation International (RAFI) asked, "The question is, who are the inventors? [The scientists] who isolated the gene? Or West African farmers who identified the value of the plant holding the gene and then developed and protected it?"[53] In valuing techno-scientific over indigenous knowledge, an intellectual property regime (IPR) regime creates an unequal relation—endangering farmers' rights to plant their crops and threatening to expropriate genetic resources developed by peasants, forest dwellers, and local communities over centuries of cultural experimentation. Gene patenting ultimately relies on an IPR regime that privileges governments and corporations as legal entities and disempowers communities and farmers by disavowing their indigenous knowledge rights.[54]

The TRIPs protocol establishes uniform standards, globally, for intellectual property rights protection, allowing exclusion of plants and animals from patent laws but insisting on intellectual property rights for "inventors" of micro-organisms, microbiological processes and products, and plant varieties, which must be either patentable or subject to an effective *sui generis* system, which states interpret to mean plant variety protection. The latter stems from the 1992 Convention on Biological Diversity (CBD), which confirmed national sovereignty over genetic resources and affirmed that nations are entitled to "fair and equitable sharing of the benefits." The CBD is a commitment to conserve biological diversity, recognizing traditional knowledges and obliging member states to conserve knowledge for biological wealth. In addition, it empowers states to enact national laws to protect biodiversity. However, how states interpret that right and obligation is part of the controversy.[55]

## CASE STUDY

## Unequal Construction of Knowledges and the
## Question of Biodiversity Protection

When the Indian government introduced the Protection of Plant Varieties and Farmers' Rights Bill in December 1999, the key question was whether the bill would promote India's food security by improving conditions for plant breeding of new seed varieties. Critics claim that the bill's provisions, modeled on the 1978 International Convention for the Protection of New Plant Varieties (UPOV)—which secured green revolution plant breeding—privilege the formal, corporate plant breeder who produces new seed varieties. Farmers, who informally employ centuries-old plant-breeding methods, are excluded from the bill's provisions and viewed as potential "bioserfs" to grow the new varieties bred by the corporate sector. Ashish Kothari—coordinator of a group formulating the Indian National Biodiversity Strategy and Action Plan and the founder-member of the environmental action organization, Kalpavriksh—recommends an alternative *sui generis* system of plant variety protection to achieve food security and enhance the genetic base that would include the following principles: legal recognition and protection of farming communities' agricultural knowledges, systems of registration at subnational and national levels to ensure protection from piracy, representation of farm communities on agricultural planning and implementation bodies, appropriate and equitable benefit-sharing arrangements with farmers and communities whose varieties and knowledges are used for commercial and scientific purposes, and so forth.

The Indian case demonstrates the tension embedded in states between Western modernity and indigenous knowledges. Internationally, as well as in WTO protocols, Western legal-scientific arrangements are deemed to be the optimal framework. This devalues the existence, integrity, and viability of non-Western knowledge and values, channeling benefits to private investors rather than communities. The TRIPs concept of intellectual property rights represents and enforces an idea of diversity for immediate benefit because of the unequal value placed on techno-scientific versus indigenous knowledge.

How is that in protecting corporate science through the TRIPs protocols, modernity, with all of its scientific resources, can discount the intricate and historical connections between cultural and ecological diversity on which our planet's sustainability may well depend?

---

*Source: Kothari (2000).*

The significance of the *sui generis* system for plants lies in its potential for alternative formulations, recognizing and securing collective rights for agricultural and medicinal plant biodiversity. A *sui generis* system premised on collective rights to biodiversity would recognize diverse cultural knowledges and practices. The *sui generis* principle was recently affirmed in the case of the Texas-based company RiceTec, Inc., which sells "Kasmati" rice and "Texmati" rice and claimed rights to basmati rice. In June 2000, under popular pressure, the Indian government successfully challenged 4 of the 20 claims for this patent on the grounds that the grain, as well as the seeds and plants producing the grain, is the product of centuries of indigenous breeding and cultivation.[56]

## 4. General Agreement on Trade in Services (GATS)

Services, unlike goods, are defined as "anything you can not drop on your foot."[57] They include public and financial services. The 1994 GATS regime opened markets for trade in services by establishing the rights to corporate "presence" in member countries for the delivery of a service in the areas of finance, telecommunications, and transport. "GATS 2000" is a fundamentally more far-reaching protocol to compel governments to provide unlimited market access to foreign service providers, without regard for social and environmental impacts of the service activities.[58] As Tony Clarke notes, GATS 2000 involves the following:

- Imposing severe constraints on the government's ability to protect environmental, health, consumer, and other public interest standards. A "necessity test" requires government proof that regulations on service provision are the "least trade restrictive," parallel with WTO rules on trade in goods.
- Restricting government funding of public works, municipal services, and social programs. Using WTO "national treatment" protocols on government procurement and subsidies, it would impede the role of government funds for public services, making them equally available to foreign-based private service corporations.
- The guaranteed access of private service corporations to domestic markets in all sectors, including health, education, and water, is accelerated by permitting commercial presence in GATS member countries.
- "Every service imaginable is on the table, including a wide range of public services in sectors that affect the environment, culture, energy and natural

resources; plus drinking water, health care, K-12 education, post-secondary education, and social security; along with transportation services, postal delivery, prisons, libraries and a variety of municipal services."[59]

- Finally, access provisions are more profound, applying to most government measures affecting "trade-in-services," such as labor laws, consumer protection, subsidies, grants, licensing standards and qualifications, market access restrictions, economic needs tests, and local content provisions.

In other words, GATS threatens to replace the social contract between state and citizen with a private contract between corporation and consumer. The democratic claims of the citizen-state (expressed in municipal contracts for construction, sewage, garbage disposal, sanitation, tourism, and water services) would yield to the private capacities of the consumer-citizen, at the expense of the public interest and its development expressions. In this proposal, we see the elimination of all vestiges of the development state and its replacement by corporate services globally.

---

**Who Is behind GATS 2000, and Who Stands to Gain?**

*The GATS 2000 agenda was drawn up by a powerful transnational coalition of corporate service providers, including the following:*

1. *U.S. Coalition of Service Industries (USCSI)—composed of electronic entertainment and telecommunication giants AOL Time-Warner, AT&T, and IBM; energy and water enterprises such as Enron and Vivendi Universal; financial empires such as Citigroup, Bank of America, and J. P. Morgan Chase; investment houses such as Goldman Sachs and General Electric Financial; health insurance corporations such as the Chubb Group; management and consultant corporations such as KPMG and Price-Waterhouse Coopers; and express delivery services such as United Parcel and Federal Express*

2. *European Services Forum—composed of 47 corporations, including financial giants Barclays PLC and Commerzbank AG; telecommunications: British Telecom, Telefonica, and Deutsche TelekomAG; water: Suez-Lyonnaise des Eaux; health insurance: the AXA Group and CGU plus Norwich Union; financial consultants: Arthur Andersen Consulting; publishing and entertainment: Bertelsmann; and brand-name empires such as Daimler-Chrysler Services and Marks and Spencer PLC*

*(Continued)*

---

(Continued)

   3. *Japan Services Network, under the leadership of the CEO of Mitsubishi*

*Since the late-1980s, on the heels of debt regime-mandated privatization, trade in services tripled to 25 percent of world trade. As Figure 5.3 shows, the global North dominates international trade in services. The Bush administration predicted in 2002 that the elimination of barriers to services would create $1.8 trillion in new global commerce annually, with $450 billion earned by U.S. firms.*

---

Sources: Clarke (2001); Phillips (2002); Watkins (2002:21).

---

The strategy used by the proponents of GATS 2000 is, to term it appealingly, a *trade agreement* and demands openness to "cross-border" provision of services (by TNCs) as a condition for opening EU and U.S. markets in garments, textiles, and agricultural products.[60] Oxfam's Kevin Watkins notes that this is a replay of the Uruguay Round, when the global North offered to open its markets in return for protection of TNC patents (which cost the global South $40 billion in increased technology costs), and suggests that while the game has changed, the rules are the same: "The West buys your bananas and shirts if you give its banks and insurance companies unrestricted access to your markets."[61] GATS advocates argue that the conversion of public entities into privately owned, profit-making concerns eliminates bureaucratic inefficiency and government debt, providing superior services on a user-pays basis. A World Development Monitor report cautions against foreign control of services—citing the liberalization of financial banking services in Aotearoa/New Zealand, where affordable financial services and low-cost loans disappeared, leading the government to propose the public establishment of a new bank, the People's Bank.[62]

### CASE STUDY
### Leasing the Rain: Privatizing the Social Contract in Bolivia

In 1997, the World Bank informed the Bolivian president that the condition for $600 million in debt relief was a commitment to privatizing

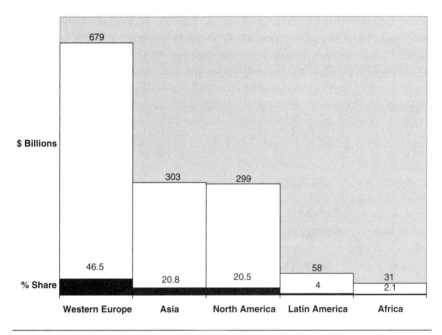

**Figure 5.3**    World Exports of Commercial Services by Region, 2001

Source: International Trade Statistics, WTO, 2001.

its third largest city's water system. Two years later, Bolivian officals leased Cochabamba's water to a subsidiary of the California engineering giant, Bechtel, for 40 years. Until then, Bolivia was touted widely by the multilateral agencies as a model for other low-income countries. Aguas del Tunari quickly doubled the city's water rates and charged citizens for rainwater collected on rooftops. Poor families found that food was now cheaper than water, which was costing workers 25 percent of their wages. Tanya Paredes, a mother of four, remarked, "What we pay for water comes out of what we have to pay for food, clothes, and the other things we need to buy our children." A resistance coalition of factory workers, farmers, environmental groups, and others named La Coordinadora (the Coalition for the Defense of Water and Life) formed and organized a city-wide general strike. The depth and courage of public outcry—fueled by state violence that resulted in the murder of an unarmed 17-year-old boy, Victor Hugo Daza, by a plainclothes army captain trained at the U.S. School of the Americas, and communicated globally by Internet (although not reported by the U.S. media)—forced the city to resume control of the water system. A year later, Bechtel filed a $25 million legal action against the Bolivian government for cost recovery at the World Bank's International Center for the Settlement of Investment Disputes. On February 25, 2003, the secretive tribunal prohibited public and media participation in the legal proceedings, silencing the civic voice.

In this instance, citizen action succeeded in decommodifying a public good. However, if GATS 2000 had been in place, such a reversal would have been practically impossible. While GATS may exclude services provided "under the exercise of government authority," it does apply to services with a commercial dimension or that compete with the private sector. It is irreversible, also.

What is it about the WTO protocols that they must be irreversible—does it have something to do with economic logic, their undemocratic origins, and/or power relations?

---

*Sources: Coates (2001:28); Farthing and Kohl (2001:9); Shultz (2003:35-36).*

## Regional Free Trade Agreements (FTAs)

The WTO regime is anticipated in the spread of free trade agreements (FTAs). These are agreements among neighboring countries to reform trade and investment rules governing their economic intercourse. Free trade agreements range from the North American FTA (known as NAFTA and including originally Canada, the United States, and Mexico) to the southern cone of Latin America (where Brazil, Uruguay, Argentina, and Paraguay participate in the Mercosur Treaty) to the South African Development Community (including Angola, Botswana, Lesotho, Malawi, Mozambique, Namibia, South Africa, Swaziland, Zambia, and Zimbabwe). The megaregions are **NAFTA,** centered on the United States; the **European Union (EU),** centered on Germany; and the **Asian Pacific Economic Community (APEC),** centered on Japan. They are considered megaregions because they produce about two-thirds of world manufacturing output and three-quarters of world exports. In fact, the market represented by the "triad" countries belonging to these three megaregions consists of more than 600 million middle-class consumers "whose academic backgrounds, income levels both discretionary and nondiscretionary, life-style, use of leisure time, and aspirations are quite similar."[63]

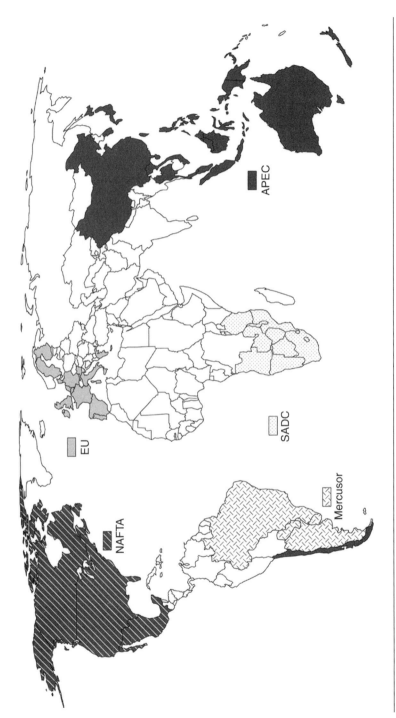

**Figure 5.4** Major Free Trade Zones

189

## The Region-State versus the Nation-State, in the Borderless World

*Japanese economist Kenichi Ohmae depicts the global economy as a "borderless world," rendering states "powerless." He argues that the "region-state" (e.g., the San Diego/Tijuana zone; the growth triangle of Singapore, Johore of southern Malaysia, and the Riau Islands of Indonesia; and the South China region, linking Taiwan, Hong Kong, and the Chinese province of Guandong) is the natural economic zone in a borderless world: "Because of the pressures operating on them, the predictable focus of nation states is on mechanisms for propping up troubled industries," whereas "region states . . . are economic not political units, and they are anything but local in focus. They may lie within the borders of an established nation state, but they are such powerful engines of development because their primary orientation is toward— and their primary linkage is with—the global economy. They are, in fact, its most reliable ports of entry." In theory, Ohmae's perspective describes the purest form of "flow governance," where the region-state ignores legitimacy issues faced by states, individually or collectively in free trade agreements, in coauthoring or authoring market rule. But in practice, states do coordinate such zones and manage the populations and social conditions included in and exploited by the zones.*

Source: Ohmae (1990:80, 89, 99).

Regionalist groupings subscribe to the principles of global free trade but implement them among neighboring states. NAFTA was logical, economically, for Canada and Mexico, which conduct 70 percent of their trade with the United States.[64] As regional integration occurs, states elsewhere respond with local regional groupings, anticipating the possible exclusion of their exports from other trading blocs. In this sense, regionalism is a defensive strategy. Thus, the three megaregions formed in defensive relation to one another, where the European Union's creation of a single currency and common market, termed *Fortress Europe*, deepened integration movements in the Asia-Pacific region and the Americas—even though the United States and Japan conduct 74 percent and 64 percent of their trade, respectively, *outside* their regions, compared with only

30 percent for the European Community members and their European Free Trade Association.[65]

Regionalism embodies the tensions around sovereignty that define the globalization project. The European Community revealed these tensions in its movement toward a common governance in the 1980s, culminating in the founding of the European Union (EU) in the 1991 Treaty of Maastricht. When the secrecy of the technocrats was challenged in the European Court of Justice, lawyers for the European Council of Ministers responded, "There is no principle of community law which gives citizens the right to EU documents." James Goldsmith argued, "The Treaty of Maastricht seeks to create a supranational, centralized, bureaucratic state—a homogenized union. It would destroy the pillars on which Europe was built—its nations. . . . The strength of the European Parliament and the [European] Commission is in inverse proportion to that of the national democratic institutions."[66]

A monetary union to create a single currency, the euro, generated further tensions, especially around the relocation of monetary policy from states to the European Central Bank (Frankfurt), which has no democratic oversight. EU legal arrangements privilege international treaties over national laws, providing a model for WTO-style governance "as a treaty-based regime which would then trump the municipal law of states adhering to the WTO—locking them in, so to speak, to the open door provisions of the WTO on services as well as trade issues, monopoly rents on intellectual property rights, etc."[67] The monetary union has been used to defer the question of a social charter (labor protections) by focusing on financial disciplines and dismantling the "social market" "to build Europe à l'americaine." One consequence of this was the highly publicized and effective strike of 5 million French public servants in 1995, protesting the prime minister's austerity plan to meet the budgetary conditions of the European Monetary Union (EMU).[68]

### CASE STUDY
### NAFTA: Regional Economic Success, Social Failure?

NAFTA, founded in 1994, regulates flows of goods, services, and capital between the three member nations (Canada, the United States, and Mexico) according to the open-door provisions of the WTO. National and local regulations regarding health, labor, and environmental standards are subordinated to market rule and managed by unelected bureaucrats—thus, NAFTA forbade the United States to restrict imports based on methods of production (e.g., child labor or negative environmental practices such as drift netting for tuna).

NAFTA formalized a decade-long process of Mexican structural adjustment. In run-up debates, opposition presidential candidate Cuauhtémoc Cárdenas argued, "Exploitation of cheap labor, energy, and raw materials, technological dependency, and lax environmental protection should not be the premises upon which Mexico establishes links with the United States, Canada and the world economy." As exports shifted from oil to manufactured goods, 85 percent of which crossed the northern border, the government secured this export relation by depressing wages further (a 60 percent decline since 1976) in return for the end of U.S. protectionism. In 1995, Mexican hourly labor costs were 9 percent of those in the United States.

While trade volume has nearly tripled and the Mexican economy is now the world's ninth largest, Mexico's 50 percent rate of poverty has not changed since the early 1980s, even though the population grew from 70 to 100 million from 1980 to 2000. The professional and business middle class, formerly Mexico's shining achievement, is unstable and in decline, while the richest 10 percent control 50 percent of Mexico's financial and real estate assets. Mexico is now considered a paradox like Brazil, where, with so many resources, there is such a polarization of wealth. Perversely enough, Mexico is now the model state for a planned hemispheric-wide **Free Trade Area for the Americas (FTAA)**—a $13 trillion market of 34 countries and nearly 800 million people—which some regard as "NAFTA on steroids," threatening living standards across South America.

Meanwhile, a "region-state" called the *Plan Puebla de Panama* (PPP), a vast infrastructure and cheap labor zone linking the Puebla state in southern Mexico to Central America, is under construction. From the Mexican government's point of view, the PPP is an attempt to colonize its southern fringes, discipline the Zapatista rebels, and revive the failed promise of NAFTA. As Tom Hayden argues, "Relocating the crisis-ridden maquiladora industry to southern Mexico, where wages are half those of the Mexican maquilas on the US border, is a desperate effort to prevent the hemorrhage of jobs to China, where 'nimble Chinese hands,' in the words of the *Los Angeles Times*, sew and stitch for 40 cents an hour, only one-sixth of the Mexican wage."

How can this "race to the bottom," embedded in the market logic of extracting resources and profits from casualized labor, be considered at one and the same time a success and a failure?

---

*Sources: Schwedel and Haley (1992:54–55); Fenley (1991:41); Resource Center Bulletin (1993:2); Fidler and Bransten (1995); Moody (1999:133); Thompson (2002a); Jordan and Sullivan (2003); Hayden (2003).*

## The Globalization Project as a Utopia

The development project was an ideal that some say was a confidence trick or an illusion because the world economy has always rested on an exploited base or periphery;[69] others say it was a success because it was never intended to be absolute:

> Some critics make the mistake of proclaiming that development has failed. It hasn't. Development as historically conceived and officially practised has been a huge success. It sought to integrate the upper echelons, say ten to forty per cent, of a given third world population into the international, westernized, consuming classes and the global market economy. This it has accomplished brilliantly.[70]

Whatever the case, it is clear that the development project was a process wherein states *attempted* to manage national economic integration, but the integration was often incomplete. Not only did states differ regarding points of departure, degrees of corruption, and resources with which to work, but also capitalist development is inherently uneven and unequal. In addition, the fixation on industrialization marginalized rural communities and populations, and cash cropping and/or cheap food imports deepened their redundancy, propelling them into urban shantytowns. States often exploited weaker communities in their hinterlands (forest dwellers, peasants) to build dams; expand mines, plantations, and commercial farms for export revenues; or relocate other displaced peasants, justifying this action in the name of national development.

Overall, large social segments of the Third World remained on the margins or experienced dislocation as the development project took hold. In fact, only about one-fifth of the world's almost 6 billion people participate in the cash or consumer credit economy. In many ways, development has been quite limited, unequal, and undemocratic—whatever its successes and however inclusive its ideals. The globalization project intensifies these outcomes. As our case studies suggest, if there is a national integrating trend under the development project, it appears to be a national disintegrating trend under the globalization project because of a global integrating trend. But global integration is neither homogeneous nor stable.

The formation of Western welfare states involved demands for expanding citizenship rights, including political mobilization by the working classes of those nations, the demand for adequate wages, job and employment protections, and the right to organize into unions.[71] This trend has subsided recently as industrial restructuring, offshore investment, public works downsizing, labor demobilization, and rising unemployment have swept across the global North. On the other side of this process, we have seen the incorporation of new labor forces across the global South into global commodity chains. Peasant contractors, *maquila* workers, child labor, casual female and male labor, sweatshop work, plantation labor, homework, and even slave labor constitute a quite heterogeneous mix of labor in the global economy. And with TNC global sourcing and states trimming their national workforces, employment insecurity rises across the world. In short, the world market may standardize consumption, but it tends to fragment production and, in the process, disorganize producing communities. Globalization has two faces.

If this is in fact the dominant scenario under the globalization project, which is likely to become more tenuous and socially disorganized, then the globalization project looks more and more like a utopia itself. Like the development project, the globalization project is an unrealizable ideal from two angles:

- First, expectations do not square with the reality in which either project has been pursued. Neither nation-states nor the world community are singularly composed of market-oriented individuals: The social divisions of class, gender, race, and ethnicity give texture to the power relationships within which (global) development operates, as well as power to its growing countermovement, insofar as these new political identities compound its demands.
- Second, as a project privileging corporate property rights, globalization generates its own tensions, expressed in the resistance movements, deep interstate rivalries in the WTO, and intra-elite disputes that animate this corporate project. The growing fractiousness of the **Washington Consensus,**

the paralysis of the WTO's 1999 Seattle Ministerial (via combination of offense taken by the African group and the Latin/Caribbean states to the global North's exclusionary tactics and new alliances among labor and environmental justice movements) and its 2003 Cancun Ministerial (because of northern protectionism and the successful mobilization of 21 southern states), and the worldwide suspicion of neoliberal rules all reveal a deeply contradictory and conflictual state of affairs.

The globalization project is the most powerful ordering force so far, in part because it has not had to confront its contradictory effects—in that it manages and controls the role and demise of the nation-state in realizing its vision but cannot or does not admit to it. Some of these effects are spelled out in the chapters to come. But one effect alarms the inner circles of global management: the fragility of a deregulated world monetary system. While financial deregulation exerts discipline over participating countries and routinely compels some to shoulder the cost of market-induced crisis, this severely erodes legitimacy of the system.

The United States is the most indebted state in the world, but because those debts are not denominated in other currencies (since trade partners accept dollars), to date it has avoided having to tighten its financial belt under the kinds of debt management conditions laid down by the IMF. In 1994, a group called the Bretton Woods Commission, headed by former Federal Reserve Board Chairman Paul Volcker, suggested overhauling the world monetary system to tame its unstable and speculative dynamic by bringing all countries (including the United States) under IMF discipline. This is not likely since the IMF is a mechanism of exporting global discipline to weaker states in a global currency hierarchy.[72] Although the G-7 countries have attempted to stabilize the system, creating an emergency fund to bail out states on the verge of national bankruptcy, the commission stated, "There has been no reliable long-term global approach to coordinating policy, stabilizing market expectations, and preventing extreme volatility and misalignments among the key currencies."[73]

This was prescient, given the massive 1997 financial crisis in East Asia, fueled by IMF monetary fundamentalism, which left these markets exposed to destabilizing withdrawals of short-term money, deepening the crisis and its widespread social impact. The financial virus spread to Russia and Latin America, settling on Argentina at century's end with the greatest severity and revealing the bankruptcy of global financial arrangements.

Whereas the United States may be in the driver's seat in the globalization project in general, as it was in the development project, its seating arrangement is only as good as the willingness of the world to use the dollar and finance its deficits—or the U.S. unwillingness to assert its military superiority globally. The twenty-first century has seen significant reversals under way. U.S. unilateralism in Iraq unravels the legitimacy gained through participation in multilateral institution building and forces the United States to admit to its imperial relation to the world. British journalist George Monbiot observes, "This admission, in turn, forces other nations to seek to resist it. Effective resistance would create the political space in which their citizens could begin to press for a more equitable multilateralism."[74] Monbiot adds,

> Already strategists in China are suggesting that the yuan should replace the dollar as East Asia's reserve currency. The euro has started to challenge the dollar's position as the international means of payment for oil. The dollar's dominance of world trade, particularly the oil market, is all that permits the US Treasury to sustain the nation's massive deficit, as it can print inflation-free money for global circulation. If the global demand for dollars falls, the value of the currency will fall with it, and speculators will shift their assets, with the result that the US economy will begin to totter.[75]

In other words, the United States would experience the austerity associated with structural adjustment, imposed through a market "blowback" mechanism rather than by the Bretton Woods institutions. The existence of an alternative world currency, the euro, poses a potential threat to the dollar (depending on European unity, weakened by the Iraq conflict). While the United States runs a persistent trade deficit in addition to its net debtor status, Europe runs a trade surplus with the rest of the world, which owes it about $1 trillion, establishing the possibility of substituting euros for dollars and obliging the United States to stop assuming that its deficits will continue to be financed because of the dollar's international reserve currency status to date.[76]

Following the East Asian financial crisis, the G-7 came up with a proposed line of credit, making billions of dollars available to prevent attacks on currencies or markets that are spillovers from economic crises elsewhere. Global financiers such as George Soros have argued for reform of the global economy along the lines of establishing an international credit insurance corporation. Other proposals are an international central bank to coordinate international private borrowing, a "Tobin tax" (named after Nobel laureate James Tobin) on international flows of capital as friction and revenue to reduce financial collapses, or the Chilean model of imposing a one-year moratorium on capital reflux, which constitutes an effective and sufficient control on the problem of capital flight.

There are three unresolved, and perhaps unresolvable, problems:

- northern states are unwilling to have global agencies regulating their financial markets,
- there is an estimated $500 billion in offshore bank accounts in the Cayman Islands alone—beyond any institutional regulation, and
- opinions are seriously divided on the degree of market rule necessary, depending in part on one's position in the global political and currency hierarchies.

Meanwhile, China, which has been expanding while the rest of East Asia has been collapsing or shrinking, has exemplified an alternative to market rule. China is perhaps exceptional in its resource base and its reservoir of cheap labor. It is also much more autonomous: "Its currency is not freely convertible, its financial system is owned and controlled by the state, and there is relatively little foreign ownership of equities. And it does not have to take orders from the IMF."[77] But there are other countries—like Malaysia, Hong Kong, Chile, and Colombia—that, in instituting modest currency and/or capital controls to stabilize their national economies, have shown the way toward strengthening national economic sovereignty.

The ultimate issues are the following:

- whether markets should be disembedded (as in the vision of the globalization project) or embedded in social institutions,
- how the project of disembedding markets provokes resistance and visions of how to embed markets in ways that address questions of social justice, and
- whether the system of states or some other cosmopolitan arrangement[78] can develop a democratic form of governance respecting multiscale needs in sustaining humane social organization.

These issues, including the unhealthy fallout from the globalization project, are the subjects of the following chapters.

## Summary

This chapter has recounted how the development project incubated a new direction in the world capitalist order, which hatched during the 1980s debt crisis. The new direction was the globalization project, an alternative way of organizing economic growth corresponding to the growing scale and power of the transnational banks and corporations. The increasing volume of economic exchanges and the greater mobility of money and firms required forms of regulation beyond the reach of the nation-state but embedded within the system of nation-states. The WTO represents one such form of regulation.

All markets are political institutions. They require certain kinds of social regulatory mechanisms to work. When monetary exchanges began to govern European productive activity in the nineteenth century and industrial labor markets emerged, central banks and state bureaucracies stepped in to regulate and protect the value and rights of these flows of money and labor, respectively. Markets in money and labor could not work automatically. Similarly, when global money markets became dominant in the 1970s and then the flows of credit needed to be protected in the 1980s, the IMF stepped in to regulate the value of international currency.

The new global regulatory system subordinated states' social protections to financial credit protection. This new balance of power marked the transition from the development project to the globalization project. Indebted states remained viable regulators of market exchanges but only through agreeing to restructure their institutions and their priorities. They were turned inside out; that is, they downgraded their social functions of subsidizing education, health, food prices, producer credit, and other social services and upgraded their financial and commercial export ministries. Overall, with variation according to capacity and indebtedness, states became surrogate managers of the global economy (or "market states"). These tendencies are replicated in regional free trade agreements, which express goals similar to those of the globalization project by locking in the open-door provisions of the neoliberal doctrine.

The imposition of austerity measures by indebted governments deepened inequalities within their societies. Their surrender of public capacity yielded power to global corporate and financial institutions. Economic liberalization and currency devaluation heightened competition among states for credit and investment, consolidating Third World

---

### What Are the Elements of the Globalization Project?

*The globalization project combines several strands:*

- *a (Washington-based) consensus among global managers/policymakers favoring market-based rather than state-managed development strategies;*
- *centralized management of global market rules by the G-7 states;*
- *implementation of these rules through multilateral agencies (World Bank, IMF, and WTO);*
- *concentration of market power in the hands of TNCs and financial power in the hands of TNBs;*
- *subjection of all states to economic disciplines (trade, financial, labor), varying by position in the state system (North/South/East), global currency hierarchy, debt load, resource endowments, and so forth;*
- *realization of global development via new gender, race, and ethnic inequalities;*
- *a countermovement at all levels, from marginalized communities to state managers to factions even within multilateral institutions, contesting and second-guessing unbridled market rule.*

---

disunity. Structural adjustment programs required the reduction of social infrastructure, privatization of public enterprise, and deregulation of protective laws regarding foreign investment, national banking, and trade policy. And so were laid the foundations for the new globalization project, the components of which are summarized in the above insert.

The standardized prescriptions for liberalization reorganize regions and locales: from the removal of Mexican *campesinos* from long-held public lands to the rapid dismantling of public ownership of the economies of Eastern Europe to the proliferation of export processing zones and agro-export platforms. Many of these mushrooming export sites suffer the instability of flexible strategies of "footloose" firms, as they pick and choose their way among global sourcing sites. Social protections decline as communities lose their resource bases (as forests dwindle) or their employment bases (as firms downsize or move offshore).

Under these conditions, globalization is everything but universalist in its consequences. It assigns communities, regions, and nation-states new niches or specialized roles (including marginalization) in the global economy. The development project proposed social integration through national economic growth under individual state supervision and according to a social contract between government and citizenry. Alternatively, the globalization project offers new forms of authority and discipline according to the laws of the market. Whether these forms of authority and discipline are based in global institutions such as the World Trade Organization or in national institutions managing the global marketplace within their territories, they perform the governance functions of the globalization project.

# 6

# The Globalization
# Project: Disharmonies

G lobal integration is not a harmonious process. Nor is it straightfor-
ward. It is, in some ways, a form of crisis management stemming
from the demise of the development project. There are many consequences of the crisis of national developmentalism, perhaps the most
striking being the intensification of inequalities and the destabilization of
social and political institutions (from the family, through national welfare,
to multilateral organizations such as the United Nations). The United
Nations (UN) reports that the richest 20 percent of the world's population
enjoyed 30 times the income of the poorest 20 percent in 1960, but by 1997,
the difference was on the order of 74.[1] The globalization project has
inequitable foundations.

The ingredients of destabilization include the casualization of labor,
displacement of populations, food insecurity and health crises such as
AIDS, political legitimacy crises, financial market volatility, and a widening band of informal activity as people make do in lieu of stable jobs, government supports, and sustainable habitats. This will be the subject of this
chapter.

The attempt to construct a liberal economic order as the new blueprint
for global development generates its own tensions in the accumulating
instabilities and resistances that define the twenty-first-century world.
Because of this, there is a profound debate among the global managers

themselves as to the speed and direction of globalization, stimulated by the contagion of financial crisis as much as by organized opposition to, and silent rejection of, market rule. While the International Monetary Fund (IMF) is busy fighting financial fires around the world, corporate elites are busy fighting to control the discursive agenda associated with the globalization project—including such terms as *comparative advantage, free trade, sustainable development, organic farming, food security, social capital,* and *best practice.*

The existence of these tensions suggests that the globalization project, as such, does not have a lock on the future. Not only is it unstable, but also it has some of the qualities of the sorcerer's apprentice about it. It promises to intensify the transformation of social structures that we associate with the development project. Intensification does not just mean a quantitative increase; it also means qualitative changes that we can only speculate about at this point. What happens if 3 billion peasants leave the land because they cannot compete in the global grain market? Where do they go, and with what consequence? How will the "nemesis effect," whereby eroding ecosystems interact (e.g., climate change impact on forest fire cycles, feeding back on climate), fundamentally alter our material environment? And what new social arrangements and health issues might emerge via new techniques of bioengineering human and plant genetic makeup?

Proponents of globalization focus on the material prosperity of global consumers, but it is by no means clear if this trend is sustainable over the long term and/or if the global consumers will expand beyond being a minority of the world's population. It is impossible to predict the social, ecological, and political impact of transformations induced or sped up by wholesale liberalization of the global economic and political order. The future is uncertain, and it is unlikely that current bureaucratic forms of global governance will suffice to "manage" the extraordinary social and ecological changes afoot. It is already clear that the globalization project includes alternative voices in the countermovements (see Chapter 7) that contest and seek to shape its discourse and direction—how effectively is anybody's guess.

In this chapter, we consider some of the disharmonies of global integration. These are (1) the problem of displacement, (2) food insecurity, (3) informalization and marginalization, (4) AIDS, and (5) problems of governance (political and financial). These provide the stimulus to the oppositional social movements examined in Chapter 7.

# Displacement

In the shadow of globalization lurks a rising dilemma: the casualization of labor and the redundancy of people. For example, in France, the gross national product (GNP) grew by 80 percent between 1973 and 1993, but unemployment grew from 420,000 to 5.1 million.[2] This is the dilemma of structural unemployment, where automation and/or offshore relocation of work sheds stable jobs and where redundant workers cease rotating into new jobs. It is matched across the world by other forms of displacement, including forced resettlement by infrastructural projects (e.g., 1.9 million peasants will be resettled in China's Three Gorges Dam project),[3] civil wars, and the destabilization of rural communities by market forces (dumping of cheap food, corporatization of agriculture, and decline of farm subsidies).

### CASE STUDY
### Neoliberalism and Food Insecurity

In the neoliberal project, food security involves growing dependence on food importing for a large minority of southern states. By the mid-1990s, half of the foreign exchange of the Food and Agriculture Organization's (FAO's) 88 low-income food deficit countries went to food imports. Food-dependent states' food bills grew, on average, 20 percent between 1994 and 1999, despite record-low prices in the late 1990s.

In southern Africa, where 15 million face starvation currently, the official "famine" threshold has been crossed. Structural adjustment policies contribute to this condition through the promotion of export agriculture and the replacement of state marketing boards with private buyers, whose purchasing decisions are governed by profit and speculation, both of which discriminate systematically against small producers. In Zambia, those living below the poverty line rose from 69 to 86 percent between 1996 and 2001. Across Lesotho, Malawi, Mozambique, Swaziland, Zambia, and Zimbabwe, 51 percent of the population live below national poverty lines. In Lesotho, two-thirds of the population live below the poverty line. This tension, whereby "free" markets exclude and/or starve populations dispossessed as a result of their implementation, is one consequence of neoliberal policies of food security via the market.

Markets are political institutions, and their behavior depends on the policies and forces constructing them. We know that 78 percent of all mal-nourished children younger than five years of age in the global South live in food surplus countries. India, for instance, has a national food self-sufficiency program with a government-managed food supply, currently stockpiling 53 million metric tons of surplus wheat. And yet 350 million Indians starve. Why? The Indian government has privileged large Punjabi farmers (green revolution beneficiaries) by purchasing their grain at increasingly inflated prices. The high domestic price of grain is maintained by government exporting of cheap surplus grains. This practice has inflated wheat prices 30 percent since 1997, pushing consumer prices beyond the reach of the poor, just as international lenders have pressured the govern-ment to reduce food subsidies. Meanwhile, the inflated market has intensi-fied corruption, stimulating informal marketing of at least a third of the grain that should be available to the poor through the half-million "ration shops"—a public distribution system that is gradually deteriorating. In the Punjab's neighboring state of Rajasthan, villagers unable to purchase wheat are forced to eat boiled leaves or discs of bread made from grass seeds, which hastens rather than slows the march of famine-induced death.

Indian agriculture, the home of tens of millions of small farmers and a source of livelihood of 75 percent of the population, is steadily being undermined by the neoliberal policies introduced in 1991. An Indian Ministry of Agriculture booklet stated in 2000, "The growth in agriculture has slackened during the 1990s. Agriculture has become a relatively unre-warding profession due to an unfavourable price regime and low value addition, causing abandoning of farming and migration from rural areas." Corporate seed prices have inflated tenfold, and cheap imports (notably of rice and vegetable oils) have undercut local farmers and processors. Meanwhile, policies promoting agro-exports of affluent com-modities such as farmed shrimp, flowers, and meat in the name of food security increase human insecurities. Every dollar of foreign exchange earned on meat exports destroys 15 dollars' worth of ecological capital stemming from the use of farm animals in sustainable agriculture.

Under these conditions, does food security for affluent consumers via the global market have to depend on a foundation of starvation, destitution, and destruction of social and ecological sustainability?

---

*Sources: LeQuesne (1997); Murphy (1999:3); Lappé, Collins, and Rosset (1998:8–11); Patel (2002a:2); Waldman (2002:3); Paringaux (2001:4); Shiva (2000:14).*

Global economic integration intensifies displacement as governments and corporations seek to position themselves in a highly competitive marketplace. The quickened movement of the global economy stratifies populations across, rather than simply within, national borders. With provocative imagery, Jacques Attali, former president of the European Bank for Reconstruction and Development, distinguishes *rich nomads* ("consumer-citizens of the privileged regions") from *poor nomads* ("boat people on a planetary scale"):

> In restless despair, the hopeless masses of the periphery will witness the spectacle of another hemisphere's growth. Particularly in those regions of the South that are geographically contiguous and culturally linked to the North—places such as Mexico, Central America, or North Africa—millions of people will be tempted and enraged by the constant stimulation of wants that can't be satisfied. . . . With no future of their own in an age of air travel and telecommunications, the terminally impoverished will look for one in the North. . . . The movement of peoples has already begun; only the scale will grow: Turks in Berlin, Moroccans in Madrid, Indians in London, Mexicans in Los Angeles, Puerto Ricans and Haitians in New York, Vietnamese in Hong Kong.[4]

Such fears, founded in latent stereotypes, underlie the concern of the global managers and many northern consumer-citizens to stem the tide of global labor migration. This has been compounded by invoking the terrorist threat, which turns the idea of enragement from deprivation into enragement from humiliation by the West (a theme in Osama bin Laden's post–September 11 speech). Consequences range from the spread of "gated communities" and the Hummer to a rollback of civil rights in the global North.

A cursory glance at the newspapers in the global North confirms a broad anxiety about the ethnic composition of the underground global labor force, often manifested in outbreaks of racist violence toward "guest workers." This attitude has been particularly manifest in Europe, where as many as 3 million "illegal" migrants (from Eastern Europe, Turkey, Central Asia, China, and Francophone West Africa) work in restaurants, construction, and farming—they "enjoy none of the workers' rights and protections or social benefits of the state . . . are paid less than the legal wage, and are often paid late, with no legal recourse." Advocates argue that legalizing the status of the *"sans papiers"* is the most effective way of reducing xenophobia.[5] The guest worker phenomenon is not unique to the twenty-first century, and the cycles of attraction and expulsion mirror economic cycles

**Figure 6.1**    Migration of Economic Refugees

Source: United Nations Commission for Human Refugees (2000, www.unchr.ch/).

Note: Refers to refugees who fall under the mandate of the United Nations Commission for Human Refugees.

in host countries. For example, in 2002, facing an economic downturn, the Malaysian government expelled 400,000 Indonesian workers, who returned home, where 40 million remain unemployed.[6] In the global North, continuing immigration is in the interests of firms needing cheap labor and of privileged people needing servants, even though it has become the focus of cultural backlash and political fear campaigns.

---

### Migrant Labor in the Global Economy: Economic and Environmental Refugees

*In the early twenty-first century, as many as 150 million people were estimated to be living as expatriate laborers around the world. Asian women are the fastest growing group of foreign workers, increasing by 800,000 each year. There are 20 million refugees and 100 million migrants, of whom 42 million are official guest workers, and 25 million are environmental migrants, who migrate from their homelands because their natural resources have been destroyed by unregulated economic growth. Vanessa Baird notes that "in countries where some of the biggest fuss is being made about the influx of refugees, the intake is puny." In 2002, refugees in Britain accounted for just over 0.1 percent of the total population, whereas Asia and Africa receive 80 percent of the world's refugees, with Tanzania's 500,000 in 2002 eclipsing the refugees entering the United States.*

*It is predicted that environmental migration will double by the year 2010. Likely sources include the following:*

- *135 million people whose land is being desertified;*
- *900 million of the world's poorest, existing on less than a dollar a day and living in areas vulnerable to soil erosion, droughts, desertification, and floods;*
- *200 million people who may face rising sea levels due to climate change;*
- *50 million people in famine-vulnerable areas subject to climate change; and*
- *550 million people already suffering from chronic water shortage.*

Sources: Montalbano (1991:F1); Boyd (1998:17); Baird (2002:10).

## Labor: The New Export

Just as money circulates the globe, seeking investment opportunities, so labor increasingly circulates, seeking employment opportunities. Migration is of course not new to the twenty-first century. The unrelenting separation of people from the land is etched into the making of the modern world. Colonialism propelled migrations of free and unfree people across the world. Between 1810 and 1921, 34 million people, mainly Europeans, immigrated to the United States alone. The difference today, perhaps, is in the feminization of global migration: 75 percent of refugees and displaced persons are women and children.[7]

During the 1980s, spurred by debt regime restructurings, there was an internal migration in the former Third World of between 300 and 400 million people.[8] This pool of labor, then, contributes to current levels of global migration from overburdened cities to metropolitan regions as migrants seek to earn money for families back home. Estimates suggest that roughly 100 million kinfolk depend on remittances of the global labor force. In the 1990s, for example, two-thirds of Turkey's trade deficit was financed by remittances from Turks working abroad. In 2001, Bangladeshi workers in Southeast Asia or the Middle East sent home $2 billion, the second largest source of foreign exchange after garment exports. Mexico, a nation of 100 million, earns more than $9 billion a year in remittances— almost as much as India, which has a population of 1 billion. And Latin America and the Caribbean received $25 billion in 2002 from remittances, which, along with foreign direct investment, are now more important sources of finance than private lending there.[9]

The significance of the remittance stream has not been lost on the home governments. The influx of foreign exchange not only supplies much-needed hard currency, but in an era of structural adjustment and privatization, remittance money supplements or subsidizes public ventures. Thus, in Indonesian villages, remittances finance schools, roads, and housing in lieu of public funding. Migrants recently invested $6 million in new roads, schools, churches, water systems, and parks in Zacatecas, Mexico, and President Fox commented, "The families that receive the money use it to buy shoes or beans, clothes, or books for their children. Now we want to channel part of that money for production for projects that generate jobs," matching, peso for peso, money remitted by migrant workers for public works projects in their home communities.[10]

Spurred by debt, labor export has become a significant foreign currency earner: Filipino overseas earnings are estimated to amount to

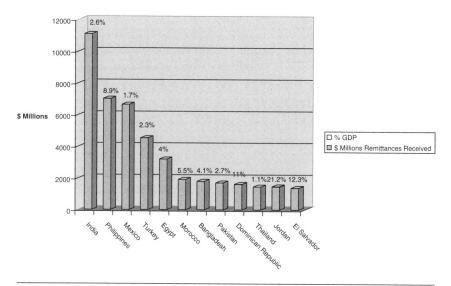

**Figure 6.2**    Top 12 Developing Country Receivers of Remittances, 1999

Sources: International Monetary Fund (2001); World Bank (2000a).

$5.7 billion, for example. About 6 million Filipinos, increasingly rural, work overseas in 130 countries as contract workers (seamen, carpenters, masons, mechanics, or maids).[11] The government of the Philippines has a de facto labor export policy, part of an export-led development strategy.[12] That is, in addition to products, labor is exported, mainly to the oil-rich Middle East, where contractors organize the ebb and flow of foreign labor. One contractor, Northwest Placement, a privately run recruiting agency, receives 5,000 pesos ($181)—the maximum allowed by the Labor Department—from Filipino applicants on assurance of a job; this covers the costs of a medical check, visas, and government clearance fees. Not surprisingly, there are plenty of unlicensed agencies operating also.[13]

### CASE STUDY
### Trafficking in Women: The Global Sex Trade versus Human Rights

Human trafficking is the fastest growing form of bonded labor in today's global market and the leading human rights violation. It is estimated that

700,000 to 2 million women and children are trafficked annually and that there are about 10 million trafficked people working at risk. After drug smuggling and gun running, human trafficking is the third largest illegal trade (annual profit of about $6 billion). Child trafficking already dwarfs the trans-Atlantic slave trade at its peak, by a magnitude of 10. Some destinations are farming, restaurant labor, domestic servitude, fishing, mail-order brides, market stall labor, shop work, and the sex trade.

Human rights exploitation of trafficked people, who lack legal status and language skills, is easy and widespread. This is particularly so for women, who constitute the majority of migrant labor from Asia today: Since 1990, about 30 million women and children have been trafficked for prostitution and sweatshop labor. The rise in trafficking is directly related to the global feminization of poverty and the use of the Internet as a sex forum.

In Thailand, female emigration took off in the 1980s, as the East Asian boom disrupted cultural traditions and family livelihoods. Young women flooded into Bangkok from the Thai countryside, looking for income to remit to their villages. Many of these women would end up in Europe, Southeast Asia, the United States, Australia, South Africa, or the Arabian Gulf in the burgeoning sex industry by deceit or by choice (being a relatively high-income trade open to uneducated women). Evidence suggests that sex tourism to Thailand contributed to the demand for Thai women overseas. By 1993, there were almost 100,000 Thai women working in the Japanese sex industry and 5,000 in Berlin alone. Research in northern Thailand has shown that about 28 percent of household income was remitted by absent daughters. A common motive is relieving poverty and debt (especially now in the wake of the Asian financial crisis), and often parents sell their daughters to agents for a cash advance to be paid off by work in the global sex industry. Alternatively, individual women pay an agent's fee of around $500. From then on, women are devoid of human rights: They work as bonded labor, are subject to arrest for illicit work and illegal residence, have no rights to medical or social services overseas, are forced to sell sex with no power to choose their customers or service, remain at high risk of contracting HIV, and are targets of racial discrimination and public humiliation if arrested.

Action against trafficking is difficult because of the collusion between families who benefit materially from absent daughters and agents of the trade; because of the underground lifestyle of the women, trapped by underground employers; and because national governments have an interest in suppressing information about the sex trade to avoid adverse publicity. Karen Booth's use of the contradictory gender ideology in the nation-state system between "national mother" (women's political and cultural value as constructed within the nation and community) and "global whore" (women's value as constructed in the international market) is relevant to this impasse.

How can global human rights agencies address the trafficking tragedy when governments are reluctant to intervene against this lucrative source of foreign exchange into their national economies?

*Sources: "Slavery in the 21st Century" (2001:18); Booth (1998); Skrobanek, Boonpakdi, and Janthakeero (1997:13-31, 68, 103); Worden (2001); Pyle (2001).*

International labor circulation combines formal policies with decidedly informal working conditions. Migrant workers routinely lack human rights. Workers in the Gulf states, for example, are indentured, with no civic rights, no choice of alternative jobs, and no recourse against poor employment conditions and low wages—which are determined by the income levels of the country of origin. Migrant workers must surrender their passports on arrival; they reportedly work 12 to 16 hours a day, seven days a week. Governments in the migrant workers' home countries in Asia, dependent on foreign currency earnings, are reportedly resigned to the exploitation of their nationals. International labor union organizations have been ineffectual, especially as Middle Eastern states have united to suppress discussion in international forums of working conditions inside their countries.[14]

In the United States, labor comes from all over the world, principally Mexico (around 60 percent in 1990), Asia (22.1 percent), Europe (7.3 percent), South America (5.6 percent), and Africa (2.3 percent). About 33 percent of the population of Los Angeles County is foreign born, a number that has tripled since 1970. "Latinos, now 28 percent of California's population, will likely be the majority by 2040."[15] The scale is large enough that immigrants retain their cultural and linguistic traditions rather than assimilate— Robert Reich comments that "the old American 'melting pot' is now cooking a variegated stew, each of whose ingredients maintains a singular taste."[16] Increasingly, given the scale of labor migration, minority cultures are forming identifiable communities in their new labor sites, maintaining a certain distance from the local culture. The inhabitants of these "transnational communities" have regular contact with their sending countries and other migrant communities through modern electronic communication and remit part of their income to families left behind.

The juxtaposing of distinct cultures in countries to which labor migrates creates this *multicultural* effect. The United States took a turn in this direction in 1965, when the Immigration and Nationality Act amendments abolished the previous policy of organizing immigration according to the already established patterns of cultural origin. "During the 1950s there were nine times as many European immigrants as there were Asians. Following the passage of the new Immigration Act, the proportions were sharply reversed."[17] However, in the context of economic restructuring in the United States, a heightened "nativism" is appearing— a backlash response to rising economic uncertainties. Since 1965, the polled percentage of Americans objecting to immigration has almost doubled—from 33 percent to 60 percent.[18]

 **CASE STUDY**
**Multiculturalism and Its Contradictions**

In France, the question of multiculturalism has been tested recently with the growing presence of the more than 3.5 million Muslims living in that country. Muslims comprise a quarter of the total immigrant population (mostly from European countries). Their presence stems from a French policy to import large numbers of North African men for factory and construction work from the 1960s through 1974, after which families were allowed to join the men. Arab and African immigrants and their French-born children form an increasingly distinct suburban underclass in French society. A principal of a Parisian school with a large immigrant population remarked, "In the 1970s and 1980s, we promoted multiculturalism. We had a day of couscous, a day of paella, it was 'vive la différence' much of the time. Now the pendulum is going the other way."

France has more than 1,000 *banlieues sensibles* ("sink estates") in which immigrants from a variety of cultures are crowded into high-rise, run-down ghettos—built originally in the 1960s and 1970s to house immigrant workers. Unemployment among 20- to 29-year-olds of North African origin runs at about 40 percent, compared with 10 percent for youths of French origin. Rampant street crime fans French fears, generating 6 million votes for the arch-conservative National Front leader, Jean-Marie Le Pen, in the 2002 presidential elections. Yasser Amri, a successful graduate of one of the largest council estates, commented, "It's the end of the republican ideal. The French republic deals with citizens, not individuals. But here, people aren't citizens. They don't know what they are. Not Algerian, or Moroccan or West African, but not French citizens either. They're unrecognised, unremembered, and unrepresented. No wonder they rebel."

Meanwhile, Tunisian-born French entrepreneur Tawfik Mathlouthi has sold more than 2 million Mecca-Colas, a new soft drink capitalizing on antipathy toward America's Middle-Eastern foreign policy, especially among Muslims. The label, "Don't drink stupid, drink committed," refers to the 10 percent of the profits earmarked for a Palestinian children's charity. Originally targeted at Muslim neighborhoods, Mecca is now stocked by a major hypermarket chain in the northern suburbs of Paris.

Why is it that representations of globalization use images of a homogeneous global market culture, rather than revealing the cultural tensions arising from the inequalities through which the project of globalization is realized?

---

*Sources: Riding (1993); Henley (2003:3); Henley and Vasagar (2003:3).*

The circulation of cultures of labor binds the world through multiculturalism. However, the conditions in which labor circulation has intensified have made multiculturalism a fragile ideal. Labor export arrangements deny rights and representation to the migrant workforce. Deteriorating economies and communities in the centers of the global economy spark exclusionist politics that scapegoat cultural minorities. In the days of the development project, a more inclusive attitude prevailed, rooted in broad-based class movements and political coalitions more committed to assimilation and the redistribution of resources. In the present context, inclusion is threatened by separatist politics. The race to the bottom is not just about wage erosion. It is also about growing intolerance for difference.

## Informal Activity

The globalization project is Janus-faced. It exaggerates the market culture at the same time as it intensifies its opposite—a growing culture of informal, or marginal, activity. This culture involves people working on the fringes of the market, performing casual and unregulated labor, working in cooperative arrangements, street vending, or pursuing what are deemed illegal economic activities. This culture did not just appear, however. With the rise of market societies, the boundaries of the formal economy were identified and regulated by the state for tax purposes, but they have always been incomplete and fluid, often by design and certainly by custom. An army of servants and housecleaners, for example, routinely works "off the books." Casual labor has always accompanied small-scale enterprise and even large-scale harvesting operations where labor use is cyclical. Also, a substantial portion of labor performed across the world every day is unpaid labor—such as housework and family farm labor.

It is somewhat artificial, then, to distinguish between a formal economy with its legal/moral connotations and an informal sector with its illegal or immoral connotations. They are often intimately connected and mutually conditioning. Economists make the distinction because their profession is defined by the measurement of monetary transactions considered to be the foundation of national accounting, which in turn is a convenient tool of state power (even if such measurement ignores and indeed marginalizes a substantial part of social activity). We continue to make the distinction here because it helps to illuminate the limits of official, formal development strategy, on the one hand, and to identify alternative, informal livelihood strategies, on the other.

Our point is that those who are bypassed or marginalized by development often form a culture parallel to the market culture. There is, of course, a question as to whether this informal culture is a real alternative or simply an impoverished margin of the formal culture. This may be an issue of scale, or it may depend on the context. For example, withdrawal from the formal economy in the countryside may revive subsistence farming that represents an improvement in living standards over working as a rural laborer or existing on the urban fringe, as long as land is available. The scale of marginalized populations grows as peasants lose their land to commercial/export agriculture and as workers lose jobs through structural unemployment. These trends are often connected, so that informalization stems from expanded formal economic activity or the concentration of resources in fewer corporate hands.

One source of the quite dramatic expansion of the informal sector has been the hyperurbanization in the global South, where more than 50 percent of the population is involved in informal activity. Agricultural modernization routinely expels peasants and rural labor from secure rural livelihoods; they migrate to urban centers where, as they hear on the radio and through migrant networks, jobs and amenities are available. One account of this trend is given by Hernando de Soto, a libertarian critic of development:

> Quite simply, Peru's legal institutions had been developed over the years to meet the needs and bolster the privileges of certain dominant groups in the cities and to isolate the peasants geographically in rural areas. As long as this system worked, the implicit legal discrimination was not apparent. Once the peasants settled in the cities, however, the law began to lose social relevance. The migrants discovered that their numbers were considerable, that the system was not prepared to accept them, that more and more barriers were being erected against them, that they had to fight to extract every right from an unwilling establishment, that they were excluded from the facilities and benefits offered by the law. . . . In short, they discovered that they must compete not only against people but also against the system. Thus it was, that in order to survive, the migrants became informals.[19]

In effect, development and marginalization go together. Of course, these *peri-urban* communities, as they are known, have been expanding throughout the twentieth century: The urban South grew from 90 million in 1900 to 2 billion in 2000, with increases of 109 percent in Africa, 50 percent in Latin America, and 65 percent in Asia. Between 1990 and 1995, southern urban populations grew by 263 million—the equivalent of a Shanghai or a Los Angeles every month. The global South's share of world urban population increased from 39 to 63 percent between 1950 and 1990, and in 2006, it will exceed 50 percent.[20]

With global integration, the lines are drawn even more clearly, on a larger scale, and possibly more rapidly. There are professional and managerial classes who participate within global circuits (involved with products, money, electronic communications, high-speed transport) linking enclaves of producers/consumers across state borders. Many of these people increasingly live and work within corporate domains. For the United States, Robert Reich termed this the *secession of the successful*, meaning the top fifth of income earners in America, who "now inhabit a different economy from other Americans. The new, *Fast World* elite is linked by jet, modem, fax, satellite and fiber-optic cable to the great commercial and recreational centers of the world, but it is not particularly connected to the rest of the nation."[21] And there are those whom these circuits bypass or indeed displace. These are the redundant labor forces, the structurally unemployed, the marginals, who live in shantytowns and urban ghettos or

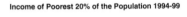

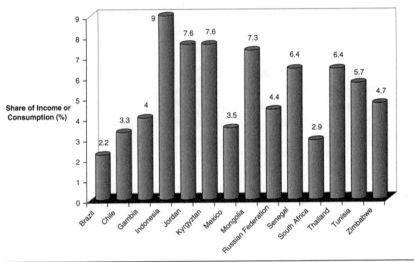

**Figure 6.3**     Income of Poorest 20 Percent of Populations of Selected
Countries, 1994–1999

Source: World Bank, *World Development Indicators*, 2002.

circulate the world. Given our definition, many of these people are part of the global labor force, even if unaccounted for by government measures—in fact, much of the global market depends on informal, unregulated labor.

Informalization is not new, but under the project of globalization, it has some different facets. One facet is the industrial decay or downsizing that occurs as the global labor market comes into play. The labor expelled in this process is quite distinct from first-generation peasants forced to leave the land. Middle-class people are now entering the ranks of the structurally unemployed daily across the global North. Another is the sheer exclusivity of the globalization project, where marginalization is a structural outcome of the shift toward privileging private, rather than public, investment, which seeks profitable outlets and shuns poverty. Joseph Kahn reported from a G-7 meeting in Mexico in 2002, "Perhaps aside from China, the only country that appears to have benefited unambiguously from the trend toward open markets world-wide is the United States, where a huge inflow of capital has helped allow Americans to spend more than they save, and to import more than they export."[22] Soon after, the UN issued the *Least Development Countries Report, 2002*, claiming that for the poorest 49 countries, the "current form of globalisation is tightening rather than loosening the international poverty trap," noting that living standards were lower now than they were 30 years ago.[23] And former European Member of Parliament James Goldsmith reported the following to a 1994 U.S. Senate inquiry, anticipating the mass displacement of peasants under a World Trade Organization (WTO) regime:

> The application of GATT [General Agreement on Trade and Tariffs] will also cause a great tragedy in the third world. Modern economists believe that an efficient agriculture is one that produces the maximum amount of food for the minimum cost, using the least number of people. . . . It is estimated that there are still 3.1 billion people in the world who live from the land. If GATT manages to impose worldwide the sort of productivity achieved by the intensive agriculture of nations such as Australia, then it is easy to calculate that about 2 billion of these people will become redundant. Some of these GATT refugees will move to urban slums. But a large number of them will be forced into mass migration. . . . We will have profoundly and tragically destabilized the world's population.[24]

## Informalization

Economic and environmental refugees enlarge the social weight of informal activities across the world. Informalization involves two related *processes*: the casualization of labor via corporate restructuring and the development of new forms of individual and collective livelihood strategies. The latter have recently become the target of World Bank and nongovernmental organization (NGO)–driven schemes, which view such informal networking as **social capital** to be "developed." Informalization (understood as a social movement of sorts) reputedly first defined the consolidation of informal activity in Africa in the 1970s, a trend that grew out of successive development failures.[25]

Informal activity has been viewed as an alternative society or set of social institutions, rather than simply an invisible economic reality that is negative or antistate. The state view of informals is negative by definition. Informals—for example, women performing unwaged work—are perceived by planners as beyond the formal realm of official statistics and, by definition, unproductive. Such negative description parallels common First World perceptions of Third World people. According to Arturo Escobar, non-European people often tend to be perceived by what they lack—capital, entrepreneurship, organization and political conscience, education, political participation, infrastructure, and rationality.[26] This perception underlay the assumptions of the development project, and it continues to prejudice understanding of this exploding other world. The positive description of the informal economy transcends the notion that informalization represents simply an antistate movement. For Fantu Cheru, the withdrawal of African peasants from a failing formal economy, including paying taxes, represents a "silent revolution." Exiting was the choice for producers and workers consistently bypassed by state policies. Self-defense "has required the resuscitation of rural co-operatives, traditional caravan trade across borders, catering services and other activities that had once fallen into disuse, depriving the state of the revenue that traditionally financed its anti-people and anti-peasant development policies."[27]

### CASE STUDY

### Informalization versus the
### African State: The Other Side of "Globalization"

Aili Mari Tripp views the elaboration of new rules of the game in the burgeoning informal sector across Africa as a form of resistance. Viewing informalization as more than a passive outcome of state or corporate restructuring, she focuses on the creative ways in which Africans have responded to the failure of development states, exacerbated by more than a decade of structural adjustment. Urban farming has proliferated in the absence of food subsidies, such that 68 percent of families in Dar es Salaam, Tanzania, now grow their own vegetables and raise livestock. Noncompliance with the state has generated new institutional resources in Tanzania:

> Hometown development associations became visible in the late 1980s as urban dwellers sought to provide assistance to the rural towns from which they originated. They used these associations to build schools, orphanages, libraries, roads, and clinics; to establish projects to conserve the environment; to provide solar electricity and water; to disburse soft loans to women's groups engaged in business; and to raise funds for flood relief and other such causes. These new associations resemble the early, ethnically based welfare and burial societies that formed in Dar es Salaam in the early 1900s to help new migrants adjust to city life, except that their focus today is to assist people in their rural towns and villages.

In addition to these new resources, traditional resources such as midwifery and craftwork are revived, often undertaken by women. And new activities—from street vending, pastry selling, and hairbraiding, to exporting seaweed—have sprung up. In some cases, informal businesses have become so successful in monetary terms that they have moved into the formal sector (e.g., in flour milling, dry cleaning, and prawn farming). The phenomenon of informalization combines individualistic market economy behavior as well as "moral economy," where community interests, rather than markets, define the values shaping economic activity.

In Tanzania, the cultural weight of informalization led to the 1991 Zanzibar Declaration, which acknowledged the legitimacy and social necessity of informal activities, outside of official corruption.

Is it possible to argue that informalization not only shapes some aspects of the formal economy but also reshapes the state, as a set of civil relationships? And is this a new form of development?

---

*Sources: Tripp (1997:13, 127, 188); O'Meara (1999:34).*

In addition to the marginalizing dynamic, informalization has gained prominence because people are disenchanted with the economic models associated with the development and globalization projects. The discovery of survival strategies among the poor and dispossessed has become an academic industry. Activists are finding these communities to be sources of hope rather than despair. Ivan Illich, for example, notes that "up to now, economic development has always meant that people, instead of doing something, are instead enabled to buy it."[28] He finds that "development castaways" constitute a proliferating culture of alternatives. Meanwhile, an NGO, Community and Institutional Development (CID), works in Cairo with informal-sector operators, whose microenterprise recycles 3,000 tons of household garbage daily, creating jobs for 40,000 people—the goal being to construct partnerships among poor communities, the private sector, donors, the Egyptian government, and alternative trading organizations as a tool for development.[29]

Serge LaTouche views the informal as

comprehensive strategies of response to the challenges that life poses for displaced and uprooted populations in peri-urban areas. These are people torn between lost tradition and impossible modernity. The sphere of the informal has, incontestably, a major economic significance. It is characterised by a neo-artisanal activity that generates a lot of employment and produces incomes comparable to those of the modern sector. . . . Resolving practical problems of living spaces and daily life has all sorts of economic ramifications, so much so that the practical importance of the "informal economy" is no longer a matter of debate. Some 50–80% of the population in the urban areas of these countries live in and from the informal, one way or another.[30]

The "lost decade" intensified pressures to consolidate new livelihood strategies in already overburdened cities. In Latin America, whereas formal employment rose by 3.2 percent annually in the 1980s, informal jobs rose at more than twice that rate. Presently, about a third of urban jobs in Asia and Latin America and more than half in Africa are estimated to be informal. And it is estimated that 90 percent of Eastern European computer software is illegally produced.[31] Among the poor in urban Mexico, collective pooling of resources to acquire land, shelter, and basic public services (water, electricity) was one widespread strategy for establishing networks among friends and neighbors to build their own cheap housing.[32] And in Brazil, working poor volunteerism, often organized by the church, proliferates: Between 1988 and 1998, volunteer organizations increased from 1,041 to 4,000, addressing adult literacy, child shelters, and day care. In a society only two decades away from military rule, the president of the Volunteer Centre of São Paulo remarked, "We understand that we have a role to play as citizens, and that's a new thing for Brazilians."[33]

Many different strategies contribute to the *culture of the new commons*, a social inventiveness arising on the fringes of industrial society and drawing on traditional collective interaction to allow people to make ends meet. Mexican intellectual Gustavo Esteva observes,

> Peasants and grassroots groups in the cities are now sharing with people forced to leave the economic centre the ten thousand tricks they have learned to limit the economy, to mock the economic creed, or to refunctionalize and reformulate modern technology. The "crisis" of the 1980s removed from the payroll people already educated in dependency on incomes and the market people lacking the social setting enabling them to survive by themselves. Now the margins are coping with the difficult task of relocating these people. The process poses great challenges and tensions for everyone, but it also offers a creative opportunity for regeneration.[34]

## Growth and Marginalization

The globalization project involves a growth/marginalization dynamic, so informalization and the culture of the new commons may spread as more and more regions across the world decay from neglect. The neglect has two sources. First is the incapacity of debt-stressed governments to support communities that do not contribute to the global project. Weaker regions of the world have no real channels of representation. And they attract attention from investors only by making themselves weaker through further structural adjustment. Poorer states, with borrowed funds earmarked to promote exports to service debt, are unable to subsidize sectors and communities on the margins. In sub-Saharan Africa, total debt servicing amounts to four times the amount spent on health and education.[35] However, the global North is not immune to this fiscal stress—the United States continues to confront its rising debt burden by cutting social services, and the European states have diminished their social contract in preparation for monetary union.

Second, the hallmark of a liberal market regime is polarization. Cross-border investment continues to concentrate in the markets of the three superregions—the United States, Europe, and Japan (the "triad")—more than one-third of such investment worldwide.[36] Of the 45 countries at the bottom of the Human Development Index, 35 are sub-Saharan African. Africa has been described as a "lost continent," where the daily caloric intake is below that of Mexico or China by a third or more, and "340 million people, or half the population, live on less than US$1 per day. . . . Only 58 percent of the population have access to safe water. The rate of illiteracy for people over 15 is 41 percent. There are only 18 mainline telephones per 1000 people in Africa, compared with 146 for the world as a whole and 567 for high-income countries."[37] Child mortality below age 5 is 174 in 1,000, compared to a world average of 89 in 1,000, and the survivors confront pneumonia, tuberculosis, malaria, and an exploding AIDS epidemic that is devastating lives and the continent's financial resources.[38]

## CASE STUDY
## The Global AIDS Crisis

Worldwide, 36 million people are infected with HIV, 70 percent of them in sub-Saharan Africa, 16 percent in South and Southeast Asia, and almost 3 percent in Latin America. In South Africa, 20 percent of adults are infected, and in 2003, there were approximately 15 million orphans. Africa has lost 12 million people from AIDS, more deaths than those in recent wars, and every day, 11,000 more cases are diagnosed.

The AIDS/poverty cycle is vicious: The erosion of subsistence agriculture removes protections against hunger, poverty renders the body more susceptible, and AIDS impoverishes many of its victims, reducing adult life expectancy and its role in generational cycles of caregivers and producers within families. At the national level, projected negative impacts of HIV/AIDS on the gross domestic product (GDP) of selected countries are as follows: 14 percent in Kenya, 19 percent in Tanzania, 7 percent in Zambia, and 6 percent in Zimbabwe.

Responses to AIDS are instructive. UN Secretary-General Kofi Annan calls, perhaps instrumentally, for corporate donations: "As AIDS creates more poverty and deepens inequalities, it fuels the growing public backlash against globalization." In five of the world's most populous nations (Russia, Ethiopia, China, Nigeria, and India), the rapid spread of the HIV virus has been declared by the United States a security threat as it could harm national economic, social, political, and military structures. Governments individualize the problem to homosexuals or to female promiscuity and focus on preventing men from being infected. South African men believe AIDS is curable through sex with virgins, and Indian males buy sex with younger girls, considering them to be safer. In Calcutta, the state absolves itself from responsibility for infected girls sold to trafficking networks. This "global whore" syndrome is the double standard by which patriarchal states (fostering a paternalistic "national mother" syndrome) ignore the needs of women who (are forced to) work in the sex trade.

In South Africa, the Treatment Action Campaign (TAC), which spearheads the campaign for affordable medicine for HIV-related illnesses (joined by Médecins Sans Frontières and Oxfam), accused the Mbeki government in 2001 of "failure . . . to act with courage, humility and urgency."

After a three-year struggle, 39 pharmaceutical transnational corporations (TNCs) were shamed (largely by the mobilizing efforts of TAC) into settling a suit *they* brought against the South African government to prevent it from purchasing brand-name drugs from third parties at cheapest possible rates.

The typical antiretroviral AIDS drug cocktail costs U.S.$10,000 to $15,000—beyond the reach of a large proportion of HIV carriers in the global South. Large countries, such as India, Egypt, Thailand, Argentina, and Brazil, manufacture cheap generic drugs (around $600) to make medicines affordable. Brazil has a model public health infrastructure geared to delivery of medicines and educating people how to practice the triple therapy involved. But these practices are challenged by pharmaceutical TNCs, citing infringements of the WTO Trade-Related Intellectual Property Rights (TRIPs) protocol, which guarantees patent protection for at least 20 years. A loophole, allowing countries to manufacture or import generic drugs for national health emergencies, challenged for several years by the companies and the United States, was ratified by the WTO in August 2003. However, Doctors Without Borders noted that U.S. conditions that countries first prove public health needs would severely limit the utility of the agreement because of the daunting bureaucratic procedures. Not only were commercial drugs largely developed with public funding and then patented by firms that spend twice as much on marketing as on research and development, but Africa, which has 80 percent of the world's AIDS patients, comprises just 1 percent of the market for the big four: Merck, Pfizer, GlaxoSmithKline, and Eli Lilly. Drug company average profit margins, more than 30 percent, are one of the highest in the world. Meanwhile, only 10 percent of the annual global health research budget targets diseases such as malaria, tuberculosis, and HIV/AIDS, which account for 90 percent of global health problems, while profitable health problems (e.g., obesity is the new El Dorado for the pharmaceutical industry) gains most attention.

In times of health crises, or indeed at any time, should intellectual property rights be used to subordinate public rights to corporate rights?

---

*Sources: Central Intelligence Agency (2000); Elliott (2001:12); Le Carre (2001:12–13); Gevisser (2001:5–6); Perlez (2001:A1); Altman (2002:A12); Ayittey (2002); Médecins Sans Frontières Web site (www.msf.org); Guardian Weekly (November 21–27, 2000:14); De Waal (2002:23); Booth (1998); Stuart (2003:21); Becker (2003:14).*

African countries have submitted to structural adjustment programs over the past two decades, with comparatively little financial aid. The Heavily Indebted Poor Countries (HIPC) debt relief package, instituted by the IMF and the World Bank in 1996, targeted 40-odd countries, 32 of which are African. Conditionality included demonstrating six years of prudent fiscal management. At the turn of the twenty-first century, failure of this initiative to spur growth or relieve poverty led to the Bank admitting failure to make Africa's foreign debt "sustainable" and to the G-8

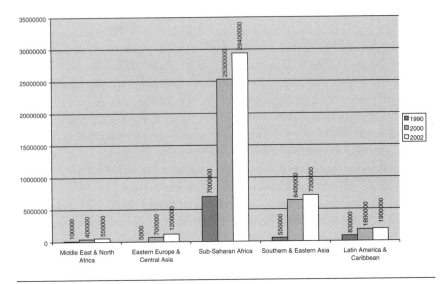

**Figure 6.4**    Number of People with HIV/AIDS, 1990–2002

Sources: www.avert.org; www.unicef.org/sowc02/g32.htm (2002).

countries shortening the six-year demonstration, requiring that aid be spent on education and health (although without the ability to ensure compliance).[39]

Meanwhile, in response to complaints by African politicians that large multilateral aid flowed quickly into Asia following the 1997 financial crisis, the IMF and World Bank admitted that their assistance to Asia reflected that region's greater significance to the global financial system.[40] By 1997, the World Bank's *Development Report* was highlighting the decay of the African state, despite the Bank's contribution to this outcome through policies to shrink states that lead to neglect of education, erosion of infrastructure and institutional capacity, and rising unemployment.[41]

The New Partnership for African Development (NEPAD), an African initiative agreed to by the Washington Consensus in 2002, continues this policy, urging African leaders to promote "democracy and human rights in their respective countries . . . [while simultaneously] instituting transparent legal and regulatory frameworks for financial markets."[42] Capital flight from every African country to open up its financial markets is endemic, with regular appeals to unknown non-Africans (including this author, who rejects the money) to participate in multimillion dollar capital flight schemes. Patrick Bond notes, "Africa's continued poverty ('marginalization') is a direct outcome of excess globalisation, not of insufficient globalisation, because of the drain from ever declining prices of raw materials (Africa's main exports), crippling debt repayments and profit repatriation to transnational corporations."[43] Nevertheless, foreshadowing the formation of the **African Union** in 2002, chaired by South African President Thabo Mbeki, NEPAD continues to promote neoliberal economic policies, offering Africa to the global elite in a poverty alleviation strategy:

> The continued marginalisation of Africa from the globalisation process and the social exclusion of the vast majority of its peoples constitute a serious threat to global stability. . . . We readily admit that globalisation is a product of scientific and technological advances, many of which have been market-driven. . . . The locomotive for these major advances is the highly industrialised nations.[44]

NEPAD commits African states to "good governance," from liberalization to peer review of human rights abuses and corruption, as a condition for financial support from the global North. Citing the failure of African states to condemn the excesses of the Mugabe government of Zimbabwe, Muna Ndulo argues that since Africa will be not able to deliver on the governance or peer review issues, "Western countries have a perfect excuse now for not delivering on NEPAD."[45]

## Legitimacy Crisis and Neoliberalism

As governments incorporate mechanisms of global governance into their administrative practices, they compromise their sovereignty and their representative role in transferring national powers upwards to the multilaterals. The globalization project intensifies a political **legitimacy crisis** as citizens lose faith in their government or its policies. Global governance erodes national sovereignty via foreign ownership of essential public resources, through the undoing of political coalitions formed around national development projects, to the dismantling of social services provided by governments to their needier populations. All these trends erode the social contract, whereby governments commit to protect civil rights and social entitlements (health, education, unemployment protection, welfare), compromising government legitimacy.

Of course, legitimacy problems are not the creation solely of the globalization project. They have profound historical roots in the disorganizing legacy of colonialism, carried into the postcolonial era when independent states struggled to develop coherent societies and economies in a global order dependent on sustaining natural resource exports to, and emerging markets for, the First World. Military aid protected this order, and governments embracing the development project privileged urban-industrial sectors.

In Africa, for example, *urban bias* channeled wealth away from the rural sector, inflating public works in the cities at the expense of the agricultural sector. While urban bias was common across the Third World, it was amplified in Africa by state patronage systems constructed during colonialism on the basis of artificial tribal hierarchies.[46] Such bifurcated power, between the centralized modern state and a "tribal authority which dispensed customary law to those living within the territory of the tribe," conditioned the current failure of African states, where neoliberalism overlays and enlarges often despotic (and ethnically based) rural social control.[47] This structure of power has facilitated the exploitation of rural areas by urban elites, enriched by foreign investment in resource extraction. For example, Kinshasa, the capital of Zaire, a "giant spider at the hub of a subcontinental web, acted as an 'overwhelming suction pump' absorbing all attainable rural resources as well as whatever might be milked from foreign donors and investors." Citizens disengage from such illegitimate political systems, pursuing informal activities such as currency exchanging, smuggling, and bartering, called by Ghanian President Rawlings the "culture of silence."[48]

*Militarization*, through aid packages from the cold war superpowers and through choices made by military or authoritarian regimes, diverted scarce funds from developmental programs. Between 1960 and 1987, military spending in the Third World rose almost three times as fast as in the First World, as the Third World more than doubled its share of global military spending—from 7 to 15 percent. Meanwhile, the Third World's share of global income stayed below 5 percent. In 1992, 18 Third World countries devoted more to military spending than to their education and health budgets, and 8 of these were among the world's poorest nations.[49] But these spending decisions reflect far more than the diversion of resources. The militarization of societies has vast consequences. Basic human rights and potential civil rights suffer in states whose regimes exercise terror and intimidation of their subject populations. Legitimacy is always compromised in states that rule through coercion rather than consent. If governments were balancing their developmental needs with security needs in a hostile world, then coercion (and military aid) was more readily justified. And there will be more of this in the so-called "age of terrorism."

## Governance Reforms

Governance reform is a key consequence of structural adjustment. This prescription was articulated in the World Bank's influential report in 1989, *Sub-Saharan Africa: From Crisis to Sustainable Growth:* "Africa needs not just less government by better government—government that concentrates its efforts less on direct [economic] interventions and more on enabling others to be productive."[50] The goal is to use liberalization to eliminate the one-party state, releasing entrepreneurial forces at all levels of society. This is the political side of the globalization project. This view, of course, matured under the conditions of the debt regime. Subsequently, the World Bank discovered the importance of the strong development state as the secret of the East Asian "miracle" and titled its 1997 *World Development Report* "The State in a Changing World."[51] In that report, the decaying African state was identified as a problem, given the Asian experience. Of course, Africa is not Asia, and development discourse routinely forgets that cultural and historical circumstances make a world of difference, so to speak. East Asian development states, for one thing, rested on a reciprocal authoritarianism, embedded in the norms of Confucianism, that sustained capitalist development in this strategic region. African geopolitics and historical cultures differ markedly.

African states inherited complex power structures from the colonial experience. European colonization combined forms of urban power directly excluding natives from civil freedoms on racial grounds, as well as forms of rule in the countryside via a reconstruction of tribal authority to rule natives indirectly. With decolonization, independence abolished racial discrimination and affirmed civil freedoms, but it also divided power within the new nation-states according to the artificial tribal constructs (ethnic, religious, regional) established during colonial rule.[52] The vulnerability of African politics stems from inheriting a centralized state and its patronage networks (common to all states), as well as a "tribalization" of politics—which reasserted itself with a vengeance in the 1990s.

When African governments were compelled to shrink the state via global governance, the growing scarcity of resources became the pivot on which political conflict, represented in racialized and/or ethnicized terms, turned. This is not to say that beneath the veneer of the African nation-state lies a primordial tribalism, which is how the tragedy of African politics is often presented. It is to say that historically, African states have been segmented in ethnicized terms. When political order erodes and resources disappear, ensuing conflict takes ethnic form because power hierarchies and political identities are structured in ethnic terms. In this way, ethnic identity organizes political conflict and undermines a politics of inclusion that is associated with Western liberal democracy, as the following case study suggests.

### CASE STUDY

 Identity Politics and the
Fracturing and Underdevelopment of Nigeria

Nigeria, with more than 250 ethnic groups, has three dominant ethnicities: the Hausa-Fulani, the Yoruba, and the Ibo, each of which have quite distinct political practices. The Hausa-Fulani in the north have roots in autocratic, bureaucratic, and hierarchical precolonial states; the Yoruba in the west have a tradition of loose confederation among centralized kingdoms where monarchs were elected by, and shared power with, a council of chiefs; and the Ibo in the south practiced decentralized and egalitarian forms of social organization. In short, not only is cultural and political unity within the nation-state compromised by interethnic competition, but the political values brought to the table are often irreconcilable, to the extent that a politics of ethnic identity governs negotiations.

Related to these historically constructed fracture lines is an elemental division of Nigeria into a Muslim north and a Christian south, exacerbated by the exploitation of the south's oil resources by the north, where oil rents have financed a string of corrupt generals since Nigeria's independence in 1960. Per capita income is now one-quarter of what it was in the 1980s. And these generals have not reinvested profits in the Niger Delta (population of 7 million) on the grounds that a developing south could attempt to secede, like the then-Republic of Biafra did in 1967. In an internationally condemned incident in 1995, Nigerian writer Ken Saro-Wiwa was executed by the regime when he protested southern underdevelopment, linking it to exploitation by the northern-dominated government and foreign oil interests and demanding compensation for the region and his Ogoni people.

Mobil, Shell, Texaco, Chevron, and other Western oil companies extract oil from the Delta; for example, Chevron's worldwide revenues of $30.6 billion in 1998 matched Nigeria's GNP of $30.7 billion in 1997 (one of Africa's biggest). Mobil, Shell, and Chevron, at least, now play a de facto government role in the absence of state investment. Local movements demanding compensation from these firms have managed to involve them in financing basic forms of community development such as running water, electricity, hospitals, and roads.

All modern states embody historic tensions between formal secularism and historical layering of race and ethnic political relations, which are exacerbated by the impact of globalization. Why should African states be any different?

---

*Sources: Sandbrook (1995:93-94); Onishi (1998:A1, A6, 1999:28–29); Cohen (1998:A1).*

The African one-party state arose out of the difficulties in securing power in and administering nation-states with artificial political boundaries drawn up in the Berlin Conference of 1885 and then reaffirmed in 1963 by the **Organization of African Unity** (OAU). At that time, early "African socialist" Presidents Léopold Senghor (Senegal) and Julius Nyerere (Tanzania) argued that the Western multiparty system would be ethnically divisive and inappropriate to the consensual African context, which lacked Western class divisions. Nyerere's attempt to base Tanzanian socialism on a collectivist ethic of self-reliant development at the village level (*ujaama*) overreached itself in rural resettlement and underestimated the corrosive individualism of agricultural modernization. The fate of this one-party state was different from that of the Western-oriented states that had no such rural community-based vision and ruled by force.[53]

Uganda's Museveni, who took power at the end of decades of bloody civil war in 1986, managed to defy international pressure for many years that made "aid contingent on democratization efforts."[54] Reportedly, he also rejected multiparty systems, viewing them as products of Western industrial societies with fluid class divisions, while African societies are divided vertically, along fixed tribal lines. He argued that a multiparty system may, therefore, divide along tribal lines, leading to ethnic conflict. Museveni's solution—"national resistance councils," organized locally to bring local concerns into the national arena—was viewed by critics as a one-party state by another name.[55]

In fact, the one-party state with its rule through patronage degenerated in the lost decade of the 1980s into what is termed **predatory rule,** where the state becomes informalized and power personalized in a dictatorship built on systematic extraction of resources from the society for enrichment of the ruler. President Mobutu, of Zaire (now the Congo), was the archetypal predatory ruler, amassing $4 billion (the equivalent of Zaire's foreign debt at the time) in foreign bank accounts.[56] Mobutu was overthrown in 1996 by a Zairian Tutsi rebellion led by Laurent Kabila, supported by the surrounding states of Rwanda, Uganda, and Angola, among others.

As the twenty-first century arrived, sub-Saharan African states experienced destabilizing forces from within and without. From *within,* as economic conditions deteriorated with little relief from structural adjustment, democratizing trends spread, drawing inspiration and example from the collapse of the Eastern European one-party states and responding to governance pressures from the global managers. But with the demise of one-party rule and in the context of declining economic opportunity, democratizing trends are complicated by internal conflict along protective ethnic lines. These lines often become the pretext for and the vehicle of civil wars and ethnicized struggles for control over national resources—as evidenced in the implosion of Rwanda and Somalia and the breakup of Ethiopia in the mid-1990s.

From *without,* African states broke with their initial (OAU) noninterference agreement and entered into a pattern of intervention in neighboring states. Conflicts between the Tutsi and Hutu groups in Rwanda escalated with the intervention of Uganda on the side of the former ethnic group in 1994. In 1996, Rwanda, Uganda, and Angola intervened in Zaire, which became Congo; in 1997, Angola participated in a civil war in the Republic of Congo; and Ethiopia, Eritrea, and Uganda have assisted rebels in the Sudan fighting a civil war against the Islamic regime. Congo was again the site of intervention from six neighboring states at the turn of the century, with President Kabila allied with Zimbabwe, Angola, Namibia, and Chad against eastern rebels supported by Uganda and Rwanda.[57] There are indications that African boundaries are no longer sacred and that intervention in states such as Congo, with its wealth of natural resources and its implications for geopolitical security, may draw Africa into an extended military contest over boundaries.

Sub-Saharan Africa struggles with enormous dilemmas, in which structural adjustment fans social and geopolitical divisions over dwindling resources. The divisions often express themselves in ethnic conflict that is externally supported, as economies stagnate and political reforms destabilize one-party states. Spreading civil war signals the inability of some states to maintain any internal authority, especially in a world where global forces are now considerably more selective. The export dependency of African states handicaps their ability to maneuver in a technologically dynamic global market. State legitimacy crises have deep roots.

One dramatic manifestation of the loss of political cohesion of some African states is an exploding refugee population, consisting of "international refugees" and "internally displaced persons." Loss of cohesion is not confined to Africa, however. Although economic and political power has been centralizing in the hands of transnational institutions, military power has remained at the state level—whether held as a monopoly of the state itself or subdivided between warring factions within the state. With these destabilizing movements, further global governance mechanisms have come into play. The United Nations is assuming an expanding role in policing the world. In 1993, U.S. marines landed in Somalia. In the absence of a functioning government, they were uninvited, but the UN Security Council approved the action on humanitarian grounds to stem the destruction of civil war.

In 1999, the Balkans conflict, culminating in the massive "ethnic cleansing" of Kosovian Albanians, saw the North Atlantic Treaty Organization (NATO) take matters into its own hands (without consulting the UN Security Council) and organize a bombing intervention against the Serbian leader, President Milosevic, on the grounds of protecting human rights. Since the same interventionist logic has not been used on behalf, say, of the Kurds in Turkey and the Tibetans in China, critics argued that the Kosovian conflict was a threshold in constructing the discourse and military actions underlying a new world order. Here, "human rights imperialism" is used to bring rogue states under control and/or to assert geopolitical power.[58] The United States used this pretext to invade Iraq in 2003, also claiming the right of preemptive strike against a state deemed threatening to U.S. national security (broadly defined given its dependence on global resources such as oil and global markets).

## Financial Crisis

In a world in which U.S.$2 trillion circulates daily, the total value of financial transactions is double that of production, and 97.5 percent of foreign exchange transactions is speculative, it is not surprising that financial crisis has become part of the landscape.[59] Management of financial crisis has become routine, but its gravity outweighs its frequency. The debt regime of the 1980s was a series of multilaterally organized bailouts of banks as a result of a crisis of *government borrowing* in the then Second and Third Worlds. The structural adjustment of scores of states was to be a proving ground for crisis management on a broad scale. In the 1990s, debt crises were triggered by *private borrowing* via capital account liberalization, which encouraged closer financial integration of money markets. The Mexican (1994) and Asian (1997) crises revealed the instability of short-term lending from portfolio investors looking to profit from the ebullience associated with NAFTA and the East Asian miracle, respectively. In each case, the attraction of funds *followed* financial liberalization.

The recent Asian crisis "marks the unraveling of a model of development," of "fast-track capitalism." Walden Bello observes,

> This model was one of high-speed growth fuelled, not principally by domestic savings and investment, as in the case of Taiwan and Korea, the classical NICs or newly industrializing countries, but mainly by huge infusions of foreign capital. The mechanism to achieve this was to liberalize the capital account as fully as possible, achieving very considerable interaction between the domestic financial market and global financial markets. The illusion that propelled the advocates of this model was that countries could . . . leapfrog the normally long arduous course to advanced country status simply by maximizing their access to foreign capital inflows.[60]

In the 1990s, structural changes in global markets (privatization, financial liberalization, economic integration) encouraged institutional investors to target the Southeast Asian markets and their high interest rates as sources of quick yields on huge savings, pension, mutual, government, and corporate funds that they managed. The tolerance shown by the Bretton Woods institutions toward the accelerating foreign debt was, arguably, because it was privately financed. As soon as currencies tumbled late in 1997, the IMF stepped in, as in Mexico, because the crisis implicated broad segments of the G-7 citizenry's savings. Again, the crisis was managed to recover the debt of the banks and institutional investors. The deeper reality is that vulnerable states (with weakened currencies) end up absorbing the crisis.

 **CASE STUDY**
**Financial Crisis Releases Indonesian Democratic Forces**

Globalization can unmask patronage in development states, releasing democratic forces. At the turn of the twenty-first century, the Indonesian state experienced a seismic shift, as a mass movement successfully challenged the military regime and its neoliberal project. First, structural adjustment intensified cronyism, as an estimated 80 percent of privatization contracts went to the president's children or friends. Second, the 1997 Asian regional financial crisis brought IMF reforms, challenging General Suharto's patronage networks, as well as a drastic reduction in living standards, as the rupiah (national currency) lost three-quarters of its value.

This episode suggests that the negotiation between states and global managers may have unintended consequences. It may be that the IMF gained more power to shape Indonesian economic policy through debt restructuring over time. But, as the IMF actually admitted, its negotiating position may have worsened the financial crisis because speculator fears (of the IMF withholding funds and of domestic social instability) undermined the value of the rupiah. A democratic opposition mushroomed, bringing down the military regime.

Arguably, this episode also revealed that the instability of global (financial) integration is triggered by politics. Changing balances of political forces affect stability and perceptions of stability, where currency traders continually evaluate financial implications of national policies. And they do this in real time, so the possibility of financial crisis is ever present where financial institutions are deregulated.

This presents a puzzle: Is the subordination of national sovereignty to global financial markets a good thing (in flushing out corrupt rule), a bad thing (in destabilizing/polarizing societies), or both?

*Sources: Erlanger (1998:A9); Sanger (1998:A1, D11).*

By integrating money markets, financial liberalization rendered the global financial system more vulnerable to financial/currency speculation. In the Asian case, states allowed their currencies to float with the dollar as a device to attract foreign capital but exercised no control over the disposition of the capital inflow, which found its way into property development, real estate schemes, tourism, golf courses, speculative mergers, and intensified natural resource extraction.[61] The increasing fragility of Southeast Asian debt eventually unnerved the currency traders, who maintain the "information standard" on states' financial health for global investors—in this case, with massive currency sales stimulating capital flight elsewhere in the world. About 18 percent of the GDP of these countries vanished.[62]

The IMF-supervised devaluation of Asian currencies, in the name of financial orthodoxy, shifted the burden onto the citizens of the adjusted states, who experienced a dramatic reversal of living standards—as a consequence of financial transactions and speculations against their national currency for which they were not responsible. The larger point is that while all states surrender power to unregulated global financial markets, some states must pay for the casino-like movement of short-term funds among national markets in search of quick profits. Market rule, via financial liberalization, obscures power relations in the "currency pyramid," where some currencies (e.g., the U.S. dollar) are more equal than others.[63] Furthermore, the notion of national responsibility for sound currencies is contradicted by unregulated currency speculation and then invoked in crisis management.

This global "protection racket" is not foolproof; even establishment voices acknowledge the risks. Thus, a proponent of free market "shock treatment" in post–cold war Eastern Europe, Jeffrey Sachs, said the following about the IMF's Asian bailout: "The IMF deepened the sense of panic not only because of its dire public pronouncements, but also because its proposed medicine—high interest rates, budget cuts, and immediate bank closures—convinced the markets that Asia indeed was about to enter a severe contraction. . . . Instead of dousing the fire, the IMF in effect screamed fire in the theatre."[64]

The globalization project, imposed through the financial markets via structural adjustment conditions, requires management of national macroeconomic policy under IMF "trusteeship." Jeffrey Sachs observed,

> Not unlike the days when the British Empire placed senior officials directly into the Egyptian and Ottoman finance ministries, the IMF is insinuated into the inner sanctums of nearly 75 developing-country governments around the world—countries with a combined population of some 1.4 billion. These governments rarely move without consulting the IMF staff, and when they do, they risk their lifelines to capital markets, foreign aid, and international respectability.[65]

 **CASE STUDY**
**South Korea in Crisis: Running Down the Showcase**

The crisis of the South Korean "miracle" is perhaps the marker of the "new world order." In the development era, South Korea was the showcase of successful development. Then, during the 1980s, South Korea was the subject of World Bank shifts of perspective on the question of managed capitalism versus free market policies. By the 1990s, the Bank was presenting Korea as a successful case of managed capitalism. But in 1995, South Korea entered into a "Faustian bargain" with the United States when it accepted wholesale liberalization of its financial institutions in exchange for membership in the Organization for Economic Cooperation and Development (OECD). When the crisis hit Korea in 1997, Washington consensus rhetoric about its origins in "crony capitalism" exploded the Korean model once and for all. In fact, in the post–cold war/Third World era, there is no more need for a showcase of development. The severe adjustment of South Korea left the Koreans stunned— particularly given their recent admission to the OECD (cf. Mexico's admission in 1994, prior to the peso collapse), which conferred on them First World status. The moral of the story is that market rule (i.e., crisis management) appears to take no prisoners.

Was South Korea, once an example of successful development, *made an example of,* through structural adjustment, to preserve global finance or global power relations?

---

*Sources: Evans (1995); Grosfoguel (1996); Amsden and Euh (1997).*

## Summary

The globalization project has many social and political consequences and implications for the future of the world. We have examined just four phenomena: displacement, informalization/marginalization, the legitimacy crisis of state organizations, and financial instability. None of these is unique to the global project. They have all appeared in previous eras but not on the qualitatively different scale found today. They are linked; indeed, they are mutually conditioning processes, being four dimensions of a single process of global restructuring affecting all countries, although with local variation.

The technological shedding of labor and the downsizing and stagnation produced by structural adjustment programs expand the informal sector. Indeed, the institution of wage labor is undergoing substantial change across the world. Not only is wage employment contracting, but wage labor is also displaying a *casualizing* trend, where jobs become part-time and impermanent. The strategies of flexibility embraced by firms contribute to this informalization as much as does the growing surplus of populations severed from their land and livelihood. Some observers see informalization as a countermovement to the official economy and to state regulation—the "new commons." Whether or not informalization is the source of future alternatives to the formal market economy, there is no doubt that it is the site of a diverse array of livelihood strategies, some of which are embedded in community or personal relations.

State legitimacy crisis is substantial under the globalization project because of the relative incapacity of states in a market regime to resolve the breakdown of social institutions. The breakdown marks the crossing of a threshold from the national development era to a new era in which international competition and global efficiency increasingly govern and privatize national policy and growth strategies. But in such breakdown, there are signs of a renewal, as people across the world push for democratic participation. Movements for democracy have emerged in the moment at which already overextended states, sometimes riddled with unproductive cronyism, are under pressure to end the pretense of development and repay the debts built up over two decades of development financing. This is exacerbated by the recent recurrence of financial crisis, from Mexico to Asia to Brazil, Russia, and Argentina. The emperor really doesn't have on any clothes, and disillusioned citizens, repressed workers, and neglected rural communities have demanded the opening of their political systems. This demand coincides with the reorganization of states as vehicles of global governance and fuels the global countermovements discussed in the following chapter.

# PART IV

## Rethinking Development

# 7

# Global Development
# and Its Countermovements

The globalization project has been a relatively coherent perspective and has had a powerful set of states, agencies, and corporations working on its behalf. Nevertheless, its discourse and rules are always in contention *because* this project is realized through various inequalities. Like the development project, the globalization project is an attempt to fashion the world around a central principle through powerful political and financial institutions. Since the principle is framed as a discourse of rights and freedom, its power ultimately depends on the interpretation and effect of these ideals.

Countermovements resist various features of globalization. But they are not simply coincidental alternatives. They shape globalization by representing the material and discursive conditions targeted by global institutions for appropriation. For example, biotechnology corporations impose a singular discursive and material logic on a culturally, ecologically, and politically diverse world—here, seed patenting reduces biodiversity to corporate monoculture in the name of world hunger and in the face of countermovements of farmers and peasant communities. And the concept of "comparative advantage" is presented as enabling an efficient allocation of global resources and benefits based on ecological and cultural endowments; but according to labor and environmental movements, it is a corporate, rather than a geographical, property. In other words, corporate goals do not simply view globalization as the path to prosperity;

they also *deny* cultural diversity, producer and consumer rights, and biodiversity as alternative forms of sustainable development.

Most governments feel the pressure to play by the new and emerging global rules, but their citizens do not always share their outlook. And where global restructuring weakens nation-states (by eroding their public welfare function, increasing social and regional polarization, and reducing state patronage systems), citizens have fresh opportunities to renew the political process. This chapter surveys some of these countermovements, exploring their origins and goals. Examining each movement offers a particular angle on the reformulation of development in the globalization project. Although the various countermovements have emerged in different ways and places and at different overlapping times, there is a sense in which they converge (as "global justice movements"). We consider the following countermovements and assess their impact in the development debate: fundamentalism, environmentalism, feminism, cosmopolitan activism, and food sovereignty.

## Fundamentalism

Fundamentalism usually expresses a desire to recover the simplicity and security of traditional codes of behavior. But it is never quite so simple. First, who decides what is traditional? There may be sacred texts, but they are open to interpretation. And fundamentalist movements are usually split by factional differences and power struggles. Second, what are the conditions in which fundamentalism comes to the fore? These conditions are likely to shape the leadership and the interpretation of tradition. In the twenty-first-century United States, the broad-based fundamentalism espousing family values can be understood only in the context of a significant decline in the proportion of the population that is actually a part of the traditional nuclear family structure. Even then, the nuclear family is not exactly traditional; the extended family is the more traditional structure. What may be "traditional" is the age-old and unquestioned power of the family patriarch. The values associated with patriarchy are deployed steadily to reshape the U.S. sociopolitical landscape as Christian fundamentalism reasserts itself in an age of excess for some and economic uncertainty for most. Indeed, first reactions of some fundamentalist TV evangelists to the September 11, 2001, attacks on New York and Washington, D.C., were represented as "God's punishment" for the toleration of homosexuality and abortion.

In uncertain times, constructing the fundamentals of what holds people together often moves to the front burner. People gravitate to fundamentalism for protection and security and to make sense of the world around them and their places in it. We have seen a variant of this in the rising use of ethnic politics as competition for jobs grows while the economy shrinks. Nothing is absolute or definite about the content of fundamentalism or about the elevation of ethnic identity as a way of drawing boundaries between people. The interpretation of ethnicity is quite plastic and depends very much on the historical and social context in which people reconstruct ethnic divisions. Nevertheless, in an increasingly confused and unstable world, the *presumed* essentialism of ethnic identity either comforts people or allows them to identify scapegoats. The current challenge to affirmative action in the United States represents one such reaction. In whatever form, fundamentalist politics has become a powerful weapon for mobilizing people as the stable political and class coalitions of the development era crumble.

In a post-2001 world, northerners equate fundamentalism with activities by people of the Islamic faith. This in itself is a fundamentalist response as, in portraying Islam in monolithic and alien terms, it ignores the variety of Islamic orders, the relationship between fundamentalism and modernity, and the fact that other religious fundamentalisms (e.g., Christian and Hindu) have displayed an equal capacity for violence. The common assumption made about fundamentalism being antithetical to modernity is evident in easy depictions of a world divided into "Jihad versus McWorld,"[1] secular versus religious states, and materialist opportunism versus absolute values. As Tariq Ali points out, "For Islamists, none of the rulers of existing Muslim states today are 'true' Muslims. Not a single one. Hence the struggle to change the existing regimes and replace them with holy emirates. Some orthodox Jews regard the very existence of Israel as a disgrace."[2] During the 1990s, such easy depictions appeared via public intellectuals—notably Samuel Huntington's *Clash of Civilizations*, which depicted a world divided into eight cultures of religion but riven between the West (valuing "individualism, liberalism, constitutionalism, human rights, equality, liberty, the rule of law, democracy, free markets") and the Rest (epitomized by the most menacing: Islam and Confucianism).[3] However, this "clash" did not prevent the United States, in pursuing a form of imperial fundamentalism itself, from supporting the most hard-line Islamic fundamentalisms against communism or progressive/secular nationalism during the cold war: the Muslim brotherhood against Egyptian president Nasser, the Sarekat-i-Islam against

Indonesian president Sukarno, the Jamaat-e-Islami against Pakistan president Bhutto, and, later, Osama bin Laden and the Taliban against the secular-communist president Najibullah of Afghanistan.[4]

The point is that fundamentalism and modernity are inextricably tied, and easy dichotomies misrepresent the complex relationship between them. And resisting the essentialism of fundamentalism with further essentialism (as dominant states tend to do) is inappropriate. At this time, a more constructive approach is to understand the appeal of fundamentalist constructions (by leaders and politicians) for people.

In the shadow of September 11, 2001, *The New York Times* reported the rise of Islam as a political force in Africa and "the stunning spread of hard-line Islamic law from one small Nigerian state in 1999 to a third of the country's 36 states today."[5] Rather than confirming the topical question asked by Americans in the post–September 11 era, "Why do they hate us?"—which projects some deep-seated envy of the West onto the Muslim world—the report detailed the limits of Western modernity in Africa:

> Islamic values have much in common with traditional African life: its emphasis on communal living, its clear roles for men and women, its tolerance of polygamy. Christianity, Muslims argue, was alien to most Africans. . . . Other Western values like democracy have been a disappointment here, often producing sham elections, continued misrule and deep poverty.[6]

An Anglican bishop noted, "For many Africans, it makes more sense to reject America and Europe's secular values, a culture of selfishness and half-naked women, by embracing Islam."[7] Under these circumstances, Muslims supported the Hisbah organization's imposition of *Shariah* (Islamic law) in Kano, Nigeria's largest Muslim city. The president of the Hisbah justified this assertion of political Islam in terms that depend on a profound encounter with modernity and its contradictions:

> It is the failure of every system we have known. We have had colonialism, which was exploitative. We had a brief period of happiness after independence, then the military came in, and everything has been going downward since then. But before all this, we had a system that worked. We had Shariah. We are Muslims. Why don't we return to ourselves?[8]

We should note how this leader not only constructs an absolute sense of the Muslim identity but also validates it by referring to an imagined past in which the justice system (which is harsh, particularly on women—but to defenders of Islamic justice, nothing like the death penalty in the West) is believed to have worked. The construction of *Shariah* as a repository of previous traditions and justice, although fundamentalist, cannot be understood outside of its encounter with modernity. As Olivier Roy has noted, "Islamism is the sharia plus electricity." This is particularly so since the return to democratic elections in Nigeria in 1999 (after years of military rule) allowed Islamic law to be reintroduced through the ballot box.[9] In other words, modernity and fundamentalism are intertwined.

## CASE STUDY
## Modernity's Fundamentalisms

As an illustration of the inextricable links between fundamentalism and modernity, consider the cases of the following two Arab intellectuals.

Exiled Saudi Arabian novelist, Abdelrahman Munif, remarked in an interview with Tariq Ali,

> The twentieth century is almost over, but when the West looks at us, all they see is oil and petrodollars. Saudi Arabia is still without a constitution, the people are deprived of all elementary rights, even the right to support the regime without asking for permission. Women, who own a large share of private wealth in the country, are treated like third-class citizens. A woman is not allowed to leave the country without a written permit from a male relative. Such a situation produces a desperate citizenry, without a sense of dignity or belonging. All our rules do is increase their own wealth while investing as little as possible in the intellectual development of our people. Why? Because they fear education. They fear change.

Alternatively, Egyptian philosopher and inspirer of al Qaeda Islamic terrorism, Sayyid Qutb (executed under President Nasser's nationalist regime), viewed the truly dangerous element in Western, particularly American, life as theological, not political, "stemming from Christianity's ancient division of the sacred and the secular, and creating a 'hideous schizophrenia' in modern life where life without reference to God was unfulfilling."

Paul Berman suggests that Qutb's philosophy drew on twentieth-century themes about the division between mind and body, between sensual and spiritual experiences, and he "put his finger on something that every thinking person can recognize, if only vaguely—the feeling that human nature and modern life are somehow at odds. . . . His deepest quarrel was not with America's failure to uphold its principles. His quarrel was with the principles. He opposed the United States because it was a liberal society, not because the United States failed to be a liberal society."

But which fundamentalism is the more authentic: the one that blends with the modern world or the one that uses or reacts to certain experiences in the modern world to justify its appeal to a seemingly unblemished tradition?

*Sources: Ali (2002); Berman (2003:26-29).*

Development, whether based in oil wealth or not, fuels fundamentalist opposition via overcrowded cities. In Egypt, a legitimacy crisis stemming from economic stagnation and political corruption in the government has emboldened Islamic fundamentalism. Its ranks have expanded among the urban poor, partly because Islam offers community and basic services in the midst of the disorder of huge, sprawling cities such as Cairo. In southern Egypt's public schools, fundamentalist teachers reimpose the veil on girls and revise schoolbooks to emphasize Islamic teachings. They argue that secularization has suppressed Egypt's deep Islamic and Arab roots in the pursuit of a communion with Western culture.[10] In Turkey, Istanbul's population has doubled every 15 years. When the modern Turkish Republic was created in 1923, only 15 percent of its population of 13 million was urban. Now, two-thirds of Turkey's 60 million people live in urban areas. These city dwellers offer fertile ground for an Islamic revival challenging Kemalism, the ruthless, secular politics of development associated with the founder of the Turkish republic (1923), Kemal Ataturk.[11] In 2002, the Islamic party, the AKP, came to power, drawing on religious fervor in the heartland, where polygamy is practiced and female illiteracy is high and from where young men with conservative values come to swell the ranks of the urban poor. The AKP has transformed this disenchantment into a political mandate for an Islamist revival that is at once modern and appeals to the European Union (as a source of investment and trade)—offering economic hope and a counterweight to fundamentalism.[12]

In the wake of the attacks on September 11, 2001, the Western press has focused on likely correlations between economic deprivation and religious fundamentalism in the Middle East. The blame for stagnating Arab economies is placed on authoritarian regimes with top-heavy public sectors that discourage private investment and entrepreneurship. While poverty is not widespread, unemployment averages 15 percent, especially among the relatively well educated (from whose ranks came some of the men involved in the attacks on the World Trade Center and the Pentagon), and "the lack of opportunities for the young and educated translates into deeply frustrated aspirations."[13]

A report filed from Pakistan touches a Western nerve by drawing attention to the demographic profile of Peshawar (as with all cities in the Middle East), where young men crowd the streets, with 63 percent of the population younger than age 25. The reporter notes that most young men are not rioting:

> Their anger is only loosely articulated, often because they are struggling to survive. . . . They live where globalization is not working or not working well enough. They believe, or can be led to believe, that America—or their pro-American government, if they live under one—is to blame for their misery. . . . Poor families do their best to send a son to school, but in the end they cannot manage. The son will get a backbreaking job of some sort, or . . . (enrol) at a madrassah, most of which offer free tuition, room and board. And that's where they learn that it is honorable to blow yourself up amid a crowd of infidels and that the greatest glory in life is to die in a jihad.[14]

The shortcomings of this kind of representation of a close relation between fundamentalism and terrorism are that the tensions between political cultures in an unequal world do not resolve themselves in such simplistic fashion. In fact, power lies in representation—whether it is the power of an imam to interpret the Koran or the power of powerful states and their publicist-journalists to identify those fundamentalisms they regard as threatening to their sense of world order. From the global South, the fundamentalism of neoliberal economics in structurally adjusting political economies, privatizing public goods, withdrawing subsidies, cutting wages, and patenting plant varieties is just as real and threatening to the stability of their communities and their sense of world order. Ultimately, the identification of which fundamentalisms lead to which kind of terror (stateless or state based) is a question of power relations.

There are significant examples in the twenty-first century of interconnected fundamentalisms and their use of forms of terror. The unilateral "imperial fundamentalism" governing the invasion of Iraq in 2003 was premised on a questionable representation of Saddam Hussein's regime as blending state and stateless al Qaeda–type terrorism. The conflict between Israel and the Palestinians matches formal and informal terrorisms and fundamentalist positioning on both sides. The South Asian conflict between India and Pakistan is driven by a blend of informal and formal (state-sponsored) fundamentalism.

Hindu fundamentalism, drawing on cultural history, has arguably revived recently as much as a consequence of the project of globalization, as of geopolitical tensions with Pakistan. India, a leader of the Non-Aligned Movement, was perhaps the last significant holdout among former Third World states against International Monetary Fund (IMF)–style economic liberalization. In 1991, the Indian Finance Ministry accepted the borrowing conditions set out by the IMF, and India joined the "structural adjustment" club. Right-wing Hindu groups, once advocates of economic liberalism, then organized a "Buy Indian" campaign against imports and the efforts to "globalize" the Indian economy on the part of Prime Minister P. V. Narasimha Rao. The Swadeshi Jagran Manch (SJM), an organization promoted by a Hindu revivalist group (Rashtriya Swayamsewak Sangh), urged Indians to boycott foreign-made goods such as toothpaste, shaving cream, soaps, detergents, cosmetics, soft drinks, paint, canned food, and even crayons. The convenor of the SJM, S. Gurmurthy, wore homespun cotton clothes, invoking the economic nationalism of India's beloved anticolonial leader Mahatma Gandhi. Gurmurthy declared,

> We want to create a nationalist feeling that every nation has to evolve a mind of its own in economics. The integration of India with the rest of the world will be restricted to just one percent of our population. A nation should largely live within its means and produce for its own market with trans-country commerce restricted to its needs.[15]

More recently, Hindu fundamentalism has gathered steam via the nationalist Bharatiya Janata Party (BJP), which won an overwhelming majority in the Indian parliament in 2002. While campaigning, the chief minister of Gujarat, Narendra Modi, drew some disturbing lessons from an earlier experience of a religious riot in his home state. An officially unrestrained Hindu rampage, after Muslims killed 59 Hindu pilgrims, resulted in the massacre of more than 2,000 of their Muslim neighbors. Modi used the incident to incite a new, aggressive platform of Hindutva (chauvinist Hindu supremacism), campaigning against "Muslim terrorism" in neighboring Pakistan but, by implication, within Gujarat, where Muslims account for just 9 percent of the population. This kind of neofascist politics, targeting a minority as the basis for an electoral mobilization, illustrates the way fundamentalism can be deployed to achieve powerful ends.[16]

In sum, the fundamentalist movements abroad in the world have two main features. First, they articulate the uncertainties and legitimacy deficit that populations experience as a result of the limits of developmentalism and the increasing selectivity of globalization. Second, they often take the form of ethnonationalist resurgence against perceived threats to cultural integrity. The combination may involve contesting the "fundamentalisms" of globalization (financial, institutional, or imperial) and offering alternative ways of organizing social life—whether in defensive or aggressive terms. The point is that what gets represented as fundamentalism is usually one-sided, obscuring its political roots in modernity.

## Environmentalism

Environmentalism as a countermovement involves questioning modern assumptions that nature and its bounty are infinite. It has two main strands. One derives from growing environmental awareness among citizens in the West, most recently inspired by the publication of Rachel Carson's *Silent Spring* in 1962. This path-breaking book documented the disruption in the earth's ecosystems that was being caused by modern economic practices such as the use of agricultural chemicals. Its title refers to the absence of birdsongs in the spring. Carson's metaphor dramatized the dependence of life on sustainable ecological systems. It also emphasized the shortcomings of Western rationalism's perception of nature as "external" to society. This perception encourages the belief that nature is an infinitely exploitable domain.[17]

A range of "green" movements has mushroomed throughout the First World as the simple truths revealed by Carson's study have gained an audience. First World "greens" typically challenge the assumptions and practices of unbridled economic growth, arguing for scaling back to a renewable economic system of resource use. One of their foci is agricultural sustainability—that is, reversing the environmental stress associated with capital- and chemical-intensive agriculture. A key goal is maintaining a natural aesthetic to complement the consumer lifestyle, the emphasis being on preserving human health, on the one hand, and enhancing leisure activities, on the other.

The second strand of environmentalism appears in active movements to protect particular bioregions from environmentally damaging practices. Across the world, where rural populations produce 60 percent of their food, human communities depend greatly on the viability of regional ecologies for their livelihood. Such movements are therefore often distinguished by their attempts to protect existing cultural practices. In contrast to First World environmentalism, which attempts to regulate the environmental implications of the market economy, southern environmentalism questions market forces. This is especially true where states and firms seek to "monetize" and harvest natural resources on which human communities depend.

Local communities have always challenged environmentally damaging practices where natural conservation is integral to local culture. Opposition has come from eighteenth-century English peasants, who protested the enclosure of the commons; nineteenth-century Native Americans, who resisted the takeover of their lands and the elimination of the buffalo; and Indians, who struggled against British colonial forestry practices.

In the late twentieth century, forest dwellers across the tropics grabbed the world's attention as they attempted to preserve tropical rain forests from the extensive timber cutting associated with commercial logging. Timbering and the pasturing of beef cattle in degraded forest areas intensified with the agro-export boom of the 1980s, amplifying southern environmentalism. Demands for northern-style environmental regulation gathered momentum to address environmental stresses from resource mining and river damming to the overuse of natural resources resulting in desertification, excessive water salinity, and chemical contamination associated with the green revolution.

The common denominator of most environmental movements is a belief that natural resources are not infinitely renewable. The finiteness of nature has been a global preoccupation, from the neo-Malthusian specter of population growth overwhelming land supplies and the food grown on it to anxiety about the dwindling supplies of raw materials, such as fossil fuels and timber, that sustain modern economies.

Lately, however, this rather linear perspective has yielded to a more dynamic one that sees a serious threat to essential natural elements such as the atmosphere, climates, and biodiversity. Trees may be renewable through replanting schemes, but the atmospheric conditions that nurture them may not be so easily replenished. As Paul Harrison implies, the world has moved to a new threshold of risk to its sustainability:

> It used to be feared that we would run out of non-renewable resources— things like oil, or gold. Yet these, it seems, are the ones we need worry least about. It is the renewables—the ones we thought would last forever—that are being destroyed at an accelerating rate. They are all living things, or dynamic parts of living ecosystems.[18]

Furthermore, the very survival of the human species is increasingly at risk as pollution and environmental degradation lead to public health epidemics. These include lead poisoning, new strains of cancer, cataracts from ozone destruction, immune suppression by ultraviolet radiation, and loss of genetic and biological resources for producing food and medicines.[19]

Destruction of renewable resources increasingly is understood as undermining the sustainability of formal economic activity. While a tree plantation may provide timber products, it cannot perform the regenerative function that natural systems perform because it is a monoculture and lacks natural diversity. Robert Repetto, of the World Resources Institute, articulated the shortcomings of conventional economic notions of value:

> Under the current system of national accounting, a country could exhaust its mineral resources, cut down its forests, erode its soils, pollute its aquifers, and hunt its wildlife and fisheries to extinction, but measured income would not be affected as these assets disappeared. . . . [The] difference in the treatment of natural resources and other tangible assets confuse the depletion of valuable assets with the generation of income. . . . The result can be illusory gains in income and permanent losses in wealth.[20]

As a consequence of the appreciation of "nature's services," a form of **ecological accounting** is emerging—for example, it was recently estimated that the economic value of the world's ecosystem services is currently around $33 trillion a year, exceeding the global gross national product (GNP) of $25 trillion. Whether or not it is appropriate to value nature in this way, this trend is an antidote to traditional economics reasoning, which invisibilizes environmental impact.[21]

The change in thinking has been stimulated from several quarters. In the first place, there are the **new social movements** (conceptualized in the following insert), some of which are the subject of this chapter. Their appearance on the historical stage reflects the demise of developmentalism and the search for new directions of social and political action.[22]

---

**What Are the New Social Movements?**

---

*The new social movements, such as the greens, feminism, global justice,* **participatory action research,** *and grassroots or basismo politics,*

*(Continued)*

(Continued)

*share criticism of developmentalism. Where developmentalism advocates national/global economic management, the new movements tend to reject centralism and stress decentralized, or accountable, forms of social organization instead. Where developmentalism emphasizes industrialism and material abundance, the new movements emphasize appropriate technology and ecological balance, and where developmentalism champions state and market institutions, the new social movements seek autonomy and the embedding of markets in cooperative social arrangements. In short, the new social movements are distinguished by an expressive politics and their challenge to the economism and instrumental politics of the "developed society" model. They have grown as the institutions of the welfare state have receded, and they express the declining legitimacy of development in its national and global incarnations.*

Sources: Buttel (1992); Lehman (1990).

The second indication of a change in thinking is a growing awareness of the limits of "spaceship earth." From the late 1960s, space photographs of planet Earth dramatized the biophysical finiteness of our world. The dangerous synergies arising from global economic intercourse and ecology were driven home by the Brundtland Commission's declaration in 1987: "The Earth is one but the world is not. We all depend on one biosphere for sustaining our lives." In 1997, the Environmental Defense Fund warned that the burning of the Amazon forests would have "potentially enormous global consequences."[23]

Third, various grassroots movements focus attention on the growing conflict on the margins between local cultures and the global market. For example, the Kayapo Indians of the Amazon strengthened their demands by appealing to the global community regarding defense of their forest habitat from logging, cattle pasturing, and extraction of genetic resources. One response by the Brazilian government to this kind of demand was the creation of self-managing **extractive reserves** for native tribes and rubber tappers to protect them from encroaching ranchers and colonists. These reserves are relatively large areas of forestland set aside, with government protection, for extractive activities by forest dwellers.[24]

Finally, from the 1970s on, the pressure on natural resources from the rural poor has intensified. This pressure stems from the long-term impoverishment of rural populations forced to overwork their land and fuel sources to eke out a subsistence. As land and forest were increasingly devoted to export production in the 1980s, millions of rural poor were pushed into occupying marginal tropical forest ecosystems. Environmental degradation, including deforestation, resulted. Environmental movements have proposed both solutions under the mantle of "sustainable development"—including the idea of self-organizing development versus the dominant centralizing version. Resistance to the Narmada Dam is a case in point.

Since the 1980s, the Indian government has been implementing a huge dam project in the Narmada River valley, with financial assistance from the World Bank. This massive development project involves 30 large and more than 3,000 medium and small dams on the Narmada River, expected eventually to displace more than 2 million people. In 1992, at the time of the Earth Summit, there was an embarrassing simultaneous release of an independent review (the first ever) of the Bank's Sardar Sarovar dam project in India. Commissioned by the Bank president, the review claimed "gross delinquency" on the part of the Bank and the Indian government in both the engineering and the forcible resettlement of displaced peasants. These revelations and the growing resistance movement, the Narmada Bachao Andolan (Movement to Save the Narmada), had considerable success in forcing the Bank to withdraw its support for this project. Members of the grassroots opposition to the dam argue that the resistance

articulates . . . the critical legacy of Mahatma Gandhi . . . of the struggles all over the country that continue to challenge both the growing centralization and authoritarianism of the state and the extractive character of the dominant economic process—a process which not only erodes and destroys the subsistence economies of these areas, but also the diversity of their systems. . . . The movement is therefore representative of growing assertions of marginal populations for greater economic and political control over their lives.[25]

## Sustainable Development

The concept of **sustainable development** gained currency as a result of the 1987 Brundtland report, titled *Our Common Future*. The report defined sustainable development as "meet[ing] the needs of the present without compromising the ability of future generations to meet their own needs."[26] How to achieve this remains a puzzle. The Brundtland

Commission suggested steps such as conserving and enhancing natural resources, encouraging grassroots involvement in development, and adopting appropriate technologies (smaller scale, energy conserving). While acknowledging that "an additional person in an industrial country consumes far more and places far greater pressure on natural resources than an additional person in the Third World," the commission nevertheless recommended continued emphasis on economic growth to reduce the pressure of the poor on the environment.[27]

The report did not resolve the interpretive debate over the root cause of environmental deterioration—whether the threat to our common future stems from poverty or from affluence:

- Those who argue the poverty cause consider the gravest stress on the environment to be impoverished masses pressing on resources. Population control and economic growth are the suggested solutions.
- Those who identify affluence as the problem believe that the gravest stress on the environment comes from global inequality and the consumption of resources to support affluent lifestyles.

Measures of this latter effect abound, one of the more provocative being the claim that each U.S. citizen contributes 60 times more to global warming than each Mexican and that a Canadian's contribution equals that of 190 Indonesians.[28] This perspective has generated former World Bank economist Herman E. Daly's "impossibility theorem": that "a U.S.-style high-resource consumption standard for a world of 4 billion people is impossible."[29]

## The Earth Summit

The terms of this debate infused the 1992 United Nations Conference on Environment and Development (UNCED). Popularized as the Rio de Janeiro "Earth Summit," it was the largest diplomatic gathering ever held. The United Nations Environment Program (UNEP) organized the conference to review progress on the Brundtland report. Conference preparations resulted in a document, known as Agenda 21, detailing a global program for the twenty-first century and addressing all sides of the debate, which continued through the decade, to the rather low-key and ineffectual follow-up 2002 World Summit on Sustainability in Johannesburg.

The South, for instance, recognizes that the First World has an interest in reducing carbon dioxide emissions and preserving biodiversity and the tropical rain forests for planetary survival. It has agreed to participate in the global program in return for financial assistance, arguing that "poverty is the greatest polluter," a phrase once used by the now deceased Indian president Indira Gandhi. Accordingly, it has called for massive investment by the First World in sustainable development measures in the South, including health, sanitation, education, technical assistance, and conservation.[30]

However, UNCED detoured from the question of global inequities, stressing environmental protection to be a development priority, but "without distorting international trade and investment."[31] The outcome was a shift in emphasis from the Brundtland report: (1) privileging *global* management of the environment over local/national concerns and (2) maintaining the viability of the global economy rather than addressing deteriorating economic conditions in the South. The globalization project was alive and well.

### CASE STUDY
### Deforestation under the
### Globalization Project, Post–Earth Summit

Since the Rio de Janiero Earth Summit, deforestation has continued unabated and, in fact, has intensified. The United States has suspended national forest laws to facilitate logging; the Siberian and Eastern Russian boreal forests have been plundered; the rate of Amazonian deforestation has risen by one-third, and burning has tripled; and, after destroying more than 50 percent of Southeast Asian forests, logging companies from Burma, Indonesia, Malaysia, the Philippines, New Guinea, and South Korea moved on to Amazonia, where they received the blessing of the Brazilian government (having submitted an environmental impact study and become licensed), although government studies estimate that 60 to 70 percent of licensees operate illegally.

Brazil moved expeditiously to situate Amazonia as the logging frontier of the twenty-first century—allowing private interests to legally challenge indigenous land titles, building a huge transport infrastructure as a subsidy to private investment in Brazilian natural resources, implementing plans to resettle thousands of Brazilians under pressure from the Sem Terra landless workers' movement, and privatizing 39 of its national forests to attract foreign loggers. Meanwhile, under the terms of the IMF bailout of Indonesia in the 1997 crisis, that country's forests are open to foreign ownership. And in Mexico, the North American Free Trade Agreement (NAFTA) has no provision for protecting forests. Following the peso crash in 1994, the International Paper Corporation leveraged reform of Mexican laws regarding forest exploitation, removing protections for biodiversity, soil, and water quality and gaining generous federal subsidies. A new Forest Reform Law legalized private industrial tree plantations in the indigenous reserves and *ejido* lands, where 80 percent of Mexican forests are located. International Paper plans a 100,000-hectare eucalyptus and pine plantation in Chiapas. Meanwhile, the World Trade Organization (WTO) prepares a national treatment code requiring foreign investors to claim the same rights as domestic ones, which threatens to institutionalize "cut-and-run" logging around the world.

How can we have long-term global environmentalism when states themselve facilitate the exploitation of natural resources for short-term profit and foreign exchange needs?

---

*Sources: Tautz (1997); Menotti (1998:352-62; 1999:181).*

## Managing the Global Commons

Environmental management is as old as the need for human communities to ensure material and cultural survival. *Global* environmental management seeks to preserve planetary resources, but there is no resolution as yet as to what end. This question is posed and resolved on a continuing basis by struggles between communities and countermovements, on the one hand, and private interests, states, and global institutions, on the other. Within the terms of the globalization project, it is not difficult to see that states, strapped for foreign exchange and sometimes required to undergo reform to earn foreign exchange, are beholden to wealthy corporations that want to exploit natural resources and/or secure control over their supply in the future. In many cases, it is left up to local inhabitants, as well as their nongovernmental organization (NGO) supporters, to question the commercialization and degradation of environments to which they are historically and spiritually attached. Southern grassroots movements, in particular, regard global environmental managers and their powerful state allies as focused on managing the global environment to ensure the profitability of global economic activity. This includes regulating the use of planetary resources and global waste sinks such as forests, wetlands, and bodies of water. Instead of linking environmental concerns to issues of social justice and resource distribution, the new "global ecology" has converged on four priorities:

- reducing greenhouse gas emissions, primarily from automobiles and burning forests;
- protecting biodiversity, mainly in tropical forests;
- reducing pollution in international waters;
- curbing ozone-layer depletion.

The institutional fallout from UNCED strengthened global economic management. A **Global Environmental Facility (GEF)** was installed, geared to funding global ecology initiatives. The World Bank initiated the establishment of the GEF to channel monies into global environmental projects, especially in the four areas identified above; 50 percent of the projects approved in the GEF's first tranche were for biodiversity protection. In addition, UNCED, via the **Food and Agricultural Organization (FAO)**, planned to zone southern land for cash cropping with the assistance of national governments. Under this facility, subsistence farming would be allowed only where "natural resource limitations" or "environmental or socioeconomic constraints" prevent intensification. And where governments deem marginal land to be over-populated, the inhabitants would be forced into transmigration or resettlement programs.[32]

The logic of this scenario is that of managing the "global commons" and viewing surplus populations and their relation to scarce natural resources as the immediate problem, rather than situating the problem of *surplus* population in a broader framework that recognizes extreme inequality of access to resources. In Brazil, for example, less than 1 percent of the population owns about 44 percent of the fertile agricultural land, and 32 million people are officially considered destitute. Structural adjustment policies, grain imports, and expansion of soy export production have dispossessed small peasants. Under conditions where Brazilian social ministries have been gutted, those landless peasants who do not join the Sem Terra (see below) or the mass migration to the towns or the frontier are incorporated into NGO-organized "poverty management" programs, constituting a cheap labor force for wealthy landowners.[33]

## CASE STUDY
Managing the Global Commons:
The GEF and Nicaraguan Biosphere Reserves

In 1997, the Global Environmental Facility developed a strategy for protecting the Bosawas rainforest region in Nicaragua on the grounds that it is globally significant biodiversity under threat of *campesino* colonization and unregulated logging by transnational firms attracted to the abundant timber, cheap labor, and relatively lawless conditions. The GEF strategy proposed "institutional strengthening" for the "participation of local stakeholders" and "decentralized management of protected areas." A GEF grant of $7.1 million, combined with European aid of $12.8 million, was promised the Nicaraguan government in return for brokering this strategy of biospheric reserve management on behalf of the indigenous communities of the Mayangna Indians. The GEF views the Indians as guards and guardians of the high biodiversity areas: "By strengthening and reinforcing land and natural resource rights of indigenous communities . . . when indigenous communities have fairly secure tenure of their land, they can represent formidable barriers to the expansion of the agricultural frontier." The GEF pledged money for demarcation and titling of indigenous lands.

Instituting this plan ran into formidable obstacles since the Nicaraguan government was juggling the GEF "sustainable development" program and a program of broad logging concessions. These were contested through physical demonstrations, as well as challenge in the courts (including the Inter-American Commission on Human Rights), by the Indians. They claim use of two-thirds of the land conceded by the state to a subsidiary of a Korean clothing transnational corporation (TNC) for hunting, burial sites, and areas of spiritual significance. The sticking point is that *indigenas* are not inclined to accept land parcels that fragment collectively used forests to complement private logging concessions. The state is caught between its embracing "sustainable development" and its revenue-enhancing relationship to the logging firms.

How does this episode help us understand the contradictory interests between a global agency responsible for planetary biodiversity (and therefore responsive to indigenous guardianship) and states managed by powerful patronage networks and driven by the need to earn foreign exchange?

*Source: Weinberg (1998).*

Global ecology, geared to environmental management on a large scale, has priorities for sustainability that often differ from those of the remaining local environmental managers. It is estimated that there are 200 to 300 million forest dwellers in South and Southeast Asia, distinct from lowland communities dependent on irrigated agriculture. Some of these people have been given official group names assigning them a special—and usually second-class—status in their national society: India's "scheduled tribes" (*adivasis*), Thailand's "hill tribes," China's "minority nationalities," the Philippines's "cultural minorities," Indonesia's "isolated and alien peoples," Taiwan's "aboriginal tribes," and Malaysia's "aborigines." Challenging their national status and elevating their internationally common bonds, these groups have recently redefined themselves as "indigenous."[34]

Indigenous and tribal people around the world have had their rights to land and self-determination enshrined in the International Labor Organization Convention. Nevertheless, they are routinely viewed from afar as marginal. The World Bank, in adopting the term *indigenous* in its documents, stated in 1990, "The term indigenous covers indigenous, tribal, low caste and ethnic minority groups. Despite their historical and cultural differences, they often have a limited capacity to participate in the national development process because of cultural barriers or low social and political status."[35]

Viewed through the development lens, this is a predictable perspective, and it carries a significant implication. On the one hand, it perpetuates the often unexamined assumption that these cultural minorities need guidance. On the other hand, it often subordinates minorities to national development initiatives, such as commercial logging or government forestry projects involving tree plantations. More often than not, such indigenous peoples find themselves on the receiving end of large-scale resettlement programs justified by the belief that forest destruction is a consequence of their poverty. This has been the case recently on the Indonesian island of Kalimantan, where the state has been actively encouraging commercial logging at the expense of a sophisticated and centuries-old rattan culture practiced by the Dayak Indians. They have formed their own resistance, documenting their ownership of cultivars in the forest.[36]

The focus on poverty as the destroyer of forests guided the establishment of the Tropical Forest Action Plan (TFAP) in the 1980s by a global management group consisting of the World Bank, the Food and Agricultural Organization, the **United Nations Development Program,** and the World Resources Institute. TFAP was designed to pool funds to provide alternative fuel-wood sources, strengthen forestry and environmental institutions, conserve protected areas and watersheds, and promote social forestry. It became the "most ambitious environmental aid program ever conceived" and, as such, attracted requests for aid from 62 southern states looking for new, seemingly "green," sources of funds for extraction of forest products for export. TFAP projects were completed in Peru, Guyana, Cameroon, Ghana, Tanzania, Papua New Guinea, Nepal, Colombia, and the Philippines. Seeing their effects, however, and charging that the TFAP projects furthered deforestation through intervention and zoning, a *worldwide rain forest movement* mobilized sufficient criticism (including that of Britain's Prince Charles) that the TFAP initiative ended. Forestry loans, however, continued through the World Bank.[37]

### CASE STUDY
### Chico Mendes, Brazilian Environmentalist by Default

As the leader of Brazil's National Council of Rubber Tappers, Chico Mendes concerned himself with the safety of his tappers as ranchers tried to force them off their land. By the Catholic Church's reckoning, between 1964 and 1988, 982 murders over land disputes in the Amazon occurred, largely by ranchers' hired guns. Under these circumstances, the Brazilian government obtained a forestry loan from the World Bank for "agro-ecological zoning" in the Brazilian Polonoroeste area of Rondônia and Mato Grosso to set aside land for farmers, extractive reserves for the rubber tappers (so they could supplement their tapping wages with sales of other forest products), and protected Indian reserves in addition to national parks, forest reserves, and other protected forest areas. The minorities affected were not consulted, even though Mendes lobbied the World Bank in Washington on behalf of the rubber tappers in 1988. He feared a repetition of the mistakes made in the 1980s, when Rondônia was occupied by impoverished settlers who burned the Amazonian jungle in vain hopes of farming, observing,

> We think that the extractive reserves included in Polonoroeste II only serve to lend the Government's project proposal to the World Bank an ecological tone—which has been very fashionable lately—in order to secure this huge loan. . . . What will be created will not be extractive reserves, but colonization settlements with the same mistakes that have led to the present disaster of Polonoroeste. In other words, a lot of money will be spent on infrastructures which do not mean anything to the peoples of the forest and the maintenance of which will not be sustainable.

Mendes was later murdered by a hired gun for his part in championing the rubber tappers' cause to secure their land. While he was a forest worker, he left an environmentalist's legacy in the idea of the extractive reserve, which is still taking root. At the very moment that the Rondônian Natural Resources Management Project loan was approved in 1992, the Brazilian land agency, the INCRA, "was proceeding with plans to settle some 50,000 new colonists a year in areas that were supposed to be set aside as protected forests and extractive reserves for rubber tappers under the Bank project."

Was the legacy of Chico Mendes the idea of extractive reserves or of the power of resisting the violence of development?

---

*Sources: Rich (1994:167-69); Schemo (1998:A3).*

On the other side of the world, a similar resettlement project was under way in Indonesia. In this transmigration project, millions of poor peasants were moved from densely populated inner islands of Indonesia, notably Java, to the outer islands of Kalimantan, Irian Jaya, and Sumatra to settle and cultivate cash crops for export, such as cacao, coffee, and palm oil. The outer islands were inhabited by non-Javanese indigenous tribes and contained 10 percent of the world's remaining rain forests. Critics saw this project as both a money spinner for the Indonesian government and a security project against non-Javanese people who desired autonomy from the military government. Building on the Indonesian government's initial resettlement of more than half a million people since 1950, the World Bank assisted a further resettlement of 3.5 million people between 1974 and 1990, with that many again moving to the outer islands as private colonizers. The project, by the Bank's accounting, simply redistributed poverty spatially, from the inner to the outer islands; in addition, it eliminated roughly 4 percent of the Indonesian forests.[38]

## Environmental Resistance Movements

In all these cases, there is a discernible pattern of collaboration between the multilateral financiers and governments concerned with securing territory and foreign exchange. Indigenous cultures, on the other hand, are typically marginalized. Indonesia's Forestry Department controls

74 percent of the national territory, and the minister for forestry claimed in 1989, "In Indonesia, the forest belongs to the state and not to the people. . . . They have no right of compensation" when their habitats fall to logging concessions.[39]

Under these conditions, grassroots environmental movements proliferate. They take two forms: (1) active resistance, which seeks to curb invasion of habitats by states and markets, and (2) adaptation, which exemplifies the centuries-old practice of renewing habitats in the face of environmental deterioration. In the latter practice lie some answers to current problems.

Perhaps the most dramatic form of resistance was undertaken by the Chipko movement in the central Himalaya region of India. Renewing an ancient tradition of peasant resistance in 1973, the Chipko adopted a Gandhian strategy of nonviolence, symbolized in tree-hugging protests led primarily by women against commercial logging. Similar protests spread across northern India in a move to protect forest habitats for tribal peoples. Emulating the Chipko practice of tree planting to restore forests and soils, the movement developed a "pluck-and-plant" tactic. Its members uprooted eucalyptus seedlings—the tree of choice in official social forestry, even though it does not provide shade and does ravish aquifers—and replaced them with indigenous species of trees that yield products useful to the locals. Success of these movements has been measured primarily in two ways: (1) by withdrawal of Bank involvement and the redefinition of forestry management by the government and (2) by the flowering of new political associations, sometimes called "user groups," that are democratic and dedicated to reclaiming lands and redefining grassroots development.[40]

Environmental activism like this is paralleled across the South. In Thailand, where the state has promoted eucalyptus plantations that threaten massive displacement of forest dwellers, there has been

an explosion of rural activism. . . . Small farmers are standing up to assassination threats; weathering the contempt of bureaucrats; petitioning cabinet officials; arranging strategy meetings with other villagers; calling on reserves of political experience going back decades; marching; rallying; blocking roads; ripping out seedlings; chopping down eucalyptus trees; burning nurseries; planting fruit, rubber and forest trees in order to demonstrate their own conservationist awareness. . . . Their message is simple. They want individual land rights. They want community rights to local forests which they will conserve themselves. They want a reconsideration of all existing eucalyptus projects. And they want the right to veto any commercial plantation scheme in their locality.[41]

In the Philippines, a successful reforestation program undertaken by the Ikalahan of the eastern Cordillera followed the decentralization of resource control from the Department of Energy and Natural Resources to management by the local community in the 1980s. The state in effect transferred ancestral land back to the community. On the island of Mindanao, indigenous communities have reclaimed state and pastoral lands for subsistence farming, organizing themselves democratically along Chipko lines.[42]

As grassroots environmentalism mushrooms across the South, community control gains credibility by example. At the same time, the institutional aspects of technology transfer associated with the development project come under question. An ex-director of forestry at the Food and Agricultural Organization commented in 1987,

> Only very much later did it dawn on the development establishment that the very act of establishing new institutions often meant the weakening, even the destruction of existing indigenous institutions which ought to have served as the basis for sane and durable development: the family, the clans, the tribe, the village, sundry mutual aid organizations, peasant associations, rural trade unions, marketing and distribution systems and so on.[43]

Forest dwellers have *always* managed their environment. From the perspective of colonial rule and the developers, these communities did not appear to be involved in management because their practices were alien to the rational, specialized pursuit of commercial wealth characterizing Western ways beginning under colonialism. Local practices were therefore either suppressed or ignored.

Now, where colonial forestry practices erased local knowledge and eroded natural resources, recent grassroots mobilization, such as the Green Belt Movement in Kenya organized by women, has reestablished intercropping to replenish soils and tree planting to sustain forests. Where development agencies and planners have attempted to impose irrigated cash cropping, such as in eastern Senegal, movements such as the Senegalese Federation of Sarakolle Villages have collectively resisted in the interests of sustainable peasant farming (sustainable in the social as well as the ecological sense).[44]

**CASE STUDY**

**Local Environmental Managers in Ghana**

Hundreds of local communities have evolved new resource management practices as livelihood strategies, often with the aid of **nongovernmental organizations** (NGOs). A case in point is the revival of local environmental management in the Manya Krobo area of southeastern Ghana, in the wake of environmental deterioration visited on the forestland by cash cropping. British colonialism promoted the production of palm oil, followed by cocoa cultivation, for export. The displacement of forest cover by monocultural cocoa crops led to severe degradation of the soils. With cocoa prices falling in the second half of the twentieth century, local farmers shifted to growing cassava and corn for local food markets; they also cultivated oil palms and activated a local crafts industry (distilling) used for subsistence rather than for export. Forest restoration technologies, combined with food crops, have emerged as a viable adaptation. These restoration methods are based on the preservation of pioneer forest species rather than the fast-growing exotics (with purchasable technological packages) promoted by development agencies as fuel-wood supplies and short-term forest cover.

When a community is attempting to recover a stable livelihood, which includes developing technologies appropriate to retaining ecological balance, does that count as development?

*Source: Amanor (1994:64).*

The challenge for grassroots environmental movements in the former Third World is twofold: (1) to create alternatives to the capital- and energy-intensive forms of specialized agriculture and agro-forestry that are appropriate to the goal of restoring and sustaining local ecologies and (2) to build alternative models to the bureaucratic, top-down development plans that have typically subordinated natural resource use to commercial, rather than to sustainable, social ends. Perhaps the fundamental challenge to southern environmental movements is the perspective stated in the Bank's world development report for 1992: "Promoting development is the best way to protect the environment."[45] Whether development, understood from the Bank's perspective, is a source of sustainability is the question.

# Feminism

Where southern grassroots movements entail protection of local resources and community, women typically play a defining role. This has always been so, but one consequence of colonialism is that this activity has become almost exclusively a women's preserve. As private property in land emerged, women's work tended to specialize in use of the commons for livestock grazing, firewood collection, game hunting, and seed gathering for medicinal purposes. These activities allowed women to supplement the incomes earned by men in the commercial sector. Women assumed a role as environmental managers, often forced to adapt to deteriorating conditions as commercial extractions increased over time.

The establishment of individual rights to property under colonialism typically privileged men. The result was to fragment social systems built on the complementarity of male and female work. Men's work became specialized: In national statistics, it is routinely counted as contributing to the commercial sector. Conversely, the specialization of women's labor as "non-income-earning" work remains outside the commercial sector. Oppositions such as waged versus nonwaged work or productive versus nonproductive work emerged. In modern national accounting systems, only productive work is counted or valued, leaving much of women's work invisible. The domain of invisible work includes maintaining the commons.

When we trace the development of feminism, we find that it has circled back toward recovery of this sense of the commons. The journey has been both practical and theoretical—moving from bringing women into development to an alternative conception of the relationship of women to development. It began with the movement to integrate women into development in the early 1970s. The first UN world conference on women was held in Mexico City in 1975 and concentrated on extending existing development programs to include women. This movement was known as women in development (WID). Since then, the movement has changed gears, shifting from what Rounaq Jahan terms an "integrationist" to an "agenda-setting" approach, which challenges the existing development system of thought with a feminist perspective.[46] The goal includes involving women as decision makers concerned with empowering all women in their various life situations.

## Feminist Formulations

The shift from integration to transformation of the development model has involved a redefinition of feminism from WID to women, environment, and alternative development (WED). The redefinition symbolizes a movement from remedies to alternatives.[47] There are two aspects to this shift. First, the WID position emerged to redress the absence of gender issues in development theory and practice. The arguments are familiar: Women's contributions were made invisible by economic statistics that measured only the contributions to development of income-earning units (waged labor and commercial enterprises). WID feminists have identified problems and formulated remedies in the following ways:

- Women have always been de facto producers, but because of their invisibility, their technological and vocational supports have been minimal. Planners should therefore recognize women's contributions, especially as food producers for rural households and even urban markets, where males labor when not migrating to the agro-export or cash crop sector.
- Women also bear children, and a more robust understanding of development would include education, health care, family planning, and nutrition as social supports.
- Finally, because of patriarchal expectations that women perform unpaid household/farm labor in addition to any paid labor, development planners should pursue ameliorative measures. Findings reveal that where women can be incorporated into income-earning activities, a net benefit accrues to community welfare since male income is often dissipated in consumer/urban markets.

By contrast, the WED feminist position includes critiques and remedies as follows:

- Conventional economics is hierarchical and male oriented in its assumptions about development strategy. It excludes the contributions of women and nature from its models.
- Development practices, when informed by economic theory, reveal a predatory relationship in which women are exploited and socially and economically marginalized, and nature is plundered.
- In developing an alternative understanding of the world and its need for renewal, "the task is not simply to add women into the known equation but to establish a new development paradigm."[48] Economic theory is incapable of reform because its rationalist (Eurocentric) approach abstracts knowledge from practice and history and presumes its universal application. An alternative form of knowledge is practical and rooted in cultural traditions. Scholar-activists have formed the Association of Feminist Economics.
- Western traditions of rational science have devalued and displaced practical knowledge through colonialism and development.[49] That is, local

cultures in both the European and the non-European worlds have been subordinated to market rationality. Craft traditions have been mechanized; multiple cropping and animal husbandry combinations have been separated, specialized, and infused with chemical inputs; and Western medical science overrides traditional health practices.

- Finally, "the work of caring for the environment, and women's role as nurturers, are also undervalued in the logic of development."[50]

The difference between WID and WED feminism is further explored in the following insert.

---

### What Is the Difference between WID and WED Feminism?

*The difference in the two perspectives is not just one of emphasis. It involves how we look at the world, including what we take account of. WID feminism tends to accept the developmentalist framework and look for ways within development programs to improve the position of women. For example, pushing for new jobs for women in the paid workforce occurs because women's unpaid work was implicitly devalued and removed from consideration as an activity contributing to livelihoods. The movement from WID to WED follows a conceptual shift from a universalist (rational) toward a diverse (expressive) understanding of the world. It is a shift from a linear to an interrelational view of social change. Thus, WED feminists question the separation in Western thought between nature and culture, where nature is viewed as separate from and acted on by culture rather than each shaping the other. In the WED view, stewardship of nature is understood as integral to the renewal of culture rather than being constructed as a program per se.*

---

The WED position argues that, within the WID paradigm, women are presumed to be universally subordinate to men. Furthermore, development is redefined as a mechanism of emancipation of women. But this perspective is flawed insofar as it tends to judge Third World women's position against the ideal of the emancipated (economically independent) woman of the First World.[51]

In making this comparison, WED feminism stresses that development is a relative, not a universal, process, and we should be aware of how our ideals shape our assumptions about other societies. Concerns for the empowerment of women in Third World settings should refer to those circumstances, not to abstract ideals of individual emancipation. In other words, women's role in sustaining cultural and ecological relations is complex, place specific, and incapable of being reduced to universal formulas.

### CASE STUDY
### Human Rights versus Cultural Rights:
### The Ritual of Female Genital Mutilation

Genital cutting, formerly known as female circumcision, retains prominence in some cultures today as a rite of passage for young females. Global opposition to the ritual, in the name of human rights, is met by defense of it as a valued cultural ritual. In Sudan, where 89 percent of women are circumcised, justifications for the ritual include a custom originating in religious practice (sanctioned, if not required, by Islamic law), the clitoris' evil properties, and the fertility-enhancing and male pleasure–enhancing consequences of circumcision. But subtler cultural functions associated with the patriarchal valuation of women, including the necessity of virginity at marriage, contribute to this ritual. Human rights activists view female genital mutilation as a violation of the rights of women and children across the globe, claiming that its pain and harm to women's sexual pleasure and physical and psychological health are cruel and unnecessary. The UN and NGOs pressure governments to stop the ritual, but often such pressure, including advocating education (which has been shown to change women's attitudes to circumcision), is experienced as *cultural imperialism.* Alternative ceremonies have evolved—such as in Kenya, where the ritual is changed into a rite of passage through a weeklong program of counseling—that still validate the cultures and their practitioners. In eastern Uganda, the Sabiny people use a symbolic ritual pioneered by the Elders Association, who also counsel parents about the medical risks of cutting in terms of exposing females to HIV/AIDS and compromising childbirth later on.

When confronted with a conflict between human and cultural rights, who has the power to decide what is good for the people involved, and what is a solution that is sensitive to the needs of a healthy cultural practice?

*Sources: Crossette (1998b:A8); Kohli and Webster (1999); Sobieszczyk and Williams (1997).*

## Women and the Environment

At the practical level, women engage in multifaceted activity. Across the world, women's organizations have mobilized to manage local resources, empower poor women and communities, and pressure governments and international agencies on behalf of women's rights. Countless activities of resource management undertaken by women form the basis of these practices. Perhaps most basic is the preservation of biodiversity in market and kitchen gardens. In Peru, the Aguarunu Jivaro women nurture more than 100 varieties of manioc, the local staple root crop. Women have devised ingenious ways of household provisioning beside and within the cash-cropping systems managed by men. Hedgerows and wastelands become sites of local food crops.[52] Forest products (game, medicinal plants, condiments) are cultivated and harvested routinely by women. In rural Laos, more than 100 different forest products are collected chiefly by women for home use or sale. Women in Ghana process, distribute, and market game. Indian women anchor household income—with an array of nontimber forest products amounting to 40 percent of total Forest Department revenues—as do Brazilian women in Acre, working by the side of the male rubber tappers.[53]

In Kenya, the Kikuyu women in Laikipia have formed 354 women's groups to help them coordinate community decisions about access to and use of resources. Groups vary in size from 20 to 100 neighbors, both squatters and peasants; members contribute cash, products, and/or labor to the group, which in turn distributes resources equally among them. The groups have been able to pool funds to purchase land and establish small enterprises for the members. One such group, the Mwenda-Niire, formed among landless squatters on the margins of a large commercial estate. Twenty years later, through saving funds, by growing maize and potatoes among the owner's crops, and through political negotiation, the group purchased the 567-hectare farm, allowing 130 landless families to become farmers. Group dynamics continue through labor-sharing schemes, collective infrastructure projects, and collective marketing. Collective movements such as this go beyond remedying development failures. They restore women's access to resources removed from them under colonial and postcolonial developments.[54]

## Women, Poverty, and Fertility

Women's resource management is often ingenious, but often poverty subverts their ingenuity. For example, where women have no secure rights to land, they are less able to engage in sustainable resource extraction. Environmental deterioration may follow. When we see women stripping forests and overworking fragile land, we are often seeing just the tip of the iceberg. Many of these women have been displaced from lands converted for export cropping, or they have lost common land on which to subsist.

Environmental damage stemming from poverty has fueled the debate surrounding population growth in the former Third World. Population control has typically been directed at women—ranging from female infanticide to forced sterilization (as in India) to family planning interventions by development agencies. In Peru, government agencies seized the initiative from women and founding NGOs, deploying a women's health program to perform 80 percent of sterilizations in a broad sterilization campaign that has cut Peru's fertility rate almost in half since 1961.[55] Feminists entered this debate to protect women from such manipulation of their social and biological contributions.

Feminists demand the enabling of women to take control of their fertility without targeting women as the source of the population problem. On a global scale, the current world population of almost 6 billion is expected to double by 2050, according to UN projections, unless more aggressive intervention occurs. Studies suggest that female education and health services reduce birthrates. The 1992 World Bank report pointed out that women without secondary education, on average, have seven children; if almost half these women receive secondary education, the average declines to three children per woman.[56]

In addition, recent evidence based on the results of contraceptive use in Bangladesh has been cited as superseding conventional theories of "demographic transition." Demographic theory extrapolates from the Western experience a pattern of demographic transition whereby birthrates decline significantly as economic growth proceeds. The threshold is the shift from preindustrial to industrial society, in which education and health technologies spread. This is expected to cause families to view children increasingly as an economic liability rather than as necessary hands in the household economy or as a response to high childhood mortality rates.

Evidence from Bangladesh, one of the 20 poorest countries of the world, shows a 21 percent decline in fertility rates during the decade and a half (1975–1991) in which a national family planning program was in effect. The study's authors claimed that these findings "dispute the notion that 'development is the best contraceptive,'" adding that "contraceptives are the best contraceptive."[57]

Feminist groups argue that family planning and contraception need to be rooted in the broader context of women's rights. Presently, almost twice as many women as men are illiterate, and that difference is growing. Poor women with no education often do not understand their rights or contraceptive choices. The International Women's Health Coalition identified the Bangladesh Women's Health Coalition, serving 110,000 women at 10 clinics around the country, as a model for future United Nations planning. This group began in 1980, offering abortions. With suggestions from the women it served, the coalition has expanded into family planning, basic health care services, child immunizations, legal aid, and training in literacy and employment skills.[58]

The correlation between women's rights and low fertility rates has ample confirmation. In Tunisia, the 1956 Code of Individual Rights guaranteed women political equality, backed with family planning and other social programs that included free, legal abortions. Tunisia is a leader in Africa, with a population growth rate of only 1.9 percent. The director-general of Tunisia's National Office of Family and Population, Nebiha Gueddana, claims that successful family planning can occur in a Muslim society: "We have thirty years of experience with the equality of women and . . . none of it has come at the expense of family values."[59] And in Kerala, where the literacy rate for women is two and a half times the average for India and where the status of women has been high throughout the twentieth century relative to the rest of the country, land reforms and comprehensive social welfare programs were instrumental in achieving a 40 percent reduction in the fertility rate between 1960 and 1985, reducing the population growth rate to 1.8 percent in the 1980s.[60]

With supportive social conditions, fertility decisions by women can have both individual and social benefits. Fertility decisions by individual women usually occur within patriarchal settings—households or societies—as well as within definite livelihood situations. It is these conditions that the feminist movements and women's groups have identified as necessary to the calculus in fertility decisions. Over the past decade, the population issue has incorporated elements of the feminist perspective, which emphasizes women's reproductive rights and health, in the context of their need for secure livelihoods and political participation.[61] This view was embedded in the document from the 1994 UN Conference on Population and Development. Although contested by the Vatican and some Muslim nations (particularly Iran), the document states that women have the right to reproductive and sexual health, defined as "a state of complete physical, mental and social well-being" in all matters relating to reproduction.[62]

## Women's Rights

Feminism has clearly made an impact on the development agenda since the days of WID's inception. However, the improvement of women's material condition and social status across the world has not followed in step, even if the statistical reporting of women's work in subsistence production has improved.[63] In 1989, at the end of a decade of structural adjustment, the United Nations made the following report in its World Survey on the Role of Women in Development:

> The bottom line shows that, despite economic progress measured in growth rates, at least for the majority of developing countries, economic progress for women has virtually stopped, social progress has slowed, and social well-being in many cases has deteriorated, and because of the importance of women's social and economic roles, the aspirations for them in current development strategies will not be met.[64]

Five years later, the United Nation's *Human Development Report 1994* found that "despite advances in labor-force participation, education and health, women still constitute about two-thirds of the world's illiterates, hold fewer than half of the jobs on the market and are paid half as much as men for work of equal value."[65] Even so, feminism has put its stamp on the reformulations of development; the UN 1994 report declared the following in response to the crisis in the former Third World:

> It requires a long, quiet process of sustainable human development . . . [a] development that not only generates economic growth but distributes its benefits equitably, that regenerates the environment rather than destroying it; that empowers people rather than marginalizing them. It is development that gives priority to the poor, enlarging their choices and opportunities and providing for their participation in decisions that affect their lives. It is development that is pro-people, pro-nature, pro-jobs and pro-women.[66]

In Muslim cultures, with considerable variation, women's rights remain subordinated to Islamic law or, as Muslim feminists claim, to male interpretation of the Koran. In Morocco, for example, women require permission of male relatives to marry, name their children, or work. Sisters inherit half that of brothers, and male coercion in marriage is customary. Islamic women's groups across the Muslim world are mobilizing against what they term *Muslim apartheid*, especially since the UN Fourth World Conference on Women in Beijing, 1995. In the Mediterranean region, rapid urbanization has produced more educated and professional women who focus on changing secular laws to make an end run around Islamic law.[67] Women within more traditional communities who resist custom also resist the neat adoption/imitation of modern practices and beliefs.

Finally, in an evaluation of the Beijing conference, titled "Mapping Progress: Assessing Implementation of the Beijing Platform 1998," the Women's Environment and Development Organization reported that 70 percent of 187 national governments had laid plans to improve women's rights, 66 countries have offices for women's affairs, and 34 of these have legislative input. Pressure from local and international women's organizations since the Beijing conference, in countries as different as Mexico, Germany, New Zealand, and China, has made some gains, such as instituting laws against domestic violence.[68]

# Cosmopolitan Activism

Perhaps the litmus test of the globalization project is that as global integration intensifies, the currents of cosmopolitan activism deepen. Class or ethnic-based communities, regions, and networks mobilize to challenge and provide alternatives to the global order. Such challenges occur at or across different scales. Cosmopolitan activism recognizes that environmental issues are simultaneously labor issues and that women's issues are not just confined to fertility, reproduction, and women's work but also include housing, credit, and health—where each of these dimensions of development is gendered in a project realized through multiscale patriarchal structures.

Cosmopolitan activism includes cooperatives that reorganize a community around democratic values and restoring local ecological balance. Indigenous movements may assert their cultural rights to regional territories. The fair trade movements may organize transnational networks to revalue producers and what is produced in relation to social justice concerns shared with distant consumers. These multilayered initiatives contribute to new thinking about governance: from the idea of "subsidiarity" (locating decision making at the appropriate level, whether global or municipal) to David Held's related call for a **"cosmopolitan project"**[69] to Wolfgang Sachs's notion of **"cosmopolitan localism,"** based in the valuing of diversity as a universal right:

> Today, more than ever, universalism is under siege. To be sure, the victorious march of science, state and market has not come to a stop, but the

enthusiasm of the onlookers is flagging. . . . The globe is not any longer imagined as a homogeneous space where contrasts ought to be levelled out, but as a discontinuous space where differences flourish in a multiplicity of places.[70]

Cosmopolitan activisms question the assumption of uniformity in the global development project and assert the need to respect alternative cultural traditions as a matter of global survival. They represent different initiatives to preserve or assert human and democratic rights within broader settings, whether a world community or individual national or subnational arenas. This is the spirit behind the concept of "cosmopolitan democracy."[71]

## CASE STUDY
### Andean Counterdevelopment, or "Cultural Affirmation"

Cosmopolitan localism takes a variety of forms. One form is a dialogical method of privileging the local worldview, including an evaluation of modern Western knowledge from the local standpoint. This means learning to value local culture and developing a contextualized understanding of foreign knowledges, so that they do not assume some universal truth and inevitability, as claimed by Western knowledge and its officialdom. In this sense, modernity is understood as a peculiarly Western cosmology arising from European culture and history, which includes universalist claims legitimizing imperial expansion across the world. In the Peruvian Andes, indigenous writers and activists formed an NGO in 1987 called PRATEC (Proyecto Andino de Tecnologias Campesinas), which is concerned with recovering and implementing traditional Andean peasant culture and technologies via education of would-be rural developers. PRATEC links the Andean cosmology to its particular history and local ecology. It does not see itself as a political movement but rather as a form of cultural politics dedicated to revaluing Andean culture and affirming local diversity over abstract homogenizing knowledges associated with modernity. One PRATEC peasant explained, "We have great faith in what nature transmits to us. These indicators are neither the result of the science of humans, nor the invention of people with great experience. Rather, it is the voice of nature itself which announces to us the manner in which we must plant our crops." Andean peasants grow and know some 1,500 varieties of quinoa, 330 of kaniwa, 228 of tarwi, 3,500 of potatoes,

610 of oca (another tuber), and so on. In situating this cultural affirmation, a core founding member of PRATEC explained that "to decolonize ourselves is to break with the global enterprise of development." In the context of the collapse of Peru's formal economy, the delegitimization of government development initiatives, and environmental deterioration, PRATEC is the vehicle of a dynamic alternative, rooted in indigenous ecology, and a participatory culture that puts the particularity of the Western project in perspective.

When local cultures or communities are revalued like this, how can their romanticization (including privileging customary hierarchies of class, gender, or ethnicity) be avoided?

*Source: Apffel-Marglin (1997).*

The most potent example of cosmopolitan activism was the peasant revolt in Mexico's southern state of Chiapas, a region in which small peasant farms are surrounded by huge cattle ranches and coffee plantations. About a third of the unresolved land reforms in the Mexican agrarian reform department, going back more than half a century, are in Chiapas. The government's solution over the years has been to allow landless *campesinos* to colonize the Lacandon jungle and produce subsistence crops, coffee, and cattle. During the 1980s, coffee, cattle, and corn prices all fell, and *campesinos* were prohibited from logging—even though timber companies continued the practice.[72] The revolt had these deepening class inequalities as its foundation. But the source of the inequalities transcended the region.

On New Year's Day, 1994, hundreds of impoverished peasants rose up against what they perceived to be the Mexican state's continued violation of local rights. Not coincidentally, the revolt fell on the day NAFTA was implemented. To the Chiapas rebels, NAFTA symbolized the undermining of the revolutionary heritage in the Mexican Constitution of 1917, by which communal lands were protected from alienation. In 1992, under the pretext of structural adjustment policies and the promise of NAFTA, the Mexican government opened these lands for sale to Mexican and foreign agribusinesses. In addition, NAFTA included a provision to deregulate commodity markets—especially the market for corn, the staple peasant food.

The Chiapas revolt illustrates cosmopolitan localism well because it linked the struggle for local rights to a political and historical context. That is, the *Zapatistas* (as the rebels call themselves, after Mexican revolutionary Emilio Zapata) perceive the Mexican state as the chief agent of exploitation of the region's cultural and natural wealth. In one of many communiqués aimed at the global community, Subcomandante Marcos, the *Zapatista* spokesperson, characterized the Chiapas condition as follows:

> Oil, electric energy, cattle, money, coffee, bananas, honey, corn, cocoa, tobacco, sugar, soy, melons, sorghum, mamey, mangos, tamarind, avocados, and Chiapan blood flow out through a thousand and one fangs sunk into the neck of Southeastern Mexico. Billions of tons of natural resources go through Mexican ports, railway stations, airports, and road systems to various destinations: the United States, Canada, Holland, Germany, Italy, Japan—but all with the same destiny: to feed the empire. . . . The jungle is opened with machetes, wielded by the same campesinos whose land has been taken away by the insatiable beast. . . . Poor people cannot cut down trees, but the oil company, more and more in the hands of foreigners, can. . . . Why does the federal government take the question of national politics off the proposed agenda of the dialogue for peace? Are the indigenous Chiapan people only Mexican enough to be exploited, but not Mexican enough to be allowed an opinion on national politics? . . . What kind of citizens are the indigenous people of Chiapas? "Citizens in formation?" [73]

In these communiqués, the Ejército Zapatista de Liberación Nacional (EZLN) movement addresses processes of both decline and renewal in Mexican civil society. The process of decline refers to the dismantling of the communal tradition of the Mexican national state symbolized in the infamous reform of Article 27 of the Constitution. The article now privileges private (foreign) investment in land over the traditional rights of *campesinos* to petition for land redistribution within the *ejido* (Indian community land held in common) framework. The *Zapatistas* argue that this reform, in conjunction with NAFTA liberalization, undermines the Mexican smallholder and the basic grains sector. The *Zapatistas* understand that the U.S. "comparative advantage" in corn production (6.9 U.S. tons versus 1.7 Mexican tons per hectare, including infrastructural disparities) seriously threatens Mexican maize producers, especially because under NAFTA, the Mexican government has agreed to phase out guaranteed prices for staples such as maize and beans.[74] With an estimated 200 percent rise in corn imports under NAFTA's full implementation by 2008, it is expected that more than two-thirds of Mexican maize production will not survive the competition.[75] The NGO, Global Food Watch, estimates that 1.8 million Mexican maize farmers have been undermined recently by heavily subsidized corn imports from the United States.[76]

Renewal involves the "citizenship" demands by the Chiapas movement—meaning the need for free and fair elections in Chiapas (and elsewhere in Mexico), adequate political representation of *campesino* interests (as against those of Chiapas planters and ranchers), and the elimination of violence and authoritarianism in local government. The EZLN's demands included a formal challenge to a centuries-old pattern of *caciquismo* (local strongman tradition) in which federal government initiatives have been routinely thwarted by local political and economic interests.[77]

The renewal side also includes the demonstration effect of the Chiapas revolt because communities throughout Mexico have since mobilized around similar demands—especially because local communities face common pressures, such as market reforms. In challenging local patronage politics, the *Zapatistas* elevated demands nationally for inclusion of *campesino* organizations in political decisions regarding rural reforms, including equity demands for small farmers as well as farm workers. They also advanced the cause of local and/or indigenous development projects that sustain regional ecologies and cultures.[78]

What is distinctive about the Chiapas rebellion is the *texture* of its political action. Timed to coincide with the implementation of NAFTA, it wove together a powerful and symbolic critique of the politics of globalization. This critique had two goals. First, it opposed the involvement of national elites and governments in implementing neoliberal economic reforms on a global or regional scale, reforms that undo the institutionalized social entitlements associated with political liberalism. Second, it asserted a new agenda of renewal involving a politics of rights that goes beyond individual or property rights to human, and therefore community, rights. The push for regional autonomy challenged local class inequalities and demanded the empowerment of *campesino* communities. It also asserted the associative political style of the EZLN, composed of a coalition of *campesino* and women's organizations. Within the *Zapatista* movement, women have questioned the premise of official indigenous state policies that dichotomizes modernity and tradition, insisting on "the right to hold to distinct cultural traditions while at the same time changing aspects of those traditions that oppress or exclude them."[79] This involves blending the formal demand for territorial and resource autonomy with the substantive demand for women's rights to political, physical, economic, social, and cultural autonomy.

The *Zapatista* program rejects integration into outside development projects, outlining a plan for land restoration, abolition of peasant debts, and reparations to be paid to the Indians of Chiapas by those who have exploited their human and natural resources. Self-determination involves the development of new organizational forms of cooperation among different groups in the region. These have evolved over time into a "fabric of cooperation" woven among the various threads of local groupings. They substitute fluid organizational patterns for the bureaucratic organizational forms associated with modernist politics—such as political parties, trade unions, and hierarchical state structures.[80] In these senses, whether the *Zapatistas* survive the Mexican army's continuing siege of Chiapas and the current move to undercut the rebels with a regional investment and trade corridor (the Plan Pueblo de Panama—tapping into a low-cost pool of displaced labor that can compete in the "race-to-the-bottom" dynamic spearheaded by China), the movement they have quickened will intensify the unresolved tension between global governance and political representation.

## CASE STUDY
### The New Labor Cosmopolitanism:
### Social Movement Unionism

One consequence of the globalization project is labor union decline, as well as the casualization of labor associated with the restructuring of work and corporate downsizing, as firms and states pursue efficiency in the global economy. Another is the relocation of union activities from the global North to the newly industrialized countries (NICs). A new labor internationalism is emerging to present a solid front to footloose firms that divide national labor forces and to states that sign the free trade agreement's (FTA's) weakening labor benefits.

The new labor internationalism was a key part of the political debate surrounding NAFTA. Led by the rank and file, organized labor joined a national political coalition of consumers, environmentalists, and others in opposing the implementation of NAFTA, arguing that, since Mexican unions were organs of the state, which maintained a low minimum wage, NAFTA could not protect U.S. labor from unfair competition.

Subsequently, cross-border unionism to protect labor on either side has taken off. The stranglehold of the Mexican government on union organization frayed, evidenced by the formation of an independent union, the Authentic Labor Front, which formed an alliance with the U.S. United Electrical Workers, Teamsters, Steel Workers, and four other U.S. and Canadian unions in the early 1990s. The American Federation of Labor and Congress of Industrial Organizations (AFL-CIO) has since sought alliances with independent Mexican unions, including calling for independent labor organizing in the *maquiladores*. On December 12, 1997, following a long struggle, the Korean-owned Han Young plant in Tijuana agreed to the formation of an independent union among its *maquila* factory workers, a 30 percent pay raise, and reinstatement of fired activists.

On International Women's Day (March 8) in 2002, the International Confederation of Free Trade Unions launched a three-year campaign, targeting female workers in export processing zones (EPZs) as well in the informal sector, realizing that in the latter is a growing segment of future membership.

This development mirrors movements elsewhere in the global South, where independent unions respond to global integration. For instance, the Transnationals Information Exchange (TIE) forged networks of labor organization across the world, targeting the production of the "world car," and formed the Cocoa-Chocolate Network, based on the global commodity chain, whereby TIE linked European industrial workers with Asian and Latin American plantation workers and peasants, linking chocolate factories to the cacao bean fields. TIE practiced **social movement unionism,** connecting casualized labor across national boundaries, organizing regionalized networks of labor, and addressing issues of racism and immigrant workers. It evolved a flexible, decentralized structure that mirrors the age of lean production, empowering labor and its activists across the networks. Such social movement unionism is spreading in middle-income states such as Brazil, South Africa, Taiwan, and South Korea, where unions spearhead broad coalitions demanding democratization of political systems, linking economic rights (working conditions) with political rights (independent organization) and social rights (restoration of the social contract and responsiveness to social justice concerns). Their employment in globally competitive industries often lends them a strategic power through the strike.

If labor organizes transnationally, what cosmopolitan institutional mechanisms, beyond the nation-state, does it need to protect and sustain its rights to secure employment, fair wages, and just working conditions?

---

*Sources: Silver (2003); Ross and Trachte (1990); Brecher and Costello (1994:153-54); Benería (1995:48); Calvo (1997); Moody (1999:255-62); Dillon (1997, 1998); Rowling (2001:24); Seidman (1994).*

## Food Sovereignty Movements

At the turn of the twenty-first century, 815 million people (777 million in the global South) remain food insecure, that is, unable to meet their daily energy requirements. Meanwhile six corporations handle 85 percent of the world grain trade, and integrated, centralized control of the food chain (from gene to supermarket shelf) intensifies. In the name of globalization, this northern model (including risks associated with factory farming and food scares) is exported as the solution to food insecurity, displacing northern and southern farmers. Canadian farmer Nettie Wiebe remarks, "The difficulty for us, as farming people, is that we are rooted in the places where we live and grow our food. The other side, the corporate world, is globally mobile."[81]

Resistances to the global conception of food security are mushrooming—framed by the alternative conception of **food sovereignty.** This means not just protecting local farming but revitalizing democratic, cultural, and ecological processes at the subnational level. The several million-strong farmers' transnational movement, Via Campesina, asserts that "farmers' rights are eminently collective" and "should therefore be considered as a different legal framework from those of private property." Via Campesina, formed in 1992, unites local and regional chapters of landless peasants, family farmers, agricultural workers, rural women, and indigenous communities across Africa, Europe, Asia, and North, Central, and South America. It claims that "biodiversity has as a fundamental base the recognition of human diversity, the acceptance that we are different and that every people and each individual has the freedom to think and to be. Seen in this way, biodiversity is not only flora, fauna, earth, water and ecosystems; it is also cultures, systems of production, human and economic relations, forms of government; in essence it is freedom."[82]

Food sovereignty, in this vision, is "the right of peoples, communities and countries to define their own agricultural, labour, fishing, food and land policies which are ecologically, socially, economically and culturally appropriate to their unique circumstances."[83] Via Campesina argues that food should not come under the WTO regime: Food production plays a unique social role and should not be subordinated to market dictates. Food self-reliance comes first, *followed* by trade. The movement would subordinate trade relations to the question of access to land, credit, and fair prices, set politically via the rules of fair trade to be negotiated in the United Nations Conference on Trade and Development (UNCTAD), with active participation of farmers in building democratic definitions of agricultural and food policies. While the consumer movement (e.g., the 60,000 towns and villages of the European slow food movement) has discovered that "eating has become a political act," Via Campesina adds, "Producing quality products for our own people has also become a political act . . . this touches our very identities as citizens of this world."[84] Access to land is a first step, and Via Campesina declares,

> Access to the land by peasants has to be understood as a guarantee for survival and the valorisation of their culture, the autonomy of their communities and a new vision of the preservation of natural resources for humanity and future generations. Land is a good of nature that needs to be used for the welfare of all. Land is not, and cannot be, a marketable good that can be obtained in whatever quantity by those that have the financial means.[85]

Perhaps the most significant chapter of Via Campesina is the Brazilian landless workers' movement, the Movimento dos Trabalhadores Rurais Sem Terra (MST). In the past 17 years, the MST has settled more than 400,000 families on 15 million acres of land seized by takeovers of unworked land. The stimulus has been a Brazilian development model of structural adjustment, in a context where 1 percent of landowners own (but do not necessarily cultivate) 50 percent of the land, leaving 4.8 million families landless. While Brazil's extensive system of agricultural subsidies was withdrawn, the Organization for Economic Cooperation and Development (OECD) member states' agricultural subsidies have continued at U.S.$360 billion a year. As the MST Web site notes, "From 1985 to 1996, according to the agrarian census, 942,000 farms disappeared, 96% of which were smaller than one hundred hectares. From that total, 400 thousand establishments went bankrupt in the first two years of the Cardoso government, 1995–96." Between 1985 and 1996, rural unemployment rose by 5.5 million, and between 1995 and 1999, a rural exodus of 4 million Brazilians occurred. While in the 1980s, Brazil imported roughly U.S.$1 million worth of wheat, apples, and products not produced in Brazil, from "1995 to 1999, this annual average leapt to 6.8 billion dollars, with the importation of many products cultivable . . . in Brazil."[86]

The landless workers' movement draws legitimacy for its land occupations from the Brazilian constitution's sanctioning of the confiscation of uncultivated private property: "It is incumbent upon the Republic to expropriate for social interest, for purposes of agrarian reform, rural property, which is not performing its social function."[87] The MST is organized in 23 states of Brazil, and while dispossessed farmers comprise 60 percent of its membership, it also includes unemployed workers and disillusioned civil servants.

Land seizures—under the slogan of "Occupy! Resist! Produce!"—lead to the formation of cooperatives, which involve social mobilization "transforming the economic struggle into a political and ideological struggle."[88] Democratic decision making is practiced to develop cooperative relations among workers and alternative patterns of land use, financed by socializing a portion of settlement income. Participatory budgeting allocates funds for repairs, soil improvement, cattle feeding, computers, housing, teachers' salaries, child care, mobilization, and so on. Fundamental to this social project is the Freirian dictum that "a settlement, precisely because it is a production unit . . ., should also be a whole pedagogic unit."[89] Education starts from children's daily perspective, building on the learner's direct experience and communicating the inherent value of rural life. This differs from the production focus of the corporate economic model, including its disregard for rural well-being, farmer knowledges, and farmer rights.[90] Joao Pedro Stedile, president of the MST, observes,

> Under the objective economic conditions, our proposal for land reform has to avoid the oversimplification of classical capitalist land reform, which merely divides up large landholdings and encourages their productive use. We are convinced that nowadays it is necessary to reorganize agriculture on a different social base, democratize access to capital, democratize the agroindustrial process (something just as important as landownership), and democratize access to know-how, that is, to formal education.[91]

The MST's 1,600 government-recognized settlements include medical clinics and training centers for health care workers and 1,200 public schools employing an estimated 3,800 teachers serving about 150,000 children at any one time. A UNESCO grant enables adult literacy classes for 25,000, and the MST sponsors technical classes and teacher training. MST cooperative enterprises generate $50 million annually. They produce not only jobs for thousands of members but also (increasingly organic) foodstuffs and clothing for local, national, and global consumption. The priority given to producing staple foods for low-income consumers (rather than foods for affluent consumers in cities and abroad) led to a 2003 agreement with the da Silva government for the direct purchase of settlement produce for the national Zero Hunger campaign.

And, as one commentator notes,

> These collective enterprises show why the MST is considered a leader in the international **fair trade** movement. The movement is supplying a real, workable alternative to corporate globalization, putting community values and environmental stewardship before profit-making. MST co-ops offer a glimpse of what environmentally sustainable and socially just commerce would look like.[92]

## CASE STUDY
### The Case for Fair Trade

The idea of fair trade paralleled the intensification of global integration, with aid agencies sponsoring links between craftspeople from the global South and northern consumers with a taste for "ethnic" products. Fair trade has now blossomed as a method of transcending abuses in the free trade system and rendering more visible the conditions of production of globally traded commodities to establish just prices, environmentally sound practices, healthy consumption, and direct understanding between producers and consumers of their respective needs.

Fair trade exchanges have an annual market value of $400 million, and the market for fair trade products (organic products such as coffee, bananas, cocoa, honey, tea, and orange juice—representing about 60 percent of the fair trade market, alongside organic cotton jeans and an array of handicrafts) expands at between 10 and 25 percent a year. Three fair trade labels—Transfair, Max Havelaar, and Fairtrade Mark—broke into European markets in the late 1980s and are now united under the Fairtrade Labelling Organizations International (FLO), an umbrella NGO that harmonizes different standards and organizes a single fair trade market (in the absence of national regulations). FLO aims to "raise awareness among consumers of the negative effects on producers of international trade so that they exercise their purchasing power positively." Laura Raynolds notes that certification of fair trade practices requires "democratically organized associations of small growers or plantations where workers are fully represented by independent democratic unions or other groups . . .[and] labor conditions . . . uphold basic ILO conventions (including rights to association, freedom from discrimination, prohibition of child and forced labor, minimum social conditions, and rights to safe and healthy work conditions)." Above world market prices are guaranteed. In Costa Rica, for instance, a cooperative, Coopetrabasur, achieved Fairtrade registration to supply bananas, eliminating herbicide use, reducing chemical fertilizers, building democratic union procedures, raising wages, and establishing a "social premium" set aside for community projects such as housing improvement, electrification, and environmental monitoring.

But will fair trade remain a parallel movement only, encouraging TNCs such as Starbucks to offer a fair trade variety at the most and primarily offering a fair outlet for dependent tropical producers, or can it mobilize public education and consumer purchasing power to democratize the global market and transform its corporate management?

*Sources: Raynolds (2000:298, 301, 306); Ransom (2001b); J. Smith (2002:40-41).*

## Summary

We have toured some of the world's hot spots in this chapter, noting the particular forms in which social movements respond to the failures of developmentalism and the further disorganizing impact of globalism. Responses range from withdrawal into alternative projects (e.g., women's cooperatives, recovery of noncapitalist agro-ecological practices) to attempts to reframe development as a question of rights and social protections (such as the feminist movement, social environmentalism, local rebellions, and right-wing fundamentalism). All these responses express the uncertainties of social arrangements under globalizing tendencies. Many express a fundamental desire to break out of the homogenizing and disempowering dynamics of the globalization project and to establish a sustainable form of social life based on new forms of associative politics.

Other forms of resistance to the globalization project include mushrooming consumer advocacy. One broad consumer movement has been the United Students Against Sweatshops (USAS), formed in 1998 after several years of campus organizing against the link between U.S. universities and offshore sweatshops producing logo-emblazoned clothing. Approximately 160 colleges support an anti-sweatshop code proposed by the Collegiate Licensing Company, which purchases apparel from the manufacturers. Continuing contention about the stringency of the code has led to building occupations and mass meetings at a number of campuses, including Duke, Wisconsin, Georgetown, Stanford, and Cornell. Nike responded by raising wages for its workers in Indonesia, even though the financial crisis has undermined their real purchasing power.[93] In related human rights areas, consumer movements have successfully focused attention on child labor stitching soccer balls in Pakistan, although monitoring remains incomplete.

In sum, the road to the political future has several forks. Across the world, countermovements form in regional cereal banks in Zimbabwe, ecological campaigns by women's groups in West Bengal, *campesino* credit unions in Mexico, the emergence of solidarity networks among labor forces, food safety campaigns in Europe, and the defense of forest dwellers throughout the tropics. How effectively these movements will interconnect politically—at the national, regional, and global levels—is an open question. Another question is how these movements will negotiate with existing states over the terms of local and/or cultural sustenance. Potentially, the new movements breathe new life into politics. They transcend the centralizing thrust of the development states of the postwar era and present models for the recovery of democratic forms of social organization at different scales, as well as the extension of the meaning of civil society. Overriding questions include how new political movements will articulate with states and whether they will replenish or replace nation-states. Many of the people and communities left behind by the development and globalization projects look to NGOs, rather than to states or international agencies, to represent them and meet their needs. Indeed, we are currently in a phase of "NGOization," in that national governments and international institutions have lost much of their legitimacy, and NGOs take considerable initiative in guiding grassroots development activities.

In sum, the opportunity presented by the globalization project is precisely the more complete disrobing of the emperor, as the global market is revealed to be social invention with decidedly antisocial tendencies. Even the global managers recognize this. In 1996, the World Economic Forum, an organization of executives from the top 1,000 global corporations that meets annually in Davos, Switzerland, produced an article titled "Start Taking the Backlash to Globalization Seriously," which states that "a mounting backlash to economic globalization is threatening a very disruptive impact on the economic activity and social stability in many countries" and that globalization "leads to winner-take-all situations; those who come out on top win big, and the losers lose even bigger."[94] While "a very disruptive impact" can be taken both ways, there is no doubt that the battle lines regarding the assumptions and content of the global development project are being drawn and redrawn daily. In the following and concluding chapter, we examine how our future and the future of development are shaping up.

# 8

# Whither Development?

In an age of unilateralism, pursued by the remaining world superpower, it is not yet clear what may happen to the project of global development. Some say we are in transition to a new, imperial project, where the United States will use its military supremacy and bilateral trade deals to manage its rivals and its access to resources and markets. Others say this has been a pattern all along, even if multilateralism appears to be losing salience. Still others believe that transnational corporations (TNCs) are sufficiently powerful that global integration through the market will remain a strong force. Whatever the case, there is no doubt that the commitment to liberalization on the part of the United States and other G7 states is less than absolute. Countries may be equal in theory, but some are more equal than others in practice. Where does this leave development?

Development has always been a handmaiden to power. Development discourse may represent change in such a way as to serve powerful interests. This does not mean that there has been no positive movement in basic development indicators (literacy, health, standard of living, innovation). What it does mean is that the identification of development with measures that record cash transactions has privileged monetary relations and therefore those who manage monetary relations and those who turn money into capital. Privileging monetary measures discounts a range of other relations that matter: unpaid labor, informal knowledges, biodiversity, habitat, family/community care, local markets, and so forth.

Some say development as an ideal has lost its credibility, given recent reports from the United Nations that more than 100 countries have experienced declining living standards over the past two decades.[1] Others say development has been redefined in the age of globalization and that the "trickle down" of wealth now depends not on individual national policies but on the dynamism and prosperity of the global economy, as well as the ability of populations to find their niche in this process. Still others say that development (culminating in an "age of high mass consumption") can no longer be realized because of "planetary overload" or because of the rapid polarization of wealth/poverty or power/marginalization in a global market system. Political mechanisms to sustain and redistribute resources and equalize power relations appear to be ineffectual and/or crisis ridden.

The nineteenth-century European social thinkers, who gave us our theories of development, saw social development evolving along rational industrial lines. Eventually, the European colonies were expected to make the same journey. Development spoke to the human condition, with universal expectation. This expectation was formalized in the development project, which proved to be an unrealizable ideal. It was replaced with another unrealizable ideal, the globalization project, which speaks a similar economic language but at a different scale with different rules. It is old wine in a new bottle.

In this chapter, we reflect on the legacies of the development project and the limits of the globalization project—including the movement toward an imperial project.

## Legacies of the Development Project

Three observations can be made about the development project and its underlying message.

- It took the fork in the historical road favoring the Western model over possible alternatives.
- This fork privileges economic power and rationality over other ecological conceptions of social organization.
- As a result, the world faces an uncertain future, and development itself is in serious question.

### Historical Choices

Historical choices were made in the 1940s, but they grew out of global power relations. Development is a longstanding European idea combining, uneasily, two elements of Enlightenment thought: the belief in unlimited progress and the promise of self-organization.[2] Progressivism legitimized Europe's emergence as the world capitalist power, which was committed to an endless accumulation of wealth as a rational economic activity and premised on subjugation of the non-European world. The inevitable and unreflective comparison Europeans made between their civilization and the apparently backward culture of their colonial subjects produced a *particular* conception of modernity *universalized* as human destiny. This conception governed the choice to institutionalize development on a world scale.

The development project took the fork that led toward unlimited progress, defined by the Western experience and bundled up in the discourse of national economic growth. It rejected the other fork, the one of self-definition. From the West's perspective, the colonial world was too valuable, in economic terms, to let go; from many newly independent political elites' perspective, the West was also too tempting a source of aid and legitimacy to let go. As postcolonial nations achieved independence, membership of the United Nations came with a system of national accounting that standardized the meaning of development across the world of states.

## Reductionism

Henceforth, only measurable (monetized) human activity would be counted as economic or productive. All other activity was defined as "dependent," or "undeveloped" or "backward." The way was clear to impose the Western model of political economy on the world that counted. Women, assigned to the household, would not be counted, and indigenous peasants, nomads, and forest dwellers could be marginalized or displaced as unproductive. Nation-states have managed this process of development in the name of modernity.

Reductionism does not just discriminate; it is also a flimsy paradigm on which to depend for our survival. Reductionism includes the homogenization of diets—symbolized in the explosion of fast food (Beijing already has 80 McDonald's outlets) and the associated physiological problems of obesity and heart disease. It also includes linguistic genocide: Only 50 percent of the world's 6,000 to 7,000 spoken languages will exist by 2100, and because linguistic diversity is highly correlated with biodiversity, the world is rendered increasingly vulnerable with the onset of monoculture: "The potential for the new lateral thinking that might save us from ourselves in time lies in having as many and as diverse languages and cultures as possible."[3] In the same vein, the embrace of transgenic technology threatens sustainability in general, substituting monopoly for diversity. Just a century ago, hundreds of millions of farmers across the world controlled their seed stocks and their reproduction, whereas today "much of the seed stock has been bought up, engineered, and patented by global companies and kept in the form of intellectual property," where farmers become simply a new market for genetically altered seeds.[4]

Reductionism links people's fortunes (and determines their futures) to the logic of a seemingly independent force: the economy. As we have seen, the project of globalization has subordinated the social contract to market forces. Employment security has declined as firms have either downsized to remain competitive in a global market or relocated production to lower rungs on the global wage ladder. These changes have been in part responsible for the declining living standards and growing racial/ethnic tensions in the global North. Ever-enlarging portions of the labor force assume part-time, low-skill, and low-paying jobs as lean production generates a labor force with diminishing guarantees of benefits. One-third of U.S. jobs are estimated to be at risk to the growing productivity of low-wage labor in China, India, Mexico, and Latin America.[5] Meanwhile, workplace casualties are endemic in frenetic Chinese export industries. In 2002, 140,000 people died in work-related accidents, and hundreds of thousands more were injured "as the price of economic progress."[6]

Erosion of the historic benefits of citizenship in the global North is matched by violations of human rights across the world as the competitive dynamics of the global market forces a lowering of standards everywhere. Under these circumstances, where the future is unpredictable, development is becoming an *uncertain paradigm*. Certainly, it is cropping up all over in alternative guises. But this plethora of development alternatives does not seek a singular, paradigmatic status like the development project.

## Fouling Our Nest for an Uncertain Future

The third observation has to do with global environmental degradation. We do have a common future in that we all face growing environmental limits. The pressing issue now is whether the social and physical world can sustain current economic growth trends with current forms of energy. There are two angles here.

## Cumulative Deterioration

We face astounding problems in the depletion of our physical environment. In the United States, for example, 1 million acres disappear annually to urban-industrial development, and 2 million acres of farm-land are lost annually to erosion, soil salinization, and flooding or soil saturation by intensive agriculture, which consumes groundwater 160 percent faster than it can be replenished.[7] Meanwhile, the world has crossed the threshold to declining rates of agricultural productivity, 80 countries already experience serious water shortages, more than 1 billion people lack adequate access to clean water, and by 2025, two-thirds of the world's people will face water stress.[8]

In China, we find a veritable economic revolution under way that has serious long-term implications. Until the sudden acute respiratory syndrome (SARS) outbreak in 2003, China had been growing for two decades by 8 to 10 percent annually, and the average citizen now earns almost twice as much a year than the average Indian.[9] Factories spring up overnight in the roughly 3,000 development zones, displacing rice paddies and farmlands.[10] Foreign investors have been taking advantage of the $2- to $4-a-day wage rates for literate, healthy employees, and companies such as Volkswagen and Ford Motor Company invest in expectations of huge automobile markets.[11] Despite China's remarkable gains in industrial efficiency since the early 1980s, it ranks third in carbon dioxide emissions, behind the United States and the former Soviet Union. By some predictions, China could pass the United States in carbon dioxide emissions by 2025. Meanwhile, intensive agriculture has accelerated. Chinese soils are deteriorating from reduced crop rotation, erosion, overfertilization, and the loss of organic content of soils once nourished by manure-based farming. More than 2,000 square kilometers of land turn to desert annually.[12] Millions of Chinese farmers have abandoned farming for higher paying urban jobs, and analysts predict a resultant global grain crisis.[13] As a powerhouse in the twenty-first century, Chinese demand for resources will have major impacts on serious global environmental stress.

Another cumulative scenario is the unpredictability associated with global environmental changes. The United Nations (UN) World Commission on Environment and Development has noted that "major, unintended changes are occurring in the atmosphere, in soils, in waters, among plants and animals, and in relationships among these. . . . The rate of change is outstripping the ability of scientific disciplines and our capabilities to assess and advise." Epidemiologist A. J. McMichael suggests that these changes foretell threats to global public health arising from "planetary overload, entailing circumstances that are qualitatively different from the familiar, localised problem of environmental pollution"—threats such as immune suppression from ultraviolet radiation, indirect health consequences of climate change on food production and the spread of infections, and loss of biological and genetic resources for producing medicines. He observes,

> This is not to deny the health gains associated with agrarian and industrial settlement, but it emphasizes that human cultural evolution has produced distortions of ecological relationships, causing four main types of health hazard. First came infectious diseases. Then came diseases of industrialisation and environmental pollution by toxic chemicals. Simultaneously, in rich populations, various "lifestyle" diseases of affluence (heart disease, assorted cancers, diabetes, etc.) emerged. Today we face the health consequences of disruption of the world's natural systems.[14]

We cannot pin these cumulative trends on the development project itself; they have had a longer cultural gestation stemming from a long-held belief in the West that the natural world should be subordinated to human progress. But industrial development hastened these changes, and the development project acted as midwife to their universalization.

## Maldistribution of Wealth

The other angle on the sustainability question is a *relational* one, concerning the distribution of global wealth. About 80 percent of the world's income is produced and consumed by 15 percent of the world's population. Meanwhile, despite positive indices of economic growth, the World Bank has estimated that 200 million more people were living in abject poverty at the end of the 1990s than at the beginning of that decade.[15]

Global resources are disproportionately controlled and consumed by a small minority of the world's population, residing mainly in the First World. For example, grains fed to U.S. livestock equal as much food consumed by the combined populations of India and China.[16] Northern nations account for 75 percent of the world's energy use and have produced two-thirds of the greenhouse gases altering the earth's climate. Since 1950, the world's population has consumed as many goods and services, and the U.S. population has used as many mineral resources, as those consumed by all previous generations of people.[17] In short, the practice of development has brought us up sharply against growing environmental,

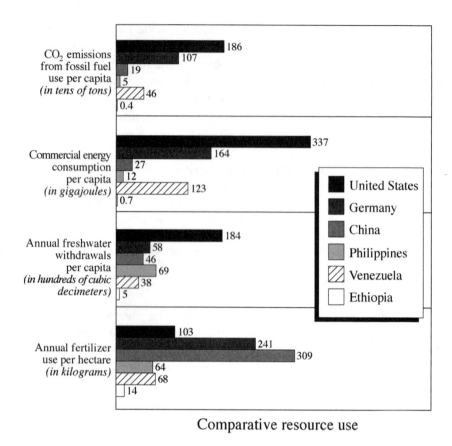

Comparative resource use

**Figure 8.1**    Resource Use in Selected Countries

Source: World Resource Institute, *World Resources 1998–99* (1998).

resource, and health limits. It is too early to know whether humans are the ultimate "endangered species."

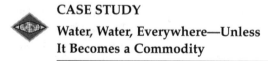

**CASE STUDY**

**Water, Water, Everywhere—Unless It Becomes a Commodity**

When a resource is commodified, it inevitably becomes the property of only those who can afford to buy it. Its availability on the market for some constructs scarcity for others. In Vellor, India, Coca-Cola's bottling plant mines water from surrounding borewells, parching the lands of more than 2,000 people residing within 1.2 miles of the plant and contaminating the remaining water, forcing women to walk much further to obtain it. Globalize this, and a market-induced water shortage threatens.

If oil wars marked the end of the twentieth century, water wars will define the twenty-first century, according to a World Bank vice president. Aside from the fact that 90 percent of wastewater in the global South is still discharged into rivers and streams, the looming global water crisis has two sources: (1) the skewing of water use priorities (agribusiness vs. small farmers; export processing zones [EPZs] vs. citizen needs; urban flush toilets vs. equitable distribution of safe drinking water) and (2) pressures to privatize water.

Water is understood to be the last infrastructure frontier for private investors, according to a member of the European Bank for Reconstruction and Development. Only 5 percent of water services are in private hands, and expansion opportunities are estimated at a trillion dollars. Water privatization is dominated by two French TNCs: Vivendi SA and Suez Lyonnaise des Eaux. Other TNCs involved include Bechtel, Enron, and General Electric. The General Agreement on Trade in Services (GATS) protocol (see Chapter 5) favors privatization of this public good, and implementation is anticipated by a provision in the North American Free Trade Agreement (NAFTA) that forbids a country from discriminating in favor of its own firms in the commercial use of its water resources. Meanwhile, the International Monetary Fund (IMF) and the World Bank demand privatization of water services as a funding condition.

A case in point is Ghana, where an IMF loan tranche in 2002 was only released on condition that the government aimed for "full cost recovery" in all public utilities, including water. Vivendi, Suez, and Saur of France and Biwater of Britain use this kind of edict to cherry-pick lucrative contracts, leaving sewerage, sanitation, urban poor, and rural water provision for local authorities and communities. While the national budget is downsized to save money for loan repayment, a public service disappears, and water prices go through the roof. One community member exclaimed, "The rain does not fall only on the roofs of Vivendi, Suez, Saur and Biwater, neither does it fall only on the roofs of the World Bank and the IMF; it falls on everyone's roof. Why are they so greedy?"

Meanwhile, water privateers are planning mass exports of bulk water, which will be possible should the GATS protocol be implemented. Scottish citizens resisted a plan to sell water to Spain, Morocco, and the Middle East, and Canada banned the export of water. Global Water Corporation, a Canadian firm, signed an agreement with Sitka, Alaska, to export 18 billion gallons of glacier water per year to China for bottling in a cheap-labor EPZ.

Maude Barlow distinguished between *water trading* and *water sharing:* "In a commercially traded water exchange, those who really need the water would be least likely to receive it. . . . Importing water for only those who could afford it would reduce the urgency and political pressure to find real, sustainable and equitable solutions to water problems in water-scarce countries." She suggests that "with current technologies and methods available today, a conservative estimate is that agriculture could cut its water demands by close to 50 percent, industry by 50 to 90 percent, and cities by one-third without sacrificing economic output or quality of life. What is missing is political will and vision."

Should the availability and distribution of a basic and precious resource such as water or food be governed by market forces, which tend to favor only those with purchasing power and compromise human rights?

Sources: *www.corpwatchindia.org/issues/PID.jsp?articleid=1603; Godrej (2003:12); Amenga-Etego (2003:20-21); Barlow (1999:2, 7, 14, 18, 27, 33, 38).*

# Rethinking Development

Development is at an important crossroads as the twenty-first century gets under way. Global development looks increasingly like a rerun of the colonial era. Certainly, the top decile of the population of the global South has joined the world's affluent segment. But liberalization turns back the clock and intensifies the exploitation of southern resources (including labor) to feed the insatiable appetites of a global consumer class, buoyed by easy credit from a deregulated financial system. Massive population displacements are accompanied by the elimination of staple foods for near-subsistence dwellers who constitute the majority of the world's population. Resource access and resource use are governed by financial and trade rules, which unsurprisingly but consistently favor market forces, whether TNCs or consumer purchasing power. This is capitalist development, but is it human development?

As noted earlier, the UN Declaration of Human Rights offered the world a paradigm of fundamental human rights, including the social contract between state and citizenry, designed to promote equity and personal dignity. While this revolutionary paradigm informed development ideals, development has been realized through inequalities, especially those that systematically compromise human rights (e.g., class, patriarchy, food insecurity, privatization).

The role of the United Nations has always been to safeguard economic, social, and cultural rights through the mutual relations of its member states. But as state sovereignty has been weakened by the mechanisms of global governance (e.g., structural adjustment, trade rules) instead of the UN protecting sovereign rights, it has been subject to these mechanisms itself (either because of dwindling revenues or because of dwindling multilateralism). The UN has established a "global compact" with the corporate world to give "a human face to the global market," consulting with firms about universal labor and environmental and human rights principles in return for UN support of liberalization. In turn, the UN Development Program (UNDP) sells corporate sponsorship for a new program: the Global Sustainable Development Facility. To encourage corporate investment in impoverished areas of the world, the UN leases its prestigious image and invaluable networks to the TNCs. Whether global firms such as Dow Chemical, Royal Dutch/Shell, and British mining colossus Rio Tinto can address the needs of the poor for basic health, education, and food is a reasonable question posed by human rights and environmental groups who are concerned that UN-sanctioned corporations will only improve their ability to "greenwash" their global activities.[18]

Where does this leave "development," then? Its status as an *organizing myth* has perhaps become clearer to us, and arguably, it is clearer to more and more people who either participate or cannot participate in the consumer economy. As an organizing myth, development mobilized all societies via appeals to universalistic economic rationality, anchored in the ideal of national self-determination. It was a powerful idea, with some tangible benefits across the world; in retrospect, it seems progressive compared to the globalization project.

Public disillusionment with global development echoes across the world. The Alternative Forum: The Other Voices of the Planet is a group representing networks of nongovernmental organizations (NGOs) that now challenge the project of global development. Its 1994 proclamation is worth quoting in full because of how it is framed:

> To overcome the myth of development, to develop more locally self-sufficient economic systems and to disassociate from traditional technocratic and economic indicators, does not imply perpetuating the *status quo* between the supposedly developed North and the supposedly underdeveloped South. Obviously, the production of goods and services in the South has to increase and must be directed primarily towards meeting the enormous number of basic needs that are not being covered. With or without the permission of the North, the countries of the South have to use up the world natural resources needed for this increase in production. However, out of pure self interest they should try to adapt their productive systems as far as possible to local ecological conditions, rather than copying the irresponsible and unsustainable models of the North. This, above all, means generating and using as much of production locally as possible because this is the level at which real human needs are most clearly expressed. . . . The end of the Development Era will be harder for the North than for the South. In fact, if we take the level of social conflict, the fear of the future and the social fulfillment of people, as general indicators, the North is probably already starting to experience this process.[19]

The sentiments expressed here speak to several issues in the process by which development is being reconceived: rejection of market rule (where social organization is subordinated to economic laws), elevation of the need to sustain community and ecology, and the substantive democracy of decentralized social systems. Decentralization may mean embracing the idea of "subsidiarity," situating decision-making power at the lowest appropriate levels/loci, transforming sovereignty into a "relative rather than an absolute authority," or strengthening local communities.[20] Of course, local systems do not have a monopoly on virtue—they are often the site of patriarchy and authoritarianism undiluted by individual rights. Strengthening them means engaging in reflexive learning to overcome historic inequities, as practiced by the Movimento dos Trabalhadores Rurais Sem Terra (MST) and Proyecto Andino de Tecnologias Campesinas (PRATEC) (see Chapter 7).

It is interesting to observe that the members of the Alternative Forum perceive Westerners as being at a comparative disadvantage because they are much more thoroughly incorporated into and therefore more thoroughly affected by the reversals of the development myth. One reversal that is currently redefining the politics of the global North is the perceived threat of formerly colonized peoples—whether through global migration or terrorism. This has been referred to as "blowback." As Wolfgang Sachs warned in the early 1990s,

> For the first time the Northern countries themselves are exposed to the bitter results of Westernizing the world. Immigration, population pressure, tribalism with mega-arms, and above all, the environmental consequences of worldwide industrialization threaten to destabilize the Northern way of life. It is as if the cycle which had been opened by Columbus is about to be closed at the end of this century.[21]

These are admittedly alarming notions, but it is necessary to remember that the first rule in responding to gloomy predictions is to recognize that the more we can understand the process, the better we can respond to it. Most important, it allows us to see that the history of development wove together the fate of people on opposite sides of the world.

## Governance and Security

In an era when foreign aid faces growing skepticism, the prime minister of Denmark, Poul Nyrup Rasmussen, explained the rationale for continuing aid: "We have a good argument now, a very concrete one, for ordinary people, which is, if you don't help the third world, if you don't help northern Africa, if you don't help eastern and central Europe with a little part of your welfare, then you will have these poor people in our society."[22] The notion of security, with its underlying racism, has assumed greater prominence in the wake of September 11, 2001, and the subliminal insecurities people feel across a world marked by instability and upheaval. UN Secretary-General Kofi Annan has articulated, on several occasions, the view that "if we cannot make globalization work for all, in the end it will work for none."[23] Programmatically, this has led to a blending of two forms of global governance: liberalization and new forms of loan conditionality—assistance on the condition that governments attend to stabilizing their populations. This factor has been included in the World Bank's new lending criteria, concerned with "state effectiveness." This is part of a broad strategy of stabilization to sustain the idea of "globalization" as the path to economic well-being. Thus, the Bank stated in its world development report of 1997 the following:

> The cost of not opening up will be a widening gap in living standards between those countries that have integrated and those that remain outside.

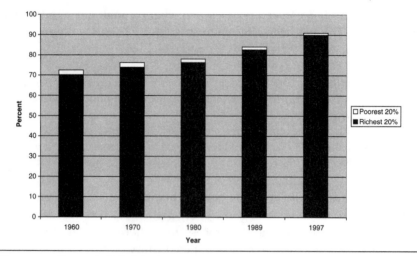

**Figure 8.2.** Share of Global Income over Time

Source: Sarah Anderson and John Cavanagh, *Field Guide to the Global Economy* (2000).

> For lagging countries the route to higher incomes will lie in pursuing sound domestic policies and building the capability of the state. Integration gives powerful support to such policies—and increases the benefits from them—but it cannot substitute for them. *In that sense, globalization begins at home. But multilateral institutions such as the World Trade Organization have an important role to play in providing countries with the incentive to make the leap.*[24]

The leap may be a leap of faith: faith in institutions created to sponsor liberalization. The Asian financial crisis of the late 1990s weakened faith in liberalization—emphasizing that financial deregulation promotes destabilizing speculation rather than social investment. The Bank became more circumspect in light of Malaysia's relative success in implementing capital controls in defiance of the Washington consensus (see Chapter 5) and, in 2002, acknowledged that privatization had done little to improve the fiscal position of Latin American governments.[25] Meanwhile, emphasis on governance includes decentralization to partner private entrepreneurship and the release of social capital. In a context of state shrinking via structural adjustment ($900 billion public assets sold in the 1990s), responsibility devolves "downward" to municipal authorities, communities, and their NGO supporters.[26] The World Bank's world development report of 1999–2000 urges participatory policymaking, observing that "institutions of good governance that embody such processes are critical for development and should encompass partnerships among all elements of civil society." The Bank's reflex is to stabilize populations impoverished by structural adjustment and continuing debt service. This may be a new development strategy, under the guise of responding to the voice of poverty (see the World Bank's [2000b] *Voices of the Poor*), but it displaces responsibility from the development establishment to the poor. In so doing, it disconnnects deteriorating local conditions from their global political-economic context and depoliticizes poverty. Through this redefinition of the problem and the governance solution, the development establishment seeks to preserve its hegemony.

## CASE STUDY
### Global Meets Local: The Microcredit Business

Microcredit is one of the fastest growing world industries today. Its popularity stems from the model of the Grameen Bank, begun by Muhammad Yunus in 1976 in a village near Chittagong, Bangladesh, to assist impoverished villagers. With a high rate of payback of 90 percent or more and a loan volume of $500 million in 1995, this bank has rapidly become known as the champion of poor women across the South. It extends small amounts of commercial credit for microenterprise to cells of five women, each of whom receives a loan and guarantees that all members of the cell will repay their own loans at an interest rate of about 20 percent. Grameen has been so successful that it no longer requires subsidies from donor governments or the International Fund for Agricultural Development.

Microcredit has mushroomed, with liberal assistance from intenational donor agencies such as the Ford Foundation, UNDP, and the Swiss Agency for Development and Cooperation. Interest rates for microcredit range between 20 and 100 percent, so multilateral development banks embrace microcredit as an opportunity to replace capital-intensive "development as charity" with the more profitable "development as business." And the business is shared around. In India, for example, banks lend to NGOs at 9 percent, NGOs are allowed to lend to self-help groups (SHGs) at rates up to 15 percent, and SHGs in turn charge up to 30 percent to individual borrowers. The expectation is that the poor will use the credit for commercial purposes, but, as Gayatri Menon has shown, the loans are often used to meet daily consumption needs. Nonetheless, the development community is riding the microcredit bandwagon, given that it is consistent with the dominant paradigm of self-help, decentralization, and stimulating "social capital" at the local level to promote community-based entrepreneurship and given that structural adjustment programs have forced the poor into self-employment.

The World Bank established a microlending arm, the Consultative Group to Assist the Poorest (CGAP), at the Fourth World Conference on Women in Beijing in 1995, with the goal of "systematically increasing resources in microfinance." And while the CGAP program comes with conditions governed by profitability considerations, such as countries privatizing their microlending institutions and strengthening their debt collection laws, there are other microcredit operations such as the Self-Employed Women's Association (SEWA) of Ahmedabad, India, that focus on empowering women with practical support programs such as labor advocacy, provision of health care, training, and so forth.

How is it possible that a well-intentioned idea of empowering poor women with credit could become a method of incorporating "informals" into the formal economy and exposing them to its financial disciplines and mechanisms of governance and surveillance?

---

*Sources: Tyler (1995:A1); Kane (1996); Singh and Wysham (1997); Menon (2001).*

## Development in Contention

Where does this leave the concept of development, then? Let us retrace its steps. Initially, development theory was formalized as part of the foundation of the development project. It took its cues from nineteenth-century European social thought, which was concerned primarily with different aspects of the rise of capitalism and industrialism. European social theory has recently been criticized for its Eurocentric "grand narrative" of history and social progress, and, of course, this progressivism in turn shaped and formalized development theory in the mid-twentieth century, giving rise to the development project.

A powerful theoretical critique of developmentalism came in Immanuel Wallerstein's formulation of **world-system analysis** in the early 1970s. The argument he made was twofold. First, since the rise of the sixteenth-century European capitalist world economy under colonialism, the world has been a hierarchical system organized into unequal zones of specialization—with Europe in the center and the colonial and postcolonial world in the periphery. Like the middle classes of industrial society, there is also a buffer zone between the poles: the semiperiphery, comprising the middle-income states. In the postwar world, the newly industrializing countries joined other semiperipheral states such as Australia, New Zealand, and Canada; the southern European states; and the Soviet bloc countries. Second, Wallerstein critiqued developmentalism as an organizing myth, both because of its misapplication as a national strategy in a hierarchical world, where only some states can "succeed," and because it has displaced other, more equitable, notions of social organization.[27]

As the development project proceeded, development was redefined in response to changing conditions. Growing Third World poverty provoked the 1970s "basic needs" approach, new socialist/dependency interpretations of underdevelopment as a historical condition, and redefinitions by the UNDP of human development indexes.[28] The rise of the newly industrializing countries produced the World Bank's notion of development as participation in the world market in 1980. When the 1980s debt crisis punctured illusions of development, debt management became the new orthodoxy. The debt regime was a dress rehearsal for a reformulation of the development enterprise as a global project. This project institutionalized rules drawn from neoliberal economics emphasizing openness and downgrading of the development state. Accompanying and shaping these developments, countermovements have emerged with alternatives that propose reembedding markets in society, reducing the intensity of resource use, and democratizing political and social decisions at all scales.

The countermovement challenges the belief and outcomes of neoliberalism. Neoliberal globalists believe in the rationality of an open world economy. The level playing field that is supposed to drive this operation is a fiction at best and an assertion of power at worst. Such globalists deploy free trade arguments to "open" national economies to privileged investors and transnational corporations; they propose deregulated money markets that encourage financial speculation and huge, destabilizing capital flight as wealthy nationals shift their—and sometimes the public's—money to more inviting regions of the global economy. Neoliberal globalizers meet annually, by invitation only, in Davos, Switzerland, at the World Economic Forum (WEF), known colloquially as the "rich man's club." In 2001, the WEF theme was the fragility (and therefore the growing illegitimacy) of the global system.

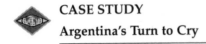

**CASE STUDY**
**Argentina's Turn to Cry**

Argentina experienced financial crises in 1995 (part of the tequila effect related to the Mexican peso crisis) and 1998–1999 (contagion from the 1997 Asian financial crisis). In 2001, the IMF, after years of "second-generation structural adjustment" (linking a line of credit to "good governance"—designed to thoroughly privatize the economy), turned off the cash spigots (until September 2003, by which time it was necessary to bail Argentina, and its own credibility, out). The economy minister declared a *corralito* on bank deposits, whereby Argentinians could withdraw only 1,000 pesos a month. The fiction of parity of the peso with the dollar, maintained by the ruling elite (and in a world where the United States could finance its deficits, but Argentina could not), finally collapsed. Argentina's economy shrunk by 20 percent between 1998 and 2002, official unemployment was 22 percent and rising, and 43 percent of the population was impoverished (20 percent officially destitute). In 2002, NGOs estimated that 8,000 *nupos* (new poor) entered Buenos Aires every day from the surrounding provinces and that there were 3,000 homeless. Staple foods doubled in price, and what was once called the world's breadbasket was awash in hunger.

Ann Pettifor, of Jubilee Plus in London, declared that Argentina needed an international bankruptcy court to provide justice for debtors and creditors, contrasting Argentina with Enron:

> Enron has had its debt payments suspended. Argentina has to pay the IMF, the World Bank, and Spain. Enron is forced to open up its books, and the whole of US business is having to clean up its act fast. Argentina is still a big secret. At Enron the advisors to the company are in shit street. The shareholders had a process. Compare that to Argentina. The IMF is still calling the shots.

What is so instructive about Argentina's financial crisis is that it was the IMF's model Latin student in the 1990s; as one journalist, Larry Elliott, put it in 2002, the country "has been transformed from the blue-eyed boy of Latin American globalisation into a country imploding economically, politically, and socially." Interestingly enough, the "blue-eyed boy" reference resonates with an observation of the Uruguayan-born, celebrated author, Eduardo Galeano, who noted the universal implications of this crisis:

> There is a universal perplexity because people don't understand how such a thing could happen in a white, well-nourished country without a demographic explosion. The event itself calls into question the theories of [social scientists] who, for example, identify underdevelopment and poverty with social explosions—things they say occur in obscure regions of the planet, regions condemned by destiny to suffer poverty because of the color of their skin, as a result of miscegenation that did not bear good fruit.

Meanwhile, the civic response to this market-enforced crisis has demonstrated citizen action that is outside of regular institutional frameworks for political involvement. Direct forms of democracy have mushroomed, born of hunger by people who, unlike their leaders, have nothing to lose. The new direct democracy movement comprises a mix of neighborhoods, small businesses and merchants, and the middle-class (*caserolazos*), workers, and the unemployed (*piqueteros*) who appropriate public spaces and maintain factory operations, producing for the populace. They set up barter arrangements, exchanging everything from old video games to homemade food or skilled services; brainstorm new forms of civic organization to address the health crisis; manage provincial budgets; and organize community kitchens, libraries, schooling, gardens, and so forth. As Toronto-based journalist Naomi Klein remarked, "They are developing tactics that allow some of the most marginal people on earth to meet their own needs without using terror—by blockading roads, squatting in buildings, occupying land and resisting displacement."

Is it not ironic that when citizens are disciplined with grinding austerity in the name of financial security and maintaining global development, they discover the self-organizing principles that anchor the Enlightenment and yet have been submerged in the historic project to develop the world?

---

*Sources: P. Lewis (1997:D1); Frasca (2002:26, 28); Legrand (2002:30); Elliott (2002:10); Aviles (2002); Klein (2003:10); Young and Guagnini (2002); Nogueira, Bretbart, and Strohm (2003).*

The global system's legitimacy problem only intensified when Joseph Stiglitz, 2001 Nobel laureate and former chief economist of the World Bank, published a book titled *Globalization and Its Discontents.*[29] Defining globalization as "the closer integration of the countries and peoples of the world which has been brought about by the enormous reduction to costs of transportation and communication, and the breaking down of artificial barriers to the flows of goods, services, capital, knowledge, and (to a lesser extent) people across borders," he celebrated the creation of new institutions (the WTO) to join with existing ones (such as the UN, the International Labor Organization, and the World Health Organization [WHO]) to work across borders, as well as the expansion of international civil society (to join organizations such as the International Red Cross). He went on to say,

> Many, perhaps most, of these aspects of globalization have been welcomed everywhere. . . . It is the more narrowly defined economic aspects of globalization that have been the subject of controversy, and the international institutions that have written the rules, which mandate or push things like liberalization of capital markets. . . . The result for many people has been poverty and for many countries social and political chaos. The IMF has made mistakes in all the areas it has been involved in: development, crisis management, and in countries making the transition from communism to capitalism. . . . Underlying the problems of the IMF and the other international economic institutions is the problem of governance: who decides what they do. The institutions are dominated not just by the wealthiest industrial countries but by commercial and financial interests in those countries, and the policies of the institutions naturally reflect this. . . . While almost all of the activities of the IMF and the World Bank today are in the developing world (certainly, all of their lending), they are led by representatives from the industrialized nations. . . . The institutions are not representative of the countries they serve.[30]

The legitimacy problem Stiglitz identified is underlined by, among other trends, a growing dissatisfaction with neoliberalism across Latin America (significant regime shifts in Brazil, Venezuela, and Ecuador, for example) and the emergence, in 2001, of the World Social Forum (WSF) as a countersummit in Porto Alegre—stronghold of the Brazilian Workers' Party and famous for its practice of participatory budgeting, in which citizens decide on the allocation of half of the municipal budget. Each January, synchronized with the WEF meeting, hundreds of global civil society organizations meet at the WSF (more than 100,000 delegates in 2003). While the WSF slogan is "another world is possible," it celebrates difference, viewing itself as a process, not an organization. Its Charter of Principles declares that it is a body "representing world civil society." It is not a "locus of power," as such; rather, it is a plural, diversified *context* that, "in a decentralized fashion, interrelates organizations and movements engaged in concrete action at levels from the local to the international to build another world . . . [and] encourages its participant organizations and movements to situate their actions as issues of planetary citizenship."[31] The WSF is a broad movement to reembed markets socially, viewing the choice facing the world as between a path of exclusion, monoculture, and corporate rights and a path of inclusion, diversity, and citizen rights.

A spokesperson for the Living Democracy Movement, Vandana Shiva, critiques globalization thus:

> The philosophical and ethical bankruptcy of globalization was based on reducing every aspect of our lives to commodities and reducing our identities to that of mere consumers in the global marketplace. Our capacities as producers, our identity as members of communities, our role as custodians of our natural and cultural heritage were all to disappear or be destroyed. Markets and consumerism expanded. Our capacity to give and share was to shrink. But the human spirit refuses to be subjugated by a world-view based on the dispensability of our humanity.[32]

Perhaps the distinguishing mark of this world countermovement is its commitment to building solidarity out of a respect for diversity. The WSF is a springboard for constructing enduring networks of relationships among diverse civic and cultural initiatives, forging an alternative organizational and discursive space to that occupied by corporate globalization. Previous antisystemic social movements (e.g., labor movements, women in development [WID]) worked to reform or institutionalize counterveiling power within institutions or societies. While this has been an indispensable part of giving substance to modernity, it has privileged the universalist themes of modernity—which of course crystallized in the project of development and are now the target of a new sensibility that challenges the singular, reductionist vision of development. This is not to say that the global justice movement should not work to reform or transform existing institutions, but it also has the historic opportunity to do this by drawing on and supporting alternative models that are not paralyzed by the logic of economic reductionism and political rationality.

## Toward an Imperial Project?

The open-world rhetoric of the globalization project has always been honored in its breach. The WTO has been deployed as a weapon to shrink states and social protections, expand trade, and secure intellectual property rights. Made up of member states, the WTO is also accountable to them or at least their competitive relations. Because of this, the inequality among states regularly asserts itself (particularly as the WTO makes decisions by consensus, not by vote). The most glaring contradiction concerns agricultural trade rules, where the global North continues to protect its farms with huge subsidies while pressuring the global South to open its agricultural markets to food surplus dumping (see Chapters 5 and 6). This asymmetry of power has brought the WTO to a virtual standstill over agriculture, evident in the breakdown of the WTO Ministerial in September 2003, in Cancun, Mexico. Multilateralism may be shared in principle but not in practice. At the Doha Ministerial of the WTO in 2001, the global North continued its use of threats to obtain free trade and investment concessions from countries in the global South. Since then, there has been much talk about the threat to globalization of rising bilateralism and unilateralism. The incoming director-general of the WTO, Supachai Panitchpakdi, remarked delicately about impending war in Iraq in 2003, "I can feel the sense of trepidation. Whatever happens, if the U.S. will maintain the way we use multilateral solutions, it will be highly appreciated."[33]

During the 1990s, a unilateralist strain emerged within the higher reaches of the American state. A think tank, named Project for the New American Century (PNAC), was founded in 1997 by conservative interventionists concerned to consolidate a global empire. A PNAC report issued in 2000 stated, "At no time in history has the international security order been as conducive to American interests and ideals. The challenge of this coming century is to preserve and enhance this 'American peace.'" At that time, PNAC identified Iran, Iraq, and North Korea as key short-term targets, well before President Bush referred to them as the "axis of evil" in 2001.

Not unlike the ordering of the world in the 1940s, minus the liberal internationalism, this bastardized twenty-first-century *Pax Americana* would require "constabulary duties" (the United States as policeman of the world), and such actions "demand American political leadership rather than that of the United Nations." The report advocated an expansion of the U.S. military presence beyond the 130 nations already in deployment, with a plan for permanent U.S. military and economic domination of every region of the world (within and beyond Western Europe and northeast Asia), unrestricted by international treaty. The men who created the project joined the Bush administration, running the Pentagon, the Defense Department, and the White House. After the September 11,

2001, attacks on New York and Washington, D.C., President Bush elaborated the elements of this **imperial project** in the National Security Strategy of the United States of America (NSSUSA), with its new military doctrine of *preemptive* (or preventive) war, subsequently used against Iraq in 2003, with little or no regard for world opinion, international law, or the sensibilities of the United Nations.[34]

The NSSUSA document argues that the twentieth century produced a "single, sustainable model for national success: freedom, democracy, and free enterprise," values to be protected "across the global and across the ages." The United States "enjoys a position of unparalleled military strength and great economic and political influence" and "will use this moment of opportunity to extend the benefits of freedom across the globe. We will actively work to bring the hope of democracy, *development*, free markets and free trade to every corner of the world."[35] Here, national security is foreign policy. The document went on to identify multilateral institutions as explicit instruments of U.S. national security, insisting that the World Bank's development assistance is tied to "measurable goals and concrete benchmarks," and "our long-term objective should be a world in which all countries have investment-grade credit ratings that allow them access to international capital markets and to invest in their future."[36]

As managing director of the world's largest bond investment firm (PIMCO) remarked at the time, "American imperialism is, by definition, a retreat away from global capitalism. It's a retreat from the invisible hand of markets in favor of a more dominant role for the visible fist of governments."[37] Meanwhile, in August 2003, Chile and Singapore signed a bilateral trade deal with the United States, in which those states agreed to surrender capital controls in return for more favorable U.S. market access, signaling a movement to revive the Multilateral Agreement on Investment (MAI), defeated in 1998 (largely by countermobilization of citizens and NGOs concerned about unregulated financial flows).[38] But is this simply a shift in emphasis in the hand-fist relationship? As the pro–free market journalist, Thomas Friedman, put it,

> The hidden hand of the market will never work without a hidden fist— McDonald's cannot flourish without McDonnell Douglas, the builder of the F-15. And the hidden fist that keeps the world safe for Silicon Valley's technologies is called the United States Army, Air Force and Marine Corps.[39]

The moral of this story is that the United States entered the new century with a new project to strengthen its position in the globalization project. That is, while the goals of the globalization project remain, its mechanisms may assume a more explicit use of bilateral agreements and military and other imperial force. Neoliberalism, as we have seen, brings instability, skepticism, and outright disaffection. It has never achieved international hegemonic status as a universalist ideology (like development). It has therefore always sought to "lock in" market reforms to prevent states from backsliding—as in the strong clauses of NAFTA and the current attempt to extend it to the whole hemisphere as the Free Trade Area of the Americas (FTAA).[40] In an era of flawed multilateralism; loss of edge in electronics, biotechnology, and pharmaceuticals; and rising resistance movements across the world, a more powerful U.S. approach to ordering the world was bound to appear—accelerated by the legitimacy gained through the September 11 attacks (even though the PNAC vision was already in motion). Quite possibly, "regime change" in Afghanistan and Iraq was a first step in the reordering of the power balance in the Middle East, as a precondition for a reordering of the world power balance, as the United States seeks to neutralize (via control of oil) potential rivals in the European Union, China, and a reunited Korea (with bomb) and maintain a revenue stream to service its rising imbalance of payments.

Given the circumstances of such a unilateralist move, it is unlikely that a new conception of development will emerge. In fact, from the development project to the globalization project to an emerging imperial project, the universalist appeal of development has shrunk progressively toward a crystallization of its core power relation: that of securing resources and markets to sustain a dominant consumer state. It is not surprising that the distinguishing feature of this incipient imperial project is its concern with security. This concept manages foreign relations to maintain the supply lines and internal relations via information management.

As with all imperial ventures, overreach is often highly correlated with mounting resistances. This is likely to be the case as the twenty-first century wears on. February 2003 saw millions of people demonstrating across the world against war in Iraq, many of whom also identify with various strands of the global countermovement. This gathering of peoples has been referred to already as the world's other superpower. Alongside of this instant antiwar movement (that of the Vietnam War era took years to develop), new cosmopolitan practices, perhaps characterized in terms of strategic diversity and "self-organization from below," are mushrooming in relation and as alternatives to the narrowing, or indeed bankruptcy, of global and now imperial forms of development.[41]

These currents came together dramatically to forestall the WTO's Cancun Ministerial (2003). The failure of the previous Doha Ministerial

(2001) to make credible progress on the so-called "Development Round" consolidated forces from the previous Seattle Ministerial (1999). These forces—a renewed solidarity within the global South and a parallel solidarity among civil society and global justice groups—converged decisively at Cancun. New partnerships between the **Group of 20 (G-20)**, led by Brazil, India, and China, and a panoply of NGOs effectively called into question undemocratic northern-managed WTO proceedings and issues ranging from agricultural trade rules to the GATS and Trade-Related Intellectual Property Rights (TRIPs) agreements. The fallout from the failed Ministerial is that the U.S./European Union agenda will require modification in context of a revitalized segment of the global South, future negotiations are less likely to reproduce an asymmetrical agenda across North-South lines, and, in the meantime, bilateralism along regional lines will substitute for an impaired multilateralism.

## Conclusion

This concluding chapter brings some closure to the story of the ongoing transformation of the development paradigm. Development was a powerful organizing ideal that was institutionalized on a world scale. This text focuses on the changing assumptions, practices, and social legacies of development as a world-historical project—citing individual case histories as instances of global dynamics, tensions, and trends. These legacies continue, even as global development displaces the historic project of national development. While states endure, their public capacities—those geared to comprehensive citizenship—are under threat across the world in varying degrees. Many international agencies, governments, NGOs, and people continue to pursue development at the national scale, but that development is increasingly beholden to global developments as public goods and infrastructures (education, health care, unemployment security) erode. A protective global countermovement also pursues development, of a different kind, seeking to reinvigorate democratic traditions, shore up the social contract, give substance to human rights, and experiment with new scale technologies and methods of social organization geared to revaluing social life and ecology rather than the omnipresent commodity.

Human sustainability will depend on more than environmental conservation and less on economic growth. It requires preservation of community (at all levels, from micropolitics to macropolitics) in inclusive terms rather than the exclusive or specialized terms of economic globalization. The globalization project is not just a successor to the development project. Its prescriptions are double-edged because its conception of the future erases the past—a past created by movements for social protection. As the development project has subsided, a *general* reversal of thinking has emerged. The present is no longer the logical development of the past; rather, it is increasingly the hostage of the future. Those who define the future will frame the debate about development.

At present, world debate pivots on the adequacy of the market as a guardian of social and environmental sustainability. But this is a prelude to a broader, historical set of questions concerning the scale of human community and governance, as well as the growing tension between material affluence and survival of the human species.

# Notes

## Introduction: Development and Globalization

1. Crossette (1997).
2. Hellman (1994:157).
3. Norberg-Hodge (1992:95, 97–98).
4. José Maria Arguedes, "A Call to Certain Academics," translated from the Quechua by William Rowe.
5. Ruggiero (1996, 1998).
6. Neville (1997:48–49).
7. *The Washington Post* (January 5, 1999:3B).
8. Rosenberg (1998:A38).
9. Norberg-Hodge (1994–1995:2).
10. Hedland and Sundstrom (1996: 889).
11. Crossette (1997).
12. Korzeniewicz (1994).
13. Collins (1995).
14. Barnet and Cavanagh (1994:383).
15. *UNDP Human Development Report,* quoted in Rist (1997:9).

## Chapter 1: Instituting the Development Project

1. Cowan and Shenton (1996).
2. Mitchell (1991:68–75, 96).
3. Davidson (1992:83, 99–101).
4. Quoted in Rist (1997:58).
5. Bujra (1992:146).
6. Quoted in Stavrianos (1981:247).

7. Chirot (1977:124).
8. Davis (2001:26, 299).
9. Wolf (1982:369, 377).
10. Ali (2002:168).
11. Wacker (1993:132–34).
12. Mitchell (1991:175).
13. Cooper and Stoler (1997).
14. James (1963).
15. Quoted in Davidson (1992:164).
16. Memmi (1967:74).
17. Fanon (1967:254–55).
18. F. Cooper (1997:66–67).
19. Stavrianos (1981:624).
20. Quoted in Clarke and Barlow (1997:9).
21. Adams (1993:2–3, 6–7).
22. Quoted in Esteva (1992:6).
23. Quoted in Davidson (1992:167).
24. Esteva (1992:7).
25. Rist (1997:79).
26. Ake (1996:36).
27. Cited in F. Cooper (1997:79).
28. Quoted in Davidson (1992:203).
29. Davidson (1992:183–84).
30. Rostow (1960).
31. Agarwal (1988:18).
32. Quoted in Hettne (1990:3).
33. Quoted in Dube (1988:16).
34. Bose (1997:153).
35. Lehman (1990:5–6).
36. Lehman (1990:5–6).
37. Cardoso and Faletto (1979: 129–31).
38. Kemp (1989:162–65).

## Chapter 2: The Development Project: International Dimensions

1. Block (1977:76–77).
2. Quoted in Brett (1985:106–7).
3. Quoted in Kolko (1988:17).
4. Cleaver (1977:16).
5. R. E. Wood (1986:38–61).
6. Magdoff (1969:124).
7. Ideas and quotes from Rich (1994:55, 56).
8. Rich (1994:72).
9. Rich (1994:58); George and Sabelli (1994:15).
10. Rich (1994:73).
11. The examples in the next four paragraphs are from Rich (1994:10–13, 39, 41, 94).
12. Rich (1994:75).
13. Adams (1993:68–69).
14. Quoted in Magdoff (1969:54).
15. Magdoff (1969:124); Chirot (1977:164–65).
16. Quoted in G. Williams (1981: 56–57).
17. Brett (1985:209); R. E. Wood (1986:73); Rist (1997:88).
18. Brett (1985:209); R. E. Wood (1986:73).
19. Adams (1993:73).
20. Rich (1994:84).
21. Harris (1987:28).
22. Harris (1987:102).
23. Grigg (1993:251).
24. Revel and Riboud (1986:43–44).
25. Grigg (1993:243–44); Bradley and Carter (1989:104). Self-sufficiency measures do not necessarily reveal the state of nutrition in a country or region, as a country—for example, Japan—may have a low self-sufficiency because its population eats an affluent diet, which depends on imports.
26. H. Friedmann (1982).
27. Quoted in Magdoff (1969:135).
28. Quoted in George (1977:170).
29. Raikes (1988:175, 178).
30. H. Friedmann (1992:373).
31. H. Friedmann (1992:373).
32. Chung (1990:143).
33. To be sure, Korean farmers protested, and in the 1970s the state modernized rice-farming regions to raise rural incomes, but this policy ran out of steam as rice consumption continued to decline with the changing Korean diet (McMichael and Kim 1994).
34. Dudley and Sandilands (1975); H. Friedmann (1990:20).
35. Morgan (1980:301).
36. Quoted in George (1977:170).
37. H. Friedmann (1990:20).
38. H. Friedmann (1992:373).
39. McMichael and Raynolds (1994:322). The terms *peasant foods* and *wage foods* are from de Janvry (1981).
40. Hathaway (1987:13).
41. P. McMichael (2003).
42. Revel and Riboud (1986:62).
43. de Janvry (1981:179).
44. Middleton, O'Keefe, and Moyo (1993:129).
45. Wessel (1983:158).
46. Berlan (1991:126–27); see also Dixon (2002).
47. Burbach and Flynn (1980:66); George (1977:171).
48. Quoted in George (1977: 171–72).
49. H. Friedmann (1992:377).
50. Dalrymple (1985:1069); Andrae and Beckman (1985); Raikes (1988).
51. George (1977:174–75).
52. Agarwal (1994:312).
53. Griffin (1974); Pearse (1980); Byres (1981); Sanderson (1986a); Dhanagare (1988); Raikes (1988); Llambi (1990).
54. Griffin (1974); Athreya, Djurfeldt, and Lindberg (1990).
55. Lipton (1977).
56. McMichael and Kim (1994); Araghi (1995).
57. Grigg (1993:103–4, 185); Araghi (1995).
58. Rich (1994:95, 155).
59. Rich (1994:91, 97); Feder (1983:222).
60. de Janvry (1981); Araghi (1995).

# Chapter 3: The Global Economy Reborn

1. Arrighi (1994:68).
2. Bello, Cunningham, and Rau (1994:7).
3. Hoogvelt (1987:43–45).
4. Harris (1987:75).
5. Hoogvelt (1987:40).
6. Knox and Agnew (1994:340).
7. The term *newly industrializing countries* (NICs) was coined by the Organization for Economic Co-operation and Development in 1979 and included four southern European countries: Spain, Portugal, Yugoslavia, and Greece. The common attributes of NICs were (1) rapid penetration of the world market with manufactured exports, (2) a rising share of industrial employment, and (3) an increase in real gross domestic product per capita relative to the First World (Hoogvelt 1987:25).
8. Brett (1985:185–86).
9. Hoogvelt (1987:28).
10. Brett (1985:188).
11. Knox and Agnew (1994:347).
12. Hoogvelt (1987:64).
13. Knox and Agnew (1994:331). (Between 1975 and 1989, this group enlarged to include China, South Africa, Thailand, and Taiwan; Argentina dropped out.)
14. Martin and Schumann (1997: 100–1).
15. Quoted in Brett (1985:188).
16. Gereffi (1989).
17. Cf. Evans (1995).
18. Cf. Barndt (2002).
19. Hoogvelt (1987:26–31). At the same time, as a consequence of import-substitution industrialization and the buoyancy of the export-oriented industrialization strategy in the 1970s, the composition of imports mainly from the First World moved from manufactured consumer goods to capital goods.
20. Landsberg (1979:52, 54).

21. See Gereffi (1994).
22. Quoted in Baird and McCaughan (1979:130).
23. Baird and McCaughan (1979: 130–32); Bernard (1996). For an excellent and detailed study of the *maquiladora* industry, see Sklair (1989).
24. Henderson (1991:3).
25. Reich (1992:81, 113).
26. Sivanandan (1989:2, 8); Strom (1999:A3); Stimson (1999:A1).
27. M. B. Brown (1993:46).
28. See Harris (1987). See also Gereffi (1994) for an alternative formulation of the world product as a series of commodity chains.
29. Barnet and Cavanagh (1994: 300); Dicken (1998:131); Ellwood (2001:68).
30. For an extended account of the gendered restructuring of the world labor force, see Mies (1991) and Benería and Feldman (1992).
31. Baird and McCaughan (1979: 135–36).
32. Baird and McCaughan (1979: 135).
33. Hobsbawm (1992:56); Araghi (1999).
34. *Pacific Basin Reports* (August 1973:171).
35. Fröbel, Heinrichs, and Kreye (1979:34–36).
36. Henderson (1991:54).
37. Korzeniewicz (1994:261).
38. Henderson (1991).
39. *The Economist* (June 3, 1995:59); "Slavery in the 21st Century" (2001:8).
40. Moody (1999:183, 188).
41. Lang and Hines (1993:24); Holusha (1996).
42. Woodall (1994:24); Martin and Schumann (1997:100–1).
43. Milbank (1994:A1, A6).
44. Quoted in Bonacich and Waller (1994:90).
45. Cited in Lewin (1995:A5).
46. *The Nation* (November 8, 1993:3).
47. *The Economist* (June 3, 1995:59).
48. Heffernan and Constance (1994:

42–45); Kneen (1990:10); Heffernan (1999:4).

49. P. McMichael (1993a).
50. Watts (1994:52–53).
51. Goss, Burch, and Rickson (2000).
52. Sanderson (1986b); Raynolds et al. (1993); Raynolds (1994).
53. DeWalt (1985).
54. Friedland (1994).
55. Schoenberger (1994:59).
56. Quoted in Appelbaum and Gereffi (1994:54).
57. Daly and Logan (1989:13); Schoenberger (1994:59–61); Chossudovsky (1997:87–88); Herbert (1996).
58. Uchitelle (1993); Harper (1994).
59. Jordan and Sullivan (2003:33).
60. Daly and Logan (1989:13); Schoenberger (1994:59–61); Chossudovsky (1997:87–88); Herbert (1996).
61. Templin (1994:A10); Meredith (1997).
62. Crook (1993:16).
63. Hayden (2003).
64. Uchitelle (1994:D2); Barboza (1999).

# Chapter 4: Demise of the Third World

1. Hoogvelt (1987:58).
2. Berger (2004).
3. Pilger (2002:29).
4. Pilger (2002:25).
5. Pilger (2002:28).
6. Pilger (2002:26–39).
7. Quoted in Magdoff (1969:53).
8. Berger (2004).
9. George (1988:6).
10. Amin (1997:28).
11. Quoted in R. E. Wood (1986:197).
12. Quoted in Adams (1993:123).
13. Hoogvelt (1987:80–87).
14. Rist (1997:152–53).
15. Schaeffer (1997:49); Helleiner (1996:171–75).
16. Adams (1993:127).
17. Hoogvelt (1987:87–95).
18. Strange (1994:112).
19. Crook (1992:10).
20. Helleiner (1994:111–19).
21. Strange (1994:107).
22. Quoted in Brecher and Costello (1994:30).
23. The New Internationalist (August 1993:18); Kolko (1988:24).
24. Debt Crisis Network (1986:25).
25. Kolko (1988:26).
26. Roodman (2001:21).
27. George (1988:33).
28. Lissakers (1993:66).
29. Roodman (2001:26).
30. Lissakers (1993:59).
31. Lissakers (1993:56).
32. Lissakers (1993:69–73).
33. R. E. Wood (1986:247, 253, 255); Evans (1979).
34. George (1988:6).
35. Walton and Seddon (1994:13–14).
36. George (1988:28–29).
37. Lissakers (1993:67).
38. A. Singh (1992:141).
39. A. Singh (1992:144).
40. George (1988:60).
41. Quoted in Roodman (2001:30).
42. Economic Commission for Latin America and the Caribbean (1989:123).
43. de la Rocha (1994:270–71).
44. Barkin (1990:101, 103).
45. de la Rocha (1994:270–71).
46. George (1988:139, 143).
47. Cheru (1989:24, 27–28, 41–42).
48. Cheru (1989:24, 27–28, 41–42); Redding (2000).
49. Rich (1994:186–87).
50. A. Singh (1992:138–39, 147–48).
51. Bello et al. (1994).
52. George (1992:xvi).
53. George (1992:97).
54. Cox (1987:301).
55. Calculated from Crook (1993: 16); Avery (1994:95); Hoogvelt (1997: 138).
56. George (1988:97).
57. Crook (1992:9).
58. Crook (1993:16).
59. Arrighi (1990); Khor, quoted in Danaher and Yunus (1994:28).
60. Payer (1974).

61. Canak (1989).

62. Salinger and Dethier (1989); McMichael and Myhre (1991); Myhre (1994); Barry (1995:36, 43–44, 144).

63. Bangura and Gibbon (199219); World Bank (1981).

64. Gibbon (1992:137).

65. Bernstein (1990:17).

66. Beckman (1992:99).

67. Gibbon (1992:141).

68. Stephany Griffith-Jones, quoted in Crook (1991:19).

69. Cahn (1993:161, 163); Rich (1994); Corbridge (1993:127).

70. Cahn (1993:168, 172).

71. Gill (1992).

72. World Bank (1990:10–11).

## Chapter 5: Implementing Globalization as a Project

1. Ruggiero (2000:xiii, xv).

2. Quoted in Bello et al. (1994:72).

3. Ricardo ([1821] 1951).

4. George (1992:11).

5. Acharya (1995:22).

6. Nash (1994:C4).

7. Bello et al. (1994:59).

8. Rich (1994:188).

9. Quoted in Bello et al. (1994:63).

10. Rich (1994:188).

11. Denny (2002:6).

12. Rohter (2002:A9); Vidal (2001:20).

13. Hathaway (1987:40–41); World Bank (2000:14, 25).

14. Black (2002:62).

15. Kolko (1988:271–72).

16. The South Centre (1993:13).

17. Clarke and Barlow (1997:12–13).

18. P. McMichael (1993b).

19. Adams (1993:196–97).

20. Quoted in Watkins (1991:44).

21. Middleton et al. (1993:127–29).

22. Watkins (1991:43).

23. See P. McMichael (2003).

24. Kolko (1988:215).

25. Quoted in Ritchie (1994).

26. Quoted in Ritchie (1993:11).

27. Quoted in Ritchie (1993, n. 25).

28. Quoted in Schaeffer (1995:268).

29. See Raghavan (1990).

30. Wallach and Sforza (1999:x).

31. Quoted in Ransom (2001a:27).

32. Quoted in Wallach and Sforza (1999:21).

33. Quoted in Wallach and Sforza (1999:x).

34. Tabb (2000:9).

35. Ritchie (1999).

36. Lehman and Krebs (1996).

37. Gorelick (2000:28–30); Madeley (2000:75); Carlsen (2003).

38. Karen Dawkins (1999).

39. LeQuesne (1997).

40. Bailey (2000); Murphy (1999:3).

41. Quoted in Madeley (2000:79).

42. Madeley (2000:54–55).

43. Salmon (2001:22).

44. Clarke and Barlow (1997:21).

45. Quoted in Schott (2000:237).

46. Moran (2000:235).

47. Moran (2000:224–26)

48. Moran (2000:231–32).

49. Kristin Dawkins (2000).

50. Tuxill (1999).

51. ActionAid (2000:2).

52. Madden and Madeley (1993:17).

53. Quoted in Weissman (1991:337).

54. Greenfield (1999).

55. Pollack (1999).

56. GRAIN (1998).

57. Juhasz (2002).

58. Clarke (2001).

59. Clarke (2001).

60. Wallach (2003).

61. Watkins (2002:21).

62. Juhasz (2002).

63. Ohmae (1985:xvi–xvii).

64. Baer (1991:132).

65. Baer (1991:146).

66. Goldsmith (1994:66, 67, 77).

67. Gowan (2003:23–24).

68. Moody (1999:125–26, 181).

69. See, for example, Wallerstein (1983); Arrighi (1990).

70. George and Sabelli (1994:147).

71. Rueschemeyer, Stephens, and Stephens (1992).

72. Benjamin Cohen (1998).

73. Bacon (1994:A1).
74. Monbiot (2003:11).
75. Monbiot (2003:11).
76. Thurow (1999:22–23); R. Cohen (1999).
77. Weisbrot (1999:20); Global Intelligence Update (1999).
78. See Held (1995).

## Chapter 6: The Globalization Project: Disharmonies

1. United Nations Development Program (1997).
2. Goldsmith (1994:18). (The official French figure for unemployment is 3.3 million, but according to Goldsmith, the government's own statistics show the omission of categories consisting of an additional 1.8 million people.)
3. Quing (1998:3).
4. Attali (1991:5, 14).
5. Richburg (2002:29).
6. Perlez (2002:10).
7. Enzenburger (1994:112); www.unfpa.org/modules/factsheets/emergencies_overview.htm.
8. Montalbano (1991:H7); Graw (1999); Ride (1998:9).
9. Montalbano (1991:F1); Sengupta (2002:3); Thompson (2002b: A3); World Bank Press Release No: 2003/266/S.
10. Thompson (2002b:A3); Perlez (2002:10); The Economist (February 23, 2002:42).
11. Tan (1991a).
12. Ball (1990).
13. Tan (1991b).
14. MacShane (1991).
15. Andreas (1994:52).
16. Reich (1991:42).
17. Goldsmith (1994:64–65).
18. Andreas (1994:45).
19. de Soto (1990:11).
20. King and Schneider (1991:164); Harrison (1993:170); O'Meara (1999:15).
21. Reich (1991:42).
22. Kahn (2002:7).
23. Denny and Elliott (2002:14).
24. Goldsmith (1994:38–39).
25. LaTouche (1993:130).
26. Escobar (1995, chap. 2).
27. Cheru (1989:8, 19).
28. Quoted in LaTouche (1993:158).
29. Kamel (1999).
30. LaTouche (1993:133–34).
31. Ayres (1996:12).
32. de la Rocha (1994).
33. Buckley (2001:27).
34. Esteva (1992:21).
35. Darnton (1994a:A8); Castells (1998:83, 85).
36. Lang and Hines (1993:84); Hoogvelt (1997:129).
37. Quoted in Patel (2002b).
38. Crossette (1998c:1).
39. Hawkins (1998:I); The Economist (June 26, 1999:23–25).
40. French (1997:A3).
41. Herbert (1998:A15).
42. Patel (2002b).
43. Bond (2002).
44. Quoted in Bond (2002).
45. Ndulo (2002:9).
46. Davidson (1992:206, 257).
47. Bond (2001:53); and Mamdani (2003).
48. Mamdani (1996:17–20).
49. Rothchild and Lawson (1994: 257–58).
50. World Bank (1989:5).
51. World Bank (1997); Berger and Beeson (1998).
52. Mamdani (1996:17–20).
53. Sandbrook (1995:92); Rist (1997: 130–32).
54. Lorch (1995:A3).
55. Darnton (1994b:A9).
56. Castells (1998:96–98).
57. Fisher and Onishi (1999:A1, A9); French (1997:A1).
58. E. M. Wood (1999:1).
59. Korten (1995); Lietaer (1997:7).
60. Bello (1998:).
61. Bernard (1999).
62. Sydney Morning Herald (June 17, 1998).
63. B. Cohen (1998:129).

64. J. Sachs (1998:17).
65. J. Sachs (1998:17).

## Chapter 7: Global Development and Its Countermovements

1. Barber (1996).
2. Ali (2002:256).
3. Huntington (1993).
4. Ali (2002:275).
5. Onishi (2001:A14).
6. Onishi (2001:A14).
7. Quoted in Onishi (2001:A14).
8. Onishi (2001:A14).
9. Roy (1998:52); S. Smith (2002:30).
10. Ibrahim (1994:A1, A10).
11. Cowell (1994:A14).
12. Woollacott (2002:14).
13. Blustein (2002:37).
14. Maass (2001:50).
15. Swamy (1995).
16. Harding (2002:4).
17. A. J. McMichael (1993:51); Carson (1962).
18. Harrison (1993:54).
19. See A. J. McMichael (1993).
20. Quoted in Abramovitz (1999:12).
21. Abramovitz (1999:18–19).
22. Amin et al. (1990).
23. Quoted in W. Sachs (1992:107); quoted in Schemo (1997:3).
24. Stewart (1994:108–9).
25. Kothari and Parajuli (1993:233).
26. Quoted in Rich (1994:197).
27. Quoted in Middleton et al. (1993:19).
28. Agarwal and Nurain, cited in Rich (1994:262).
29. Quoted in J. Friedmann (1992:123).
30. Rich (1994:244–45).
31. Middleton et al. (1993:25).
32. Hildyard (1993:32–34).
33. Chossudovsky (1997:187–88).
34. Colchester (1994:71–72).
35. Quoted in Colchester (1994:72).
36. Fried (2003).

37. Rich (1994:160–65).
38. Rich (1994:34–37).
39. Quoted in Colchester (1994:78).
40. Colchester (1994:83, 88).
41. Lohmann (1993:10).
42. Colchester (1994:88).
43. Quoted in Colchester (1994:89).
44. Rau (1991:156–57, 160).
45. Quoted in George and Sabelli (1994:170).
46. Jahan (1995:13).
47. Harcourt (1994:4).
48. Harcourt (1994:5).
49. Apffel-Marglin and Simon (1994).
50. Harcourt (1994:19).
51. Apffel-Marglin and Simon (1994:33).
52. Rocheleau (1991).
53. Abramovitz (1994:201).
54. Wacker (1994:135–39).
55. Boyd (1998).
56. "Battle of the Bulge" (1994:25).
57. Robey, Rutstein, and Morris, quoted in Stevens (1994:A8).
58. Chira (1994:A12).
59. Crossette (1994:A8).
60. Bello (1992–1993:5).
61. Sen (1994:221).
62. Quoted in Hedges (1994:A10).
63. Benería (1992).
64. Quoted in Jahan (1995:77).
65. Quoted in Jahan (1995:109).
66. Quoted in Jahan (1995:109).
67. Simons (1999:A1, A6); Moghadam (1993).
68. Crossette (1998a:A14).
69. Held (1995).
70. W. Sachs (1992:112).
71. Held (1995).
72. Fox (1994).
73. Communiqués No. 1, 22, quoted in AVA 42, 31, 1994, p. 1.
74. Harvey (1994:14).
75. Watkins (1996:253).
76. Mittal (1998:101).
77. Hernández (1994:51); Harvey (1994:20).
78. Harvey (1994:36–37); Fox (1994:18).
79. Eber (1999:16).

80. Cleaver (1994:154–55).

81. "Food and Farming" (2003:20); Ainger (2003:10–11) (Wiebe quote).

82. http://ns.rds.org.hn/via/theme.biodiversity.htm

83. Quoted in Ainger (2003:11).

84. http://ns.rds.org.hn/via/(Seattle Declaration, December 3, 1999).

85. http://ns.rds.org.hn/via/theme-agrarian.htm

86. www.mstbrazil.org/Economic Model.html

87. Article 184, quoted in Lappé and Lappé (2002:70).

88. Flavio de Almeida and Sanchez (2000).

89. Quoted in Dias Martins (2000).

90. Lappé and Lappé (2002:86–87).

91. Quoted in Orlanda Pinnasi, Cabral, and Lourencao (2000).

92. Mark (2001).

93. M. Cooper (1999:12, 14); Moberg (1999:16).

94. Quoted in Menotti (1996:1).

## Chapter 8: Whither Development?

1. United Nations Development Program (1997).

2. Rist (1997).

3. Skutnabb-Kangas (2001:3).

4. Rifkin (1998:114).

5. Uchitelle (1993); Chase (1995:16).

6. Kahn (2003:3).

7. Segelken (1995:5).

8. Barlow (1999); United Nations Environment Program (2002).

9. Bradsher (2002:A1, A8).

10. Lappin (1994:193).

11. WuDunn (1993).

12. L. R. Brown (2001:19).

13. Tyler (1994:D8); L. R. Brown (1994:19).

14. A. J. McMichael (1993:336).

15. Ihonvbere (1993–1994:8); Borosage (1999:19).

16. Hildyard (1993:30).

17. Durning (1993:14–15).

18. The Economist (April 8, 1995:34).

19. The Alternative Forum (of NGOs), "Borrador Conclusiones," Global Forum, Madrid, May 1994.

20. Brecher, Costello, and Smith (2000:44).

21. W. Sachs (1993:20).

22. Quoted in Crossette (1995:A5).

23. Houtart and Polet (2001).

24. World Bank (1997:12, emphasis added).

25. B. Edwards (2003:15).

26. Kikeri and Nellis (2002).

27. World Bank (2000:3); see also Chase-Dunn (1998); Hall (2002).

28. Wallerstein (1983). See also Sklair (2002) for a global sociology of the current world economy.

29. Stiglitz (2002).

30. Stiglitz (2002:9–10, 18–19).

31. World Social Forum (2003: 355–57).

32. Shiva (2003:115).

33. Becker (2003:5).

34. Bookman (2002); Pitt (2003); quoted in "U.S. Imperial Ambitions and Iraq" (2002:5).

35. Quotes from Research Unit for Political Economy (2003:68, emphasis added).

36. Research Unit for Political Economy (2003:72–73).

37. Quoted in Olive (2003).

38. K. Singh (2003).

39. Friedman (1999).

40. Panitch (1996).

41. Starr (2000); Brecher et al. (2000).

# References

Abramovitz, Janet N. 1994. "Biodiversity and Gender Issues." In *Feminist Perspectives on Sustainable Development,* edited by Wendy Harcourt. London: Zed.

———. 1999. "Nature's Hidden Economy." *World Watch* 11 (1): 10–19.

Acharya, Anjali. 1995. "Plundering the Boreal Forests." *World Watch* 8 (3): 2–29.

ActionAid. 2000. "Crops and Robbers: Biopiracy and the Patenting of Staple Food Crops." Retrieved from www.actionaid.org

Adams, Nassau A. 1993. *Worlds Apart: The North-South Divide and the International System.* London: Zed.

Agarwal, Bina. 1988. "Patriarchy and the 'Modernising State': An Introduction." In *Structures of Patriarchy: The State, the Community and the Household,* edited by Bina Agarwal. London: Zed.

———. 1994. *A Field of One's Own: Gender and Land Rights in South Asia.* Cambridge, UK: Cambridge University Press.

Ainger, Katherine. 2003. "The New Peasants' Revolt." *New Internationalist* 353 (January/February): 9–13.

Ake, Claude. 1996. *Democracy and Development in Africa.* Washington, DC: Brookings Institute.

Ali, Tariq. 2002. *The Clash of Fundamentalisms: Crusades, Jihads, and Modernity.* London: Verso.

Alperovitz, Gar. 2003. "Tax the Plutocrats!" *The Nation,* January 27, pp. 15–18.

Altman, Lawrence K. 2002. "AIDS in 5 Nations Called Security Threat." *The New York Times,* October 1, p. A12.

Amanor, Kojo. 1994. "Ecological Knowledge and the Regional Economy: Environmental Management in the Asesewa District of Ghana." In *Environment & Development: Sustaining People and Nature,* edited by Dharam Ghai. Oxford, UK: Blackwell.

Amenga-Etego, Rudolf. 2003. "Stalling the Big Steal." *New Internationalist* 354:20–21.

Amin, Samir. 1997. *Capitalism in the Age of Globalization.* London: Zed.

Amin, Samir, Giovanni Arrighi, Andre Gunder Frank, and Immanuel Wallerstein. 1990. *Transforming the Revolution: Social Movements and the World System.* New York: Monthly Review Press.

Amsden, Alice and Yoon-Dae Euh. 1997. "Behind Korea's Plunge." *The New York Times,* November 27, p. D1.

Anderson, Sarah and John Cavanagh, with Thea Lee. 2000. *Field Guide to the Global Economy*. New York: New Press.

Andrae, Gunilla and Björn Beckman. 1985. *The Wheat Trap*. London: Zed.

Andreas, Peter. 1994. "The Making of Amerexico." *World Policy Journal*, Summer, pp. 45–56.

Apffel-Marglin, Frédérique. 1997. "Counter-Development in the Andes." *The Ecologist* 27 (6): 221–24.

Apffel-Marglin, Frédérique and Suzanne L. Simon. 1994. "Feminist Orientalism and Development." In *Feminist Perspectives on Sustainable Development*, edited by Wendy Harcourt. London: Zed.

Appelbaum, Richard P. and Gary Gereffi. 1994. "Power and Profits in the Apparel Commodity Chain." In *Global Production: The Apparel Industry in the Pacific Rim*, edited by Edna Bonacich, Lucie Cheng, Norma Chinchilla, Nora Hamilton, and Paul Ong. Philadelphia: Temple University Press.

Araghi, Farshad. 1995. "Global Depeasantization, 1945–1990." *The Sociological Quarterly* 36 (2): 337–68.

———. 1999. "The Great Global Enclosure of Our Times: Peasants and the Agrarian Question at the End of the Twentieth Century." Pp. 145–60 in *Hungry for Profit: The Agribusiness Threat to Farmers, Food, and the Environment*, edited by Fred Magdoff, John Bellamy Foster, and Frederick H. Buttel. New York: Monthly Review Press.

Arrighi, Giovanni. 1990. "The Developmentalist Illusion: A Reconceptualization of the Semiperiphery." Pp. 11–42 in *Semiperipheral States in the World Economy*, edited by William G. Martin. Westport, CT: Greenwood.

———. 1994. *The Long Twentieth Century: Money, Power, and the Origins of Our Times*. London: Verso.

Athreya, Venkatesh B., Göran Djurfeldt, and Staffan Lindberg. 1990. *Barriers Broken: Production Relations and Agrarian Change in Tamil Nadu*. Newbury Park, CA: Sage.

Attali, Jacques. 1991. *Millennium: Winners and Losers in the Coming World Order*. New York: Times Books.

Avery, Natalie. 1994. "Stealing from the State." Pp. 95–101 in *50 Years Is Enough: The Case against the World Bank and the IMF*, edited by Kevin Danaher and Muhammad Yunus. Boston: South End.

Aviles, Jaime. 2002. "Argentina 'Obedient' Victim: Interview with Eduardo Galeano." La Jornada, April 14. Retrieved from www.zmag.org/content/Argentina/jornada_galeano.cfm

Ayittey, Georg. 2002. "AIDS Scourge Saps Africa's Vitality." *The Financial Gazette*, April 18.

Ayres, Ed. 1996. "The Shadow Economy." *WorldWatch* 9 (4): 10–23.

Bacon, Kenneth M. 1994. "Politics Could Doom a New Currency Plan." *Wall Street Journal*, May 9, p. A1.

Baer, M. Delal. 1991. "North American Free Trade." *Foreign Affairs* 70 (4): 132–49.

Bailey, Mark. 2000. "Agricultural Trade and the Livelihoods of Small Farmers." Oxfam GB Discussion Paper No. 3/00, Oxfam, GB Policy Department Oxford, UK. Retrieved from www.oxfam.org.uk/policy/papers/agricultural_trade/agric.htm

Baird, Peter and Ed McCaughan. 1979. *Beyond the Border: Mexico & the U.S. Today*. New York: North American Congress on Latin America.

Baird, Vanessa. 2002. "Fear Eats the Soul." *New Internationalist*, October, pp. 9–12.

Ball, Rochelle. 1990. "The Process of International Contract Labor Migration from the Philippines: The Case of Filipino Nurses." Ph.D. dissertation, Department of Geography, University of Sydney, Australia.

Bangura, Yusuf and Peter Gibbon. 1992. "Adjustment, Authoritarianism and Democracy in Sub-Saharan Africa: An Introduction to Some Conceptual and Empirical Issues." In *Authoritarianism, Democracy and Adjustment: The Politics of Economic Reform in Africa*, edited by Peter Gibbon, Yusuf Bangura, and Arve Ofstad. Uppsala, Sweden: Nordiska Afrikainstitutet.

Barber, Benjamin. 1996. *Jihad versus McWorld: How Globalism and Tribalism Are Reshaping the World*. New York: Ballantine.

Barboza, David. 1999. "Pluralism under Golden Arches." *The New York Times*, February 12, pp. D1, D7.

Barkin, David. 1990. *Distorted Development: Mexico in the World Economy*. Boulder, CO: Westview.

Barlow, Maude. 1999. *Blue Gold*. San Francisco: International Forum on Globalization.

Barndt, Deborah. 1997. "Bio/cultural Diversity and Equity in Post-NAFTA Mexico (or: Tomasita Comes North While Big Mac Goes South)." Pp. 55–69 in *Global Justice, Global Democracy*, edited by Jay Drydyk and Peter Penz. Winnipeg/Halifax: Fernwood.

———. 2002. *Tangled Routes: Women, Work, and Globalization on the Tomato Trail*. New York: Rowman & Littlefield.

Barnet, Richard J. and John Cavanagh. 1994. *Global Dreams: Imperial Corporations and the New World Order*. New York: Touchstone.

Barry, Tom. 1995. *Zapata's Revenge: Free Trade and the Farm Crisis in Mexico*. Boston: South End.

"Battle of the Bulge." 1994. *The Economist*, September 3, p. 25.

Beams, Nick. 1999. "UN Figures Show: International Production System Developing." Retrieved from www.wsws.org/articles/1999/Oct1999/un-o09.html

Becker, Elizabeth. 2003. "U.S. Unilateralism Worries Trade Officials." *The New York Times*, March 17, p. 5.

———. 2003. "Poor Nations Can Purchase Cheap Drugs under Accord." *The New York Times*, August 31, p. 14.

Beckman, Björn. 1992. "Empowerment or Repression? The World Bank and the Politics of African Adjustment." In *Authoritarianism, Democracy and Adjustment: The Politics of Economic Reform in Sub-Saharan Africa*, edited by Peter Gibbon, Yusuf Bangura, and Arve Ofstad. Uppsala, Sweden: Nordiska Afrikainstitutet.

Bello, Walden. 1992–1993. "Population and the Environment." *Food First Action Alert*, Winter, p. 5.

———. 1998. "Addicted to Capital: The Ten-Year High and Present-Day Withdrawal Trauma of Southeast Asia's Economies." In *FOCUS on the Global South*. Bangkok: Chulalongkorn University.

Bello, Walden, with Shea Cunningham and Bill Rau. 1994. *Dark Victory: The United States, Structural Adjustment and Global Poverty*. London: Pluto Press, with Food First and Transnational Institute.

Benería, Lourdes. 1992. "Accounting for Women's Work: The Progress of Two Decades." *World Development* 20 (11): 1547–60.

————. 1995. "Response: The Dynamics of Globalization" (Scholarly Controversy: Global Flows of Labor and Capital). *International Labor and Working-Class History* 47:45–52.

Benería, Lourdes and Shelley Feldman, eds. 1992. *Unequal Burden: Economic Crises, Persistent Poverty, and Women's Work*. Boulder, CO: Westview.

Berger, Mark. 2004. "After the Third World? History, Destiny and the Fate of Third Worldism." *Third World Quarterly* 25 (1): 1–47.

Berger, Mark T. and Mark Beeson. 1998. "Lineages of Liberalism and Miracles of Modernisation: The World Bank, the East Asian Trajectory and the International Development Debate." *Third World Quarterly* 19 (3): 487–504.

Berlan, Jean-Pierre. 1991. "The Historical Roots of the Present Agricultural Crisis." In *Towards a New Political Economy of Agriculture*, edited by W. Friedland, L. Busch, F. Buttel, and A. Rudy. Boulder, CO: Westview.

Berman, Paul. 2003. "The Philosopher of Islamic Terror." *The New York Times Magazine*, March 23, pp. 24–67.

Bernard, Mitchell. 1996. "Beyond the Local-Global Divide in the Formation of the Eastern Asian Region." *New Political Economy* 1 (3): 335–53.

————. 1999. "East Asia's Tumbling Dominoes: Financial Crises and the Myth of the Regional Model." In *Global Capitalism versus Democracy: Socialist Register 1999*, edited by Leo Panitch and Colin Leys. London: Merlin.

Bernstein, Henry. 1990. "Agricultural 'Modernization' and the Era of Structural Adjustment: Observations on Sub-Saharan Africa." *Journal of Peasant Studies* 18 (1): 3–35.

Bienefeld, Manfred. 2000. "Structural Adjustment: Debt Collection Device or Development Policy?" *Review* 23 (4): 533–82.

Black, Maggie. 2002. *The No-Nonsense Guide to International Development*. London: Verso.

Block, Fred L. 1977. *The Origins of International Economic Disorder: A Study of United States International Monetary Policy from World War II to the Present*. Berkeley: University of California Press.

Blustein, Paul. 2002. "Arab Economies Lie at the Root of Unrest." *Guardian Weekly*, February 14–20, p. 37.

Bonacich, Edna and David V. Waller. 1994. "The Role of U.S. Apparel Manufacturers in the Globalization of the Industry in the Pacific Rim." In *Global Production: The Apparel Industry in the Pacific Rim*, edited by Edna Bonacich, Lucie Cheng, Norma Chinchilla, Nora Hamilton, and Paul Ong. Philadelphia: Temple University Press.

Bond, Patrick. 2001. "Radical Rhetoric and the Working Class during Zimbabwean Nationalism's Dying Days." *Journal of World-Systems Research* 7 (1): 52–89.

————. 2002. "NEPAD." Retrieved from www.ifg.org/analysis/un/wssd/bondZnet.htm

Bookman, Jay. 2002. "The President's Real Goal in Iraq." Retrieved from http://globalresearch.ca/articles/BOO21A.html

Booth, Karen. 1998. "National Mother, Global Whore, and Transnational Femocrats: The Politics of AIDS and the Construction of Women at the World Health Organization." *Feminist Studies* 24 (1): 115–39.

Borosage, Robert L. 1999. "The Global Turning." *The Nation*, July 19, pp. 19–22.

Borthwick, Mark. 1992. *Pacific Century: The Emergence of Modern Pacific Asia.* Boulder, CO: Westview.

Bose, Sugata. 1997. "Instruments and Idioms of Colonial and National Development: India's Historical Experience in Comparative Perspective." Pp. 45–63 in *International Development and the Social Sciences,* edited by Frederick Cooper and Randall Packard. Berkeley: University of California Press.

Boyd, Stephanie. 1998. "Secrets and Lies." *The New Internationalist* 303:16–17.

Bradley, P. N. and S. E. Carter. 1989. "Food Production and Distribution—and Hunger." In *A World in Crisis? Geographical Perspectives,* edited by R. J. Johnston and P. J. Taylor. Oxford, UK: Blackwell.

Bradsher, Keith. 1995. "White House Moves to Increase Aid to Mexico." *The New York Times,* January 12, p. D6.

———. 2002. "India Slips Far behind China, Once Its Closest Rival." *The New York Times,* November 29, pp. A1, A8.

Brandt Commission (Independent Commission on International Development Issues). 1983. *Common Crisis: North, South & Cooperation for World Recovery.* London: Pan.

Brecher, Jeremy and Tim Costello. 1994. *Global Village or Global Pillage? Economic Reconstruction from the Bottom Up.* Boston: South End.

Brecher, Jeremy, Tim Costello, and Brendan Smith. 2000. *Globalization from Below: The Power of Solidarity.* Cambridge, MA: South End.

Brett, E. A. 1985. *The World Economy since the War: The Politics of Uneven Development.* London: Macmillan.

Brown, Lester R. 1994. "Who Will Feed China?" *World Watch* 7 (5): 10–19.

———. 1995. "China's Food Problem: The Massive Imports Begin." *World Watch* 8 (5): 38.

———. 2001. "Bad Tidings on the Wind for Chinese." *Guardian Weekly,* June 7–13, p. 19.

Brown, Michael Barratt. 1993. *Fair Trade.* London: Zed.

Bruno, Kenny. 1998. "Monsanto's Failing PR Strategy." *The Ecologist* 28 (5):287–93.

Buckley, Stephen. 2001. "Brazil's Poor Learn to Help Themselves." *Guardian Weekly,* February 8–14, p. 27.

Bujra, Janet. 1992. "Diversity in Pre-Capitalist Societies." In *Poverty and Development in the 1990s,* edited by Tim Allen and Allan Thomas. Oxford, UK: Oxford University Press.

Burbach, Roger and Patricia Flynn. 1980. *Agribusiness in the Americas.* New York: Monthly Review Press.

Buttel, Frederick H. 1992. "Environmentalization: Origins, Processes, and Implications for Rural Social Change." *Rural Sociology* 57 (1): 1–28.

Byres, Terry J. 1981. "The New Technology, Class Formation and Class Action in the Indian Countryside." *Journal of Peasant Studies* 8 (4): 405–54.

Cahn, Jonathan. 1993. "Challenging the New Imperial Authority: The World Bank and the Democratization of Development." *Harvard Human Rights Journal* 6:159–94.

Calvo, Dana. 1997. "Tijuana Workers Win Labor Battle." Retrieved from tw-list@essential.org

Canak, William L. 1989. "Debt, Austerity, and Latin America in the New International Division of Labor." In *Lost Promises: Debt, Austerity, and*

*Development in Latin America,* edited by William L. Canak. Boulder, CO: Westview.

Cardoso, Fernando H. and Enzo Faletto. 1979. *Dependency and Development in Latin America.* Berkeley: University of California Press.

———. 2003. "The Mexican Farmers' Movement: Exposing the Myths of Free Trade," America's Program Policy Report, March. Retrieved from www.americaspolicy.org/reports/2003/0302farm.html

Carson, Rachel. 1962. *Silent Spring.* Boston: Houghton Mifflin.

Castells, Manuel. 1998. *End of Millennium.* Oxford, UK: Blackwell.

Central Intelligence Agency. 2000. "The Global Infectious Disease Threat and Its Implications for the United States." Retrieved from www.cia.gov/cia/publications/nie/report/nie99-17d.html

Chan, Anita. 1996. "Boot Camp at the Shoe Factory." *Guardian Weekly,* November 17, pp. 20–21.

Chase, Edward T. 1995. "Down and Out in London, Paris and New York." *The Bookpress (Ithaca),* March, p. 16.

Chase-Dunn, Christopher. 1998. *Global Formation: Structures of the World-Economy.* Boulder, CO: Rowman & Littlefield.

Chatterjee, Partha. 2001. *Nationalist Thought and the Colonial World.* Minneapolis: University of Minnesota Press.

Cheru, Fantu. 1989. *The Silent Revolution in Africa: Debt, Development and Democracy.* London: Zed.

Chira, Susan. 1994. "Women Campaign for New Plan to Curb the World's Population." *The New York Times,* April 13, p. A12.

Chirot, Daniel. 1977. *Social Change in the Twentieth Century.* New York: Harcourt Brace Jovanovich.

Chomsky, Noam. 1994. *World Orders Old and New.* New York: Columbia University Press.

Chossudovsky, Michel. 1997. *The Globalisation of Poverty: Impacts of IMF and World Bank Reforms.* Penang: Third World Network.

Chung, Youg-Il. 1990. "The Agricultural Foundation for Korean Industrial Development." In *The Economic Development of Japan and Korea,* edited by Chung Lee and Ippei Yamazawa. New York: Praeger.

Clarke, T. and M. Barlow. 1997. *MAI: The Multilateral Agreement on Investment and the Threat to Canadian Sovereignty.* Toronto: Stoddart.

Clarke, Tony. 2001. "Serving Up the Commons." *Multinational Monitor* 22 (4). Retrieved from www.essential.org/monitor/mm2001/01april/corp2.html

Cleaver, Harry. 1977. "Food, Famine and the International Crisis." *Zerowork* 2:7–70.

———. 1994. "The Chiapas Uprising." *Studies in Political Economy* 44:141–57.

Coates, Barry. 2001. "Big Business at Your Service." *Guardian Weekly,* March 15–21, p. 28.

Cohen, Benjamin J. 1998. *The Geography of Money.* Ithaca, NY: Cornell University Press.

Cohen, Roger. 1998. "High Claims in Spill Betray Depth of Nigerian Poverty." *The New York Times,* September 20, pp. A1, A6.

———. 1999. "Shiny, Prosperous 'Euroland' Has Some Cracks in Façade." *The New York Times,* January 3, pp. A1, A6.

Colchester, Marcus. 1994. "Sustaining the Forests: The Community-Based Approach in South and Southeast Asia." In *Development & Environment: Sustaining People and Nature,* edited by Dharam Ghai. Oxford, UK: Blackwell.

Collins, Jane. 1995. "Gender and Cheap Labor in Agriculture." In *Food and Agrarian Orders in the World-Economy,* edited by Philip McMichael. Westport, CT: Praeger.

Collins, Joseph and John Lear. 1996. *Chile's Free Market Miracle: A Second Look.* Oakland, CA: Food First Books.

Cooper, Frederick. 1997. "Modernizing Bureaucrats, Backward Africans, and the Development Concept." Pp. 64–92 in *International Development and the Social Sciences,* edited by Frederick Cooper and Randall Packard. Berkeley: University of California Press.

Cooper, Frederick and Ann Laura Stoler, eds. 1997. *Tensions of Empire: Colonial Cultures in a Bourgeois World.* Berkeley: University of California Press.

Cooper, Helene and Thomas Kuhn. 1998. "Much of Europe Eases Its Rigid Labor Laws and Temps Proliferate." *Wall Street Journal,* June 4, pp. A1, A5.

Cooper, Marc. 1999. "No Sweat," *The Nation,* June 7, pp. 11–14.

Corbridge, Stuart. 1993. "Ethics in Development Studies: The Example of Debt." In *Beyond the Impasse: New Directions in Development Theory,* edited by Frans J. Schuurman. London: Zed.

Cowan, M. P., and R. W. Shenton. 1996. *Doctrines of Development.* London: Routledge Kegan Paul.

Cowell, Alan. 1994. "Muslim Party Threatens Turk's Secular Heritage." *The New York Times,* November 30, p. A14.

Cox, Robert W. 1987. *Production, Power, and World Order: Social Forces in the Making of History.* New York: Columbia University Press.

Crook, Clive. 1991. "Sisters in the Wood: A Survey of the IMF and the World Bank." *The Economist,* Special Supplement, October 12, pp. 5–48.

———. 1992. "Fear of Finance: A Survey of the World Economy." *The Economist,* Special Supplement, September 19, pp. 5–48.

———. 1993. "New Ways to Grow: A Survey of World Finance." *The Economist,* Special Supplement, September 25, pp. 3–22.

Crossette, Barbara. 1994. "A Third-World Effort on Family Planning." *The New York Times,* September 7, p. A8.

———. 1995. "Talks in Denmark Redefine 'Foreign Aid' in Post–Cold-War Era." *The New York Times,* March 10, p. A5.

———. 1997. "Kofi Annan's Astonishing Facts!" In *Human Development Report 1997.* New York: United Nations Development Program.

———. 1998a. "Women See Key Gains since Talks in Beijing." *The New York Times,* March 8, p. A14.

———. 1998b. "A Uganda Tribe Fights Genital Cutting." *The New York Times,* July 16, p. A8.

———. 1998c. "Where the Hunger Season Is Part of Life," *The New York Times,* Week in Review, August 16, pp. 1, 5.

Cumings, Bruce. 1987. "The Origin and Development of the Northeast Asian Political Economy: Industrial Sectors, Product Cycles, and Political Consequences." In *The Political Economy of the New Asian Industrialism,* edited by Frederic C. Deyo. Ithaca, NY: Cornell University Press.

Dalrymple, D. 1985. "The Development and Adoption of High-Yielding Varieties of Wheat and Rice in Developing Countries." *American Journal of Agricultural Economics* 67:1067–73.

Daly, M. T. and M. I. Logan. 1989. *The Brittle Rim: Finance, Business and the Pacific Region*. Ringwood, Victoria: Penguin.

Danaher, Kevin and Muhammad Yunus, eds. 1994. *50 Years Is Enough: The Case against the World Bank and the International Monetary Fund*. Boston: South End.

Darnton, John. 1994a. "In Poor, Decolonized Africa Bankers Are New Overlords." *The New York Times*, June 20, p. A1.

———. 1994b. "Africa Tries Democracy, Finding Hope and Peril." *The New York Times*, June 21, p. A9.

Davidson, Basil. 1992. *The Black Man's Burden: Africa and the Curse of the Nation-State*. New York: Times Books.

Davis, Mike. 2001. *Late Victorian Holocausts: El Nino Famines and the Making of the Third World*. London: Verso.

Dawkins, Karen. 1999. "Agricultural Prices and Trade Policy: Evaluating and Correcting the Uruguay Round Agreement on Agriculture." Paper submitted to UNCTAD/NGLS Consultation with NGOs, December 12–14, Geneva.

Dawkins, Kristin. 2000. "Battle Royale of the 21st Century." *Seedling* 17 (1): 2–8.

de Castro, Josué. 1969. " Introduction: Not One Latin America." In *Latin American Radicalism*, edited by Irving Louis Horowitz, Josué de Castro, and John Gerassi. New York: Vintage.

de Janvry, Alain. 1981. *The Agrarian Question and Reformism in Latin America*. Baltimore: Johns Hopkins University Press.

de la Rocha, Mercedes Gonzaléz. 1994. *The Resources of Poverty: Women and Survival in a Mexican City*. Cambridge, MA: Blackwell.

de Soto, Hernando. 1990. *The Other Path: The Invisible Revolution in the Third World*. New York: Harper & Row.

Denny, Charlotte. 2002. "Poor Always the Losers in Trade Game." *Guardian Weekly: Earth*, August, p. 6.

Denny, Charlotte and Larry Elliott. 2002. "Millions More Must Survive on $1 a Day." *Guardian Weekly*, June 25–July 3, p. 14.

Devraj, Ranjit. 2001. "Room at the Top." *New Internationalist* 334 (May): 17.

De Waal, Alex. 2002. "What AIDS Means in a Famine." *The New York Times*, November 19, p. 25.

DeWalt, Billie. 1985. "Mexico's Second Green Revolution: Food for Feed." *Mexican Studies/Estudios Mexicanos* 1:29–60.

Deyo, Frederic C. 1991. "Singapore: Developmental Paternalism." In *Mini-Dragons: Fragile Economic Miracles in the Pacific*, edited by Steven M. Goldstein. Boulder, CO: Westview.

Dhanagare, D. N. 1988. "The Green Revolution and Social Inequalities in Rural India." *Bulletin of Concerned Asian Scholars* 20 (2): 2–13.

Dias Martins, Monica. 2000. "The MST Challenge to Neoliberalism." *Latin American Perspectives* 27 (5): 33–45.

Dicken, Peter. 1998. *Global Shift: Transforming the World Economy*. New York: Guilford.

Dickinson, Torry D. and Robert K. Schaeffer. 2001. *Fast Forward: Work, Gender, and Protest in a Changing World*. Lanham, MD: Rowman & Littlefield.

Dillon, Sam. 1997. "After 4 Years of Nafta, Labor Is Forging Cross-Border Ties." *The New York Times*, December 20, pp. A1, A7.

———. 1998. "U.S. Labor Leader Seeks Union Support in Mexico." *The New York Times*, January 23, p. A3.

Dixon, Jane. 2002. *The Changing Chicken: Chooks, Cooks, and Culinary Culture.* Sydney, Australia: UNSW Press.

Dube, S. C. 1988. *Modernization and Development—The Search for Alternative Paradigms.* London: Zed.

Dudley, Leonard and Roger Sandilands. 1975. "The Side Effects of Foreign Aid: The Case of Public Law 480 Wheat in Colombia." *Economic Development and Cultural Change* 23 (2): 325–36.

Durning, Alan Thein. 1993. "Supporting Indigenous Peoples." In *State of the World,* edited by Lester Brown. New York: Norton.

Dwyer, Michael. 1998. "IMF Starts to Query Its Own Ideology." *The Australian Financial Review,* November 30, p. 4.

Eber, Christine E. 1999. "Seeking Our Own Food: Indigenous Women's Power and Autonomy in San Pedro Chenalhó, Chiapas (1980–1998)." *Latin American Perspectives* 26 (3): 6–36.

Economic Commission for Latin America and the Caribbean (ECLAC). 1989. *Transnational Bank Behaviour and the International Debt Crisis.* Santiago, Chile: ECLAC/UN Center on Transnational Corporations.

Edwards, Beatrice. 2003. "IDB Plan to Sell the Public Sector. The Cure or the Ill?" *NACLA* 36 (4): 13–19.

Elliott, Larry. 2001. "Evil Triumphs in a Disease-Ridden World." *Guardian Weekly,* February 14–21, p. 12.

———. 2002. "Spare a Tear for Argentina." *Guardian Weekly,* June 13–19, p. 10.

Ellwood, Wayne. 1993. "Multinationals and the Subversion of Sovereignty." *New Internationalist* 246:4–7.

———. 2001. *The No-Nonsense Guide to Globalization.* Oxford, UK: New Internationalist.

Enzenburger, Hans Magnus. 1994. *Civil Wars: From L.A. to Bosnia.* New York: The New Press.

Erlanger, Steven. 1998. "Suharto Fostered Rapid Economic Growth, and Staggering Graft." *The New York Times*, May 22, p. A9.

Escobar, Arturo. 1995. *Encountering Development: The Making and Unmaking of the Third World.* Princeton, NJ: Princeton University Press.

Esteva, Gustavo. 1992. "Development." Pp. 6–25 in *The Development Dictionary,* edited by Wolfgang Sachs. London: Zed.

Evans, Peter. 1979. *Dependent Development.* Princeton, NJ: Princeton University Press.

———. 1995. *Embedded Autonomy: States and Industrial Transformation.* Princeton, NJ: Princeton University Press.

Faison, Seth. 1997. "Detours behind It, the Giant Follows Asian's Growth Path." *The New York Times*, March 4, pp. A1, D4.

Fanon, Frantz. 1967. *The Wretched of the Earth.* Harmondsworth, UK: Penguin.

Farthing, Linda and Ben Kohl. 2001. "Bolivia's New Wave of Protest." *NACLA Report on the Americas* 34 (5): 8–11.

Feder, Ernst. 1983. *Perverse Development*. Quezon City, Philippines: Foundation for Nationalist Studies.

Fenley, Lindajoy. 1991. "Promoting the Pacific Rim." *Business Mexico*, June, p. 41.

Fernandez Kelly, Patricia. 1983. *For We Are Sold, I and My People: Women and Industry in Mexico's Frontier*. Albany, NY: SUNY Press.

Fickling, David. 2003. "Rag-Trade Slaves Face Misery in America's Pacific Outpost." *Guardian Weekly*, March 20–26, p. 5.

Fidler, Stephen and Lisa Bransten. 1995. "Mexican Sell-Offs to Help Solve the Debt Crisis." *Financial Times*, August 1, p. 1.

Fisher, Ian and Norimitsu Onishi. 1999. "Congo's Struggle May Unleash Broad Strife to Redraw Africa." *The New York Times*, January 12, pp. A1, A9.

Flavio de Almeida, Lucio and Felix Ruiz Sanchez. 2000. "The Landless Workers' Movement and Social Struggles against Neoliberalism." *Latin American Perspectives* 22 (5): 11–32.

"Food and Farming: The Facts." 2003. *New Internationalist*, January–February, pp. 20–21.

Fox, Jonathan. 1994. "The Challenge of Democracy: Rebellion as Catalyst." *Akwe:kon* 11 (2): 13–19.

Frantz, Douglas. 2002. "Turkey, Well along Road to Secularism, Fears Detour to Islamism." *The New York Times*, January 8, p. A8.

Frasca, Tim. 2002. "The Sacking of Argentina." *The Nation*, May 6, pp. 26–30.

Freeman, Carla. 2000. *High Tech and High Heels in the Global Economy: Women, Work, and Pink-Collar Identities in the Caribbean*. Durham, NC: Duke University Press.

"Free Trade: The ifs, ands and buts." 1993. *Resource Center Bulletin*, July, pp. 31–32.

French, Howard W. 1997. "A Century Later, Letting Africans Draw Their Own Map." *The New York Times*, November 23, pp. A1, A3.

Fried, Stephanie. 2003. "Writing for Their Lives: Bentian Authors and Indonesian Development Discourse." In *Forests, Coasts, and Seas: Culture and the Question of Rights to Southeast Asian Environmental Resources*, edited by C. Zerner. Durham, NC: Duke University Press.

Friedland, William H. 1994. "The Global Fresh Fruit and Vegetable System: An Industrial Organization Analysis." In *The Global Restructuring of Agro-Food Systems*, edited by Philip McMichael. Ithaca, NY: Cornell University Press.

Friedman, Thomas. 1999. "A Manifesto for the Fast World." *New York Times Magazine*, March 28. Retrieved from www.globalpolicy.org/nation/fried99.htm

Friedmann, Harriet. 1982. "The Political Economy of Food: The Rise and Fall of the Postwar International Food Order." *American Journal of Sociology* 88S:248–86.

———. 1990. "The Origins of Third World Food Dependence." In *The Food Question: Profits versus People?* edited by Henry Bernstein, Ben Crow, Maureen Mackintosh, and Charlotte Martin. New York: Monthly Review Press.

———. 1992. "Distance and Durability: Shaky Foundations of the World Food Economy." *Third World Quarterly* 13 (2): 371–83.

Friedmann, John. 1992. *Empowerment: The Politics of Alternative Development*. Cambridge, UK: Blackwell.

Fröbel, Folker, Jürgen Heinrichs, and Otto Kreye. 1979. *The New International Division of Labor*. New York: Cambridge University Press.

Gardner, Gary and Brian Halweil. 2000. "Underfed and Overfed: The Global Epidemic of Malnutrition." Worldwatch Paper No. 150, Worldwatch Institute, Washington, DC.

George, Susan. 1977. *How the Other Half Dies: The Real Reasons for World Hunger.* Montclair, NJ: Allenheld, Osmun and Co.

———. 1988. *A Fate Worse Than Debt: The World Financial Crisis and the Poor.* New York: Grove.

———. 1992. *The Debt Boomerang: How Third World Debt Harms Us All.* Boulder, CO: Westview.

George, Susan and Fabrizio Sabelli. 1994. *Faith and Credit: The World Bank's Secular Empire.* Boulder, CO: Westview.

Gereffi, Gary. 1989. "Rethinking Development Theory: Insights from East Asia and Latin America." *Sociological Forum* 4 (4): 505–33.

———. 1994. "The Organization of Buyer-Driven Global Commodity Chains: How U.S. Retailers Shape Overseas Production Networks." In *Commodity Chains and Global Capitalism,* edited by Gary Gereffi and Miguel Korzeniewicz. Westport, CT: Praeger.

Gevisser, Mark. 2001. "AIDS: The New Apartheid." *The Nation,* May 14, pp. 5–6.

Gibbon, Peter. 1992. "Structural Adjustment and Pressures toward Multipartyism in Sub-Saharan Africa." In *Authoritarianism, Democracy and Adjustment: The Politics of Economic Reform in Sub-Saharan Africa,* edited by Peter Gibbon, Yusuf Bangura, and Arve Ofstad. Uppsala, Sweden: Nordiska Afrikainstitutet.

Gill, Stephen. 1992. "Economic Globalization and the Internationalization of Authority: Limits and Contradictions." *Geoforum* 23 (3): 269–83.

Global Intelligence Update. 1999. "World Bank Reverses Position on Financial Controls and on Malaysia." Retrieved from www.stratfor.com

Godrej, Dinyar. 2003. "Precious Fluid." *New Internationalist* 354:9–12.

Golden, Tim. 1995. "Mexicans Find Dream Devalued." *The New York Times,* January 8, p. 5.

Goldsmith, James. 1994. *The Trap.* New York: Carroll & Graf.

Gorelick, Sherry. 2000. "Facing the Farm Crisis." *The Ecologist* 30 (4): 28–32.

Goss, Jasper, David Burch, and Roy E. Rickson. 2000. "Agri-Food Restructuring and Third World Transnationals: Thailand, the CP Group and the Global Shrimp Industry." *World Development* 28 (3): 513–30.

Gowan, Peter. 2003. "The American Campaign for Global Sovereignty." Pp. 1–27 in *Fighting Identities: Socialist Register,* edited by Leo Panitch and Colin Leys. London: Merlin.

GRAIN. 1998. "Biopiracy, TRIPS and the Patenting of Asia's Rice Bowl: A Collective NGO Situationer on IPRs and Rice." Retrieved from www.grain.org/publications/reports/rice/htm

Graw, Stephen. 1999. "Overseas Labor Remittances: Spare Change or New Changes?" Paper presented at annual meeting of the Association for Asian Studies, April, Boston.

Greenfield, Gerard. 1999. "The WTO, the World Food System, and the Politics of Harmonised Destruction." Retrieved from www.labournet.org/discuss/global/wto/html

Greider, William. 2001. "A New Giant Sucking Sound." *The Nation,* December 31, pp. 22–24.

Griffin, K. B. 1974. *The Political Economy of Agrarian Change: An Essay on the Green Revolution*. Cambridge, MA: Harvard University Press.

Grigg, David. 1993. *The World Food Problem*. Oxford, UK: Blackwell.

Grosfoguel, Ramon. 1996. "From Cepalismo to Neoliberalism: A World-Systems Approach to Conceptual Shifts in Latin America." *Review* 19:131–54.

Hall, Thomas D. 2002. "World-Systems Analysis and Globalization Directions for the Twenty First Century." Pp. 81–122 in *Theoretical Directions in Political Sociology for the 21st Century*, vol. 2, edited by T. Buzzell. New York: Elsevier Science.

Harcourt, Wendy. 1994. "Introduction." In *Feminist Perspectives on Sustainable Development*, edited by Wendy Harcourt. London: Zed.

Harding, Luke. 2002. "Election Threatens India's Secular Future." *Guardian Weekly*, December 19–25, p. 4.

Harper, Doug. 1994. "Auto Imports Jump in Mexico." *The New York Times*, July 7, p. D1.

Harris, Nigel. 1987. *The End of the Third World: Newly Industrializing Countries and the Decline of an Ideology*. Harmondsworth, UK: Penguin.

Harrison, Paul. 1993. *The Third Revolution: Population, Environment and a Sustainable World*. Harmondsworth, UK: Penguin.

Harvey, Neil. 1994. *Rebellion in Chiapas: Rural Reforms, Campesino Radicalism, and the Limits to Salinismo*. San Diego: Center for U.S.-Mexican Studies.

Hathaway, Dale E. 1987. *Agriculture and the GATT: Rewriting the Rules*. Washington, DC: Institute for International Economics.

Hawkins, Tony. 1998. "At the Heart of Further Progress." *Financial Times*, June 2, pp. I–VI.

Hayden, Tom. 2003. "Seeking a New Globalism in Chiapas." *The Nation*, April 7, pp. 18–23.

Hedges, Chris. 1994. "Key Panel at Cairo Talks Agrees on Population Plan." *The New York Times*, September 13, p. A10.

Hedland, Stefan and Niclas Sundstrom. 1996. "The Russian Economy after Systemic Change." *Europe-Asia Studies* 48 (6): 889.

Heffernan, William D. 1999. "Consolidation in the Food and Agriculture System." Report to the National Farmers Union. Retrieved February 5, 1999, from www.nfu.org/whstudy.html

Heffernan, William D. and Douglas H. Constance. 1994. "Transnational Corporations and the Globalization of the Food System." In *From Columbus to ConAgra: The Globalization of Agriculture and Food*, edited by Alessandro Bonanno, Lawrence Busch, William Friedland, Lourdes Gouveia, and Enzo Mingione. Lawrence: University Press of Kansas.

Held, David. 1995. *Democracy and the Global Order: From the Modern State to Cosmopolitan Governance*. Stanford, CA: Stanford University Press.

Helleiner, Eric. 1996. *States and the Reemergence of Global Finance: From Bretton Woods to the 1990s*. Ithaca, NY: Cornell University Press.

Hellman, Judith Adler. 1994. *Mexican Lives*. New York: Free Press.

Henderson, Jeffrey. 1991. *The Globalisation of High Technology Production*. London: Routledge Kegan Paul.

Henley, Jon. 2003. "French Citizenship Ideal Dies in a High-Rise Hell." *Guardian Weekly*, January 16–22, p. 3.

Henley, Jon and Jeevan Vasagar. 2003. "Think Muslim, Drink Muslim, Says New Rival to Coke." *Guardian Weekly*, January 16–22, p. 3.

Herbert, Bob. 1996. "Nike's Pyramid Scheme." *The New York Times*, June 10, p. 33.

———. 1998. "At What Cost?" *The New York Times*, June 7, p. A15.

Hernández, Luis Navarro. 1994. "The Chiapas Uprising." In *Rebellion in Chiapas*, edited by Neil Harvey. San Diego: University of California–San Diego, Center for U.S./Mexican Studies.

Hettne, Björn. 1990. *Development Theory and the Three Worlds*. White Plains, NY: Longman.

Hightower, Jim. 2002. "How Wal-Mart Is Remaking Our World." Pamphlet #7, Ithaca, NY.

Hildyard, Nicholas. 1993. "Foxes in Charge of Chickens." In *Global Ecology: A New Arena of Political Conflict*, edited by Wolfgang Sachs. London: Zed.

Hobsbawm, Eric J. 1992. "The Crisis of Today's Ideologies." *New Left Review* 192:55–64.

Holusha, John. 1996. "Squeezing the Textile Workers." *The New York Times*, February 21, pp. D1, D20.

Hoogvelt, Ankie M. M. 1987. *The Third World in Global Development*. London: Macmillan.

———. 1997. *Globalization and the Postcolonial World: The New Political Economy of Development*. London: Macmillan.

Houtart, Francois and Francois Polet, eds. 2001. *The Other Davos: The Globalization of Resistance to the World Economic System*. London: Zed.

Huntington, Samuel, P. 1993. "The Clash of Civilizations." *Foreign Affairs* 72 (3): 22–50.

Ibrahim, Youssef M. 1994. "Fundamentalists Impose Culture on Egypt." *The New York Times*, February 3, pp. A1, A10.

Ihonvbere, Julius O. 1993–1994. "The Third World and the New World Order in the 1990s." In *Third World 94/95: Annual Editions*, edited by Robert J. Griffiths. Guildford, CT: Dushkin.

International Monetary Fund. 2001. "Balance of Payment Statistics." Retrieved from www.imf.org/external/up/sta/bop/bop.htm

Jahan, Rounaq. 1995. *The Elusive Agenda: Mainstreaming Women in Development*. London: Zed.

James, C. L. R. 1963. *The Black Jacobins: Toussaint L'Ouverture and the San Domingo Revolution*. New York: Vintage.

Jenkins, Rhys. 1992. "Industrialization and the Global Economy." In *Industrialization and Development*, edited by Tom Hewitt, Hazel Johnson, and Dave Wield. Oxford, UK: Oxford University Press.

Jordan, Mary and Kevin Sullivan. 2003. "Trade Brings Riches, but Not to Mexico's Poor." *Guardian Weekly*, April 3–9, p. 33.

Juhasz, Antonia. 2002. "Servicing Citi's Interests: GATS and the Bid to Remove Barriers to Financial Firm Globalization." *Multinational Monitor* 23 (4). Retrieved from www.multinationalmonitor.org/mm2002/02April/April02 corp3.html

Kagarlitsky, Boris. 1995. *The Mirage of Modernization*. New York: Monthly Review Press.

Kahn, Joseph. 2002. "Losing Faith: Globalization Proves Disappointing." *The New York Times*, March 21, p. 7.

————. 2003. "China's Workers Risk Limbs in Export Drive." *The New York Times*, April 7, p. 3.

Kaldor, Mary. 1990. *The Imaginary War: Understanding the East-West Conflict.* Oxford, UK: Blackwell.

Kamel, Laila Iskandar. 1999. "The Urban Poor as Development Partners." *Cooperation South* 2:127–33.

Kane, Hal. 1996. "Micro-Enterprise." *World Watch* 9 (2): 11–19.

Karliner, Joshua. 1997. *The Corporate Planet: Ecology and Politics in the Age of Globalization.* San Francisco: Sierra Club Books.

Kemp, Tom. 1989. *Industrialization in the Non-Western World.* London: Longman.

Kernaghan, Charles. 1995. *Zoned for Slavery: The Child behind the Label* [Videotape]. New York: National Labor Committee.

Kikeri, Sunita and John Nellis. 2002. "Privatization in Competitive Sectors: The Record to Date." World Bank Policy Research Working Paper 2860, World Bank, Washington, DC.

Kilvert, Andrew. 1998. "Golden Promises." *New Internationalist*, September, pp. 16–17.

King, Alexander and Bertrand Schneider. 1991. *The First Global Revolution: A Report by the Council to the Club of Rome.* New York: Pantheon.

Klein, Naomi. 2003. "No Peace without a Fight." *The Nation*, March 31, p. 10.

Kneen, Brewster. 1990. *Trading Up: How Cargill, the World's Largest Grain Company, Is Changing World Agriculture.* Toronto: N.C. Press.

Knox, Paul and John Agnew. 1994. *The Geography of the World Economy.* London: Edward Arnold.

Kohli, Geeta and Kim Webster. 1999. "Female Circumcision: A Ritual Worth Continuing?" Unpublished term paper, Rural Sociology, Cornell University, New York.

Kolko, Joyce. 1988. *Restructuring the World Economy.* New York: Pantheon.

Korten, David. 1995. *When Corporations Rule the World.* New York: Kumarian.

Korzeniewicz, Miguel. 1994. "Commodity Chains and Marketing Strategies: Nike and the Global Athletic Footwear Industry." In *Commodity Chains and Global Capitalism,* edited by Gary Gereffi and Miguel Korzeniewicz. Westport, CT: Praeger.

Kothari, Ashish. 2000. "Farmers or Corporations: Who Does the Plant Varieties Bill Benefit?" Retrieved from www.biotech-info.net/farmers_corps.html

Kothari, Smitu and Pramod Parajuli. 1993. "No Nature without Social Justice: A Plea for Cultural and Ecological Pluralism in India." In *Global Ecology: A New Arena of Political Conflict,* edited by Wolfgang Sachs. London: Zed.

Landsberg, Martin. 1979. "Export-Led Industrialization in the Third World: Manufacturing Imperialism." *Review of Radical Political Economics* 2 (4):50–63.

Lang, Tim. 1998. "Dietary Impact of the Globalization of Food Trade." *IFG News, International Forum on Globalization* 3:10–12.

Lang, Tim and Colin Hines. 1993. *The New Protectionism: Protecting the Future against Free Trade.* New York: The New Press.

Lappé, Frances Moore, Joseph Collins, and Peter Rosset, with Luis Esparza. 1998. *World Hunger: Twelve Myths.* 2d ed. New York: Grove.

Lappé, Frances Moore and Anna Lappé. 2002. *Hope's Edge.* New York: Tarcher/Putnam.

Lappin, Todd. 1994. "Can Green Mix with Red?" *The Nation*, February 14, p. 193.

LaTouche, Serge. 1993. *In the Wake of the Affluent Society: An Exploration of Post-Development*. London: Zed.

Le Carre, John. 2001. "In Place of Nations." *The Nation*, April 9, pp. 11–13.

Legrand, Christine. 2002. "Argentina's New Poor Battle against Hunger." *Guardian Weekly*, July 11–17, p. 30.

Lehman, David. 1990. *Democracy and Development in Latin America*. Philadelphia: Temple University Press.

Lehman, K. and A. Krebs. 1996. "Control of the World's Food Supply." Pp. 122–30 in *The Case against the Global Economy, and for a Turn toward the Local*, edited by J. Mander and E. Goldsmith. San Francisco: Sierra Club Books.

LeQuesne, C. 1997. "The World Trade Organization and Food Security." Talk to UK Food Group, July 15, London.

Lewin, Tamar. 1995. "Family Decay Global, Study Says." *The New York Times*, May 30, p. A5.

Lewis, Paul. 1997. "IMF Seeks Argentine Deal Linking Credit to Governing." *The New York Times*, July 15, pp. D1, D19.

Lietaer, Bernard. 1997. "From the Real Economy to the Speculative." *International Forum on Globalization News* 2:7–10.

Lipton, Michael. 1977. *Why Poor People Stay Poor: Urban Bias in World Development*. London: Temple Smith.

Lissakers, Karin. 1993. *Banks, Borrowers, and the Establishment: A Revisionist Account of the International Debt Crisis*. New York: Basic Books.

Llambi, Luis. 1990. "Transitions to and within Capitalism: Agrarian Transitions in Latin America." *Sociologia Ruralis* 30 (2): 174–96.

Lohmann, Larry. 1993. "Resisting Green Globalism." In *Global Ecology: A New Arena of Political Conflict*, edited by Wolfgang Sachs. London: Zed.

London, Christopher. 1997. "Class Relations and Capitalist Development: Subsumption in the Colombian Coffee Industry." *Journal of Peasant Studies* 24 (4): 269–95.

Lorch, Donatella. 1995. "Ugandan Strongman a Favorite of World Lenders." *The New York Times*, January 29, p. A3.

Lucas, Caroline. 2001. "The Great Food Swap." Retrieved from www.greeparty. org.uk/reports/2001/globalisation/greatfoodswap.html

Maass, Peter. 2001. "Emroz Khan Is Having a Bad Day." *The New York Times Magazine*, October 21, pp. 48–51.

MacShane, Denis. 1991. "Working in Virtual Slavery: Gulf Migrant Labor." *The Nation*, March 18, pp. 325, 343–44.

Madden, Peter and John Madeley. 1993. "Winners and Losers: The Impact of the GATT Uruguay Round in Developing Countries." *Christian Aid*, December, p. 17.

Madeley, John. 2000. *Hungry for Trade*. London: Zed.

Magdoff, Harry. 1969. *The Age of Imperialism*. New York: Monthly Review Press.

Mamdani, Mahmood. 1996. *Citizen and Subject: Contemporary Africa and the Legacy of Late Colonialism*. Princeton, NJ: Princeton University Press.

———. 2003. "Making Sense of Political Violence in Post-Colonial Africa." Pp. 132–51 in *Fighting Identities: Race, Religion and Ethno-Nationalism: Socialist Register 2003*, edited by Leo Panitch and Colin Leys. London: Merlin.

Mark, Jason. 2001. "Brazil's MST: Taking Back the Land." *Multinational Monitor* 22:10–12.

Martin, Hans-Peter and Harold Schumann. 1997. *The Global Trap: Globalisation and the Assault on Democracy and Prosperity.* London: Zed.

McMichael, A. J. 1993. *Planetary Overload: Global Environmental Change and the Health of the Human Species.* Cambridge, UK: Cambridge University Press.

McMichael, Philip. 1993a. "World Food System Restructuring under a GATT Regime." *Political Geography* 12 (3): 198–214.

———. 1993b. "Agro-Food Restructuring in the Pacific Rim: A Comparative-International Perspective on Japan, South Korea, the United States, Australia, and Thailand." In *Pacific-Asia and the Future of the World-System*, edited by Ravi Palat. Westport, CT: Greenwood.

———. 2001. "The Impact of Globalisation, Free Trade and Technology on Food and Nutrition in the New Millennium." *Proceedings of the Nutrition Society* 60 (2): 215–20.

———. 2003. "Food Security and Social Reproduction." Pp. 169–89 in *Power, Production and Social Reproduction: Human In/security in the Global Political Economy*, edited by Stephen Gill and Isabella Bakker. London: MacMillan Palgrave.

McMichael, Philip and Chul-Kyoo Kim. 1994. "Japanese and South Korean Agricultural Restructuring in Comparative and Global Perspective." In *The Global Restructuring of Agro-Food Systems*, edited by Philip McMichael. Ithaca, NY: Cornell University Press.

McMichael, Philip and David Myhre. 1991. "Global Regulation versus the Nation-State: Agro-Food Systems and the New Politics of Capital." *Capital & Class* 43 (2): 83–106.

McMichael, Philip and Laura T. Raynolds. 1994. "Capitalism, Agriculture, and World Economy." In *Capitalism and Development*, edited by Leslie Sklair. London: Routledge Kegan Paul.

Memmi, Albert. 1967. *The Colonizer and the Colonized.* Boston: Beacon.

Menon, Gayatri A. 2001. "The Multivalency of Microcredit: The Cultural Politics of Credit and Citizenship in India." Master's thesis, Development Sociology, Cornell University, New York.

Menotti, Victor. 1996. "World Leaders Warn of 'Backlash to Globalization.'" *International Forum on Globalization News*, Fall, pp. 1, 7.

———. 1998. "Globalization and the Acceleration of Forest Destruction Since Rio." *The Ecologist* 28 (6): 354–62.

———. 1999. "Forest Destruction and Globalisation." *The Ecologist* 29 (3): 180–81.

Meredith, Robyn. 1997. "Auto Giants Build a Glut of Asian Plants, Just as Demand Falls." *The New York Times*, November 5, pp. D1, D8.

Middleton, Neil, Phil O'Keefe, and Sam Moyo. 1993. *Tears of the Crocodile: From Rio to Reality in the Developing World.* Boulder, CO: Pluto.

Mies, Maria. 1991. *Patriarchy and Accumulation on a World Scale: Women in the International Division of Labor.* London: Zed.

Milbank, Dana. 1994. "Unlike Rest of Europe, Britain Is Creating Jobs but They Pay Poorly." *Wall Street Journal*, March 28, pp. A1, A6.

Mitchell, Timothy. 1991. *Colonising Egypt.* Berkeley: University of California Press.

Mittal, Anuradha. 1998. "Freedom to Trade vs. Freedom from Hunger: Food Security in the Age of Economic Globalization." In *WTO as a Conceptual Framework for Globalization,* edited by Eva Harton and Claes Olsson. Uppsala, Sweden: Global Publications Foundation.

Moberg, David. 1999. "Bringing Down Niketown." *The Nation,* June 7, pp. 15–18.

Moghadam, Valentine M. 1993. *Modernizing Women: Gender and Social Change in the Middle East.* Boulder, CO: Lynne Reinner.

Mohan, Dia. 2003. "Scripting Power and Changing the Subject: The Political Theatre of Jana Sanskriti in Rural Bengal." Doctoral dissertation, Development Sociology, Cornell University, New York.

Monbiot, George. 2003. "Out of the Wreckage." *Guardian Weekly,* March 6–12, p. 11.

Montalbano, William D. 1991. "A Global Pursuit of Happiness." *Los Angeles Times,* October 1, p. F1.

Moody, Kim. 1999. *Workers in a Lean World: Unions in the International Economy.* London: Verso.

Moran, Theodore H. 2000. "Investment Issues." Pp. 223–42 in *The WTO after Seattle,* edited by Jeffrey J. Schott. Washington, DC: Institute for International Economics.

Morgan, Dan. 1980. *Merchants of Grain.* Harmondsworth, UK: Penguin.

Murphy, Sophia. 1999. "WTO, Agricultural Deregulation and Food Security." Paper presented at the Globalization Challenge Initiative, December. Retrieved from www.foreignpolicy-infocus.org/briefs/vol14n34wto_body.html

Myers, Norman. 1981. "The Hamburger Connection: How Central America's Forests Became North America's Hamburgers." *Ambio* 10 (1): 3–8.

Myerson, Allen R. 1997. "In Principle, a Case for More 'Sweatshops.'" *The New York Times,* June 22, p. 5.

Myhre, David. 1994. "The Politics of Globalization in Rural Mexico: Campesino Initiatives to Restructure the Agricultural Credit System." In *The Global Restructuring of Agro-Food Systems,* edited by Philip McMichael. Ithaca, NY: Cornell University Press.

Nash, Nathaniel C. 1994. "Vast Areas of Rain Forest Are Being Destroyed in Chile." *The New York Times,* May 31, p. C4.

Ndulo, Muna. 2002. "International Trade, Development, and Africa." *Africa Notes* (Institute for African Development, Cornell University), September–October, pp. 6–10.

Neville, Richard. 1997. "The Business of Being Human." *Good Weekend (The Age,* Melbourne), August 23, pp. 48–50.

Nogueira, Ana, Josh Bretbart, and Chris Strohm. 2003. "Rebellion in Argentina." Retrieved from www.zmag.org/Zmag/articles/may02nogueira_breitbart_strohm.htm

Norberg-Hodge, Helena. 1992. *Ancient Futures: Learning from Ladakh.* San Francisco: Sierra Club.

———. 1994–1995. "Globalization versus Community." *ISEC/Ladakh Project* 14:1–2.

Ohmae, Kenichi. 1985. *Triad Power: The Coming Shape of Global Competition.* New York: Free Press.

———. 1990. *The End of the Nation-State: The Rise of Regional Economies.* New York: Free Press.

Olive, David. 2003. "Global Cooling." *Toronto Star,* April 6. Posted April 8, 2003, by mritchie@iatp.org

O'Meara, Molly. 1999. "Reinventing Cities for People and the Planet." Worldwatch Paper No. 147, Worldwatch, Washington DC.

Ong, Aihwa. 1997. "The Gender and Labor Politics of Postmodernity." Pp. 61–97 in *The Politics of Culture in the Shadow of Capital,* edited by Lisa Lowe and David Lloyd. Durham, NC: Duke University Press.

Onishi, Norimitsu. 1998. "Nigeria Combustible as South's Oil Enriches North." *The New York Times,* November 22, pp. A1, A6.

———. 1999. "Deep in the Republic of Chevron." *The New York Times Magazine,* July 4, pp. 26–31.

———. 2001. "Rising Muslim Power in Africa Causes Unrest in Nigeria and Elsewhere." *The New York Times,* November 1, p. A14.

Orlanda Pinnasi, Maria, Fatima Cabral, and Mirian Claudia Lourencao. 2000. "An Interview with Joao Pedro Stedile." *Latin American Perspectives* 27 (5): 46–62.

Panitch, Leo. 1996. "Rethinking the Role of the State." Pp. 83–113 in *Globalization: Critical Reflections,* edited by James H. Mittelman. Boulder, CO: Lynne Reinner.

Paringaux, R.-P. 2001. "The Deliberate Destruction of Agriculture: India: Free Markets, Empty Bellies." *Le Monde Diplomatique,* September, 1–9.

Patel, Raj, with A. Delwiche. 2002a. "The Profits of Famine: Southern Africa's Long Decade of Hunger." *Backgrounder, Food First* 8, 4. Retrieved from www.foodfirst.org/pubs/backgrdrs/2002/f02v8n4.html

———. 2002b. "What Does NEPAD Stand For?" Retrieved from http://voiceof-theturtle.org/show_article.php?aid=97

Payer, Cheryl. 1974. *The Debt Trap.* New York: Monthly Review Press.

Pearse, A. 1980. *Seeds of Plenty, Seeds of Want.* Oxford, UK: Clarendon.

Perlez, Jane. 2001. "U.N. Chief Calls on U.S. Companies to Donate to AIDS Fund." *The New York Times,* June 2, p. A1.

———. 2002. "For Some Indonesians, Echoes of 'Coolie' Nation." *The New York Times,* August 18, p. 10.

Phillips, Michael M. 2002. "U.S. to Push Service-Sector Trade in a Sweeping Liberalization Plan." *Wall Street Journal,* July 1, p. 5.

Pilger, John. 2002. *The New Rulers of the World.* London: Verso.

Pitt, William Rivers. 2003. "be afraid...." *The Ecologist* 33 (3): 21–22.

Place, Susan E. 1985. "Export Beef Production and Development Contradictions in Costa Rica." *Tijdschrift voor Econ. en Soc. Geografie* 76 (4): 288–97.

Pollack, Andrew. 1999. "Biological Products Raise Genetic Ownership Issues." *The New York Times,* November 26, p. A9.

Public Citizen. 2001. "Down on the Farm: NAFTA's Seven-Year War on Farmers and Ranchers in the U.S., Canada and Mexico." Retrieved from www.citizen.org

Pyle, Jean L. 2001. "Sex, Maids, and Export Processing: Risks and Reasons for Gendered Global Production Networks." *International Journal of Politics, Culture and Society* 15 (1): 55–76.

Quing, Dai. 1998. "The Three Gorges Project: A Symbol of Uncontrolled Development in the Late Twentieth Century." In *The River Dragon Has Come!*

*The Three Gorges Dam and the Fate of China's Yangtze River and Its People,* edited by Dai Quing. London: M. E. Sharpe.

Raghavan, Chakravarthi. 1990. *Recolonization: GATT, the Uruguay Round and the Third World.* Penang, Malaysia: Third World Network.

Raikes, Philip. 1988. *Modernising Hunger: Famine, Food Surplus & Farm Policy in the EC and Africa.* London: Catholic Institute for International Affairs.

Ransom, David. 2001a. "A World Turned Upside Down." *New Internationalist* 334:9–11.

———. 2001b. *The No-Nonsense Guide to Fair Trade.* London: Verso.

Rau, Bill. 1991. *From Feast to Famine: Official Cures and Grassroots Remedies to Africa's Food Crisis.* London: Zed.

Raynolds, Laura T. 1994. "The Restructuring of Export Agriculture in the Dominican Republic: Changing Agrarian Relations and the State." In *The Global Restructuring of Agro-Food Systems,* edited by Philip McMichael. Ithaca, NY: Cornell University Press.

———. 2000. "Re-Embedding Global Agriculture: The International Organic and Fair Trade Movements." *Agriculture and Human Values* 17:297–309.

Raynolds, Laura T. 2001. "New Plantations, New Workers: Gender and Production Politics in the Dominican Republic." *Gender & Society* 15 (1): 7–28.

Raynolds, Laura T., David Myhre, Philip McMichael, Viviana Carro-Figueroa, and Frederick H. Buttel. 1993. "The 'New' Internationalization of Agriculture: A Reformulation." *World Development* 21 (7): 1101–21.

Redding, Sean. 2000. "Structural Adjustment and the Decline of Subsistence Agriculture in Africa." Retrieved from http://womencrossing.org/redding.html

Reich, Robert B. 1991. "Secession of the Successful." *The New York Times Magazine,* January 20, p. 42.

———. 1992. *The Work of Nations: Preparing Ourselves for 21st Century Capitalism.* New York: Vintage.

Research Unit for Political Economy. 2003. *Behind the Invasion of Iraq.* New York: Monthly Review Press.

Revel, Alain and Christophe Riboud. 1986. *American Green Power.* Baltimore: Johns Hopkins University Press.

Ricardo, David. [1821] 1951. *On the Principles of Political Economy and Taxation.* 3d ed. In *The Works and Correspondence of David Ricardo,* vol. 1, edited by P. Sraffe with the collaboration of M. M. Dobb. Reprint, Cambridge, UK: Cambridge University Press.

Rich, Bruce. 1994. *Mortgaging the Earth: The World Bank, Environmental Impoverishment and the Crisis of Development.* Boston: Beacon.

Richburg, Keith B. 2002. "Illegal Workers Do Europe's Dirty Work." *Guardian Weekly,* August 15–21, p. 29.

Ride, Anouk. 1998. "Maps, Myths and Migrants." *New Internationalist* 305:9.

Riding, Alan. 1993. "France, Reversing Course, Fights Immigrants' Refusal to Be French." *The New York Times,* December 5, pp. A1, 14.

Rifkin, Jeremy. 1992. *Beyond Beef: The Rise and Fall of the Cattle Culture.* New York: Penguin.

———. 1998. *The Biotech Century: Harnessing the Gene and Remaking the World.* New York: Tarcher/Putnam.

Rist, Gilbert. 1997. *The History of Development: From Western Origins to Global Faith.* London: Zed.

Ritchie, Mark. 1993. *Breaking the Deadlock: The United States and Agriculture Policy in the Uruguay Round.* Minneapolis: Institute for Agriculture and Trade Policy.

———. 1994. "GATT Facts: Africa Loses under GATT." Working paper, Institute for Agriculture and Trade Policy, Minneapolis, MN.

———. 1999. "The World Trade Organization and the Human Right to Food Security." Paper presented at the International Cooperative Agriculture Organization General Assembly, August 29, Quebec City, Canada. Available: www.agricoop.org/activities/mark_rithcie.pdf

Rocheleau, Dianne E. 1991. "Gender, Ecology, and the Science of Survival: Stories and Lessons from Kenya." In *Feminist Perspectives on Sustainable Development,* edited by Wendy Harcourt. London: Zed.

Rohter, Larry. 2002. "Amazon Forest Still Burning Despite the Good Intentions." *The New York Times,* August 23, pp. A1, A9.

Roodman, David Malin. 2001. "Still Waiting for the Jubilee: Pragmatic Solutions for the Third World Debt Crisis." Worldwatch Paper No. 155, Worldwatch, Washington, DC.

Rosenberg, Tina. 1998. "Trees and the Roots of a Storm's Destruction." *The New York Times,* November 26, p. A38.

Ross, Robert J. S. and Kent C. Trachte. 1990. *Global Capitalism: The New Leviathan.* Albany, NY: SUNY Press.

Rostow, Walt W. 1960. *The Stages of Economic Growth: A Non-Communist Manifesto.* Cambridge, UK: Cambridge University Press.

Rothchild, Donald and Letitia Lawson. 1994. "The Interactions between State and Civil Society in Africa: From Deadlock to New Routines." In *Civil Society and the State in Africa,* edited by John W. Harbeson, Donald Rothchild, and Naomi Chazan. Boulder, CO: Lynne Rienner.

Rowley, C. D. 1974. *The Destruction of Aboriginal Society.* Ringwood, Victoria: Penguin.

Rowling, Megan. 2001. "Sea Change." *New Internationalist* 341:23–24.

Roy, Olivier. 1998. *The Failure of Political Islam.* Cambridge, MA: Harvard University Press.

Rueschemeyer, Dietrich, Evelyne Huber Stephens, and John Stephens. 1992. *Capitalist Development and Democracy.* Chicago: University of Chicago Press.

Ruggiero, Renato. 1996. "Trading Towards Peace?" Address to the MENA II Conference, December 11, Cairo, Egypt.

———. 1998. "From Vision to Reality: the Multilateral Trading System at Fifty." Address presented at the Brookings Institution Forum, December, Washington, DC.

———. 2000. "Reflections from Seattle." Pp. xiii–xvii in *The WTO after Seattle,* edited by Jeffrey Schott. Washington, DC: Institute for International Economics.

Sachs, Jeffrey. 1998. "The IMF and the Asian Flu." *The American Prospect,* March–April, pp. 16–21.

Sachs, Wolfgang. 1992. "One World." Pp. 102–15 in *The Development Dictionary,* edited by Wolfgang Sachs. London: Zed.

———. 1993. "Global Ecology and the Shadow of 'Development.'" In *Global Ecology: A New Arena of Political Conflict,* edited by Wolfgang Sachs. London: Zed.

Salinger, Lynn and Jean-Jacques Dethier. 1989. "Policy-Based Lending in Agriculture: Agricultural Sector Adjustment in Mexico." Paper presented at World Bank Seminar on Policy-Based Lending in Agriculture, May 17–19, Baltimore.

Salmon, Katy. 2001. "Where There Are No Subsidies." *New Internationalist* 334:22.

Sandbrook, Richard. 1995. *The Politics of Africa's Economic Recovery.* Cambridge, UK: Cambridge University Press.

Sanderson, Steven. 1986a. *The Transformation of Mexican Agriculture: International Structure and the Politics of Rural Change.* Princeton, NJ: Princeton University Press.

———. 1986b. "The Emergence of the 'World Steer': Internationalization and Foreign Domination in Latin American Cattle Production." In *Food, the State and International Political Economy,* edited by F. L. Tullis and W. L. Hollist. Lincoln: University of Nebraska Press.

Sanger, David E. 1998. "Dissension Erupts at Talks on World Financial Crisis." *The New York Times,* October 7, p. A6.

Schaeffer, Robert. 1995. "Free Trade Agreements: Their Impact on Agriculture and the Environment." In *Food and Agrarian Orders in the World-Economy,* edited by Philip McMichael. Westport, CT: Praeger.

———. 1997. *Understanding Globalization: The Social Consequences of Political, Economic, and Environmental Change.* New York: Rowman & Littlefield.

Schemo, Diana Jean. 1997. "Rising Fires Renew Threat to Amazon." *The New York Times,* November 2, p. A6.

———. 1998. "Data Show Recent Burning of Amazon Is Worst Ever." *The New York Times,* January 27, p. A4.

Schneider, Cathy Lisa. 1995. *Shantytown Protest in Pinochet's Chile.* Philadelphia: Temple University Press.

Schoenberger, Erica. 1994. "Competition, Time, and Space in Industrial Change." In *Commodity Chains and Global Capitalism,* edited by Gary Gereffi and Miguel Korzeniewicz. Westport, CT: Praeger.

Schott, Jeffrey J. 2000. "The WTO after Seattle." Pp. 3–40 in *The WTO after Seattle,* edited by Jeffrey J. Schott. Washington, DC: Institute for International Economics.

Schwedel, S. and K. Haley. 1992. "Foreign Investment in the Mexican Food System." *Business Mexico* (Special Edition) 2:48–55.

Segelken, Roger. 1995. "Fewer Foods Predicted for Crowded Future Meals." *Cornell Chronicle,* February 23, p. 5.

Seidman, Gay. 1994. *Manufacturing Militance: Workers' Movements in Brazil and South Africa, 1970–1985.* Berkeley: University of California Press.

Sen, Gita. 1994. "Women, Poverty, and Population: Issues for the Concerned Environmentalist." In *Feminist Perspectives on Sustainable Development,* edited by Wendy Harcourt. London: Zed.

Sengupta, Somini. 2002. "Money from Kin Abroad Helps Bengalis Get By." *The New York Times,* June 24, p. 3.

Shenon, Philip. 1993. "Saipan Sweatshops Are No American Dream." *The New York Times,* July 18, pp. A1, A10.

Shiva, Vandana. 2000. *Stolen Harvest: The Hijacking of the Global Food Supply.* Beacon: South End.

———. 2003. "The Living Democracy Movement: Alternatives to the Bankruptcy of Globalization." Pp. 115–24 in *Another World Is Possible,* edited by William F. Fisher and Thomas Ponniah. London: Zed.

Shultz, Jim. 2003. "Bolivia: The Water War Widens." *NACLA Report on the Americas* 36 (4): 34–37.

Silver, Beverly. 2003. *Forces of Labor: Worker's Movements and Globalization since 1870*. Cambridge, UK: Cambridge University Press.

Simons, Marlise. 1999. "Cry of Muslim Women for Equal Rights Is Rising." *The New York Times*, February 24, pp. A1, A6.

Singh, Ajit. 1992. "The Lost Decade: The Economic Crisis of the Third World in the 1980s: How the North Caused the South's Crisis." *Contention* 2:58–80.

Singh, Kavaljit. 2003. "Washington Reigns Supreme." *Tribune (London)*, April 18. Posted April 26, 2003, by mritchie@iatp.org

Singh, Kavaljit and Daphne Wysham. 1997. "Micro-Credit: Band-Aid or Wound?" *The Ecologist* 27 (2): 42–43.

Sivanandan, A. 1989. "New Circuits of Imperialism." *Race & Class* 30 (4): 1–19.

Sklair, Leslie. 1989. *Assembling for Development: The Maquila Industry in Mexico and the United States*. Boston: Unwin Hyman.

———. 2002. *Globalization. Capitalism & Its Alternatives*. Oxford, UK: Oxford University Press.

Skrobanek, Siripan, Nattaya Boonpakdi, and Chutina Janthakeero. 1997. *The Human Realities of Traffic in International Women*. London: Zed.

Skutnabb-Kangas, Tove. 2001. "Murder That Is a Threat to Survival." *Guardian Weekly*, March 22–28, p. 3.

"Slavery in the 21st Century." 2001. *New Internationalist*, July–August, pp.18–19.

Smith, Jeremy. 2002. "An Unappealing Industry." *The Ecologist* 32 (3): 40–41.

Smith, Stephen. 2002. " 'Political Sharia' Poses Threat to Nigeria's Unity." *Guardian Weekly*, January 31–February 6, p. 30.

Sobieszczyk, Teresa and Lindy Williams. 1997. "Attitudes Surrounding the Continuation of Female Circumcision in the Sudan: Passing the Tradition to the Next Generation." *Journal of Marriage and the Family* 59:966–81.

The South Centre. 1993. *Facing the Challenge: Responses to the Report of the South Commission*. London: Zed.

Starr, Amory. 2000. *Naming the Enemy: Anti-Corporate Movements Confront Globalization*. London: Zed.

Stavrianos, L. S. 1981. *Global Rift: The Third World Comes of Age*. New York: William Morrow.

Stevens, William K. 1994. "Poor Lands' Success in Cutting Birth Rate Upsets Old Theories." *The New York Times*, January 2, p. A8.

Stevenson, Richard W. 1993. "Ford Sets Its Sights on a 'World Car.'" *The New York Times*, October 27, pp. D1, D4.

Stewart, Douglas Ian. 1994. *After the Trees: Living on the Amazon Highway*. Austin: University of Texas Press.

Stiglitz, Joseph E. 2002. *Globalization and Its Discontents*. New York: Norton.

Stimson, Robert L. 1999. "General Motors Drives Some Hard Bargains with Asian Suppliers." *Wall Street Journal*, April 2, pp. A1, A6.

Strange, Susan. 1994. *States and Markets*. London: Pinter.

Strom, Stephanie. 1999. "In Renault-Nissan Deal, Big Risks and Big Opportunities." *The New York Times*, March 28, p. A3.

Stuart, Liz. 2003. "Journey's End for Trafficked Humans." *Guardian Weekly*, February 13–19, p. 21.

Swamy, M. R. Narayan. 1995. "Hindu Groups Step Up 'Buy Indian' Campaign." *IA News*, January 10, p. 1.

Tabb, William. 2000. "After Seattle: Understanding the Politics of Globalization." *Monthly Review* 51 (10): 1–18.

Tan, Abby. 1991a. "Paychecks Sent Home May Not Cover Human Losses." *Los Angeles Times*, October 1, pp. H2–H3.

———. 1991b. "The Labor Brokers: For a Price, There's a Job Abroad—Maybe." *Los Angeles Times*, October 1, p. H1.

Tautz, Carlos Sergio Figueiredo. 1997. "The Asian Invasion: Asian Multinationals Come to the Amazon." *Multinational Monitor* 18 (9): 1–5.

Templin, Neal. 1994. "Mexican Industrial Belt Is Beginning to Form as Car Makers Expand." *Wall Street Journal*, June 29, pp. A1, A10.

Thompson, Ginger. 2002a. "Free Market Grinds Mexico's Middle Class." *The New York Times*, September 4, p. 3.

———. 2002b. "Big Mexican Breadwinner: The Migrant Worker." *The New York Times*, March 25, p. A3.

Thurow, Lester C. 1999. "The Dollar's Day of Reckoning." *The Nation*, January 11, pp. 22–24.

Tripp, Aili Mari. 1997. *Changing the Rules: The Politics of Liberalization and the Urban Informal Economy in Tanzania*. Berkeley: University of California Press.

Tuxill, John. 1999. "Nature's Cornucopia: Our Stake in Plant Diversity." WorldWatch Paper No. 148, WorldWatch, Washington, DC.

Tyler, Patrick E. 1994. "China Planning People's Car to Put Masses behind Wheel." *The New York Times*, September 22, pp. A1, D8.

———. 1995. "Star at Conference on Women: Banker Who Lends to the Poor." *The New York Times*, September 14, p. A6.

Uchitelle, Louis. 1993. "Stanching the Loss of Good Jobs." *The New York Times*, January 31, Section 3, pp. 1, 6.

———. 1994. "U.S. Corporations Expanding Abroad at a Quicker Pace." *The New York Times*, July 25, pp. A1, D2.

Udesky, Laurie. 1994. "Sweatshops behind the Labels." *The Nation*, May 16, pp. 665–68.

Ufkes, Fran. 1995. "Industrial Restructuring and Agrarian Change: The Greening of Singapore." In *Food and Agrarian Orders in the World Economy*, edited by Philip McMichael. Westport, CT: Praeger.

United Nations. 1997. *United Nations Development Report*. New York: Oxford University Press.

———. 2002. *Human Development Report 2002*. New York: Oxford University Press.

United Nations Environment Program (UNEP). 2002. *Global Environmental Outlook 3 Earthwatch*. Retrieved from www.unep.net

"U.S. Imperial Ambitions and Iraq." 2002. *Monthly Review* 54 (7): 1–13.

Vidal, John. 2001. "Brazil Sets Out on the Road to Oblivion." *Guardian Weekly*, July 19–25, p. 20.

Wacker, Corinne. 1994. "Sustainable Development through Women's Groups: A Cultural Approach to Sustainable Development." In *Feminist Perspectives on Sustainable Development*, edited by Wendy Harcourt. London: Zed.

Waldman, Amy. 2002. "Poor in India Starve as Surplus Wheat Rots." *The New York Times*, December 2, p. 3.

Wallach, Lori. 2003. "What the WTO Didn't Want You to Know." Retrieved March 8, 2003.

Wallach, Lori and Michelle Sforza. 1999. *Whose Trade Organization? Corporate Globalization and the Erosion of Democracy.* Washington, DC: Public Citizen.

Wallerstein, Immanuel. 1983. *Historical Capitalism.* London: Verso.

Walton, John and David Seddon. 1994. *Free Markets & Food Riots: The Politics of Global Adjustment.* Oxford, UK: Blackwell.

Washington Post. 1999. "Coffee Drinkers: Where Are Your Beans Grown?" Reprinted in *The Ithaca Journal,* January 5, p. 3B.

Watkins, Kevin. 1991. "Agriculture and Food Security in the GATT Uruguay Round." *Review of African Political Economy* 50:38–50.

———. 1996. "FreeTrade and Farm Fallacies: From the Uruguay Round to the World Food Summit." *The Ecologist* 26 (6): 244–55.

———. 2002. "Money Talks." *The Guardian Weekly,* May 9–15, p. 21.

Watts, Michael. 1994. "Life under Contract: Contract Farming, Agrarian Restructuring and Flexible Accumulation." In *Living under Contract: Contract Farming and Agrarian Transformation in Sub-Saharan Africa,* edited by Peter D. Little and Michael J. Watts. Madison: University of Wisconsin Press.

Weinberg, Bill. 1998. "La Miskitia Rears Up: Industrial Recolonization Threatens the Nicaraguan Rainforests—An Indigenous Response." *Native Americas* 15 (2): 22–33.

Weisbrot, Mark. 1999. "How to Say No to the IMF." *The Nation,* June 21, pp. 20–21.

Weissman, Robert. 1991. "Prelude to a New Colonialism: The Real Purpose of GATT." *The Nation,* March 18, p. 337.

Wessel, James. 1983. *Trading the Future: Farm Exports and the Concentration of Economic Power in Our Food System.* San Francisco: Institute for Food and Development Policy.

Williams, Gwyneth. 1981. *Third-World Political Organizations: A Review of Developments.* Montclair, NJ: Allenheld, Osmun & Co.

Williams, Robert G. 1986. *Export Agriculture and the Crisis in Central America.* Chapel Hill: University of North Carolina Press.

Wolf, Eric. 1982. *Europe and the People without History.* Berkeley: University of California Press.

Wood, Ellen Meiksins. 1999. "Kosovo and the New Imperialism." *Monthly Review* 51 (2): 1–8.

Wood, Robert E. 1986. *From Marshall Plan to Debt Crisis: Foreign Aid and Development Choices in the World Economy.* Berkeley: University of California Press.

Woodall, Pam. 1994. "War of the Worlds: A Survey of the Global Economy." *The Economist,* Special Supplement, October 1, p. 24.

Woollacott, Martin. 2002. "Islamism after Copenhagen." *Guardian Weekly,* December 19–25, p. 14.

Worden, Scott. 2001. "E-Trafficking." *Foreign Policy,* Spring. Retrieved from www.foreignpolicy.com/issue_marapr_2001/gnsprint.html

Working, Russell. 1999. "Russia's Patchwork Economy: Korean Companies, Chinese Workers and U.S. Entrée." *The New York Times,* March 18, pp. D1, D23.

World Bank. 1981. *Accelerated Development in Sub-Saharan Africa: An Agenda to Action.* Washington, DC: World Bank.

——. 1989. *Sub-Saharan Africa: From Crisis to Sustainable Growth.* Washington, DC: World Bank.

——. 1990. *World Development Report.* Washington, DC: World Bank.

——. 1997. *World Development Report.* Washington, DC: World Bank.

——. 1998–1999. *World Development Report.* Washington, DC: World Bank.

——. 2000a. *World Development Report.* Washington, DC: World Bank.

——. 2000b. *Voices of the Poor.* New York: Oxford University Press.

World Social Forum. 2003. "Charter of Principles." Pp. 354–57 in *Another World Is Possible,* edited by W. F. Fisher and T. Ponniah. London: Zed.

World Trade Organization. 2001. "International Trade Statistics." Retrieved from www.wto.org/english/res_e/statis_e/its2001_e/its01_toc_e.htm

WuDunn, Sheryl. 1993. "Booming China Is Dream Market for West." *The New York Times,* February 15, pp. A1–A6.

Young, Gerardo and Lucas Guagnini. 2002. "Argentina's New Social Protagonists." *World Press Review,* December 11. Retrieved from www.zmag.org/content/showarticle.cfm?SectionID=42&ItemID=2735

# Glossary/Index

# Supplementary Web Site Guide

Alliance for Responsible
Trade, USA
www.art-us.org

Behind the Label, USA
www.behindthelabor.org

Bretton Woods Project, USA
(watchdog group)
www.brettonwoodsproject.org

Corporate Watch, USA
www.corpwatch.org

Development Group for
Alternative Policies
(Development GAP), USA
www.igc.org/dgap

The Ecologist, UK
www.theecologist.org

Ejercito Zapatista de Liberacion
Nacional (EZLN), Mexico
www.ezln.org

Equal Exchange, USA
www.equalexchange.com

Erosion, Technology &
Concentration (formerly Rural
Advancement Foundation
International, Canada)
www.etcgroup.org

Fairtrade Labelling Organizations
International (FLO), Germany
www.fairtrade.net

Fair Trade Federation (FTF), USA
www.fairtradefederation.org

Fair Trade Resource Network
(FTRN), USA
www.fairtraderesource.org

Fifty Years Is Enough: U.S.
Network for Global Economic
Justice, USA
www.50years.org

Focus on the Global South,
Thailand
www.focus.web

Food and Agriculture
Organization (FAO), UN, Italy
www.fao.org

Food First (Institute for Food and
Development Policy), USA
www.foodfirst.org

Friends of the Earth International
(FOE), Netherlands
www.foei.org

Genetic Resources Action
International (GRAIN)
www.grain.org/front/index:cfm

Global Environment
Facility, USA
www.gefweb.org/main.htm

Global Exchange, USA
www.globalexchange.org

Grameen Bank, Bangladesh
www.grameen-info.org

Greenpeace International,
Netherlands
www.greenpeace.org

Human Rights Watch, USA
www.hrw.org

Independent Media Center, USA
www.indymedia.org

Institute for Agriculture and
Trade Policy (IATP), USA
www.iatp.org

International Coalition for
Development Action, Belgium
www.icda.be

International Forum on
Globalization (IFG), USA
www.ifg.org

International Labor
Organization, UN
www.ilo.org

International Labor Rights
Fund, USA
www.laborrights.org

International Monetary Fund
(IMF), USA
www.imf.org

International Society for Ecology
and Culture, UK
www.isec.org.uk

Jubilee +, UK (debt issues)
www.jubileeplus.org

Jubilee South, Nicaragua,
Philippines, South Africa
www.jubileesouth.org

Maquila Solidarity Network,
Canada
www.maquilasolidarity.org

Multinational Monitor, USA
www.essential.org/monitor

New Internationalist (NI), UK
www.newint.org

OneWorld, UK
www.oneworld.net

Oxfam International, UK
www.oxfam.org

Public Citizen Global Trade
Watch, USA
www.citizen.org/pctrade/tradeho
me.html

Rainforest Action Network
(RAN), USA
www.ran.org

Research Foundation for Science,
Technology, and Ecology, India
www.vshiva.net

Resource Center of the
Americas, USA
www.americas.org

South Asian Women's Network,
Canada
www.sawnet.org

Structural Adjustment Policy
Review International
Network, USA
www.saprin.org

**Survival International, UK (tribal people's rights)**
www.survival-international.org

**Sweatshop Watch, USA**
www.sweatshopwatch.org

**Third World Network (TWN), Malaysia**
www.twnside.org.sg

**Trade Justice Movement, UK**
www.tradejusticemovement.org.uk

**TransAfrica Forum, USA**
www.transafricaforum.org

**TransFair USA**
www.transfairusa.org

**Transnational Institute, Netherlands**
www.tni.org

**United Nations Development Program, USA**
www.undp.org/

**United Students Against Sweatshops (USAS), USA**
www.usasnet.org

**Women Working Worldwide, UK**
www.poptel.org.uk/women-ww

**World Bank, USA**
www.worldbank.org

**World Development Movement (WDM), UK**
www.wdm.org.uk

**World Economic Forum (WEF), Switzerland**
www.weforum.org

**World Health Organization (WHO), Switzerland**
www.who.int/en/

**World Social Forum, Brasil**
www.portoalegre2003.org/
publique/index02I.htm

**World Trade Organization (WTO)**
www.wto.org

**Via Campesina, Honduras (transnational farmers' organization)**
www.viacampesina.org